Communications
in Computer and Information Science 1842

Rationale

The CCIS series is devoted to the publication of proceedings of computer science conferences. Its aim is to efficiently disseminate original research results in informatics in printed and electronic form. While the focus is on publication of peer-reviewed full papers presenting mature work, inclusion of reviewed short papers reporting on work in progress is welcome, too. Besides globally relevant meetings with internationally representative program committees guaranteeing a strict peer-reviewing and paper selection process, conferences run by societies or of high regional or national relevance are also considered for publication.

Topics

The topical scope of CCIS spans the entire spectrum of informatics ranging from foundational topics in the theory of computing to information and communications science and technology and a broad variety of interdisciplinary application fields.

Information for Volume Editors and Authors

Publication in CCIS is free of charge. No royalties are paid, however, we offer registered conference participants temporary free access to the online version of the conference proceedings on SpringerLink (http://link.springer.com) by means of an http referrer from the conference website and/or a number of complimentary printed copies, as specified in the official acceptance email of the event.

CCIS proceedings can be published in time for distribution at conferences or as post-proceedings, and delivered in the form of printed books and/or electronically as USBs and/or e-content licenses for accessing proceedings at SpringerLink. Furthermore, CCIS proceedings are included in the CCIS electronic book series hosted in the SpringerLink digital library at http://link.springer.com/bookseries/7899. Conferences publishing in CCIS are allowed to use Online Conference Service (OCS) for managing the whole proceedings lifecycle (from submission and reviewing to preparing for publication) free of charge.

Publication process

The language of publication is exclusively English. Authors publishing in CCIS have to sign the Springer CCIS copyright transfer form, however, they are free to use their material published in CCIS for substantially changed, more elaborate subsequent publications elsewhere. For the preparation of the camera-ready papers/files, authors have to strictly adhere to the Springer CCIS Authors' Instructions and are strongly encouraged to use the CCIS LaTeX style files or templates.

Abstracting/Indexing

CCIS is abstracted/indexed in DBLP, Google Scholar, EI-Compendex, Mathematical Reviews, SCImago, Scopus. CCIS volumes are also submitted for the inclusion in ISI Proceedings.

How to start

To start the evaluation of your proposal for inclusion in the CCIS series, please send an e-mail to ccis@springer.com.

Frans Coenen · Ana Fred · David Aveiro ·
Jan Dietz · Jorge Bernardino · Elio Masciari ·
Joaquim Filipe
Editors

Knowledge Discovery, Knowledge Engineering and Knowledge Management

14th International Joint Conference, IC3K 2022
Valletta, Malta, October 24–26, 2022
Revised Selected Papers

Springer

Editors
Frans Coenen
University of Liverpool
Liverpool, UK

David Aveiro
Universidade da Madeira and Madeira-ITI
Funchal, Portugal

Jorge Bernardino
Polytechnic Institute of Coimbra - ISEC
Coimbra, Portugal

Joaquim Filipe
Polytechnic Institute of Setúbal and INSTICC
Setúbal, Portugal

Ana Fred
Instituto de Telecomunicações and University
of Lisbon
Lisbon, Portugal

Jan Dietz
Delft University of Technology
Delft, The Netherlands

Elio Masciari
University of Naples Federico II
Naples, Italy

ISSN 1865-0929   ISSN 1865-0937 (electronic)
Communications in Computer and Information Science
ISBN 978-3-031-43470-9   ISBN 978-3-031-43471-6 (eBook)
https://doi.org/10.1007/978-3-031-43471-6

This Springer imprint is published by the registered company Springer Nature Switzerland AG
The registered company address is: Gewerbestrasse 11, 6330 Cham, Switzerland

Paper in this product is recyclable.

Preface

The present book includes extended and revised versions of a set of selected papers from the 14th International Joint Conference on Knowledge Discovery, Knowledge Engineering and Knowledge Management (IC3K 2022), held in Valletta, Malta, from 24–26 October, 2022.

The purpose of IC3K is to bring together researchers, engineers and practitioners in the areas of Knowledge Discovery, Knowledge Engineering and Knowledge Management. IC3K is composed of three co-located conferences, each specialized in at least one of the aforementioned main knowledge areas.

IC3K 2022 received 127 paper submissions from 39 countries, of which 20% were included in this book.

The papers were selected by the event chairs and their selection is based on a number of criteria that include the classifications and comments provided by the program committee members, the session chairs' assessment and also the program chairs' global view of all papers included in the technical program. The authors of selected papers were then invited to submit revised and extended versions of their papers having at least 30% innovative material.

The papers selected to be included in this book contribute to the understanding of relevant trends of current research on Knowledge Discovery, Knowledge Engineering and Knowledge Management, including: Natural Language Processing, Communication, Collaboration and Information Sharing, Machine Learning, KM Strategies and Implementations, Semantic Web, Ontology Development, Knowledge Representation and Acquisition, Business Intelligence and Information Systems, Big Data and Analytics, Deep Learning, Clustering and Classification Methods, and Information Technology and Information System Research.

We would like to thank all the authors for their contributions and also the reviewers who have helped to ensure the quality of this publication.

October 2022

Frans Coenen
Ana Fred
David Aveiro
Jan Dietz
Jorge Bernardino
Elio Masciari
Joaquim Filipe

Organization

Conference Chair

Joaquim Filipe   Polytechnic Institute of Setubal / INSTICC, Portugal

Program Co-chairs

KDIR

Frans Coenen   University of Liverpool, UK
Ana Fred   Instituto de Telecomunicaçoes and University of Lisbon, Portugal

KEOD

David Aveiro   University of Madeira, NOVA-LINCS and ARDITI, Portugal
Jan Dietz   Delft University of Technology, The Netherlands

KMIS

Jorge Bernardino   Polytechnic Institute of Coimbra - ISEC, Portugal
Elio Masciari   University of Napoli Federico II, Italy

KDIR Program Committee

Mayer Aladjem   Ben-Gurion University of the Negev, Israel
Eva Armengol   IIIA CSIC, Spain
Rafael Berlanga   Universitat Jaume I, Spain
Marko Bohanec   Jožef Stefan Institute, Slovenia
Gloria Bordogna   CNR - National Research Council, Italy
Amel Borgi   Université de Tunis El Manar, Institut Supérieur d'Informatique, Tunisia
Jesús Carrasco-Ochoa   INAOE, Mexico
Zhiyuan Chen   University of Maryland Baltimore County, USA

KDIR Additional Reviewers

Israel Cuevas	University of Arkansas, USA
Delia Irazú Hernández-Farias	INAOE, Mexico
Lucio La Cava	Università della Calabria, Italy
Andrew Mackey	University of Arkansas, USA

KEOD Program Committee

Mara Abel	Universidade Federal do Rio Grande do Sul, Brazil
Michael Bada	University of Colorado Anschutz Medical Campus, USA
Stephen Balakirsky	GTRI, USA
Claudio Baptista	Universidade Federal de Campina Grande, Brazil
Rafael Berlanga	Universitat Jaume I, Spain
Fernando Bobillo	University of Zaragoza, Spain
Bert Bredeweg	University of Amsterdam, The Netherlands
Vladimír Bureš	University of Hradec Králové, Czech Republic
Guoray Cai	Penn State University, USA
Werner Ceusters	State University of New York at Buffalo, USA
Soon Chun	City University of New York, USA
João Costa	University of Coimbra, Portugal
John Edwards	Aston University, UK
Maria Ganzha	Warsaw University of Technology, Poland
Francisco García-Sánchez	University of Murcia, Spain
Xudong He	Florida International University, USA
Yongqun He	University of Michigan, USA
Gabriela Henning	Universidad Nacional del Litoral, Argentina
Stijn Hoppenbrouwers	HAN University of Applied Sciences, The Netherlands
Martina Husáková	University of Hradec Králové, Czech Republic
Jakub Klímek	Charles University and Czech Technical University in Prague, Czech Republic
Konstantinos I. Kotis	University of the Aegean, Greece
Tomislava Lauc	University of Zagreb, Croatia
Antoni Ligeza	AGH University of Science and Technology, Poland
Paulo Maio	Polytechnic of Porto, Portugal
Philippe Martin	University of Reunion Island, France
Riccardo Martoglia	University of Modena and Reggio Emilia, Italy

Nives Mikelic Preradovic	University of Zagreb, Croatia
Michele Missikoff	ISTC-CNR, Italy
Regina Motz	Universidad de la República, Uruguay
Hervé Panetto	University of Lorraine, France
Carlos Periñán-Pascual	Universitat Politècnica de València, Spain
Colette Rolland	Université Paris 1 Panthéon-Sorbonne, France
Duncan Ruiz	Pontifical Catholic University of Rio Grande do Sul, Brazil
Lloyd Rutledge	Open University of the Netherlands, The Netherlands
Nuno Silva	Polytechnic Institute of Porto, Portugal
Stian Soiland-Reyes	University of Manchester, UK
Sergio Tessaris	Free University of Bozen-Bolzano, Italy
Petr Tucnik	University of Hradec Králové, Czech Republic
Jouni Tuominen	Aalto University, Finland
Hironori Washizaki	Waseda University, Japan
Diedrich Wolter	University of Bamberg, Germany
Nianjun Zhou	IBM, USA
Qiang Zhu	University of Michigan, Dearborn, USA

KEOD Additional Reviewers

Mariano Ferreirone	CRAN, CNRS, University of Lorraine, France
Nicolas Leutwyler	CRAN, CNRS, University of Lorraine, France
Mario Lezoche	CRAN - Université de Lorraine, France

KMIS Program Committee

Leon Abdillah	Bina Darma University, Indonesia
Giuseppe Berio	University of South Brittany, France
Kelly Braghetto	University of São Paulo, Brazil
Eric Cheng	Education University of Hong Kong, China
Vincent Cheutet	Université de Lyon, INSA Lyon, DISP (EA4570), France
Chin Wei Chong	Multimedia University, Malaysia
Ritesh Chugh	Central Queensland University, Australia
Susan Cuddy	Commonwealth Scientific and Industrial Research Organisation, Australia
Roberta Cuel	University of Trento, Italy
John Davies	BT, UK

Joan-Francesc Fondevila-Gascón	CECABLE, UPF, URL, UdG (EU Mediterrani) and UOC, Spain
Matteo Gaeta	University of Salerno, Italy
Francisco García-Sánchez	University of Murcia, Spain
Bogdan Ghilic-Micu	Academy of Economic Studies, Romania
Severin Grabski	Michigan State University, USA
Michele Grimaldi	University of Cassino, Italy
Gabriel Guerrero-Contreras	University of Cádiz, Spain
Jennifer Harding	Loughborough University, UK
Keith Harman	Oklahoma Baptist University, USA
Mounira Harzallah	LS2N, University of Nantes, France
Vincent Hilaire	UTBM, France
Eli Hustad	University of Agder, Norway
Anca Daniela Ionita	University Politehnica of Bucharest, Romania
Dominique Laurent	ETIS Laboratory CNRS UMR 8051 - CY Cergy Paris University - ENSEA, France
Michael Leyer	University of Rostock, Germany
Kecheng Liu	University of Reading, UK
Carlos Malcher Bastos	Universidade Federal Fluminense, Brazil
Federica Mandreoli	University of Modena and Reggio Emilia, Italy
Ra'ed Masa'deh	University of Jordan, Jordan
Nada Matta	University of Technology of Troyes, France
Brahami Menaouer	National Polytechnic School of Oran, Algeria
Benito Mignacca	University of Cassino and Southern Lazio, Italy
Michele Missikoff	ISTC-CNR, Italy
Luis Molina Fernández	University of Granada, Spain
Vincenzo Moscato	Università degli Studi di Napoli Federico II, Italy
Wilma Penzo	University of Bologna, Italy
Filipe Portela	University of Minho, Portugal
Nicolas Prat	Essec Business School Paris, France
Arkalgud Ramaprasad	University of Illinois at Chicago, USA
Spiros Skiadopoulos	University of the Peloponnese, Greece
Marian Stoica	Bucharest University of Economic Studies, Romania
Costas Vassilakis	University of the Peloponnese, Greece
Anthony Wensley	University of Toronto, Canada
Uffe Wiil	University of Southern Denmark, Denmark

KMIS Additional Reviewers

Sara Balderas-Díaz	University of Cadiz, Spain

Invited Speakers

Bart Verheijen	GuruScan, The Netherlands
Giancarlo Guizzardi	Free University of Bolzano-Bozen, Italy and University of Twente, The Netherlands
Catholijn Jonker	Delft University of Technology, The Netherlands
Rudolf Kruse	Otto von Guericke University Magdeburg, Germany

Contents

Knowledge Management and Information Systems

Knowledge Discovery and Information Retrieval

Electrocardiogram Two-Dimensional Motifs: A Study Directed at Cardio Vascular Disease Classification

Hanadi Aldosari[1,4(✉)], Frans Coenen[1], Gregory Y. H. Lip[2], and Yalin Zheng[2,3]

[1] Department of Computer Science, University of Liverpool, Liverpool, UK
{H.A.Aldosari,Coenen}@liverpool.ac.uk
[2] Liverpool Centre for Cardiovascular Science, University of Liverpool and Liverpool Heart and Chest Hospital, Liverpool, UK
{Gregory.Lip,Yalin.Zheng}@liverpool.ac.uk
[3] Department of Eye and Vision Science, University of Liverpool, Liverpool, UK
[4] College of Computer Science and Engineering, Taibah University, Madinah, Saudi Arabia
hdosari@taibahu.edu.sa

Abstract. A process is described, using the concept of 2D motifs and 2D discords, to build classification models to classify Cardiovascular Disease using Electrocardiogram (ECG) data as the primary input. The motivation is that existing techniques typically first transform ECG data into a 1D signal (waveform) format and then extract a small number of features from this format for classification purposes. It is argued here that this transformation results in missing data, and that the consequent feature selection means that only a small part of the original ECG data is utilised. The approach proposed in this paper works directly with the image format, no transformation takes place. Instead, motifs and discords are extracted from the raw data and used as features in a homogeneous feature vector representation. The reported evaluation demonstrates that more effective classification results than that which can be achieved using the waveform format. The proposed 2D motif and discord extraction mechanism is fully described. The proposed process was evaluated using three distinct ECG data sets. A best accuracy of 85% was obtained, compared with a best accuracy of 68.48% using a comparable 1D waveform approach.

Keywords: 2D motifs · 2D discords · Cardiovascular disease classification · ECG classification

1 Introduction

Cardiovascular Disease (CVD) is an umbrella term for a range of conditions that affect the heart and/or blood vessels, of which heart disease and stoke are perhaps the best known. Collectively, CVDs are the most common global cause of mortality, and the major contributor to reduced quality of life in the 21st century [24]. According to the World Health Organisation (WHO) some 17.9 million people died from CVDs in 2019, representing 32% (approximately one third) of all global deaths [30]. The majority of

F. Coenen et al. (Eds.): IC3K 2022, CCIS 1842, pp. 3–27, 2023.
https://doi.org/10.1007/978-3-031-43471-6_1

these deaths (85%) were as a result of heart attacks or stroke. CVDs are most commonly caused by irregularities in the normal rhythm of the heart, the sinus rhythm. The sinus rhythm is between 60 and 100 beats per minute (bpm). A rate of less than 60 bpm (sinus bradycardia) or above 100 bpm (sinus tachycardia) is considered abnormal. The standard tool for monitoring heart rate is the Electrocardiogram (ECG). ECGs are obtained using an ECG machine which detects and records the electrical signals produced by a patient's heart as it beats, using sensors attached to the patient's skin. Clinicians and cardiologists can then use the ECG data to assist in determining the presence, or otherwise, of CVD. This is achieved by examining individual heart cycles within the ECG trace in terms of what are referred to as the P wave, the QRS complex and the T wave. To speed up the ECG analysis process there has been significant interest in using the tools and techniques of machine learning. Especially the application of supervised learning to ECG data to build classification models of various kinds [11, 15, 21, 26].

Supervised learning requires labelled examples to which machine learning can be applied to generate a model that can then be used to label previously unseen examples. The labelled examples are usually divided into a training set and a test set. The first is used to "learn" the desired model, and the second is to evaluate the resulting model. The process of labelling the examples is often a time consuming and therefore a challenging task. A second challenge is how best to represent the examples so that machine learning can be applied. Most machine learning algorithms use a feature vector representation where the examples are represented using a numeric vector when each numeric value relates to a data attribute (feature, dimension). Generating such a representation is fairly straightforward if the data under consideration is in a numeric tabular format where each row represents a record and each column an attribute. This becomes much more challenging if our data is in the form of images, as in the case of ECG data.

ECG machines typically produced hard copy printouts. The first stage in the process of generating training and test data is thus to scan the paper format ECGs so that they are available in a digitised image format. The second stage is then to extract the ECG signal trace from the digitised images so that the data is in a waveform format. Once the transformation has taken place the next stage is to extract features from the waveform data so that a feature vector representation can be derived. Usually, the features identified are associated with the P wave, the QRS complex, and the T wave, used in the manual analysis of ECG data; examples can be found in [14, 18, 25, 31, 32]. The consequence, it is argued here, is that the resulting labelling (classification) of previously unseen examples is not as good as it might be because of: (i) the approximations used to generate the waveform format and (ii) the small number of features typically considered.

To address the above, in [1], a solution was presented founded on the use of motifs [2]. The solution moved away from the traditional idea of applying machine learning to a small number of features extracted from ECG data that had first been transformed into a 1D waveform format, by considering the ECG data in its entirety as an image. The idea presented was to extract 2D motifs directly from ECG image data and use these motifs as the attributes in a Homogeneous Feature Vector Representation (HFVR). In this context, a motif is a frequently repeating pattern which is considered to be indicative of a particular CVD label (class). In 1D a motif is a sub-sequence of points within a larger point (time) series. In 2D this is sub-matrix within a larger matrix of points (pixels). The concept of motifs, in the 1D context, is most frequently used in time series analysis [3,20,23,38]. In the 2D context, motifs have been applied to image analysis [4,13]; although, with the exception of [1], not with respect to ECG data (at least to the best knowledge of the authors).

In [1] evidence was provided indicating that the use of 2D motifs for generating CVD classification models, using supervised learning, outperformed models generated using more traditional approaches. The evaluation was conducted using a subset of the Guangzhou Heart Study data set [9], a subset directed at Atrial Fibrillation (AF), a common form of CVD that is indicated by an irregular, and often unusually fast, heart rate (140 bpm) caused by the "twitching" of the top (atria) chambers of the heart. AF is the most common form of irregular heart beat. If untreated the presence of AF increases the risk of stroke and heart failure. However, a criticism of the work presented in [1] is that the AF versus no AF Guangzhou data set comprised only 120 records. The work presented in this paper revisits the work presented in [1] by re-analysing the claims made using a much more rigorous evaluation than was originally presented. Two additional stages have also been added to the proposed model in [1], for the cases of large numbers of motifs/discords being generated or when we have imbalanced input data. For the evaluation presented here three data sets were used: (i) the AF versus no AF Guangzhou data sets also used in [1], (ii) the entire Guangzhou Heart Study data set of 1172 records categorised as normal versus abnormal and (iii) the Liverpool Heart and Chest data set. The later is a recently acquired data set, curated by the authors, directed at AF with reoccurrence versus AF without reoccurrence (a much more challenging classification than in the case of the two other data sets considered).

In [1] a Support Vector Machine (SVM) classification model was used. A SVM classification model was also used with respect to the work presented in this paper. Partly so that fair comparisons with the work presented in [1] could be made, and partly because SVMs are frequently used with respect to reported work directed at more traditional CVD classification, see for example [33].

The rest of this paper is structured as follows. A review of previous work relevant to the work presented in this paper is given in Sect. 2. Section 3 then presents a formal definition of the 2D motif extraction problem (in the context of ECG data). A more extensive description of the approach to 2D motif feature extraction, and the utilisation of these motifs, than that presented in [1], is given in Sect. 4. Section 5 then provides a critical and comprehensive evaluation of the approach. The paper is completed, in Sect. 6, with a summary, some key conclusions and some suggested avenues for future work.

2 Related Work

Detection and classification of anomalies within ECG data has become a significant area of research in the context of CVD studies. The motivation is the observation that the manual interpretation of ECG data is time consuming, and requires prior knowledge and skills, knowledge and skills that are often in short supply. A range of Machine Learning (ML) and Deep Learning (DL) algorithms have therefore been proposed with the aim of addressing the challenge associated with the human interpretation of ECG data [14,18,25,32].

As noted in the introduction to this paper, a particular challenge of applying ML and DL to ECG data is that the raw data is typically in a paper format. Thus the starting point for any form of classification model generation, using ML or DL, is the scanning (digitising) of the paper format data into a 2D image format. As also noted earlier, the practice is then to transform the 2D digitised ECG data into a 1D waveform format. There are a range of tools available to convert 2D digitised ECG data to a 1D waveform format [5,6,12,16,19,22,29,34]. Using these tools the resulting wave forms, generated from digitized paper ECG data, can be in a variety of formats; both txt or xml are popular. Some of these tools provide additional functionality. Therefore the tools available can be divided into three groups according to the functionality that they provide: (i) Digitization + transformation (no additional functionality) (ii) digitizing + transformation + feature extraction, and (iii) digitizing + transformation + feature extraction + classification. Examples of the first can be found in [5,6,12,29]. Example of the second can be found in [19,22]. The idea here is to extract a small number of global characteristics from the ECG wave form data. As noted earlier, these characteristics are typically the amplitude and interval values of what are referred to as P wave, the QRS complex, and the T wave. The extracted characteristics can then be used to build a classification model. The last of the above tool groupings describes tools that incorporate classification model generation, not the case with respect to the previous two. Examples can be found in [16,34]. In [16], morphological features were extracted to be used with two classification models, kNN coupled with Dynamic Time Warping (DTW) and Adaboost, to detect three different types of cardiovascular abnormalities. The digitisation tool used, in this case, was the same as that presented in [12]. In [34], the focus was on four specific types of waveform. The reported evaluation indicated that SVM model generation produced the best classification results.

An alternative to the waveform format, and that is explored in this paper, is to extract discriminatory features from the 2D scanned ECG image data without transformation to a 1D format, this can avoid the information loss associated with such transformations. The challenge is then the nature of the image features to be extracted. Classic approaches which involve the extraction of "low-level" features, such as colour or texture, are deemed to be ineffective for CVD disease classification [7]; More advanced feature extraction mechanisms are required. The solution proposed in [1] was to use 2D *motifs*. Motifs, as noted earlier, are repeating patterns found in data that can be used in tasks like clustering, classification, and anomaly detection. The idea of 2D motifs was first proposed in [4] and used in [13] for the purpose of classifying digital images featuring buildings, and images extracted from video news clippings, using a K-Nearest Neighbors (kNN) classification model. The work presented in this paper builds on the work presented in [3].

3   Problem Definition

This section provides a formal problem definition for the work presented in this paper. The main goal is to generate a classification model that can be used to label previously unseen *digital ECG images* according to a given set of classes $C = \{c_1, c_2\}$. Each image I comprises a $n \times m$ pixel matrix such that p_{ij} is the pixel at row i and column j.

The input data D comprises a set of tuples of the from $\langle I, c \rangle$ where I is an ECG image and c_i is a class label taken from a set of classes C.

To generate the desired CVD classification model we aim to extract a set of features from each digital ECG image I. The idea proposed in this paper is that the most appropriate features to identify are 2D *motifs* and *discords*. A 2D motif M is a $p \times q$ sub-matrix of an image I, where $p < n$ and $q < m$, that occurs with maximal frequency. The intuition here is that because the sub-matrix occurs frequently it is likely to be a good discriminator of class. A motif set, $\mathbf{M} = \{M_1, M_2, \dots\}$, is a set of 2D motifs extracted from the images held in D, distributed according to class, one class per set of motifs. In other words, there is a one to one correspondence between the set $\mathbf{M}$ and the set of classes C, each subset $M_i \in \mathbf{M}$ is the set of motifs associated with the class $c_i \in \mathbf{C}$. Not all the motifs in $\mathbf{M}$ will be good discriminators of class, so it is necessary to prune $\mathbf{M}$. A two step process was adopted to achieve this, intra-class pruning to give the set M' and then inter-class pruning to give the set $\mathbf{M}''$.

A 2D discord S, in turn, is a $p \times q$ sub-matrix of an image I, of width p and height q, that occurs with minimal frequency (thus the opposite of a motif). The intuition here is that because the sub-matrix occurs infrequently it is likely to also be a good discriminator of class. A discord set, $\mathbf{S} = \{S_1, S_2, \dots\}$, is set of 2D discords extracted from the images held in D, again distributed according to class. As in the case of the motif set of sets $\mathbf{M}$, not all the discords in $\mathbf{S}$ are assumed to be good discriminators of class. Therefore, as in the case of motifs, we apply intra-class pruning to $\mathbf{S}$ to give S', and then inter-class pruning to give $\mathbf{S}''$. Further discussion concerning the intra- and inter-class pruning processes, with respect to the sets $\mathbf{M}$ and $\mathbf{S}$, is presented in Sub-sect. 4.2.

4   Cardiovascular Disease Classification Model Generation

This section builds on the approach proposed in [1], adding two additional stages required when large numbers of motifs/discords are generated and/or when we have imbalanced input data. A schematic of the process is presented in Fig. 1. From the figure it can be seen that the approach comprises seven stages:

1. Data cleaning.
2. 2D motif and discord extraction.
3. Feature selection.
4. Data augmentation.
5. Feature vector generation.
6. Classification Model Generation.
7. Classification Model Usgae.

Of these, feature selection and data augmentation are the two additional stages not originaly included in the process as first described in [1]. Detail concerning each of these five stages is presented in the following seven sub-sections, Sub-sects. 4.1 to 4.7.

8   H. Aldosari et al.

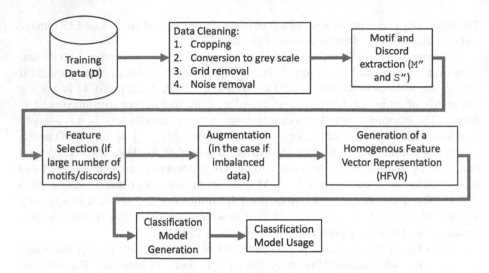

Fig. 1. Schematic of CVD Classification Model Generation Process.

4.1 Data Cleaning (Stage 1)

The first stage in the CVD classification model generation process is the cleaning of the raw image data. The input to Stage 1 was a set of ECG images $\mathbf{D} = \{\langle I_1, c_1 \rangle, \langle I_2, c_2 \rangle\}$ where I_i is an ECG image and $c_i \in C$. From Fig. 1 the Data Cleaning stage comprises four sub-processes: (i) cropping, (ii) conversion to gray scale, (iii) grid removal and (iv) noise removal. Each of the four data cleaning sub-processes is considered in the remainder of this section.

Cropping: Scanned ECG images often include spurious information around the edges of the scan. The first process was therefore to crop the image so that only the ECG signals were retained.

Conversion to Gray Scale: The cropped RGB image was then converted to a gray-scale intensity image.

Grid Removal: The third sub-processes was directed at removing all spurious data in the gray-scale ECG data, particularly the background grid which is a frequent feature of ECG digital images. This was achieved using the application of a "binarization" operation designed so that pixels related to the ECG traces were allocated the value 255 (white) and the rest of the image pixels the value 0 (black). The desired effect was that the graphical grid, and the majority of spurious data points and noise, would all be encoded as black pixels. The challenge was deciding the value of the binarisation threshold to be applied to the gray-scale image. To decide the nature of this threshold, histograms for selected ECG image files were generated. From these histograms, it was found that the background (high intensity) gray scale values were in the range 150 to 255, the threshold value was therefore set at 150. Thus, the proposed binarisation process assigned a value of 0 to each gray scale pixel whose value was greater than the 150 threshold, and a value of 255 otherwise (Eq. 1).

Noise Removal: The anticipation was that some spurious small patches of white pixels (white noise) would be retained after the application of the binarization. To remove this white noise a *morphological erosion operation* was applied whereby the pixels in the boundary of white objects were removed. This also had the effect of reducing the thickness of the ECG traces. Thus, on completion of the erosion operation a *morphological dilation operation* was applied to add pixels back to the boundaries of the retained white objects, namely the ECG trace.

$$binary(x,y) = \begin{cases} 0 & \text{if } grayscale(x,y) > threshold \\ 255 & \text{otherwise} \end{cases} \tag{1}$$

4.2 Motif and Discord Extraction (Stage 2)

The second stage in the overall process was 2D Motif and Discord extraction (discovery). The pseudo-code for the top-level motif and discord extraction algorithm is given in Algorithm 1. Note that this algorithm is similar to that given in [1]. The inputs are: (i) the data set $D = \{\langle I_1, c_1 \rangle, \langle I_2, c_2 \rangle, \ldots\}$ where each image I_i has been pre-processing during Stage 1 of the process (see above), (ii) the set of classes C, (iii) the width p and height q of the motifs and discords to be retrieved, (iv) a pre-specified similarity threshold σ used to determine whether two pixel sub-matrices are the same or not, and (v) k the number of motifs and discords to be selected. The output was a set of pruned motifs and a set of pruned discords, M'' and S'', to be used in the following stages. The algorithm commences (lines 3 to 6) by segmenting the set D into a set of subsets $D = \{D_1, \ldots D_{|C|}\}$ where each subset is associated with a class in C. Note that for the evaluation presented in Sect. 5, $|C| = 2$ was used, hence $D = \{D_1, D_2\}$. Two sets are then defined, lines 7 and 8 to hold identified motifs and discords, the sets M and S.

The set D is then processed to identify the motifs and discords held in the images associated with each class (lines 9 to 18). This involves calls to a number of sub-processes which will be discussed in further detail later in this sub-section. The output is the set $M = \{M_1, M_2, \ldots\}$ and the set $S = \{S_1, S_2, \ldots\}$; where M_i is the set of motifs associated with class $c_i \in C$, and S_i is the set of discords associated with class $c_i \in C$. As noted earlier, for the evaluation presented in Sect. 5, $|C| = 2$ was used, hence $M = \{M_1, M_2\}$, and $S = \{S_1, S_2\}$. Note that the proposed approach may result in the same motif being identified in several images, thus M and S are likely to contain repeat occurrences of motifs and discords. The intuition here for them being retained was that they would be given more significance with respect to the generation of the intended prediction model; conceptually they would be given a higher "weighting".

The sets $M = \{M_1, M_2, \ldots\}$ and $S = \{S_1, S_2, \ldots\}$ are likely to hold some motifs and discords that are unique to only one image. It was anticipated, that these would not be good discriminators of class, hence, for each set of motifs $M_i \in M$ associated with a particular class $c_i \in C$, and each set set of discords $S_i \in S$ associated with a class $c_i \in C$, intra-class pruning was applied (line 19) and unique motifs and discords removed, The retained motifs and discords were held in the sets $M' = \{M'_1, M'_2, \ldots\}$ and $S' = \{S'_1, S'_2, \ldots\}$ respectively (line 16 in Algorithm 1).

The last sub-processes in Algorithm 1, line 19, was to conduct inter-class pruning. The removal of motifs and discords, from M' and S' respectively that were associated with more than one class and hence deemed to not be useful for distinguishing between classes. The retained motifs and discords were held in the sets $\mathbf{M}'' = \{m_1, m_2, \dots\}$, and a set of discords $\mathbf{S}'' = \{s_1, s_2, \dots\}$, that were considered to be good discriminators of class.

Algorithm 1. 2D Motif and Discord Extraction [1].

1: **Input** D, C, p, q, σ, k
2: **Output** $\mathbf{M}'', \mathbf{S}''$
3: $\mathbf{D} = \{D_1 \dots D_{|C|}$ where $\forall D_i \in \mathbf{D}, D_i = \emptyset$
4: **for** $\forall \langle I_i, c_i \rangle \in D$ **do**
5:    $D_j = D_j \cup I_i$ where $j = i$
6: **end for**
7: $\mathbf{M} = \emptyset$ ▷ Define the empty set $\mathbf{M}$ to hold extracted motifs
8: $\mathbf{S} = \emptyset$ ▷ Define the empty set $\mathbf{S}$ to hold extracted motifs
9: **for** $\forall D_i \in \mathbf{D}$ **do**
10:    **for** $\forall I_j \in D_i$ **do**
11:        $\chi_i \leftarrow$ genSubMatrices(I_j, p, q) ▷ Algorithm 2
12:        $DM_i \leftarrow$ getCandidate2DmotifsAndDiscords(χ, σ) ▷ Algorithm 3
13:        $M_i, S_i \leftarrow$ topK_2DmotifsAndDiscords(DM_i, k) ▷ Algorithm4
14:        $\mathbf{M} \leftarrow \mathbf{M} \cup M_i$ ▷ Add M_i to the set $\mathbf{M}$
15:        $\mathbf{S} \leftarrow \mathbf{S} \cup S_i$ ▷ Add S_i to the set $\mathbf{S}$
16:    **end for**
17: **end for**
18: $\mathbf{M}', \mathbf{S}' \leftarrow$ intraClassPruning$(\mathbf{M}, \mathbf{S}, \sigma)$ ▷ Algorithm 5
19: $\mathbf{M}'', \mathbf{S}'' \leftarrow$ interClassPruning$(\mathbf{M}', \mathbf{S}', \sigma)$ ▷ Algorithm 6
20: **return** $\mathbf{M}'', \mathbf{S}''$

From the pseudo code given in Algorithm 1 it can be seen that the proposed 2D motif and discord extraction process comprises five sub-processes: (i) Generate sub-matrices, (ii) Generate candidate 2D motifs and discords, (iii) Get Top k 2D motifs and select discords, (iv) Intra-class pruning and (v) Inter-class pruning. Each of these is therefore discussed in further detail below.

Sub-matrix Generation. The pseudo code for the sub-matrix generation sub-process is given in Algorithm 2 (the algorithm is similar to that presented in [1]). The inputs are: (i) a pre-processed ECG image I associated with a particular class, and (ii) the desired sub-matrix window width d and height q. The sub-matrix window is slid over the image I pixel by pixel. The output is a set of sub-matrices, $\chi = \{Sub_1, Sub_2, \dots\}$ held within the image I. The algorithm commences, line 2, by defining the empty set χ in which to hold the extracted sub-matrices. Then, lines 3 to 7, the $p \times q$ sub-matrices in I are defined. We are only interested in sub-matrices that contain the ECG trace. Sub-matrices located at the edge of the image tended to be poor discriminators of class. Thus, sub-matrices that feature only black pixels and those located at the edge of the input image I were not selected for inclusion in χ. This is tested for in line 4 of the algorithm. At the end of the process χ is returned (line 8). Note that if there are only "black" images in I, the set χ would be empty, although this would be an unlikely occurrence, and indicative of a faulty ECG input image.

Algorithm 2. Generate Sub-Matrices [1].

1: **Input** I, p, q
2: $\chi = \emptyset$ ▷ Define the empty set χ to hold pixel sub-matrices
3: **for** $\forall sub_i$ of size $p \times q \in I$ **do**
4:      **if** $Sub_i \neq$ black and Sub_i not located on the edge of I **then**
5:          $\chi = \chi \cup Sub_i$
6:      **end if**
7: **end for**
8: **Return** χ

Candidate 2D Motifs and Discords. The pseudo code for generating candidate 2D motifs/discords is given in Algorithm 3, a similar algorithm was presented in [1]. The inputs are: (i) the set χ, associated with class i, of $p \times q$ sub-matrices generated using Algorithm 2, and (ii) the similarity threshold σ. The algorithm returns a set of candidate motifs/discords of the form $MD = \{\langle sub_1, count_1 \rangle, \langle sub_2, count_2 \rangle, \dots\}$ where $sub_i \in \chi$ and $count$ is the corresponding occurrence count. The algorithm starts, line 3, by defining the empty set MD. The algorithm then processes each sub-matrix sub_i in χ (lines 4 to 13). First a counter, $count_i$, is defined and set to 0 (line 5), and $\langle sub_i, count_i \rangle$ added to the set MD (line 6). Sub-matrix sub_i is then compared to every other sub-matrix sub_j in χ, whenever a similarity between sub_i and sub_j is identified the count for sub_i is incremented by one and sub_j removed from χ (so that the same sub-matrix is not counted again later in the process). The similarity between the sub-matrices, sub_i and sub_j, is determined by calculating the Euclidean distance between the two matrices using Eq. 2 given below. Euclidean distance measurement is frequently used for 1D motif similarity checking [35], and therefore was deemed to be appropriate for 2D similarity checking. The calculated Euclidean distance is then compared using the threshold σ, if the result is less than or equal to σ, sub_i and sub_j are deemed to be similar. The returned set MD will hold both candidate motifs and discords with respect to the input image (which will be associated with a particular class $c_i \in C$).

$$dist\left(sub_i, sub_j\right) = \sqrt{\sum_{h=1}^{h=(p \times q)} \left(md_{i_h} - md_{j_h}\right)^2} \qquad (2)$$

Top K 2D Motifs and Discords. Once a set of candidate motifs and discords for an image I associated with a class c_i, the set MD_i, has been identified, the next stage is to identify individual motifs and discords. Motifs will be the candidates associated with the highest counts, and discords with a count of one. The candidates in MD_i were thus ordered according to the associated frequency count and the top k were considered to be motifs, and those with a count equal to 1 to be discords. The pseudo code for achieving this is given in Algorithm 4; the algorithm is similar to that presented in [1]. The inputs are: (i) the set of candidate motifs and discords for an image i, the

Algorithm 3. Candidate 2D Motifs and Discords [1].
```
1: Input χ, σ
2: Output MDᵢ
3: MD ← ∅                          ▷ Define the empty set MD to hold extracted motifs
4: for ∀subᵢ ∈ χ do
5:     countᵢ ← 0
6:     MD ← MD ∪ ⟨subᵢ, countᵢ⟩
7:     for ∀subⱼ ∈ χ, j ≠ i do
8:         if dist (subᵢ, subⱼ) ≤ σ then
9:             countᵢ = countᵢ + 1
10:            χ ← χ with subⱼ removed
11:        end if
12:    end for
13: end for
14: Return MD
```

set $MD = \{\langle md_1, count_1 \rangle, \langle md_2, count_2 \rangle, \dots \}$ as generated using Algorithm 3, and (ii) the threshold k. The algorithm proceeds by first ordering the candidate motifs in MD according to their occurrence count (line 3). The top k are then selected as the chosen motifs and placed in M (line 4). Any candidate motifs with a count of 1 are deemed to be discords and placed in S (line 5). The sets $M = \{m_1, m_2, \dots \}$ and $S = \{s_1, s_2, \dots \}$ are then returned (line 6).

Algorithm 4. topK_2DmotifsAndDiscords [1]
```
1: input MD, k
2: output M, S
3: MDᵢ ← MD sorted in descending order
4: M ← top k candidates in MDᵢ
5: S ← candidates in MDᵢ with a count of 1
6: Return M, S
```

Intra-class Pruning. We are interested in motifs and discords that are good discriminators of class. We are therefore not interested in motifs and discords that only appear in one image. Recall that M_i is the set of motifs associated with the class c_i, and that S_i is the set of discords associated with the class c_i. Thus, we wish to remove motifs and discords, from the sets $\mathbf{M} = \{M_1, M_2, \dots \}$ and $\mathbf{S} = \{S_1, S_2, \dots \}$ respectively, that appear in only one image (intra-class pruning). The sub-process for achieving this is shown in Algorithm 5 (an identical algorithm was presented in [1]). The inputs are: (i) the set $\mathbf{M} = \{M_1, \dots, M_{|C|}\}$, (ii) the set $\mathbf{S} = \{S_1, \dots, S_{|C|}\}$ and (iii) a similarity threshold σ. The algorithm commences (lines 3 and 4) by declaring the empty sets $\mathbf{M}'$ and $\mathbf{S}'$ to hold the identified sets of motifs and discords; individual sets for individual classes. The set $\mathbf{M}$ is processed first, lines 5 to 11. For each motif m_j in the set $M_i \in \mathbf{M}$ (the set of motifs associated with class $c_i \in C$), if m_j does nor appear anywhere else in M_1 the motif is discarded, otherwise it is added to M_i'. A similar process is followed for the set $\mathbf{S}$, lines 12 to 18. At the end of the process the sets $\mathbf{M}'$ and $\mathbf{S}'$ will be returned.

Note that it might be the case that the sets $\mathbf{M}'$ and $\mathbf{S}'$ are empty. Note also that determining whether a motif appears only in a single image requires a similarity comparison with the motifs for all the other images associated with the current class. This requires the similarity threshold σ. This is therefore a computationaly expensive task.

Algorithm 5. Intra-class pruning [1].

1: **input** $\mathbf{M}, \mathbf{S}, \sigma$
2: **output** $\mathbf{M}', \mathbf{S}'$
3: $\mathbf{M}' \leftarrow \{M_1' \ldots M_{|C|}'\}$ where $\forall M_i \in \mathbf{M}', M_i = \emptyset$ ▷ Define the empty set $\mathbf{M}'$
4: $\mathbf{S}' \leftarrow \{S_1' \ldots S_{|C|}'\}$ where $\forall S_i \in \mathbf{S}', S_i = \emptyset$ ▷ Define the empty set $\mathbf{S}'$
5: **for** $\forall M_i \in \mathbf{M}$ **do**
6:      **for** $\forall m_j \in M_i$ **do**
7:          **if** m_j appears in more than one image in M_i **then**
8:              $M_i' \leftarrow M_j' \cup m_j$
9:          **end if**
10:      **end for**
11: **end for**
12: **for** $\forall S_i \in \mathbf{S}$ **do**
13:      **for** $\forall s_j \in S_i$ **do**
14:          **if** s_j appears in more than one image in S_i **then**
15:              $S_i' \leftarrow S_i' \cup m_j$
16:          **end if**
17:      **end for**
18: **end for**
19: **Return** $\mathbf{M}', \mathbf{S}'$

Inter-class Pruning. The last step in Stage 2 is to remove motifs and discords from M_1' and S_1' that are not good discriminators of class. In other words, motifs, and discords that associated with more than one class. The pseudo code for the inter-class pruning is given in Algorithm 6; the pseudo code is the same as that presented in [1]. The inputs are the sets $\mathbf{M}' = \{M_1', M_2', \ldots\}$ and $\mathbf{S}' = \{S_1', S_2', \ldots\}$ from the previous sub-process, and the similarity threshold σ. The outputs are the sets $\mathbf{M}'' = \{M_1'', M_2'', \ldots\}$, and $\mathbf{S}'' = \{S_1'', S_2'', \}$, where M_i'' is a motif and S_i'' is a discord. The algorithm commences by declaring the sets $\mathbf{M}''$ and $\mathbf{S}''$ to hold the "double" pruned sets of motifs and discords. The set $\mathbf{M}'$ is processing first (lines 5 to 11), and the set $\mathbf{S}'$ second (lines 12 to 18). Line 7 states that if the the motif m_j' does not appear in the set of motifs associated with some other class, then m_j' should be added to $\mathbf{M}''$. Line 14 should be interpreted in a similar manner but with respect to discords. On completion, line 19, $\mathbf{M}''$, and $\mathbf{S}''$ are returned. To determine whether a motif or discord appears in the context of another class again requires similarity checking, which again entails the threshold σ to determine whether two motifs (discords) are the same or not.

4.3 Feature Selection (Stage 3)

The reported evaluation presented in [1] considered a single small data set. The more extensive evaluation conducted with respect to the work presented here (see Sect. 5)

Algorithm 6. Inter-class pruning [1].

1: **input** $\mathbf{M}', \mathbf{S}', \sigma$
2: **output** $\mathbf{M}'', \mathbf{S}''$
3: $\mathbf{M}'' \leftarrow \emptyset$ ▷ Define the empty set $\mathbf{M}''$ to hold double pruned motifs
4: $\mathbf{S}'' \leftarrow \emptyset$ ▷ Define the empty set $\mathbf{S}''$ to hold dooble pruned discords
5: **for** $\forall M_i' \in \mathbf{M}'$ **do**
6:     **for** $\forall m_j' \in M_i'$ **do**
7:         **if** $\forall M_k' \in \mathbf{M}, k \neq i, m_j \notin M_k'$ **then**
8:             $\mathbf{M}'' \leftarrow \mathbf{M}'' \cup m_j$
9:         **end if**
10:     **end for**
11: **end for**
12: **for** $\forall S_i' \in \mathbf{S}'$ **do**
13:     **for** $\forall s_j' \in S_i'$ **do**
14:         **if** $\forall S_k' \in \mathbf{S}, k \neq i, S_j \notin S_k'$ **then**
15:             $\mathbf{S}'' \leftarrow \mathbf{S}'' \cup s_j$
16:         **end if**
17:     **end for**
18: **end for**
19: **return** $\mathbf{M}'', \mathbf{S}''$

revealed that if the number of extracted motifs or discords exceeded 3,000 over-fitting resulted. One solution might have been to reduce the value of the k parameter, the number of motifs extracted from an image. However, the work presented in [1] had demonstrated that $k = 5$ produced the best results. The adopted solution was therefore to include an additional stage in the overall process, Stage 3, that was invoked should the situation arise where more than 3,000 motifs were identified. The idea was to use a Dimensionality Reduction (DR) technique to reduce the number of features while attempting to keep as much of the variation in the original features set as possible [37]. There are many DR algorithms available for this purpose, for the work presented in this paper three methods were considered:

Principal Components Analysis (PCA). PCA operates using by performing a linear combination of the set of features. The combination was conducted in a given data set so as to create a smaller set of features, in such a way as to capture as much information as possible in the smallest number of features. The resulting features are referred to as "Principal Components".

Singular Value Decomposition (SVD). SVD decomposes the original features by using the concepts of Eigenvalues and Eigenvectors into three constituent matrices to remove redundant features.

T-distributed Stochastic Neighbour Embedding (T-SNE). T-SME reduces the number of features by combining them into two or three new features. In a high dimensional space, the probability similarity of points is calculated. Consequently similar points are assigned a high probability, and dissimilar points are assigned a lower probability. Then, nearby points in the high-dimensional space are mapped to the nearest points in the low-dimensional space so as to achieve dimensionality (feature) reduction.

4.4 Data Augmentation (Stage 4)

As noted above, the experiment reported in [1] focused on a single, relatively, small data set (120 records). This data set also offered the advantage that it was balanced (an equal number of examples for each class considered). In practice balanced training data is unusual. This is often the case in the context of binary classification where there tends to be more examples of "normal" cases than "abnormal" cases. To address this issue, with respect to the work presented here, an *oversampling* technique was used to augment the minority class. In "classic" oversampling the minority data is simply duplicated. However, a criticism of this approach is that it will not add any new information, only existing information. Thus, the Synthetic Minority Oversampling Technique (SMOTE) technique [8] was adopted, a technique that can be used to synthesize new examples from existing examples. For the work presented in this paper three different SMOTE variations were considered:

The original SMOTE, which operates by first selecting random records from the minority class and finding the k-nearest neighbours to these records to create "clusters". Additional synthetic records are then created using these clusters.
Support Vector Machine SMOTE (SVM-SMOTE), which is similar to the original SMOTE but instead of using the K-nearest neighbours technique, a SVM model is used.
Adaptive Synthetic (ADASYN) SMOTE, which operates by considering the data density of the minority class and generating new examples in the less dense "areas".

4.5 Feature Vector Generation (Stage 5)

The fifth stage in the proposed approach (see Fig. 1) was the generation the desired Homogeneous Feature Vectors Representation (HFVR) $H = \{V_1, V_2, \dots\}$. The idea here was that the HVRR, comprised of motifs and discords, would also allow for the addition of other features. In the evaluation presented later in this paper experiments are reported where clinical data were added. Each $V_i \in H$ is of the form $\{v_1, v_2, \dots, c\}$ where v_i is a numerical value, for example an occurrence count of a motif in $\mathbf{M}''$ or a discord in $\mathbf{S}''$, in an ECG scanned image I_i. The final element, c, is a class label taken from a set of classes C. A previously unseen record will have a null value for the variable c as this is the value we wish to predict.

4.6 Classification Model Generation (Stage 6)

Once a suitable set of feature vectors have been generated the final stage was to generate the desired CVD classification model. The feature vector representation lends it self to many classification model generators (this was why this representation was selected with respect to the work presented here. In [33] and [34], SVM model generation was adopted for CVD classification. SVM model generation was also adopted in [1]. A SVM classification model was therefore also used with respect to the work presented in this paper.

4.7   Classification Model Usage (Stage 7)

Once the desired CVD classification model had been generated it could be applied to new data. In most cases this would be straight forward. However, in some cases, we may have more than one ECG image per patient, thus *multiple learning classification*. This was a feature of one of the evaluation data sets used for evaluation purposes (as reported on in Sect. 5). Thus some kind of "conflict resolution" was required where contradictory CVD classifications were produced. Three alternative options were considered on how to deal with this situation.

Averaging. Average the motif counts for each patient when identifying the motifs to be used, regardless of the number of ECG images considered, and used

Voting. Produce multiple classifications, one for each ECG image associated with a patient, and select the class that occurs the most frequently. In the event of a tie-break situation choose the class with the most serious consequences (in other words err on the side of caution).

Using only one image input. Thus avoiding the problem all together. In this case, the most recent ECG image was selected.

5   Evaluation

The extensive evaluation (more extensive than that discussed in [1]) of the CVD classification model generation mechanism is reported in this section. For the evaluation three data sets were used: (i) the subset of the Guangzhou Heart Study data set [9] concerned with AF which was also used in [1], (ii) the Guangzhou Heart Study data set in its entirety and (iii) a data set provided by the Liverpool Heart and Chest Hospital (LHCH). More detail concerning these data sets is provided in Sub-sect. 5.1. A SVM classification model was used with respect to all the experiments reported here, with Grid Search to choose the best parameters (C, gamma, and kernel). The evaluation metrics used were: accuracy, precision, recall, F1 score and AUC. Repeated Ten-fold cross-validation was used throughout. The Friedman Test was used to determine whether or not there was a statistically significant difference between the performance. Where a statistically significant difference was identified, the Nemenyi post-hoc test was applied to identify the distinctions between the performances of the mechanisms considered. In [1] the evaluation objectives were focused on identifying the appropriate values for the parameters σ, k, p, and q. From [1] the most appropriate values were found to be:

- σ: The similarity threshold used to compare two motifs (the maximum distance between two motifs) $\sigma = 0.2$
- k: The number of most frequent candidate motifs to be selected from each image, $k = 5$
- p: The pixel matrix row size, $p = 30$
- q: The pixel matrix column size, $q = 90$

These were thus the values adopted with respect to the evaluation presented in this paper. The objectives of the evaluation were:

1. To identify the most appropriate feature selection (dimensionality reduction) and data augmentation techniques.
2. To identify the most appropriate conflict resolution technique where we have a "multiple learning classification" issue.
3. To compare the operation of the proposed approach when the motif/discord set was augmented in various ways with additional data.
4. To compare the operation of the proposed approach with a "traditional" 1D waveform approach.

Each of these objectives is discussed in further detail in the following four sub-sections, Sub-sects. 5.2, 5.3, 5.4 and 5.5.

5.1 Data Sets

As noted in the introduction to this section three data sets were used for the evaluation presented here:

1. Guangzhou Atrial Fibrillation (GAF)
2. Guangzhou Heart Study (GHS)
3. Liverpool Heart and Chest Hospital (LHCH)

Some statistics concerning these data sets are given in Table 1. GAF and GHS, the first two data sets listed, were extracted from the Guangzhou Heart Study data set [9]. This comprised 1172 patients; each patient was associated with a 12-leads ECG scanned image and patient attributes, including age and gender. Each patient record had been labeled according to arrhythmia type, either sinus arrhythmia (normal) or abnormal. The abnormal category included: (i) Atrial Fibrillation (AF) and Flutter (AFL), (ii) Premature ventricular contractions, (iii) Premature atrial contractions , (iv) ventricular tachycardia, (v) Wolff-Parkinson-White syndrome, (vi) pacing rhythm and (vii) borderline rhythm. Each image was stored using JPEG compression with a resolution of 300 dpi (dots per inch).

Table 1. Statistics Concerning Evaluation Data Sets.

Data Set	c_1				c_2			
	Label	# Rec.	# Male	# Female	Lable	# Rec.	# Male	# Female
GAF	AF	60	32	28	Not AF	60	22	38
GHS	Normal	878	283	595	Abnormal	294	116	178
LHCH	No recurrence	639	428	211	Recurrence	270	182	88

The GAF data set comprised a subset of Guangzhou Heart Study data set that featured only two labels, Atrial Fibrillation (AF) and sinus (normal) rhythm. In other words AF versus not AF. This was the data set used for evaluation purposes with respect to the work presented in [1]. The AF/not AF class split was 60/60 records (see Table 1)

The GHS data set comprised the entire Guangzhou Heart Study data set of 1172 patients. This was the largest data set considered and therefore Feature Selection was applied, Stage 3 in the proposed process given in Fig. 1. The individual patients held in the data set were categorised as being either Normal or Abnormal. The

Normal/Abnormal class split was 878/294. Thus, unlike in the case of the GAF data set, the GHS data set was significantly imbalanced. Data augmentation was therefore also applied, Stage 4 in the proposed process given in Fig. 1. It should also be noted that the GHS data set was comprised mostly of female patients, 773 (66%) compared to 399 males (34%). The age distribution was as follows: Normal class, 283 males and 595 females; Abnormal class, 116 males and 178 females. The age range of all the patients in the GHS data set was from 49 to 96, with a mean age 71.4 (a standard deviation of 6.260).

The LHCH data set was collected by the authors in collaboration with the Liverpool Heart and Chest Hospital. This data set focused on the recurrence of Atrial Fibrillation (AF) after catheter ablation which is estimated to be between 20% and 45% [10]. Accordingly, the data set comprised two classes: (i) patients who had AF and a catheter ablation where there was no recurrence, and (ii) patients who had AF and a catheter ablation where there was a recurrence. Details of all patients who had AF and a catheter ablation at the hospital, between June 2013 and December 2019, were recorded in a prospectively maintained data registry. For the LHCH data set patients were included if all their clinical and ECG data was available. ECG scanned images were only considered if they were taken within six months before the ablation. This meant that some patients had more than one ECG image associated with them. The minimum was one and the maximum was ten, but the average was two. In other words, the LHCH data set featured a "multiple learning classification" issue. Each image was stored using TIFF compression at a resolution of 300 dpi. In total, the LHCH data set comprised 909 patients and 1821 ECG images.

The LHCH data set also included information related to gender, age, body mass index (high times weight), and the presence of concomitant diseases. These features were all included because, according to Freming's study [36], these were risk factors related to AF recurrence. The following concomitant diseases were considered relevant: heart failure, hypertension, diabetes mellitus, hypercholesterolaemia, chronic kidney disease, thyroid dysfunction, and chronic obstructive pulmonary disease. These were selected because these had been identified in the study reported in [10]. The Left Atrial (LA) size was also included, because this is considered to be an effective factor for predicting AF recurrence [27].

The final LHCH data set was composed of 610 male patients (67%) against 299 female patients (33%), distributed as follows: No recurrence class, 428 males and 211 females; Recurrence class, 182 males and 88 females. Thus, as in the case of the GHS data set, the LHCH was significantly imbalanced. Therefore, referring back to the proposed process (Fig. 1), the application of Data Augmentation (Stage 4) was also applied to this data set.

Of the total of 909 patients, 176 (19%) had never used alcohol while 733 (81%) were current drinkers of alcohol. Furthermore, 506 (56%) have never smoked, 66 (7%) were current smokers and 341 (37%) were ex-smokers. Despite the minimum age of the patients being 19 years, the mean age was 60.5 years, implying that there were more elderly patients in the sample than younger. Some further statistical detail concerning the LHCH data set is given in Table 2. From the foregoing, it is clear that the LHCH data set was the most sophisticated, in terms of additional features, of the three data sets considered.

Table 2. Descriptive Statistics for LHCH data set.

Descriptive Statistics					
Risk factor	N	Minimum	Maximum	Mean	Std. Deviation
Age	909	19	84	60.5	10.711
Height	909	131	197	173.49	9.683
Weight	909	45.50	150	88.47	16.582
LA size	909	20	100	41.36	5.495

5.2 Most Appropriate Feature Selection and Data Augmentation Techniques (Objective 1)

The proposed process, as described in Sect. 4, includes a feature selection stage (Stage 3) and a data augmentation stage (Stage 4). Neither was included in the original process presented in [1]. The first is used where overfitting occurs because a large number of motifs have been derived. Empirical evidence (not reported here) suggests that overfitting occurs when the number of motifs exceeds 3000. This was the case with respect to the GHS data set. The second was used where a significant class imbalance existed. This was the case with respect to both the GHS and LHCH data sets. Referring back to Sub-sect. 4.3 three feature selection techniques were suggested: (i) Principal Components Analysis (PCA), (ii) Singular Value Decomposition (SVD) and (iii) T-distributed Stochastic Neighbor Embedding (T-SNE). Referring back to Sub-sect. 4.4 three data augmentation techniques were suggested: (i) SMOTE, (ii) SVM-SMOTE and (iii) ADASYN. The operation of all these techniques were compared to determine the most appropriate.

Table 3 shows the results obtained using SVM classification and the three feature selection techniques considered when applied to the GHS data set (best results in bold font). SMOTE data augmentation was used in all three cases because further experiments (reported later in this sub-section) indicated that this produced the best results. Inspection of the table indicates that best values were obtained using T-SNE, while the application of PCA resulted in overfitting. It was thus concluding that for feature selection T-SNE was the most appropriate choice.

Table 3. Evaluation results, using the GHS data set and SMOTE augmentation, to determine the most appropriate feature selection technique (best results in bold font).

DR Techniques	Accuracy %	Precision %	Recall %	F1 %	AUC %
PCA	Overfitting				
SVD	71.52	65.10	93.20	76.58	71.58
TSNE	**81.50**	**84.00**	**78.15**	**80.87**	**81.54**

Table 4 shows the results obtained using SVM classification and the three data augmentation techniques considered, when applied to the GHS and LHCH data sets (best

Table 4. Evaluation results, using the GHS and LHCH data sets and T-SNE feature selection, to determine the most appropriate data augmentation technique (best results in bold font)

Technique	GHS data set					LHCH data set				
	Accuracy %	Precis. %	Recall %	F1 %	AUC %	Accuracy %	Precis. %	Recall %	F1 %	AUC %
SMOTE	**81.50**	**84.00**	78.15	80.87	**81.54**	**66.82**	74.89	52.17	60.62	**66.83**
SVMSMOTE	78.49	79.86	84.86	82.21	77.17	62.76	57.49	97.15	72.15	62.67
ADASYN	79.24	82.86	75.11	78.68	79.40	64.51	62.47	80.66	70.15	63.78

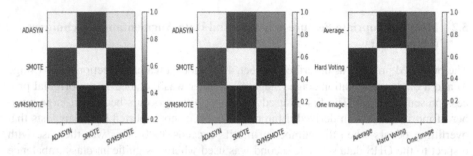

(a) Nemenyi post-hoc test for augmentation techniques using the GHS data set

(b) Nemenyi post-hoc test for augmentation techniques using the LHCH data set

(c) Nemenyi post-hoc test for conflict resolution using L-HCH data set

Fig. 2. Nemenyi post-hoc test result.

results in bold font). T-SNE feature selection was used in all three cases because this had been shown to provide the best results (as reported in Table 3). For the LHCH data set an averaging technique was used for the multiple instance learning; later experiments, reported in 5.3, indicated that this produced the best results. From Table 4, it can be seen that using SMOTE produced best results. A subsequent Friedman Test indicated a statistically significant difference with respect to all the results obtained. Figures 2a and 2b show the outcomes obtained from consequent Nemenyi post-hoc tests for the two data sets (GHS and LHCH). From the figures, it can be seen that there was a statistically significant difference when using SMOTE compared with the other methods considered. It was thus concluding that for data augmentation SMOTE was the most appropriate choice.

Table 5. Evaluation results, using the LHCH data sets, coupled with SMOTE data augmentation and T-SNE feature selection, to determine the most appropriate conflict resolution technique (best results in bold font).

DR Techniques	Accuracy %	Precision %	Recall %	F1 %	AUC %
Average	**66.82**	**74.89**	**52.17**	**60.62**	**66.83**
Voting	52.78	75.67	58.62	55.41	51.46
One Image	59.40	65.57	40.43	49.63	59.45

5.3   Most Appropriate Conflict Resolution Technique (Objective 2)

As noted earlier in Sub-sect. 5.1, the LHCH data set, in many cases, features more than one ECG image for each patient resulting in Multiple Instance Classification requiring some form of conflict resolution should contradictory classifications result. In Sub-sect. 4.7 three conflict resolution techniques were suggested: (i) Averaging, (ii) Voting and (iii) avoiding the problem by using only the most recent ECG image. The second evaluation objective, Objective 2, was to identify which of these techniques produced the most effective classification results. The results are presented in Table 5 (best results in bold font). From the table, it can be seen that the averaging produced the best results. A Friedman Test indicated a statistically significant difference in the results. The outcome of a consequent Nemenyi post-hoc test is presented in Fig. 2c. From the figure, it can be seen that there was a clear statistically significant difference in operation when using averaging.

5.4   Operation Using Additional Features (Objective 3)

Table 6. Evaluation results, coupled with (where required) SMOTE data augmentation, T-SNE feature selection and averaging conflict resolution, to determine the most appropriate data combination (best results in bold font).

Evaluation of Proposed Approach						
Data set	HFVR	Accuracy %	Precision %	Recall %	F1 %	AUC %
GAF Data set	Motifs only	84.6	84.00	86.21	83.71	85.61
	Discords only	45.00	45.00	43.00	43.98	46.50
	Clinical only	56.25	55.50	54.33	53.85	54.67
	Motifs+ Discords	77.50	73.48	85.14	76.78	77.99
	Motifs+Clinical	**86.25**	**85.83**	**86.50**	**84.88**	**85.87**
	Discords +Clinical	48.75	51.70	65.67	55.23	51.42
	Motifs+Discords +Clinical	78.75	74.83	82.57	77.00	79.62
GHS Data set	Motifs only	81.50	84.00	78.15	80.87	81.54
	Discords only	52.43	52.36	60.69	55.84	52.77
	Clinical only	64.08	64.85	61.10	62.80	63.99
	Motifs+ Discords	72.76	74.50	69.54	71.80	72.74
	Motifs+Clinical	**84.09**	**87.76**	**79.20**	**83.17**	**84.05**
	Discords +Clinical	59.87	60.27	59.65	59.56	59.95
	Motifs+Discords +Clinical	82.58	87.89	75.74	81.24	82.56
LHCH Data set	Motifs only	66.82	74.89	52.17	60.62	66.83
	Discords only	46.63	47.80	58.61	51.79	47.45
	Clinical only	82.32	78.88	88.22	83.16	82.43
	Motifs+ Discords	66.89	66.31	76.47	69.44	67.60
	Motifs+Clinical	**84.59**	**79.84**	**92.29**	**85.57**	**84.56**
	Discords +Clinical	76.61	81.16	69.87	74.79	76.81
	Motifs+Discords +Clinical	81.38	86.14	74.89	80.01	81.43

The previous sub-section described the experiments conducted to determine the best techniques to be used for: (i) feature selection, (ii) data augmentation and (iii) conflict resolution (in the event of multiple instance classification). Best results were obtained using: T-SNE feature selection, SMOTE data augmentation and averaging (where applicable). In this section, the evaluation results obtained from further experiments, conducted using additional features, are discussed. Combinations of: motifs, discords, and clinical data such as age and gender. The aim was to determine whether any advantage would be gained by adding additional features from related sources. Similar experiments were conducted in [2]; but when using 1D time series extracted from ECG traces. The reported results indicated that adding additional features improved the effectiveness of the CVD classification. Further motivation was provided from work, such as that reported in [17,28], which suggested that age, gender, smoking status, and so on, were all risk factors to be considered when classifying ECG data. Experiments were conducted using all three data sets, the GAF, GHS and LHCH. In each case seven different data combinations were considered: (i) motifs only (M), (ii) discords only (S), (iii) clinical data only (C), (iv) motifs and discords (M+S), (v) motifs and clinical data (M+C), (vi) discords and clinical data (S+C) and (vii) motifs, discords and clinical data (M+S+C). In each case, were appropriate, T-SNE feature selection, SMOTE data augmentation, and averaging conflict resolution were used.

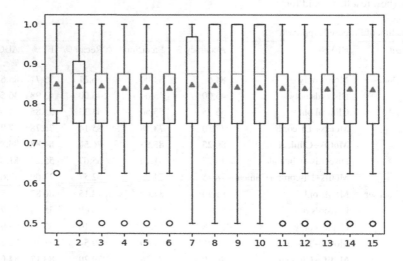

Fig. 3. Box and Whisker plots of the accuracy vs fifteen repeats for Ten-fold-cross-validation.

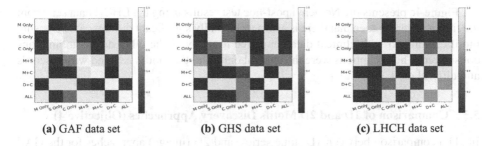

(a) GAF data set   (b) GHS data set   (c) LHCH data set

Fig. 4. Nemenyi post-hoc test when using different data combinations.

The results are presented in Table 6. From the table, it can be observed that in all three cases, the combination of motifs and clinical data produced the best results. The worst results were obtained using discords. Indeed, from the results obtained, it can be argued that the inclusion of discords had a negative effect as evidenced when discords were added to the motif and clinical data combination. It should also be noted here, with respect to the results presented in Table 6, that we re-ran the experiments for the GAF data set to calculate AUC, Unlike the case of the evaluation reported in [1] repeated Ten-cross validation was used, rather than single Ten-cross validation. Consequently, the results presented in Table 6 are not identical to the ones presented previously in [1]. The rational for using repeated Ten-fold cross-validation was that a more reliable estimate of model performance would be obtained. Note that we calculated the mean, and the standard error of the accuracy on each iteration to minimize the standard error and stabilize the mean of estimated performance.

Figure 3, shows a sequence of Box and Whisker plots for the recorded accuracy for the motifs-only model. The Y-axis gives the accuracy and the X-axis the number of cross validation repeats. From the figure, it can see that the mean seems to be around a value of 84.6 and that the standard error decreased with the increase in the number of repeats and stabilized with a value around 0.010.

A Friedman test was also applied with respect to the results obtained using each data set. The Friedman test demonstrated that there was a statistically significant difference in performance in all three cases. The results of the consequent Nemenyi post-hoc tests are presented in Fig. 4.

Figure 4a presents the Nemenyi post-hoc test results using the GAF data set. From the figure, it can be seen that there is a statistically significant difference when using motifs combined with clinical data compared to many of the other data combinations considered. The exceptions were the motifs and discords; and the motifs, discords and clinical data combinations.

Figure 4b shows the Nemenyi post-hoc test results using the GHS data set. The best overall results were obtained using the GHS data set, and particularly when motifs were combined with clinical data (an AUC of 84.05%). From the figure it can be seen that the results obtained when using motifs combined with clinical data were statistically different from most of the other combinations considered; with the exception of motifs used on their own, and motifs coupled with discords and clinical data.

Figure 4c presents the Nemenyi post-hoc test results using the LHCH data set. From the figure, it can be seen that there is also a statistically significant difference when using motifs combined with clinical data compared to many of the other data combinations considered. The exceptions were the clinical only, and the motifs coupled with discords and clinical data.

5.5 Comparison of 1D and 2D Motifs Discovery Approaches (Objective 4)

In [1] a comparison between 1D (time series) and 2D (image) approaches for the GAF data set, using motifs on their own, discords on their own, and motifs and discords combined. These results are presented in the top part of Table 7. The comparison was made to investigate the hypothesis that using 2D motifs extracted from untransformed ECG images would produce a better classification than that obtained using features selected from 1D transformed waveform representations of ECG data. For the work presented here this experiment was repeated using the GHS and LHCH data sets. To obtain the ID results the scanned GHS and LHCH images were transformed into a time series format using a recent algorithm for achieving this [12]. Following the transformation, the 1D motif approach proposed in [3] was applied. The results are presented in the lower part of Table 7. In the table best results in each case are highlighted in bold font. From the table, it can be seen that the outcomes from the experiments using GHS and LHCH data stes corroborated the results reported in [1]. That the 2D formatted data produced better results than the 1D format. Interestingly, from Table, the 1D waveform approach that using a combination of motifs as features, works well in comparison to other 1D waveform approaches. However, from Table 7, best results for the GAF and GHS data sets were obtained using 2D motifs only; while for the LHCH data set best results were obtained using 2D motifs and discords combined.

Table 7. Comparison of 1D and 2D motifs Discovery Approaches.

Data set	HFVR	2D Approach					1D Approach				
		Acc. %	Pre. %	Rec. %	F1 %	AUC %	Acc. %	Pre. %	Rec. %	F1 %	AUC %
GAF Data set	Motifs only	**85.00**	**84.00**	**86.21**	**83.71**	**85.61**	68.48	70.00	68.49	69.88	69.28
	Discords only	45.00	45.00	43.00	43.98	46.50	67.59	76.00	66.59	71.24	68.23
	Motifs + Discords	77.50	73.48	85.14	76.78	77.99	**72.35**	**78.74**	**72.50**	**75.49**	**71.92**
GHS Data set	Motifs only	**81.50**	**84.00**	**78.15**	**80.87**	**81.54**	72.119	77.96	70.01	73.22	73.00
	Discords only	52.43	52.36	60.69	55.84	52.77	69.59	74.05	68.81	70.53	70.36
	Motifs + Discords	72.76	74.50	69.54	71.80	72.74	**76.16**	**83.56**	**73.28**	**77.66**	**77.17**
LHCH Data set	Motifs only	66.82	74.89	52.17	60.62	66.83	64.69	72.60	62.96	67.08	65.41
	Discords only	46.63	47.80	58.61	51.79	47.45	64.14	72.32	62.20	66.36	65.23
	Motifs + Discords	**66.89**	**66.31**	**76.47**	**69.44**	**67.60**	**66.76**	**73.77**	**64.96**	**68.70**	**66.81**

6 Conclusion

In this paper, the approach to ECG scanned image classification using 2D motifs reported in [1] has been extended and re-analysed using additional data sets and evaluation aspects. It was assumed that the "traditional" approach to ECG classification using waveform transformation and limited features resulted in information loss due to the approximations used, and that a better classification could be obtained if the classification model was built using the original image without any transformations. To investigate this, three data sets were tested using the 2D motifs approached. The potential of including other clinical features such as age and gender were also investigated and it was found that this provided better results. The reported evaluation demonstrated that the best results were obtained when 2D motifs were extracted from an entire image compared with when the image was transformed into a 1D waveform format and 1D motifs used as features. The best accuracy of 85% was obtained using the proposed approach, and 86.25% when adding additional clinical features, in comparison with the best accuracy of 68.48% using the 1D waveform format. For future work, the authors intend to investigate: (i) improving the performance of the 2D motif extraction from scanned images process, (ii) the effect of combining 2D motifs and discords with features from other formats such as Echo data and patient data, and (iii) the application of the proposed approach to alternative CVD application domains that feature multi-class classification.

References

1. Aldosari., H., Coenen., F., Lip., G.Y.H., Zheng., Y.: Two-dimensional motif extraction from images: a study using an electrocardiogram. In: Proceedings of the 14th International Joint Conference on Knowledge Discovery, Knowledge Engineering and Knowledge Management - KDIR, INSTICC, pp. 19–28. SciTePress (2022)
2. Aldosari, H., Coenen, F., Lip, G.Y.H., Zheng, Y.: Addressing the challenge of data heterogeneity using a homogeneous feature vector representation: a study using time series and cardiovascular disease classification. In: Bramer, M., Ellis, R. (eds.) SGAI-AI 2021. LNCS (LNAI), vol. 13101, pp. 254–266. Springer, Cham (2021). https://doi.org/10.1007/978-3-030-91100-3_21
3. Aldosari, H., Coenen, F., Lip, G.Y.H., Zheng, Y.: Motif based feature vectors: towards a homogeneous data representation for cardiovascular diseases classification. In: Golfarelli, M., Wrembel, R., Kotsis, G., Tjoa, A.M., Khalil, I. (eds.) DaWaK 2021. LNCS, vol. 12925, pp. 235–241. Springer, Cham (2021). https://doi.org/10.1007/978-3-030-86534-4_22
4. Apostolico, A., Parida, L., Rombo, S.E.: Motif patterns in 2D. Theoret. Comput. Sci. **390**(1), 40–55 (2008)
5. Badilini, F., Erdem, T., Zareba, W., Moss, A.J.: ECGScan: a method for conversion of paper electrocardiographic printouts to digital electrocardiographic files. J. Electrocardiol. **38**(4), 310–318 (2005)
6. Baydoun, M., Safatly, L., Abou Hassan, O.K., Ghaziri, H., El Hajj, A., Isma'eel, H.: High precision digitization of paper-based ECG records: a step toward machine learning. IEEE J. Transl. Eng. Health Med. **7**, 1–8 (2019)
7. Bosch, A., Munoz, X., Marti, R.: Which is the best way to organize/classify images by content? Image Vis. Comput. **25**(6), 778–791 (2007)

8. Chawla, N.V., Bowyer, K.W., Hall, L.O., Kegelmeyer, W.P.: SMOTE: synthetic minority over-sampling technique. J. Artif. Intell. Res. **16**, 321–357 (2002)
9. Deng, H., et al.: Epidemiological characteristics of atrial fibrillation in southern China: results from the Guangzhou heart study. Sci. Rep. **8**(1), 1–10 (2018)
10. Dretzke, J., et al.: Predicting recurrent atrial fibrillation after catheter ablation: a systematic review of prognostic models. EP Europace **22**(5), 748–760 (2020)
11. Ebrahimi, Z., Loni, M., Daneshtalab, M., Gharehbaghi, A.: A review on deep learning methods for ECG arrhythmia classification. Expert Syst. Appl.: X **7**, 100033 (2020)
12. Fortune, J., Coppa, N., Haq, K.T., Patel, H., Tereshchenko, L.G.: Digitizing ECG image: new fully automated method and open-source software code. medRxiv (2021)
13. Furfaro, A., Groccia, M.C., Rombo, S.E.: 2D motif basis applied to the classification of digital images. Comput. J. **60**(7), 1096–1109 (2017)
14. Gupta, V., Mittal, M., Mittal, V., Saxena, N.K.: A critical review of feature extraction techniques for ECG signal analysis. J. Inst. Eng. (India): Ser. B **102**, 1–12 (2021)
15. Houssein, E.H., Kilany, M., Hassanien, A.E.: ECG signals classification: a review. Int. J. Intell. Eng. Inf. **5**(4), 376–396 (2017)
16. Jayaraman, S., Swamy, P., Damodaran, V., Venkatesh, N.: A novel technique for ECG morphology interpretation and arrhythmia detection based on time series signal extracted from scanned ECG record. In: Advances in Electrocardiograms-Methods and Analysis, pp. 127–140 (2012)
17. Joseph, P., et al.: Cardiovascular disease, mortality, and their associations with modifiable risk factors in a multi-national south Asia cohort: a PURE substudy. Eur. Heart J. **43**(30), 2831–2840 (2022)
18. Kar, A., Das, L.: A technical review on statistical feature extraction of ECG signal. In: IJCA Special Issue on 2nd National Conference-Computing, Communication and Sensor Network, CCSN, pp. 35–40 (2011)
19. Khleaf, H.K., Ghazali, K.H., Abdalla, A.N.: Features extraction technique for ECG recording paper. In: Proceeding of the International Conference on Artificial Intelligence in Computer Science and ICT (2013)
20. Liu, B., Li, J., Chen, C., Tan, W., Chen, Q., Zhou, M.: Efficient motif discovery for large-scale time series in healthcare. IEEE Trans. Industr. Inf. **11**(3), 583–590 (2015)
21. Liu, X., Wang, H., Li, Z., Qin, L.: Deep learning in ECG diagnosis: a review. Knowl.-Based Syst. **227**, 107187 (2021)
22. Loresco, P.J.M., Africa, A.D.: ECG print-out features extraction using spatial-oriented image processing techniques. J. Telecommun., Electr. Comput. Eng. (JTEC) **10**(1–5), 15–20 (2018)
23. Maletzke, A.G., et al.: Time series classification using motifs and characteristics extraction: a case study on ECG databases. In: Fourth International Workshop on Knowledge Discovery, Knowledge Management and Decision Support, pp. 322–329. Atlantis Press (2013)
24. Mensah, G.A., Roth, G.A., Fuster, V.: The global burden of cardiovascular diseases and risk factors: 2020 and beyond. J. Am. Coll. Cardiol. **74**(20), 2529–2532 (2019)
25. Mir, H.Y., Singh, O.: ECG denoising and feature extraction techniques-a review. J. Med. Eng. Technol. **45**(8), 672–684 (2021)
26. Nadakinamani, R.G., et al.: Clinical data analysis for prediction of cardiovascular disease using machine learning techniques. Comput. Intell. Neurosci., Soc. Issue Artif. Intell. Mach. Learn.-Driven Decis.-Mak. (2022)
27. Njoku, A., et al.: Left atrial volume predicts atrial fibrillation recurrence after radiofrequency ablation: a meta-analysis. Ep Europace **20**(1), 33–42 (2018)
28. Peters, S.A., et al.: Clustering of risk factors and the risk of incident cardiovascular disease in Asian and Caucasian populations: results from the Asia Pacific Cohort studies collaboration. BMJ Open **8**(3), e019335 (2018)

29. Ravichandran, L., Harless, C., Shah, A.J., Wick, C.A., Mcclellan, J.H., Tridandapani, S.: Novel tool for complete digitization of paper electrocardiography data. IEEE J. Transl. Eng. Health Med. **1**, 1800107 (2013)
30. Roth, G.A., et al.: Global burden of cardiovascular diseases and risk factors, 1990–2019: update from the GBD 2019 study. J. Am. Coll. Cariol. **76**(25), 2982–3201 (2020)
31. Sahoo, S., Dash, M., Behera, S., Sabut, S.: Machine learning approach to detect cardiac arrhythmias in ECG signals: a survey. Innov. Res. BioMed. Eng. **41**(4), 185–194 (2020)
32. Seena, V., Yomas, J.: A review on feature extraction and denoising of ECG signal using wavelet transform. In: 2014 2nd International Conference on Devices, Circuits and Systems (ICDCS), pp. 1–6. IEEE (2014)
33. Smíšek, R.: ECG signal classification based on SVM. Biomed. Eng. **1**, 365–369 (2016)
34. Thanapatay, D., Suwansaroj, C., Thanawattano, C.: ECG beat classification method for ECG printout with principle components analysis and support vector machines. In: 2010 International Conference on Electronics and Information Engineering, vol. 1, pp. V1–72. IEEE (2010)
35. Torkamani, S., Lohweg, V.: Survey on time series motif discovery. Wiley Interdisc. Rev.: Data Min. Knowl. Discov. **7**(2), e1199 (2017)
36. Truong, C.D., Nguyen, B.T., Van Cong Tran, T.: Prediction of risk factors for recurrence of atrial fibrillation in patients with arterial hypertension. Int. J. Cardiovasc. Imaging **37**(12), 3413–3421 (2021). https://doi.org/10.1007/s10554-021-02331-y
37. Velliangiri, S., Alagumuthukrishnan, S., et al.: A review of dimensionality reduction techniques for efficient computation. Procedia Comput. Sci. **165**, 104–111 (2019)
38. Wankhedkar, R., Jain, S.K.: Motif discovery and anomaly detection in an ECG using matrix profile. In: Panigrahi, C.R., Pati, B., Mohapatra, P., Buyya, R., Li, K.-C. (eds.) Progress in Advanced Computing and Intelligent Engineering. AISC, vol. 1198, pp. 88–95. Springer, Singapore (2021). https://doi.org/10.1007/978-981-15-6584-7_9

Degree Centrality Definition, and Its Computation for Homogeneous Multilayer Networks Using Heuristics-Based Algorithms

Hamza Pavel, Anamitra Roy, Abhishek Santra, and Sharma Chakravarthy[✉]

UT Arlington, Arlington, TX, USA
{hamzareza.pavel,axr9563,abhishek.santra}@mavs.uta.edu,
sharmac@cse.uta.edu
https://itlab.uta.edu/

Abstract. Centrality metrics for *simple graphs/networks* are well-defined and each has numerous main-memory algorithms. MultiLayer Networks (MLNs) are becoming popular for modeling complex data sets with multiple types of entities and relationships. When data sets are modeled using MLNs, it is imperative that algorithms for each metric (e.g., degree, betweenness, closeness, etc.) are developed including definitions. As there are no definitions and algorithms for computing centrality measures *directly* on MLNs, existing strategies are used that reduce (aggregate or collapse) MLN layers to simple graphs using Boolean AND or OR operation on layer edges. This approach negates the benefits of MLN modeling as these result in loss of structure and semantics and further are not, typically, efficient.

In this paper, we address the degree centrality metric for homogeneous MLNs (HoMLNs) starting with its definition. We then develop heuristics-based algorithms for computing degree centrality on MLNs *directly (i.e., without reducing them to simple graphs)* using the decoupling-based approach which has been shown to be efficient as well as structure and semantics preserving. We compare the accuracy and precision of our algorithms with Boolean OR-aggregated graphs of Homogeneous MLNs as ground truth. The decoupling approach is used because it can take advantage of parallelism and is more efficient than aggregation- or projection-based approaches. We also highlight through several observations and lemmas the information needs from each layer for the decoupling-based approach. Extensive experimental analysis is performed on large synthetic, real-world-like, and actual real-world data sets of varying sizes and graph characteristics to validate the accuracy, precision, and efficiency of our algorithms.

Keywords: Multilayer networks · Homogeneous MLN degree centrality definition · Heuristics-based algorithms · Decoupling-based approach

1 Motivation

Graph modeling of complex data sets provides opportunities for using graph characteristics and metrics for analysis and knowledge discovery. These metrics can quantify

F. Coenen et al. (Eds.): IC3K 2022, CCIS 1842, pp. 28–52, 2023.
https://doi.org/10.1007/978-3-031-43471-6_2

the importance of node/edge/subgraphs, which can translate to meaningful real-world inferences on the data set. For example, cities that act as airline hubs, people on social networks who can maximize the reach of an advertisement/tweet/post, identification of mobile towers whose malfunctioning can lead to maximum disruption, and so on. Centrality measures include degree centrality [9], closeness centrality [13], eigenvector centrality [36], stress centrality [35], betweenness centrality [8], harmonic centrality [7], and PageRank centrality [27], which are some of the well-defined and widely-used local and global centrality measures for simple graphs.

These centrality measurements use a set of criteria to determine the importance of a node or edge in a graph. Degree centrality metric measures the importance of a node in a graph in terms of its degree, which is the number of 1-hop neighbors[1] a node has in the graph.

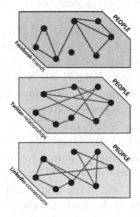

Fig. 1. Social Media HoMLN Example [26].

A multilayer network [14,17,21,32,33] is made up of layers, each of which is a simple graph[2] or a network with nodes (that correspond to entities) and edges (that correspond to relationships). Nodes within a layer are connected (termed *intra-layer* edges) based on a relationship between nodes. Nodes in a layer may also be optionally connected to nodes in other layers through *inter-layer* edges. As an example, the diverse interactions among the *same set of people* across different social media (such as Facebook, LinkedIn, and Twitter) can be modeled using a multilayer network shown in Fig. 1. In this MLN, the entities in each layer are the same, but the relationships in each layer are different (Facebook-friends, Twitter-relationships, LinkedIn-connections). This kind of MLN is referred to as homogeneous MLNs (or HoMLNs). As the edges between layers are implicit, they are not shown. It is also feasible to build

---

[1] We use degree as 1-hop neighbors in this paper without taking direction into account. However, for directed graphs, in- or out-degree can be substituted for the heuristics proposed. Hence, we discuss only undirected graphs.

[2] A simple graph has nodes that are connected by edges (optionally labeled and/or directed) with no loops or multiple edges between same nodes.

MLNs with *different types of entities and relationships* within and across layers. This type of heterogeneous MLNs (or HeMLNs) is required for modeling, for example, the DBLP data set [1] with authors, papers, and conferences [21,34]. Hybrid Multilayer networks (HyMLNs) include both types of layers.

We present formal definitions of multilayer networks below and associated analysis functions. These definitions will help us define MLN centrality definition and detection.

Definition 1. *A multilayer network $MLN(G, X)$, is defined by two sets of graphs. The set $G = \{G_1, G_2, \ldots, G_n\}$ contains* **simple** *graphs, where $G_i(V_i, E_i)$ is defined by a set of vertices V_i and a set of edges E_i. An edge $e(v, u) \in E_i$, connects vertices v and u, where $v, u \in V_i$. The set $X = \{X_{1,2}, X_{1,3}, \ldots, X_{n-1,n}\}$ consists of* **bipartite** *graphs. Each graph $X_{i,j}(V_i, V_j, L_{i,j})$ is defined by two sets of vertices V_i and V_j and a set of edges (or links) $L_{i,j}$, such that for every link $l(a, b) \in L_{i,j}$, $a \in V_i$ and $b \in V_j$, where V_i (V_j) is the vertex set of graph G_i (G_j). Some of $X_{i,j}$ can be empty.*

In a homogeneous multilayer network (HoMLN), the vertex sets are identical[3] across the constituent layers, i.e., $V_1 = V_2 = \ldots = V_n$. The vertices in each constituent network are implicitly connected to their corresponding vertices in the other layers and the set X, is not required for the HoMLN definition.

As an alternative to the traditional way of computing metrics on a MLN, we use the notion of decoupling which has several advantages. In the **decoupling approach** (elaborated in Sect. 3), the multilayer network $MLN(G, X)$ is decoupled into multiple components, $G_1, G_2, \ldots, G_m$ which are layers of the MLN. Each component is analyzed using the algorithm Ψ, and pairs of partial results are combined in a reduction like operation using a composition function Θ. We express the analysis result of the decoupling approach as MLN_Ψ^Θ. One of our goals (and challenge) is to develop algorithms for Θ so that MLN_Ψ^Θ to be the same (or close to) ground truth for the MLN as indicated by the definition. Ψ is, typically, already defined (e.g., community, degree centrality, substructure, etc.) and algorithms available as it is for a single layer or graph.

For a social network modeled as shown in Fig. 1, it will be interesting to find out the *set of people who are the most influential in a single layer (or social media) or across multiple (or a subset of) layers of social networks.* This corresponds to finding out the degree centrality nodes of a MLN using one or more layers. Since extant algorithms that calculate degree centrality metric on networks are limited to simple graphs/networks, MLNs are, typically, converted into a simple graph using type-independent aggregation [15] (e.g., Boolean AND or OR operations on layer edges) or projection [5,38]. This paper presents heuristic-based algorithms for computing degree centrality nodes (or *DC nodes* or *DC hubs*) on **HoMLNs directly** with high accuracy/precision and efficiency. The ground truth used is based on the definition as multiple definitions are possible.

We adapt the decoupling-based approach proposed in [30,31] for our algorithms. Based on this approach, we compute centrality on each layer *independently* **once** and keep Ψ results and *minimal* additional information from each layer for composing. With

---

[3] Strictly, speaking, they need not be identical. However, there is a common subset of nodes in each layer.

this, we can *efficiently* estimate the degree centrality nodes of the HoMLN. This approach has been shown to be application independent, efficient, lends itself to parallel
processing (of each layer), and is flexible for computing centrality measures on any
subset of layers. The naive decoupling-based approach to which we compare our proposed heuristic-based accuracy and precision retains no additional information from the
layers apart from the degree centrality nodes and their values (essentially Ψ results).

Contributions of this paper are:

- **Definition** of Degree Centrality for HoMLNs using Boolean OR-aggregation
- **Algorithms** for *directly* computing degree centrality nodes of HoMLNs
- **Multiple heuristics** to improve accuracy, precision, and efficiency of algorithms
- **Decoupling-based approach** to preserve structure and semantics of MLNs
- **Experimental analysis** on large number of synthetic, real-world-like, and real-
  world data sets with diverse graph characteristics
- **Accuracy, Precision, and Efficiency comparisons** with ground truth and naive app-
  roach

The rest of the paper is organized as follows: Sect. 2 discusses related work.
Section 3 introduces the decoupling approach used for MLN analysis and discusses
its advantages and challenges. Section 4 introduces the definition, and discusses ground
truth and naive approach to degree centrality. Section 4.1 presents several observations
and lemmas regarding computation using the decoupling approach. Sections 5 and 6,
respectively, describe composition-based degree centrality computation for HoMLNs
using heuristics for accuracy and precision. Section 7 describes the experimental setup
and the three types of data sets used. Section 8 discusses result analysis followed by
conclusions in Sect. 9.

1.1 Differences with the KDIR Conference Paper

As an extension of the KDIR conference paper [26], we have added additional material as suggested. We have made this paper formal by including MLN definition in
Sect. 1 and the degree centrality definition in Sect. 4. We have also added a new Sect. 4.1
with two observations to help understand why naive approach, in general, cannot give
good accuracy or precision. We have also included two lemmas to demonstrate the
amount of information needed, in general, for computing MLN degree centrality using
the decoupling-based approach to match ground truth. We have revised most sections
including the abstract, motivation, and conclusions. We have added a significant number of new experiments on real-world data sets and their analysis in Sect. 8 that were
not in the KDIR conference paper. All these extensions together add more than 30% of
material as requested.

2   Relevant Work

As complex and massive real-world data sets are becoming more popular and accessible, there is a pressing need to model them using the best approach and analyze them
efficiently in various ways. However, the use of graphs for their modeling and especially MLNs poses additional challenges in terms of computing centrality measures on

MLNs instead of simple graphs. Centrality measures including MLN centrality shed light on various properties of the network. Although there have been numerous studies on recognizing central entities in simple graphs, there have been very few studies on detecting central entities in multilayer networks. Existing research for finding central entities in multilayer networks is *use-case specific*, and there is no standard paradigm for addressing the problem of detecting central entities in a multilayer network.

Degree centrality is the most common and widely-used centrality measure. It is used to identify essential proteins [39], epidemics in animals [10], and the response of medication in children with epilepsy [42]. The most common and prominent use of degree centrality is in the domain of social network analysis. Some of the common use of degree centrality in social network analysis is identifying the most influential node [37], influential spreaders of information [23], finding opinion leaders in a social network [29], etc.

Despite being one of the most common and widely used centrality measures, very few algorithms or solutions exist to *directly* calculate the degree centrality of a MLN. In this study [9], the authors propose a solution to find degree centrality in a 10-layer MLN consisting of the Web 2.0 social network data set. Similar to the previous work, in [28], authors identify the degree centrality of nodes using the Kretschmer method. The authors in this study [43] proposed a node prominence profile-based method to effectively predict the degree centrality in a network. In another study [18], authors propose a solution to find the top-K influential person in a MLN social network using diffusion probability. More recently there has been some work in developing algorithms for MLNs using the decoupling-based approach [31].

Most degree centrality computation algorithms are **main memory based** and unsuitable for large graphs. They are also *use-case specific*. In this paper, we adopt the decoupling-based technique proposed in [31] for MLNs, where each layer can be analyzed individually and in parallel, and graph characteristics (such as degree centrality nodes) for a HoMLN can be calculated utilizing the information gathered for each layer. Our algorithms follow the network decoupling methodology, which has been demonstrated to be efficient, flexible, and scalable for other centrality measures such as the closeness centrality [25]. Achieving desired accuracy, however, is the challenge. Our approach is not strictly main-memory based as each layer (which is likely to be smaller than the aggregated graph) outputs results into a file which are used for the composition algorithm. Also, as each layer is likely to be smaller than the OR aggregated graph, larger size MLNs can be accommodated in our approach.

In this paper, we address degree centrality for HoMLNS using Boolean OR-aggregation. This is different from the work on computing centrality for HoMLNs using the Boolean AND-aggregation [31].

3   Decoupling Approach for Multilayer Networks

Existing multilayer network analysis approaches convert or transform a MLN into a simple graph for computations. Aggregating or projecting the network layers into a simple graph accomplishes this. Edge aggregation is used to bring homogeneous MLNs together into a simple graph. Although aggregating a MLN into a simple graph enables the use of currently available techniques for centrality and community discovery (of which there are many), the MLN **structure and semantics are not retained, causing information loss**.

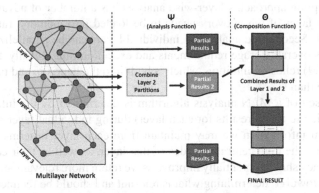

Fig. 2. MLN Decoupling Approach Overview [26].

We use the MLN decoupling strategy for analysis to overcome the aforementioned difficulties. Figure 2 shows the proposed network decoupling strategy. It entails determining two functions: one for analysis (Ψ) and the other for composition (Θ), typically, as a binary operator. Each layer is analyzed independently using the analysis function (and possibly in parallel). Partial results (as they are called) from each of the two layers are then combined using a *binary composition function/algorithm* to obtain the HoMLN results for the two layers. MLNs with more than two layers can use this binary composition repeatedly. Independent analysis permits the use of existing techniques for each layer. Decoupling, on the other hand, increases efficiency (see Sect. 8), flexibility, and scalability along with extending the existing graph analysis algorithms to compute directly on MLNs.

As the MLN decoupling method preserves the structure and semantics of the data, drill-down, and visualization of final results are easy to support. Each layer (or graph) is likely to be smaller, consume less memory than the whole MLN, and composition is done as a separate step on the partial results. The analysis function results are preserved and used in the composition. The requirement to recompute is reduced because the result of analysis for a layer can be reused by several composition functions, increasing the efficiency of the decoupling-based approach. Individual layers can be analyzed using any of the available simple graph centrality algorithms. This method is also application-independent. As a result, the decoupling-based approach can be used to extend existing centrality algorithms to MLNs. To compose the outputs of analysis functions (partial results) into the final results, we only need to develop the composition function for each type of analysis.

The challenge of the decoupling-based approach is getting accuracy/precision that is closer to the ground truth. This translates to one of the major challenges in determining the minimum *additional* information to retain as part of the layer analysis step to be used during composition to improve the overall accuracy and precision with respect to the ground truth. For many composition algorithms, we have looked into, there is a trade-off between using more information from each layer and improving accuracy or precision. Balancing this trade-off is key to developing these algorithms.

The decoupling approach's layer-wise analysis has a number of advantages. First, only a smaller layer of the network needs to be loaded into memory, rather than the whole network. Second, the analysis of individual layers can be parallelized, reducing the algorithm's overall storage requirements and execution time. Finally, the composition function (Θ) relies on intuition, which is built into the heuristic and takes substantially less time than Ψ.

The accuracy of a MLN analysis algorithm is determined by the information we keep (in addition to the Ψ results for each layer) during individual layer analysis. The basic minimum information we may maintain from each layer in terms of centrality measurements is the high centrality nodes of that layer, as well as their centrality values. The accuracy should potentially improve as we retain more relevant information for composition. However, determining what is relevant and should be retained to improve accuracy or precision is the main challenge of this approach. The key hurdles are identifying the most beneficial minimal information and the intuition for their effectiveness.

4 Degree Centrality for Graphs and Homogeneous MLNs

The degree of a node in a graph is the total number of edges that are incident on it. *Degree hubs are nodes in a network that have a degree larger than or equal to the network's average degree.* Degree hubs are defined for simple graphs. In [31], the authors have proposed three algorithms to estimate degree hubs in AND-aggregated multilayer networks. However, **there are no algorithms for calculating degree hubs for OR-aggregated HoMLNs.** If the HoMLN layers are aggregated using a Boolean operation such as OR, we can expand the notion of a hub from a simple graph to HoMLNs. In this paper, we suggest various composition functions to maximize accuracy, precision, and efficiency while estimating degree hubs in OR aggregated multilayer networks.

The ground truth is used to evaluate the performance and accuracy of our suggested heuristics for detecting the degree hubs of a homogeneous multilayer network.

Definition 2. *The degree centrality of a vertex u in a network is defined as $degree(u)$ = Number of adjacent or 1-hop neighbors. This value is divided by the maximum number of edges a vertex can have to normalize it. The equation for normalized degree centrality, $DC(u)$, in a simple graph is:*

$$DC(u) = \frac{degree(u)}{n-1} \tag{1}$$

High centrality hubs or degree hubs are the vertices with normalized degree centrality values higher than or equal to the normalized average degree values.

Even though there are different variants of degree centrality such as the group degree centrality [16], time scale degree centrality [41], and complex degree centrality [22], in this paper, we only address the normalized degree centrality for Boolean OR-aggregated, undirected, homogeneous multilayer networks. We propose **several** heuristics-based algorithms to identify high centrality hubs in Boolean OR-aggregated

MLNs. We test the accuracy, precision, and efficiency of our algorithm against the ground truth. With extensive experiments on data sets of varying graph characteristics, we show that our approaches perform better than the naive approach and are efficient compared to ground truth computation.

As there can be many definitions possible for degree centrality nodes for MLNs, we have chosen one that corresponds to an aggregation that is commonly used. Other aggregations as well as aggregation-independent definitions are possible. If an aggregation-independent definition is used, validation has to be done using only the definition without ground truth.

Definition 3. *Degree centrality of a node* v_i^j *(j^{th} node in layer i) in a HoMLN G with m layers, V being $\cup_{i=1}^m V_i$, and $|V_i| = n$, is defined as,*

$$HoMLN\_DC(v_i^j) = \frac{degree(v_i^j)\ in\ OR - aggregated\ graph\ of\ HoMLN\ layers}{n - 1}$$

(2)

where $degree(v_i^j)$ *in OR-aggregated graph* includes adjacent (or 1-hop) neighbors of node v_i^j in the aggregated graph using Boolean OR operation on edges from layers under consideration. This value is divided by the maximum number of edges a vertex can have (for a HoMLN) to normalize it. The above is the equation for normalized degree centrality.

High centrality or degree centrality hubs (or DC nodes/hubs) are the vertices with normalized degree centrality values higher than or equal to the average normalized degree for the HoMLN.

Boolean AND and OR operators used for aggregation are commutative and distributive. OR aggregation is likely to increase the size of the resulting graph (number of edges) used for ground truth. Accuracy is computed by comparing the ground truth results for the aggregated graph with the results obtained by the decoupling-based algorithm for the layers of the same graph. The naive algorithm uses only the results of each layer for the computation (in this case degree centrality) and applies the same Boolean operator to the individual results during the composition step. Typically, the naive approach does not yield good accuracy (see observations in Sect. 4.1) requiring additional information from each layer to be retained and used for the composition algorithm based on heuristics. As layers are processed *independently* (may be in parallel), no information about the other layer is assumed while processing a layer.

Based on our definition in 2, the **ground truth** for degree centrality is calculated as follows. Note that for AND-aggregation, the ground truth as well as the composition algorithm will be different, as discussed in [31].

- First, all the layers of the network under consideration are aggregated into a single graph using the Boolean OR operation on layer edges
- Degree centrality of the OR-aggregated graph is calculated using existing algorithms, and the DC hubs are identified.

For two-layer MLN, the **naive composition** (as a base decoupling-based composition algorithm for comparison) amounts to taking the DC nodes (or hubs) of each layer (using the same algorithm used for the ground truth), followed by their union (as we are using OR-aggregation). The resultant set of nodes will be the estimated DC nodes of the HoMLN layers using the naive composition approach. The naive approach is the simplest form of composition (using the decoupling approach) and does not use any additional information than the DC nodes from each layer.

4.1 Impact of Layer Information on Accuracy

In this section, we discuss a couple of important observations and prove some lemmas to understand the information needs for increasing the accuracy of the decoupling-based composition, and under what conditions it will match the ground truth. Observations 1 and 2 prove that the naive composition approach is **not guaranteed**, in general, to give ground truth accuracy, due to the *generation of false positives and false negatives*. One situation where naive accuracy coincides with the ground truth accuracy is when the two layers are topologically identical. The naive accuracy will fluctuate with respect to ground truth without reaching it in general. Lemmas 1 and 2, respectively, indicate *what additional information* from each layer is not sufficient, or sufficient for the accuracy of the composition function using the decoupling approach to match ground truth.

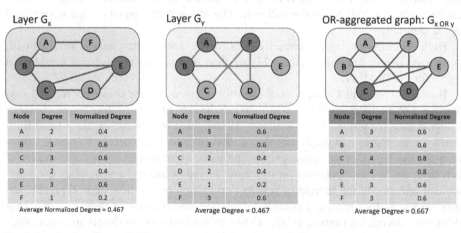

Fig. 3. Layer G_x, G_y, and OR-aggregated graph created by G_x and G_y, G_{xORy} (computed as G_x OR G_y) with the respective degree centrality for each node. Nodes highlighted in green have above average degree centrality values in each layer/graph.

Observation 1. *In spite of a node having below average degree centrality value in at least one of the HoMLN layers G_x, G_y, it may have above average degree centrality value in the OR-aggregated graph created by G_x and G_y.*

Illustration. This scenario is showcased by node **D** in Fig. 3, which in spite of not having above average degree centrality value in layers G_x and G_y, has above average degree centrality value in the OR-aggregated graph, G_{xORy}. It can be observed that the degree centrality value for other nodes (say, v) was close to the lower bound, that is, $max(DC_x$ $(v), DC_y\ (v))$. However, node **D**, due to lack of non-overlapping 1-hop neighboring nodes in participating layers, has a resulting degree close to the upper bound $DC_x\ (D)$ $+ DC_y\ (D)$ in the OR-aggregated graph. This pushed its degree centrality value above the average in the OR-aggregated graph. Node C also falls under the same category.

Observation 2. *In spite of a node having above average degree centrality value in at least one of the HoMLN layers G_x, G_y, it may have a below average degree centrality value in the OR-aggregated graph created by G_x and G_y.*

Illustration. This scenario is illustrated in Fig. 3 where node **B** in spite of *not* having below average degree centrality value in both layers G_x and layer G_y, has below average degree centrality value in the OR-aggregated graph G_{xORy}. This is because it has many neighbors that are common across the layers as compared to the other nodes. Nodes A, F, and E also fall under this category.

Lemma 1. *It is not enough, in general, to maintain for every node, the degree centrality value from the HoMLN layers, G_x and G_y, in order to compute the correct degree centrality values of nodes in the OR-aggregated graph created by G_x and G_y.*

Proof. Without loss of generality, let $deg_x(u)$ be the degree value of node u from layer G_x and $deg_y(u)$ from layer G_y. OR-aggregation is performed by retaining the union of edges from layers G_x and G_y, which will change the neighborhood of each as well. *Thus, without any information about how many of the 1-hop neighbors for the node u overlap from the two layers, it is not possible to calculate its **correct** degree in the OR-aggregated layer ($deg_{xORy}(u)$) using **only** degree information of nodes. Hence, we cannot compute the degree of any node in the OR aggregated graph using the available information and hence cannot compute the degree centrality hubs of the OR-aggregated graph.*

In general, based on maximum (complete) and minimum (no) overlap among the 1-hop neighbors, we can say that $max(deg_x(u), deg_y(u)) <= deg_{xORy}(u) <= min((deg_x(u) + deg_y(u)), (n-1))$, where n is the number of nodes. The degree of a node in the OR-aggregated graph will never go beyond $(n-1)$. This lemma contrasts with the information required for a HeMLN. In a HeMLN, it is sufficient to keep the degree information for each node in each layer to compute ground truth accuracy as shown in [24]. $\square$

Lemma 2. *It is sufficient to maintain **the set of all 1-hop neighbors** for every node (not just the hubs) in each of the HoMLN layers, G_x and G_y, in order to compute the degree centrality hubs correctly in the OR-aggregated graph created by G_x and G_y.*

Proof. Without loss of generality, we have the set of *all* 1-hop neighbors from the layers G_x and G_y for a node u. Let they be $N\_D_x(u)$ and $N\_D_y(u)$, respectively. Then, by taking set union between $N\_D_x(u)$ and $N\_D_y(u)$, we can compute the set of 1-hop neighbors for u in the OR-aggregated graph (G_{xORy}). As we can do this for each node in the OR-aggregated graph, we can compute the average degree of the OR-aggregated graph and hence the HoMLN degree hubs. $\square$

The *necessary condition* is more tricky. For some pathological cases (e.g., layers being identical), it is possible to compute the ground truth using only the 1-hop neighbors of hub nodes from each layer. But in general, it is not possible without keeping 1-hop neighbors of *all nodes* from each layer.

Given the above, the heuristics presented below compute good accuracy and even better precision using very little *additional* information from each layer. This lemma highlights the challenge faced in developing high-accuracy decoupling-based composition algorithms for MLNs and the need for heuristics based on good intuition.

5 Accuracy of Degree Centrality Heuristics

We measure accuracy with respect to ground truth using the Jaccard coefficient. An accuracy of 1 indicates an exact match with the ground truth (no false positives or false negatives generated during composition). The goal is to get the Jaccard coefficient value as close to 1 as possible with the ground truth using the decoupling approach. For most applications, high accuracy is desired. Below, we present two heuristic-based composition algorithms with better overall accuracy as compared to the naive approach.

5.1 First Heuristic for Accuracy (DC-A1)

Intuitively, with the information from each layer, we are trying to estimate the degree of a node when the layers are OR-aggregated. If we can do it effectively, we can use the approximated average degree of the OR aggregation to determine whether a node is a hub when layers are aggregated. For layers, G_x and G_y, based on the OR operator semantics, the estimated degree $estDeg_{xORy}(u)$ of a node u in the OR-aggregated graph can be $max(deg_x(u), deg_y(u))$. This is also the lower bound. This happens when the one-hop neighbor of the node u in layer G_x is a subset of the one-hop neighbor of the same node in layer G_y or vice-versa. We can use this estimated degree value of the nodes to directly calculate the degree hubs of the HoMLN in the OR-aggregated graph. Algorithm 1 describes the steps of the composition function Θ using this heuristic.

Algorithm 1. Procedure for Θ using Heuristic DC-A1 [26].

Require: $deg_x[]$, $deg_y[]$ // Arrays with degree value for each node in the layers

1: $DH'_{xORy} \leftarrow \emptyset$ // set of estimated HoMLN degree hub nodes
2: $estDeg_{xORy}[] \leftarrow 0$ // Array of estimated degree of nodes in OR-aggregated graph
3: **for** $u \in V$ **do**
4:    $estDeg_{xORy}[u] \leftarrow max(deg_x[u], deg_y[u])$
5: **end for**
6: Calculate DH'_{xORy} using $estDeg_{xORy}[u]$ values of the nodes

---

*We expect this heuristic to do much better than the naive approach. As can be seen in Fig. 4, this heuristic improves accuracy for data sets shown in Table 1 (details in Sect. 7), where the **edge distribution is equal in each layer** (x-axis values of 3, 6, 9, ...) and further accuracy improves as the data set size increases. This is as expected analytically* *as equal distribution of edges provides a better estimate of degree for this heuristic for the aggregated graph. And for data sets with a larger number of edges, even with slight deviation from non-equal distribution, the average degree of the combined layers is smoother than for small data sets. This observation holds for the other two synthetic data sets (Figs. 5 and 6) as well. For real-world-like (Fig. 7) and real-world (Fig. 8) data sets, both DC-A1 and DC-A2 (see below) are uniformly and significantly better than the naive and do not deviate much from synthetic data sets with wider coverage of edge distributions and degree distributions.*

5.2   Second Heuristic for Accuracy (DC-A2)

In the DC-A1 heuristic, we assumed that the one-hop neighbors of a node u in layer G_x are going to be a subset of one-hop neighbors of the same node in layer G_y or vice-versa. When we are estimating the degree of a node u in the OR-aggregated graph, there is a minimum value and maximum value for the estimated degree value of that node. The minimum of the estimated degree value is $max(deg_x(u), deg_y(u))$. Similarly, the maximum value of the estimated degree could be $min(((deg_x(u) + deg_y(u)), (n-1))$ when there is no common one-hop neighbor among layers G_x and G_y for node u. Here n is the number of nodes in each layer of the HoMLN. Based on intuition and observations of various data sets, the estimated degree of a node u in the OR-aggregated graph is neither the possible minimum nor possible maximum value, rather somewhere close to the average of these values. Thus, we estimate the estimated degree of node u in the OR-aggregated graph, $estDeg_{xORy}(u)$, as the average of $max(deg_x(u), deg_y(u))$ and $min(((deg_x(u)+deg_y(u)), (n-1))$. We then use the $estDeg_{xORy}(u)$ of the nodes to calculate the degree hubs of the OR-aggregated graph.

Note that, in this heuristic, we are not using any additional information than in heuristic DC-A1, but changing our estimation to a more intuitive, meaningful, and realistic value than taking an extreme. With this simple change in the heuristic, again from Fig. 4, one can see a significant improvement in accuracy over DC-A1 for the data set in Table 1. In fact, some of the accuracies reach as high as 0.98 which is commendable. One can also see that the edge distribution and data set size differences no longer have the kind of impact seen in DC-A1. Also, other synthetic data sets (Figs. 5 and 6), real-world-like (Fig. 7), and real-world (Fig. 8) data sets show the same trend.

This heuristic highlights the importance of both intuition and additional information in developing composition algorithms. Retaining more information by itself is not sufficient unless it is combined with proper intuition!

6   Heuristics for Precision

As mentioned in the previous section, we have used accuracy to compare the effectiveness of our heuristics (using the Jaccard coefficient). Based on use cases, accuracy might not be the only metric of interest for many real-world applications. Consider an airline trying to expand its operation to a new city based on the routes and operations of other competitors. This problem can be modeled as a problem to find the degree hubs of a HoMLN where each node of the HoMLN is a city and each layer represent the route of the competitors among these cities. In this scenario, a **high precision algorithm** is preferred as a false positive in identifying a hub might lead the airline to expand to an undesirable city incurring a loss. Advertising on multiple social networks also has a similar need to avoid false positives. Hence, in general, it is meaningful to identify heuristics that do not produce any false positives or any false negatives depending upon the application's need. In this section, we provide two heuristics for composition algorithms to find degree hubs of a HoMLN with high precision.

6.1   Heuristic 1 for Precision (DC-P1)

For the Boolean OR-aggregated ground truth, if a node is a degree hub (DH) in layer G_x or layer G_y, then it is likely that the node is going to be a degree hub in the OR-aggregated ground truth. We use this intuition as the basis for heuristic DC-P1 which is used to develop the first composition algorithm for the Θ function to compute high precision degree hubs.

As we previously mentioned, in the analysis function (Ψ) of the decoupling approach we analyze the layers of the HoMLN and use the partial results and additional information to obtain the final results for the MLN. In DC-P1, after the analysis (Ψ) phase of each layer (say layer G_x), we keep the set of degree hubs DH_x, the average degree $avgDeg_x$ of that layer, and the set of one-hop neighbors of each **degree hub node** u as $N\_D_x(u)^4$.

During the Θ step, we use the stored partial results and additional information to estimate the hubs for the OR-aggregation of layers G_x and G_y. As for the OR-aggregated ground-truth graph, the number of edges for a node is likely to increase. We can estimate the average degree of the OR-aggregated graph, $avgEstDeg_{xORy}$, to be the maximum between $avgDeg_x$ and $avgDeg_y$. For each node present in either DH_x or DH_y, if the union of their one-hop neighbors set is more than $avgEstDeg_{xORy}$, we consider that node a degree hub in the OR composed layer of G_x and G_y. Algorithm 2 shows the detailed steps of the composition algorithm (Θ).

Algorithm 2. Procedure for Θ using Heuristic DC-P1 [26]

Require: DH_x, $avgDeg_x$, $N\_D_x[u]$ $\forall u \in DH_x$, DH_y, $avgDeg_y$, $N\_D_y[v]$ $\forall v \in DH_y$ // degree hub sets, avg degree, 1-hop neighbor set indexed by u in hash map
1: $DH'_{xORy} \leftarrow \emptyset$
2: $avgEstDeg_{xORy} \leftarrow max(avgDeg_x, avgDeg_y)$
3: **for** $u \in DH_x \cup DH_y$ **do**
4:      **if** $|N\_D_x[u] \cup N\_D_y[u]| >= avgEstDeg_{xORy}$ **then**
5:          $DH'_{xORy} \leftarrow DH'_{xORy} \cup u$
6:      **end if**
7: **end for**

Degree hubs and their values for each layer allow us to compute the lower bound of the average for the aggregated graph. One-hop neighbor information is used to reduce or eliminate false positives. However, as these are retained only for hubs, information

---

[4] This is the additional information we retain from each layer to improve precision.

*is still not complete. Even with this limited additional information, as we will see in the experimental section (Sect. 8), there is a significant improvement in precision over the naive approach for all data sets. Using this heuristic, we get a precision of **100%** (Fig. 9) for the synthetic data sets. For real-world-like (Fig. 10) and real-world Fig. 11 data sets, we get mean precision of **96%** and **99%** respectively.*

Table 1. Summary of Synthetic Data Set 1 (Both layers with power-law degree distribution) [26].

Base Graph #Nodes, #Edges	G_{ID}	Edge Dist. % in Layers	#Edges		
			L1	L2	L1 OR L2
100KV, 500KE	1	70,30	350000	150000	499587
	2	60,40	200000	300000	499505
	3	50,50	250000	250000	499505
100KV, 1ME	4	70,30	700000	300000	998303
	5	60,40	600000	400000	998176
	6	50,50	500000	500000	997998
100KV, 2ME	7	70,30	600000	1400000	1993608
	8	60,40	1200000	800000	1992855
	9	50,50	1000000	1000000	1992207
300KV, 1.5ME	10	70,30	1050000	450000	1499463
	11	60,40	900000	600000	1499425
	12	50,50	750000	750000	1499347
300KV, 3ME	13	70,30	2100000	900000	2997825
	14	60,40	1800000	1200000	2997627
	15	50,50	1500000	1500000	2997538
300KV, 6ME	16	70,30	4200000	1800000	5991761
	17	60,40	3600000	2400000	5990599
	18	50,50	3000000	3000000	5990044
500KV, 2.5ME	19	70,30	1750000	750000	2499344
	20	60,40	1500000	1000000	2499238
	21	50,50	1250000	1250000	2499166
500KV, 5ME	22	70,30	3500000	1500000	4997388
	23	60,40	3000000	2000000	4996910
	24	50,50	2500000	2500000	4997209
500KV, 10ME	25	70,30	7000000	3000000	9989402
	26	60,40	6000000	4000000	9989190
	27	50,50	5000000	5000000	9987447

6.2   Heuristic 2 for Precision (DC-P2)

Based on how the edges are distributed in the layers of a MLN, the *actual* average degree of the OR-aggregated ground truth, $avgActDeg_{xORy}$, of layers G_x and G_y

might differ from the *estimated* $avgEstDeg_{xORy}$ in DC-P1. If $avgEstDeg_{xORy}$ is smaller than $avgActDeg_{xORy}$, a lot of false positives will be generated as hubs in the OR-aggregated graph.

To better estimate the $avgEstDeg_{xORy}$, we keep the degree of each node from each layer as additional information during the Ψ step. This allows us to estimate the individual degree of a node u in the OR-aggregated graph from its degree information in layer G_x and layer G_y. If the degree of a node u in layer G_x is $deg_x(u)$ and the degree of the same node in layer G_y is $deg_y(u)$, then the estimated degree of node u in the OR-aggregated graph, $estDeg_{xORy}(u)$, is going to be $max(deg_x(u), deg_y(u))$. Using the estimated degree $estDeg_{xORy}(u)$ of each node u, we calculate the $avgEstDeg_{xORy}$. The rest of the steps are same as Algorithm 2. As can be seen in Figs. 10 and 11, this heuristic increases the precision slightly as compared to DC-P1 for some real-world-like and real-world data sets. For synthetic data sets, both DC-P2 and DC-P1 perform equally well, as seen in Fig. 9.

7   Data Sets and Computation Environments

For validating accuracy and precision using our heuristics-based algorithms, we have used three different types of data sets to make sure they work for diverse types of graphs with different characteristics.

7.1   Data Sets

Synthetic data sets (shown in Table 1). PaRMAT [20], a parallel version of the popular graph generator RMAT [12], which uses the Recursive-Matrix-based graph generation technique, was used to create the synthetic data sets. We used PaRMAT to produce three sets of synthetic data sets for each base graph for experimentation. Our synthetic data set consists of 27 HoMLNs with two layers, each with a different edge distribution. The base graphs start with 100K vertices with 500K edges and go up to 500K vertices and 10 million edges.

For each of the above-mentioned data sets, three edge distributions (70%, 30%; 60%, 40%; and 50%, 50%) for a total of 81 HoMLNs with varied edge distributions, number of nodes, and edges are used for experimentation and validation of the proposed heuristics. Table 1 shows the different 2-layer HoMLN used in our data set used in experiments which are part of the synthetic data set 1. The synthetic data set 1 consists of HoMLN where both the layers have the power-law distribution of edges (L1: Power-law, L2: Power-law). In the second synthetic data set (not shown, but similar to Table 1), one layer (L1) follows *power-law degree distribution* and the other one (L2) follows *normal degree distribution*. In the final synthetic data set, both layers have *normal degree distribution* (again not shown, but similar to Table 1).

Real-world-like data sets (shown in Table 2), are generated from real-world-like monographs using a random number generator. The real-world-like graphs are generated using RMAT with parameters to *mimic* real-world graph data sets as discussed in [11]. As a result, the graphs are *not single connected components* and neither are their ground truth graph.

Table 2. Summary of Real-world-like Data Sets [26].

Base Graph #Nodes, #Edges	G_{ID}	Edge Dist. % in Layers	#Edges		
			L1	L2	L1 OR L2
735KV, 2.6ME	amazon-2008_1	50,50	1306357	1304863	1958865
	amazon-2008_2	70,30	1828100	784552	2063141
	amazon-2008_3	90,10	2349969	261133	2376256
325KV, 1.7ME	cnr-2000_1	50,50	876444	876383	1314919
	cnr-2000_2	70,30	1226781	525244	1384962
	cnr-2000_3	90,10	1577646	175236	1595367
100KV, 1.5ME	uk-2007-05_1	50,50	759899	761252	1141215
	uk-2007-05_2	70,30	1065435	455957	1202326
	uk-2007-05_3	90,10	1369767	152167	1385013

Finally, four **real-world data sets** (shown in Table 3) have been used from Orkut [2], LiveJournal [3], IMDB [4], and DBLP [1]. We have used these real-world data sets in two ways. In one approach, for the LiveJournal and Orkut data sets we have used a random number-based generator to generate the layers with three types of edge distributions of the original seed graph (50%, 50%; 70%, 30%; and 90%, 10%) for large graphs with millions of nodes and edges. For the second approach, for the IMDB and DBLP data sets, we have used the real-world HoMLN data sets as the layers, taking two HoMLN graphs from each data set as the layers for each experiment. In case of IMDB, the nodes are actors who are connected in 3 layers based on whether they have acted together, have worked in similar genres, or have similar average ratings. In case of DBLP, the nodes are authors who are connected in 3 layers if they have co-authored a paper published in SIGMOD, ICDM, or SIGKDD. For both IMDB and DBLP, every possible 2-layer MLN combination has been analyzed for the OR-aggregation.

7.2   Computation Environments Used

The NetworkX [19] package is used in our Python implementation. Experiments on the three synthetic data sets and real-world-like data sets were carried out on a single SDSC Expanse node [40]. Each node in the cluster runs the CentOS Linux operating system using an AMD EPYC 7742 CPU with 128 cores and 256 GB of RAM.

All experiments on the real-world data sets were carried out on a server running the CentOS Linux 7 operating system using two 2.10 GHz Intel Xeon Silver 4116 CPUs with a total of 48 cores and 780 GB of RAM. *Note that the use of different computing environments does not matter for the accuracy comparison. We are performing efficiency comparison within each data set to keep the comparison valid.*

8   Discussion of Experimental Results

In this section, we present our experimental results. We have tested our proposed heuristics-based algorithms for both accuracy and precision on large synthetic as shown

Table 3. Summary of Real-world Data Sets.

# Nodes in each layer	G_{ID}	#Edges		
		L1	L2	L1 OR L2
4.8MV	livejournal_1	21683329	21686326	32529158
	livejournal_2	30362021	13011493	34264697
	livejournal_3	39035016	4338129	39468277
3MV	orkut_1	58598766	58592102	87896056
	orkut_2	82029261	35157625	92577910
	orkut_3	105471745	11724346	106643093
9.4KV	imdb_1	996527	13945872	14591786
	imdb_2	996527	45581	1034350
	imdb_3	13945872	45581	13964023
17.2KV	dblp_1	12986	18950	30274
	dblp_2	12986	17737	30428
	dblp_3	18950	17737	36213

in Table 1 (plus 2 other distributions totaling 81 HoMLNs), real-world-like as shown in Table 2 (3 different data sets each with 3 edge distributions), and real-world as shown in Table 3 (4 data sets each with 3 edge distributions). As a measure of accuracy and precision, we use the Jaccard coefficient. While calculating the Jaccard coefficient, we consider the nodes having greater than or equal to the average degree value in the ground truth as degree hubs. We compare the execution time of our heuristics against the ground truth execution time as a measure of performance.

Table 4. Accuracy Improvement of DC-A1 and DC-A2 over Naive.

Data Set	Degree Distribution L1, L2	Mean Accuracy			
		DC-A1	DC-A2	DC-A1 vs. Naive	DC-A2 vs. Naive
Synthetic-1	Power law, Power law	90.53%	96.01%	+0.86%	**+6.96%**
Synthetic-2	Power law, Normal	64.90%	83.74%	+6.48%	**+37.38%**
Synthetic-3	Normal, Normal	76.14%	88.72%	−4.32%	**+11.47%**
Real-world-like	Power law, Power law	93.11%	98.9%	+10.03%	**+10.92%**
Real-world	Power law, Power law	96.16%	97.74%	+16.47%	**+18.05%**

Table 4 shows the mean accuracy and average percentage gain in accuracy for the synthetic, real-world-like, and real-world data sets. Across all diverse data sets, DC-A2 *outperforms* the naive approach, with **accuracy ranging from 84% to 99%**.

Figures 4, 5, and 6 show the Jaccard Coefficient for accuracy of the proposed heuristics-based approaches DC-A1, DC-A2, and the naive approach for the synthetic data set 1, data set 2, and data set 3, respectively. The heuristic DC-A2 performs the best in terms of Jaccard coefficient. It always shows higher accuracy than the naive approach. The heuristic DC-A1 performs better than the naive approach in most cases.

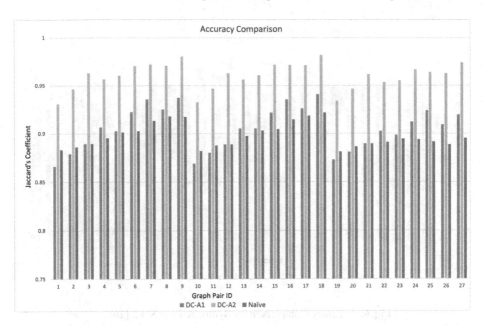

Fig. 4. Accuracy Comparison for Synthetic Data Set 1 (shown in Table 1) [26].

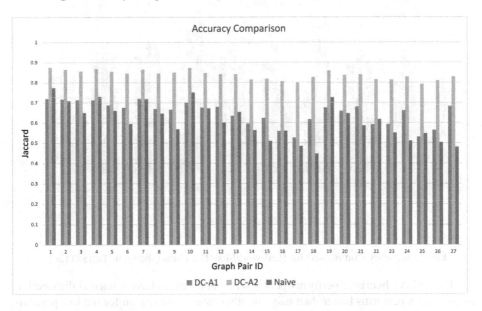

Fig. 5. Accuracy Comparison for Synthetic Data Set 2 [26].

Figures 7, and 8 show the Jaccard Coefficient for the real-world-like data sets [6] and real-world data sets, respectively. *Both heuristics DC-A1 and DC-A2 perform better than the naive approach for all the HoMLNs in the data sets.*

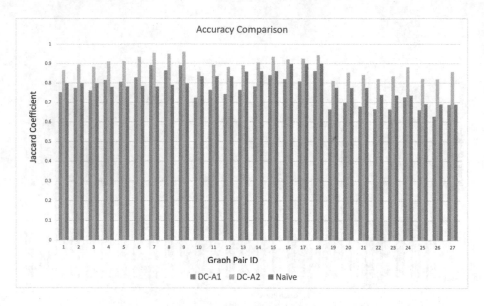

Fig. 6. Accuracy Comparison for Synthetic Data Set 3 [26].

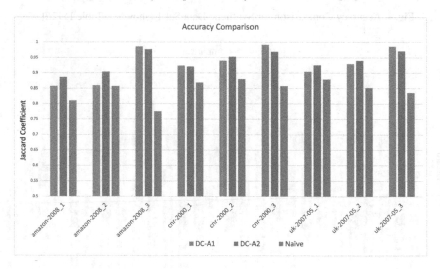

Fig. 7. Accuracy Comparison for Real-world-like Data Sets (shown in Table 2) [26].

The DC-A1 heuristic performs poorly when both layers have a normal distribution of edges, but performs better than naive in other cases. One reason for the low percentage gain compared to the naive approach is, that for Boolean OR aggregated HoMLN, the naive approach itself has relatively high accuracy.

For **precision**, DC-P1 and DC-P2 outperform DC-A1, DC-A2, as well as the naive approach. For the synthetic data sets, the precision of DC-P1 and DC-P2 is **always 100%** (Fig. 9) and more than 96% and 99% respectively for the real-world-like and real-world data sets (Figs. 10 and 11).

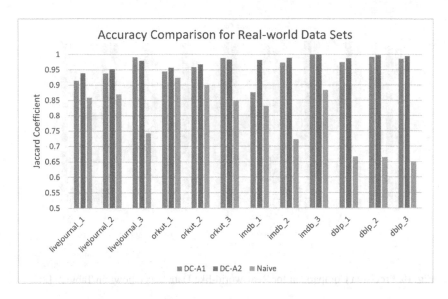

Fig. 8. Accuracy Comparison for Real-world Data Sets (shown in Table 3).

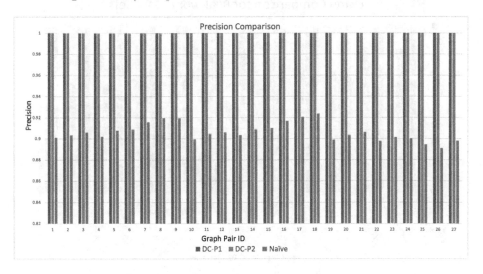

Fig. 9. Precision Comparison for Synthetic Data Set 1 (shown in Table 1) [26].

Figures 12 and 13, respectively, show the comparison of the execution time of our proposed solutions against the ground truth time for 3 of the **largest HoMLN of the synthetic data set 1** and the real-world data sets. The execution time of our approach is calculated as *maximum Ψ time of the layers + Θ time*. The ground truth time is computed as *time required to aggregate layers into a single graph using Boolean OR function + time required to find the degree hubs of the OR-aggregated graph.*

As we can see from Fig. 12, **ground truth execution time is more than an order of magnitude as compared to our proposed approaches in all cases (plotted on the**

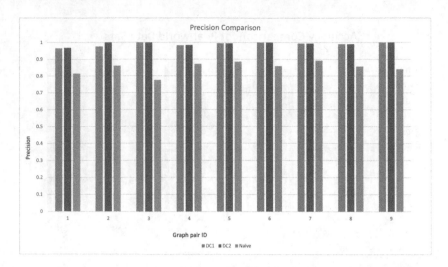

Fig. 10. Precision Comparison for Real-world-like Data Sets (shown in Table 2) [26].

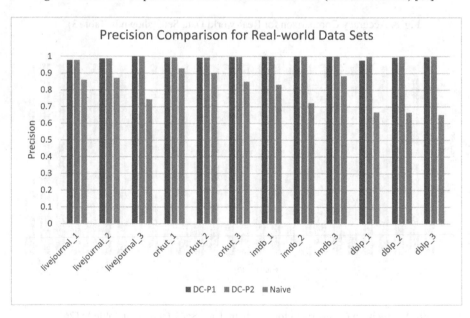

Fig. 11. Precision Comparison for Real-world Data Sets (shown in Table 3).

log scale). As for the real-world data sets, our proposed approach is significantly faster than the ground truth in all cases. The higher the density of the layers, the faster our approach is compared to the ground truth *(See Table 3)*.

Figure 14 shows the impact of additional information used from layers on the accuracy. As discussed in Sect. 4.1, more information increases the accuracy of the decoupling approach. If no additional information is kept, we are likely to get low accuracy.

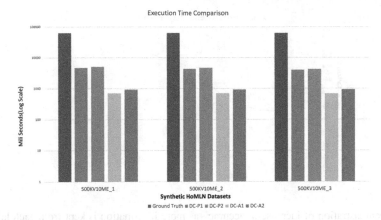

Fig. 12. Comparison of Execution Time of the Heuristics against Execution Time of Ground Truth for Synthetic Data Set 1 [26].

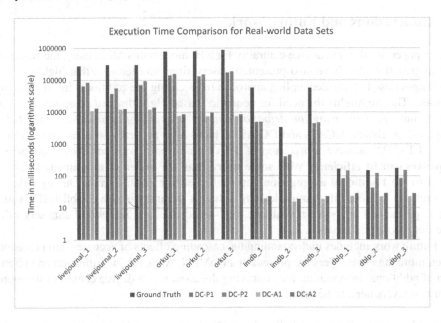

Fig. 13. Comparison of Execution Time of the Heuristics against Execution Time of Ground Truth for Real-world Data Sets.

If we keep all the one-hop neighbors of **all** the nodes, we get 100% accuracy. This is clearly illustrated in Fig. 14. Here we used a HoMLN consisting of 100K nodes from the synthetic data set 2 where the first layer follows the power-law distribution and the second layer follows the normal distribution. This HoMLN was chosen to minimize any similarity among the layers. The additional information kept is the percentage of nodes for which the one-hop neighbors are maintained from each layer. As can be clearly seen, as the percentage increases, Jaccard coefficient reaches 1 for 100% additional information indicating a match with ground truth.

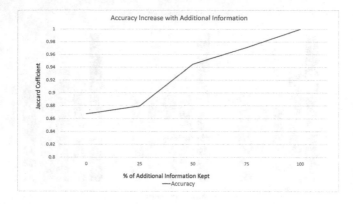

Fig. 14. Demonstration of increase in accuracy as more information is kept from each layer for DC-A2 [26].

9   Conclusions and Future Work

In this paper, we defined degree centrality for a Homogeneous MLN using the Boolean OR-aggregation. We have also presented observations and lemmas that highlight the challenges posed by the decoupling approach for deciding the additional information to be used. This highlights the need for heuristics-based algorithms to compute HoMLN degree hubs *directly using the definition and the decoupling approach*. Some of the proposed heuristics (DC-A1 and DC-A2) achieve high accuracy whereas others (DC-P1 and DC-P2) achieve a precision of 1. All proposed algorithms show **significant improvement in efficiency with some more than an order of magnitude** as compared to the traditional aggregation approach used for ground truth. Our hypothesis with respect to more information leading to higher accuracy is also established. Extensive experimental analysis on synthetic, real-world-like, and real-world data sets validate our theoretical analysis.

Future work includes understanding the cascading effects of accuracy and precision when more than two layers are present in a HoMLN. Also, the identification and retention of additional information for improving the accuracy of degree centrality for more than two layers need to be investigated.

Acknowledgments. For this work, Drs. Sharma Chakravarthy and Abhishek Santra were partly supported by NSF Grant CCF-1955798. Dr. Sharma Chakravarthy was also partly supported by NSF Grant CNS-2120393.

References

1. DBLP Data Stats. https://dblp.uni-trier.de/statistics/recordsindblp. Accessed 24 May 2020
2. http://snap.stanford.edu/data/com-Orkut.html
3. http://snap.stanford.edu/data/com-LiveJournal.html
4. The internet movie database. ftp://ftp.fu-berlin.de/pub/misc/movies/database/

5. Berenstein, A., Magarinos, M.P., Chernomoretz, A., Aguero, F.: A multilayer network approach for guiding drug repositioning in neglected diseases. PLoS (2016)
6. Boldi, P., Vigna, S.: The WebGraph framework I: compression techaniques. In: Proceedings of the Thirteenth International World Wide Web Conference (WWW 2004), Manhattan, USA, pp. 595–601. ACM Press (2004)
7. Boldi, P., Vigna, S.: Axioms for centrality. Internet Math. **10**(3–4), 222–262 (2014)
8. Brandes, U.: A faster algorithm for betweenness centrality. J. Math. Sociol. **25**(2), 163–177 (2001)
9. Bródka, P., Skibicki, K., Kazienko, P., Musiał, K.: A degree centrality in multi-layered social network. In: 2011 International Conference on Computational Aspects of Social Networks (CASoN), pp. 237–242 (2011)
10. Candeloro, L., Savini, L., Conte, A.: A new weighted degree centrality measure: the application in an animal disease epidemic. PLoS ONE **11**(11), e0165781 (2016)
11. Chakrabarti, D.: Tools for large graph mining. Carnegie Mellon University (2005)
12. Chakrabarti, D., Zhan, Y., Faloutsos, C.: R-mat: a recursive model for graph mining. In: Proceedings of the 2004 SIAM International Conference on Data Mining, pp. 442–446. SIAM (2004)
13. Cohen, E., Delling, D., Pajor, T., Werneck, R.F.: Computing classic closeness centrality, at scale. ACM, New York (2014)
14. De Domenico, M., et al.: Mathematical formulation of multilayer networks. Phys. Rev. X **3**(4), 041022 (2013)
15. Domenico, M.D., Nicosia, V., Arenas, A., Latora, V.: Layer aggregation and reducibility of multilayer interconnected networks. CoRR abs/1405.0425 (2014)
16. Everett, M.G., Borgatti, S.P.: The centrality of groups and classes. J. Math. Sociol. **23**(3), 181–201 (1999)
17. Fortunato, S., Castellano, C.: Community structure in graphs. In: Encyclopedia of Complexity and Systems Science, pp. 1141–1163 (2009). https://doi.org/10.1007/978-0-387-30440-3_76
18. Gaye, I., Mendy, G., Ouya, S., Diop, I., Seck, D.: Multi-diffusion degree centrality measure to maximize the influence spread in the multilayer social networks. In: Bissyande, T.F., Sie, O. (eds.) AFRICOMM 2016. LNICST, vol. 208, pp. 53–65. Springer, Cham (2018). https://doi.org/10.1007/978-3-319-66742-3_6
19. Hagberg, A., Swart, P., S Chult, D.: Exploring network structure, dynamics, and function using networkx. Technical report, Los Alamos National Lab. (LANL), Los Alamos, NM (United States) (2008)
20. Khorasani, F., Gupta, R., Bhuyan, L.N.: Scalable SIMD-efficient graph processing on GPUs. In: Proceedings of the 24th International Conference on Parallel Architectures and Compilation Techniques, PACT 2015, pp. 39–50 (2015)
21. Kivelä, M., Arenas, A., Barthelemy, M., Gleeson, J.P., Moreno, Y., Porter, M.A.: Multilayer networks. J. Complex Netw. **2**(3), 203–271 (2014)
22. Kretschmer, H., Kretschmer, T.: A new centrality measure for social network analysis applicable to bibliometric and webometric data. Collnet J. Inf. Manag. **1**(1), 1–7 (2007)
23. Liu, Y., Wei, B., Du, Y., Xiao, F., Deng, Y.: Identifying influential spreaders by weight degree centrality in complex networks. Chaos Solitons Fractals **86**, 1–7 (2016)
24. Mukunda, K.: Decoupling-based approach to centrality detection in heterogeneous multilayer networks. Master's thesis, The University of Texas at Arlington (2021)
25. Pavel, H.R., Santra, A., Chakravarthy, S.: Closeness centrality algorithms for multilayer networks. arXiv preprint arXiv:2207.11662 (2022)

26. Pavel, H.R., Santra, A., Chakravarthy, S.: Degree centrality algorithms for homogeneous multilayer networks. In: Coenen, F., Fred, A.L.N., Filipe, J. (eds.) Proceedings of the 14th International Joint Conference on Knowledge Discovery, Knowledge Engineering and Knowledge Management, IC3K 2022, Volume 1: KDIR, Valletta, Malta, 24–26 October 2022, pp. 51–62. SCITEPRESS (2022)
27. Pedroche, F., Romance, M., Criado, R.: A biplex approach to pagerank centrality: from classic to multiplex networks. Chaos Interdisc. J. Nonlinear Sci. **26**(6), 065301 (2016)
28. Rachman, Z.A., Maharani, W., Adiwijaya: The analysis and implementation of degree centrality in weighted graph in social network analysis. In: 2013 International Conference of Information and Communication Technology (ICoICT), pp. 72–76 (2013)
29. Risselada, H., Verhoef, P.C., Bijmolt, T.H.: Indicators of opinion leadership in customer networks: self-reports and degree centrality. Mark. Lett. **27**(3), 449–460 (2016)
30. Santra, A., Bhowmick, S., Chakravarthy, S.: Efficient community re-creation in multilayer networks using boolean operations. In: International Conference on Computational Science, ICCS 2017, 12–14 June 2017, Zurich, Switzerland, pp. 58–67 (2017)
31. Santra, A., Bhowmick, S., Chakravarthy, S.: Hubify: efficient estimation of central entities across multiplex layer compositions. In: IEEE International Conference on Data Mining Workshops (2017)
32. Santra, A., Bhowmick, S.: Holistic analysis of multi-source, multi-feature data: modeling and computation challenges. In: Big Data Analytics - Fifth International Conference, BDA 2017 (2017)
33. Santra, A., Komar, K.S., Bhowmick, S., Chakravarthy, S.: A new community definition for multilayer networks and A novel approach for its efficient computation. CoRR abs/2004.09625 (2020)
34. Santra, A., Komar, K.S., Bhowmick, S., Chakravarthy, S.: From base data to knowledge discovery - a life cycle approach - using multilayer networks. Data Knowl. Eng. **141**, 102058 (2022)
35. Shi, Z., Zhang, B.: Fast network centrality analysis using GPUs. BMC Bioinform. **12**(1) (2011)
36. Solá, L., Romance, M., Criado, R., Flores, J., García del Amo, A., Boccaletti, S.: Eigenvector centrality of nodes in multiplex networks. Chaos Interdisc. J. Nonlinear Sci. **23**(3), 033131 (2013)
37. Srinivas, A., Velusamy, R.L.: Identification of influential nodes from social networks based on enhanced degree centrality measure. In: 2015 IEEE International Advance Computing Conference (IACC), pp. 1179–1184 (2015)
38. Sun, Y., Han, J.: Mining heterogeneous information networks: a structural analysis approach. ACM SIGKDD Explor. Newsl. **14**(2), 20–28 (2013)
39. Tang, X., Wang, J., Zhong, J., Pan, Y.: Predicting essential proteins based on weighted degree centrality. IEEE/ACM Trans. Comput. Biol. Bioinf. **11**(2), 407–418 (2013)
40. Towns, J., et al.: XSeDe: accelerating scientific discovery. Comput. Sci. Eng. **16**(05), 62–74 (2014)
41. Uddin, S., Hossain, L.: Time scale degree centrality: a time-variant approach to degree centrality measures. In: 2011 International Conference on Advances in Social Networks Analysis and Mining, pp. 520–524. IEEE (2011)
42. Wang, X., Hu, T., Yang, Q., Jiao, D., Yan, Y., Liu, L.: Graph-theory based degree centrality combined with machine learning algorithms can predict response to treatment with antiepileptic medications in children with epilepsy. J. Clin. Neurosci. **91**, 276–282 (2021)
43. Yang, Y., Dong, Y., Chawla, N.V.: Predicting node degree centrality with the node prominence profile. Sci. Rep. **4**(1), 1–7 (2014)

A Dual-Stage Noise Training Scheme for Breast Ultrasound Image Classification

Yiming Bian(✉)(iD) and Arun K. Somani(iD)

Department of Electrical and Computer Engineering, Iowa State University,
Ames, IA 50010, USA
{ybian,arun}@iastate.edu

Abstract. Breast cancer is one of the most common types of cancer and among the top leading causes of death among women all around the world. An early diagnosis is extremely critical, and in-time treatments can greatly help to prevent the cancer cells from spreading. Mammography, MRI, biopsy, ultrasound, etc., are recognized as effective imaging tests for breast cancer. However, the diagnosis entirely depends on the experience and expertise of the radiologist. In the last decade, computer-aided diagnosis (CAD) systems have been developed as a secondary reference to provide an objective analysis of medical images. With the help of deep learning (DL) and convolutional neural networks (CNNs), the accuracy of intelligent systems on image tasks has been perpetually improved. In this work, we specifically focus on the breast ultrasound image classification task. We apply transfer learning to four widely used backbone CNN architectures in the medical image classification field: AlexNet, ResNet-18, ResNet-50, and VGG16. They are fine-tuned on carefully constructed noisy datasets, and the test results suggest that they all acquire remarkable noise resistance, and this immunity is almost invariant to noise intensity. We systematically formalize our methodology as a dual-stage noise training scheme and provide empirical parameter configurations for each backbone CNN. This scheme enjoys being simple, effective, and universal. We believe this study will benefit the development of the robust design of DL models in the medical area.

Keywords: Breast ultrasound image · Image Classification · Noise training scheme · Speckle noise · Robustness enhancement

1 Introduction

Breast cancer is among the most common and deadly diseases. According to the United States cancer statistics in "Leading Cancer Cases and Deaths, All Races and Ethnicities, Male and Female, 2019" by Centers for Disease Control and Prevention (CDC), there are over 129 out of $100,000$ women diagnosed with breast cancer, which leads the second place (lung and bronchus cancer) by over 169%. In addition, there are over 19 death cases per $100,000$ women, which ranks second among all types of cancer.

This work was partially supported by the Philip and Virginia Sproul Professorship.

F. Coenen et al. (Eds.): IC3K 2022, CCIS 1842, pp. 53–70, 2023.
https://doi.org/10.1007/978-3-031-43471-6_3

Surveillance, Epidemiology, and End Results (SEER) database categorizes breast cancer into localized, regional, and distant stages. [1] According to a breast cancer study by American Cancer Society, the 5-year relative survival rate of each stage when diagnosed is 99%, 86%, and 29%. Therefore, an early diagnosis is extremely critical, and regular screening, including mammograms and clinical breast exams, is recommended for women.

Ultrasound scanning is also a prevalent and effective diagnostic method. Interpreting medical images, however, completely depends on the experience and expertise of the radiologist. This is costly and sometimes inaccurate. Therefore, CAD systems are designed as a supplementary diagnosis source. They help doctors improve the accuracy and efficiency of diagnosis [2]. The use of ultrasound-based CAD for the classification of tumor diseases provides effective decision-making support and a second tool option for radiologists or diagnosticians [3].

ImageNet project [4] and ImageNet Large Scale Visual Recognition Challenge (ILSVRC) [5] greatly promoted the development of DL models for image classification tasks. Annual champion models achieved glorious and astonishing accuracies and have outperformed the average human recognition level since 2015. [6] Most image classification achievements are made in the general object area thanks to ImageNet being generously shared with the public. In the medical image area, lacking such a large amount of high-quality data holds back the development of corresponding neural architectures.

1.1 Image Data Predicament in Medical Area

Two main obstacles of medical image are data scarcity and low image quality. The absence of a large volume of high-quality medical data is an undeniable predicament. [7] Take the ultrasound medical dataset as an example, it is more difficult to obtain as the annotation of medical images requires significant professional medical knowledge. [3] In addition, patients tend to keep their health data private. To mitigate the data shortage issue, transfer learning [8, 9] and data augmentation are adopted as countermeasures.

Another obstacle is the quality of medical images As will be detailed in Sect. 2, speckle noise inherently exists in medical images, especially those acquired by coherent imaging systems. It degrades the image quality and brings great difficulty for DL models to recognize. Traditional neural networks are vulnerable to image degradation. To alleviate the noise issue, noise removal techniques and robust architecture designs are employed.

Noise removal techniques are initially designed for signal processing problems. They are simple to apply, but the restoration may bring extra degradation, such as blur. Moreover, there is a gap between a fine-quality restored image recognized by human perception and that recognized by neural networks. On the other hand, specially designed neural architectures show great robustness only in particular problems. They may not apply to interdisciplinary fields or even similar areas. For example, authors proposed a weakly supervised deep learning framework with uncertainty estimation, called Uncertainty-Driven Deep Multiple Instance Learning (UD-MIL), to address OCT image classification problem in [10]. Their framework is claimed to be robust to speckle noise. But it is unknown if this can be a backbone framework and applied to classify ultrasound or other medical images. Therefore, we decide to explore a methodology that is simple, effective, and universal. We call it a dual-stage noise training scheme.

1.2 Related Work

Previous researchers have done remarkable explorations on classifying breast ultrasound images. However, most of them adopted private datasets, and it is unrealistic to make a comprehensive comparison among these works.

Regarding speckle noise suppression in ultrasound images, a denoise algorithm based on directional average filters is proposed in [11]. Their results indicate that the noise is removed and edges are well preserved. In [12], a fast speckle noise suppression algorithm is designed using three-dimensional deep learning. The results show fast denoise and good detail preservation.

Moreover, specialized training strategies are proposed for classifying breast ultrasound images. For example, authors of [9] proposed a multistage transfer learning (MSTL) algorithm implemented using three pre-trained models: EfficientNetV2 [13], Inception-v3 [14], and ResNet-50 [6]. As breast ultrasound images are not available on a large scale. They first use easily acquired microscopic cancer cell line images to fine-tune the pre-trained network. It is claimed that learning from both natural and medical datasets improves the performance of breast ultrasound image classification. Next, the model was fine-tuned on a small breast ultrasound image dataset. The noise in ultrasound images is removed using the dilation function with 2×2 kernel.

The classification tasks of other types of ultrasound images, such as hip ultrasound images [15], kidney ultrasound images [16], etc., are also studied. They apply noise removal techniques such as non-local means (NLM) to improve image quality. The classification is done by fine-tuning various backbone CNNs.

1.3 Contributions

In this study, we focus on building a simple, effective, and universal neural network training scheme for the breast ultrasound image classification task. We identify our main contributions as follows.

- We propose a systematic dual-stage noise training scheme that grants the backbone CNN noise resilience and immunity to noise intensity.
- We design a methodology for comprehensive performance comparisons among multiple medical deep learning models.
- We provide empirical parameter configurations for the selected CNNs.

The rest of the paper is organized as follows. Section 2 provides preliminary knowledge of speckle noise. In Sect. 3, we detail the full view of the dual-stage noise training scheme, including dataset generation, backbone CNN selection, performance metrics, etc. Experiment results and analysis are presented in Sect. 4. In Sect. 5, we give concluding remarks and discuss future research directions.

2   Speckle Noise

In this section, we provide prerequisite knowledge of speckle noise. Particularly, we answer the following questions: 1) what the origin of speckle noise is, 2) why speckle noise is common, especially in medical images, 3) how speckle noise is simulated and implemented, and 4) what neural networks are widely adopted in breast ultrasound image classification.

A speckle pattern is formed when fairly coherent light is either reflected from a rough surface or propagates through a medium with random refractive index fluctuations. [17] A common source of the speckle pattern is partially coherent wavefronts of a time-varying wave field such as light and sound. Rough surfaces produce complex amplitude fluctuations. These normally distributed fluctuations are reflected and collected by the sensor. Therefore, a speckle pattern inherently exists in the output of a coherent imaging system. As this pattern degrades the quality of captured images, it is known as speckle noise.

In medical images, for example, ultrasound images, speckle noise is inevitable as the mainstream ultrasound machines are coherent imaging systems. Figure 1 shows two breast ultrasound images containing a benign nodule. Speckle noise can be easily observed.

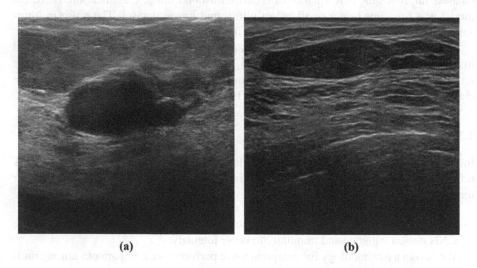

(a)   (b)

Fig. 1. (a) A Breast Ultrasound Image of a Benign Tumor (Cropped): This image is from Breast Ultrasound Images (BUSI) Dataset [18] under 'benign' folder with a filename of '000093'. This public dataset is available on Kaggle **(b)** Another Breast Ultrasound Image of a Benign Tumor (Cropped): This image is also from BUSI. It is stored under 'benign' folder, named '000087'.

Speckle noise is usually considered to be a correlated multiplicative noise but it can be transformed into additive noise by applying a logarithm operation. [19] It can be simulated as

$$O(i,j) = I(i,j) + h(i,j) \times n_{wG}(i,j) \tag{1}$$

where (i,j) is the spatial information, I is the original image, h is the point spreading function, n_{wG} is the white Gaussian noise, and O is the corrupted image with simulated speckle noise.

Two commonly adopted implementations of speckle noise generation are "imnoise()" function in MATLAB and "skimage.util.random_noise" function in Python. In our experiments, we simulate speckle noise using "imnoise()". Speckle noise is synthesized using

$$O(i,j) = I(i,j) + \sqrt{12\sigma^2} \times I(i,j) \times [\text{rand}(0,1) - 0.5] \tag{2}$$

The synthetic noise (η) in this implementation follows a uniform distribution, thus $\eta \sim \mathcal{U}(a,b)$, where $a \leq \eta \leq b$. Mean (μ) and variance (σ^2) can be expressed in a and b as given in

$$\begin{cases} \mu = \frac{1}{2}(a+b) \\ \sigma^2 = \frac{1}{12}(b-a)^2 \end{cases} \tag{3}$$

Then we have $\sqrt{12\sigma^2} = 2b - 2\mu$. Since the mean (μ) is set to 0 by default, it is simplified to $\sqrt{12\sigma^2} = 2b$. The range $[a,b]$ can be converted to $2bm$, where m is a random value ranging from -0.5 to 0.5. Therefore, $2bm$ can be written as $\sqrt{12\sigma^2} \times [\text{rand}(0,1) - 0.5]$, which explains Eq. 2.

3 Methodology

In this section, we detail the proposed dual-stage noise training methodology in the following aspects: dataset, CNN model, and performance metric. Then the complete scheme is formally stated in Sect. 3.4.

3.1 Dataset Preparation

As mentioned in Sect. 1.2, many research works in the medical image processing area adopt private datasets. In this study, we work on two small-scale public breast ultrasound image datasets. They are Breast Ultrasound Images Dataset (BUSI) [18] and MT_small [20].

Images of BUSI were acquired using LOGIQ E9 ultrasound and LOGIQ E9 Agile ultrasound system by Baheya Hospital, Cairo, Egypt in 2018. They are categorized into benign, malignant, and normal. The sample size of each class is 487, 210 and 133. MT_small has two categories: benign and malignant. Each contains 200 sample images.

In this study, we assume the presence of a nodule. Therefore, we only keep the benign and malignant classes in BUSI. In addition, we trim each dataset by removing the sample image that has a superimposed object box and annotations. The trimmed BUSI contains 335 benign images and 184 malignant images, and the trimmed

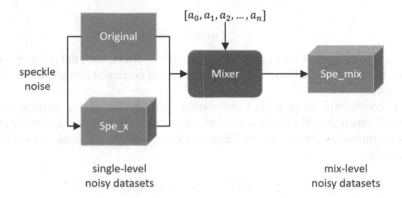

Fig. 2. Datasets generation: Two types of datasets are single-level noisy datasets and mix-level noisy datasets. Single-level noisy datasets include the original dataset and n synthesized noisy datasets by adding n levels of synthetic speckle noise to the original dataset. Mix-level datasets are generated by mixing $n + 1$ single-level datasets according to the selected proportions.

MT_small contains 187 benign images and 179 malignant images. These two trimmed datasets are generally referred to as original datasets in our proposed scheme.

Figure 2 depicts the strategy of dataset generation. It is divided into two parts: single-level noisy datasets generation and mix-level noisy datasets generation. For the first part, we add five levels of synthetic speckle noise to the original datasets. Noise level is specified by the variance of the noise. Our empirical selections of variance are from 0.02 to 0.1 at a step size of 0.02. Therefore, we obtain five synthesized noisy datasets named as "Spe_x" where $x \in \{$"002", "004", "006", "008", "010"$\}$. These six datasets, including the original dataset, are called single-level noisy datasets. The original dataset can be viewed as one added zero noise, thus "Spe_000", for a consistent notation.

To generate mix-level noisy datasets, we specify the mix proportion of single-level noisy datasets as a vector $[a_0, a_1, ..., a_n]^T$, where $\sum_{i=0}^{n} a_i = 1$. In our experiments, we mix the corresponding noisy datasets of three single-level noise retrained models with top performance. The tested proportions are $(20\%, 40\%, 40\%)$, $(25\%, 50\%, 25\%)$, $(33\%, 33\%, 33\%)$ and $(40\%, 40\%, 20\%)$. The proportions of the rest uncollected datasets are 0%, hence omitted for simplicity.

As the size of both datasets are very limited, we choose the larger BUSI for training purpose and MT_small for test purpose. To provide more evidence for performance analysis, we also consider BUSI as a test set but playing a minor role compared to MT_small. BUSI for test purposes is different from BUSI for training purposes, as will be addressed later in this section.

Another issue of the trimmed BUSI is data imbalance. The malignant sample size (184) is much smaller than the benign sample size (335), it affects both convergences during the training phase and generalization of a model on the test set [21]. We adopt oversampling to mitigate this issue. It is proven to be robust as mentioned in [22] and it outperforms all other measures such as undersampling and thresholding, with respect to the multi-class receiver operating characteristic curve (ROC AUC). [21]

Specifically, we randomly select malignant samples and crop them to create new samples. It is ensured that the nodule is present in the new sample image. This augmentation can avoid the potential overfitting issue if direct replication is used. To further avoid the overfitting risk, no synthesized image is included in the validation set. The augmented BUSI now contains two classes that have the same size (335). It is further split into a training set and a validation set at a ratio of 4 : 1. The information of every dataset used in our experiments is detailed in Table 1.

Table 1. Dataset details: Single-level noisy datasets are generated by adding synthetic speckle noise. Mix-level noisy datasets are generated by mixing single-level noisy datasets using selected proportions. In "Sample Size" column, B and M stand for benign and malignant respectively.

Purpose	Backbone Dataset	Dataset Variants	Sample Size
Training	augmented BUSI	6 single-level, 4 mix-level	B: 268
			M: 268
Validation			B: 67
			M: 67
Test	trimmed BUSI	6 single-level	B: 335
			M: 184
	timmed MT_small		B: 187
			M: 179

3.2 CNN Model Selection

In the medical image processing area, three backbone CNN architectures that are well-experimented and explored are: AlexNet [23,24], ResNet [25–28], and VGG [29–31]. We decide to carry out our experiments on these backbone CNNs and prove that these models can be applied to various medical image classification tasks after transfer learning.

Formally, we select AlexNet [32], ResNet-18 [6], ResNet-50 [6], and VGG16 [33] as the backbone CNNs. Since the pre-trained models have an output dimension of $1,000$, it is modified to 2 before retraining using transfer learning.

Based on each training set, a retrained model is generated and named "RMN_x" where the name stands for **R**etrained **M**odel on a **N**oisy dataset, and the suffix x is identical to that of the corresponding training set. For each CNN, there are 10 retrained models including 6 single-level noise trained models, named "RMN_x" where $x \in \{$"000", "002", ..., "010"$\}$, and 4 mix-level noise trained models, named "RMN_y" where $y \in \{$"204040", "255025", "333333", "404020"$\}$.

3.3 Performance Metrics

We adopt four widely used performance metrics in this study. They are accuracy, specificity, sensitivity, and F1 score. In the following equations, TP/TN and FP/FN are short for true positive/negative and false positive/negative. Positive indicates the nodule is cancerous while negative indicates otherwise.

Accuracy is the proportion of correct predictions over all types of predictions. Specificity is the proportion of predictions that if a nodule is benign, it is classified as negative. Sensitivity is the proportion of predictions that if a nodule is malignant, it is classified as positive. F1 score is the harmonic mean of precision and recall [34]. It describes the reliability of a positive prediction. These four metrics are defined as

$$\text{Accuracy}(\%) = \frac{TP + TN}{TP + TN + FP + FN} \tag{4}$$

$$\text{Specificity}(\%) = \frac{TN}{TN + FP} \tag{5}$$

$$\text{Sensitivity}(\%) = \frac{TP}{TP + FN} \tag{6}$$

$$\text{F1}(\%) = \frac{TP}{TP + \frac{1}{2}(FP + FN)} \tag{7}$$

Among them, we rank the importance as sensitivity, F1 score, accuracy, and specificity. Apart from correct predictions (TP and TN), FN is much more deadly than FP because if a malignant nodule is categorized as benign, it causes little caution. As a result, we emphasize the weight of FN in the expression, and sensitivity is the most significant metric, while specificity is the least.

3.4   A Dual-Stage Noise Training Scheme

The source code of our experiments is public on GitHub,[1] where the configuration of hyperparameters can be found. Figure 3 depicts a high-level view of the proposed dual-stage noise training scheme. Below, we explain the entire process in detail.

In Stage 1, we are initially provided with all the single-level noisy datasets, denoted as "Spe_000" to "Spe_010". We fine-tune the pre-trained model of each backbone CNN on each of them, and obtain six corresponding single-level noise trained models, named "RMN_000" to "RMN_010". We comprehensively compare their performance and determine three models with the best performance. Meanwhile, we record the noise level of the corresponding training set for the mix-level noisy dataset generation.

In Stage 2, we first construct the four mix-level noisy datasets based on the top three single-level noisy datasets and the empirical mix proportions. They are denoted as "Spe_202040" to "Spe_404020". The fine-tuned mixed-level noise trained models are named as "RMN_202040" to "RMN_404020". Next, we adopt the same comparison strategies and determine the mix-level noise trained model with the best performance. The last step is to decide the best model among the four candidates in two stages.

---

[1] https://github.com/YimingBian/Speckle_noise_IC.

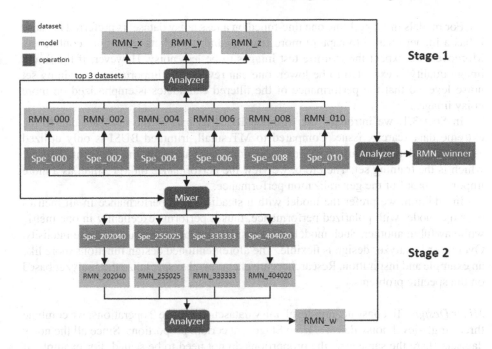

Fig. 3. An overview of the dual-stage scheme design: Three types of components are dataset (green), model (yellow), and operation (blue). The suffix of a dataset indicates the variance of the synthetic noise. Particularly, the original dataset is equivalent to a dataset that added zero synthetic noise. It is denoted as "Spe_000" as a consistent notation. The arrow between a dataset and a model indicates a retraining process. The analyzer in Stage 1 provides the top 3 single-level noisy datasets to the mixer in Stage 2. The rest arrows indicate the flow directions. (Color figure online)

Analyzer Design. We design a comprehensive performance comparison strategy to cope with the complicated nature of medical data. The model is analyzed in two aspects: performance metrics and test sets. When comparing single-level noise trained models, the training noise level is an additional aspect to be considered. We specify the order of comparison and importance ranks in Fig. 4.

	strong ⟶					weak
Metric	sensitivity		F1 score	accuracy		specificity
Training noise level (Stage 1)	Spe_000	Spe_002	Spe_004	Spe_006	Spe_008	Spe_010
Test set			MT_small		trimmed BUSI	

first ↓ last

Fig. 4. A comprehensive performance comparison design.

Four performance metrics are the core of performance analysis, as mentioned in Sect. 3.3, they are ranked as sensitivity, F1 score, accuracy, and specificity because FN scenario is highlighted. When there is a tie, we compare the following aspects.

For models in Stage 1, the one fine-tuned on a less noisy dataset is preferred because it has a higher chance to capture more features and it predicts with more confidence. Moreover, we expect the real-life test images to be less noisy. However, if the future image quality is expected to be lower, one can reverse the importance of training set noise level so that the performance of the filtered candidates is emphasized on more noisy images.

In Sect. 3.1, we introduce the trimmed BUSI as part of the test data due to the extreme data scarcity issue. Compared to MT_small, trimmed BUSI is only utilized as minor evidence because it shares some common parts with the augmented BUSI, which is the training set. Therefore, we view the performance on MT_small as a more important proof of the generalization performance.

In addition, we prefer the model with a steadily good performance in all metrics over the model with polarized performance, thus it performs excellently in one metric while awful in another. Such models are considered to be less robust to noise intensity. Overall, the analyzer design is flexible. The aforementioned design functions more like an example and inspiration. Researchers are encouraged to specialize the analyzer based on the specific problems.

Mixer Design. To construct mix-level noisy datasets for Stage 2 operations, we combine three single-level noisy datasets from Stage 1 at certain proportions. Since all the noisy datasets share the same size, the proportions do not need to be scaled. For example, if 20% of the mix-level noisy dataset comes from Spe_002, we can directly extract 20% samples from Spe_002.

The sample selection in the single-level noisy datasets should be random, one-shot, and independent. The randomness is self-explained to be necessary. Being one-shot is required to keep the proposed scheme simple. Images have different difficulties to be recognized. However, we ignore such differences and disapprove of multiple random samplings because it does not bring significant improvement. Sampling should be independent as well. Thus, if an image is selected, it is independent that its variants being selected. Therefore, it is possible that three noisy variants of the same original image exist in the mix-level noisy dataset.

Another point is that there should be no augmented image in the validation set because they may cause the overfitting issue. Since the single-level noisy validation set does not contain any oversampled images, no special action is needed to construct the mix-level noisy validation set, but it is still worth the warning. The above design principles aim to keep the mixer efficient and effective.

We provide four empirical selections of mix proportions. But this brings another problem: what is the order of three single-level noisy datasets? To answer this question, we have to recall the design of the analyzer. Three outstanding candidate models are picked after a comprehensive comparison. However, it is often the case that no model is strictly better than another, especially among the candidate models. In other words, the order of models does not matter to a large extent. Therefore, we decide to order the single-level noisy datasets regarding their noise level for simplicity. The least noisy one is placed first and the most noisy one is placed last.

4 Experiment Results

The full results of our experiments are available in the same repository on GitHub, together with the source code, for other researchers to reproduce the results and carry out further studies. In this section, we comment on the major steps and analyze the highlighted results.

4.1 Stage 1

We fine-tune the pre-trained model on six single-level noisy datasets and obtain the corresponding retrained models. They are tested on both MT_small and the trimmed BUSI regarding sensitivity, F1 score, accuracy, and specificity.

According to the comparison principles introduced in Sect. 3.4, the top three retrained models of each backbone CNN are selected after comparing their performance in the aspects of metrics, training noise level, and test set. These comparisons are visualized in Table 2 and 3. We use a dot to note the model with the best performance in each metric. The specific numbers are omitted not only for a cleaner look but the actual data space is three-dimensional. For example, the sensitivity cell of AlexNet RMN_000 contains six numbers: 82.84%, 78.03%, 74.89%, 70.8%, 66.42% and 65.31%. Each represents the sensitivity value of the model on six single-level noisy datasets.

Table 2. Performance of retrained models on MT_small.

Backbone CNN	Metric	RMN						Best Models
		000	002	004	006	008	010	
AlexNet	Sensitivity		●			●	●	RMN_002 RMN_006 RMN_008
	F1 score	●		●	●			
	Accuracy		●		●	●		
	Specificity	●		●	●			
ResNet-18	Sensitivity	●				●	●	RMN_004 RMN_006 RMN_010
	F1 score			●	●		●	
	Accuracy			●	●		●	
	Specificity			●	●		●	
ResNet-50	Sensitivity		●			●	●	RMN_002 RMN_006 RMN_008
	F1 score			●	●	●		
	Accuracy			●	●	●		
	Specificity			●	●	●		
VGG16	Sensitivity	●		●	●			RMN_000 RMN_002 RMN_004
	F1 score	●	●	●				
	Accuracy	●	●	●				
	Specificity		●	●			●	

After comprehensive performance comparisons, we obtain three candidate models of each backbone CNN as listed in Table 5.

4.2   Stage 2

With three candidate models from Stage 1, we construct four mix-level noisy datasets by combining the corresponding training and validation sets at selected mix proportions. Based on our experience, four mix proportion options are (20%, 40%, 40%), (25%, 50%, 25%), (33%, 33%, 33%), and (40%, 40%, 20%). We fine-tune the pre-trained model of each backbone CNN, and obtain four mix-level noise trained models. They are denoted as "RMN_x" where $x \in \{$ "204040", "255025", "333333", "404020"$\}$. After the comprehensive performance comparisons, we obtain the mix-level trained candidate model for each backbone CNN. They are listed in Table 5.

After acquiring all four candidate models, they are compared to determine the best model overall. In Table 4, we provide performance scores of all the AlexNet candidate models. The rest backbone CNN candidate models' performance scores are available in the repository on GitHub. We plot all the backbone CNN candidate model's performance curves in Fig. 5, 6, 7, and 8. A flat curve indicates the model is invariant to noise intensity while a skew curve means the model has a polarized performance.

In the case of AlexNet, RMN_204040 (red) has the best overall performance especially the sensitivity on Spe_000 (100%), F1 score, and accuracy on Spe_002 - Spe_010 ($\approx$ 90%), and an increasing specificity curve when the noise gets intense. Another

Table 3. Performance of retrained models on the trimmed BUSI.

Backbone CNN	Metric	RMN						Best Models
		000	002	004	006	008	010	
AlexNet	Sensitivity		●			●	●	RMN_002 RMN_008 RMN_010
	F1 score	●	●			●		
	Accuracy		●			●	●	
	Specificity	●	●		●			
ResNet-18	Sensitivity			●		●	●	RMN_000 RMN_004 RMN_010
	F1 score			●	●		●	
	Accuracy	●		●			●	
	Specificity	●		●	●			
ResNet-50	Sensitivity	●	●			●		RMN_000 RMN_002 RMN_008
	F1 score	●	●			●		
	Accuracy	●	●			●		
	Specificity		●	●	●			
VGG16	Sensitivity	●		●	●			RMN_000 RMN_002 RMN_004
	F1 score	●	●	●				
	Accuracy	●	●	●				
	Specificity	●	●	●				

Table 4. The metric scores of four AlexNet candidate models on MT_small: six scores in a row indicate the performance on each single-level noisy test set. The percent sign is omitted due to the width limit.

Model	Accuracy						Specificity					
RMN_204040	81.52	90.22	90.76	91.03	89.67	89.95	73.44	86.89	90.10	94.29	94.12	96.32
RMN_002	84.78	89.13	88.04	88.32	89.67	88.59	77.27	84.58	85.29	87.56	89.89	91.48
RMN_006	85.33	90.49	91.03	90.49	89.13	86.41	79.91	90.05	93.30	97.52	99.33	99.29
RMN_008	87.23	90.49	88.86	89.95	84.78	84.24	80.79	85.58	84.83	85.45	79.46	78.51
Model	Sensitivity						F1 score					
RMN_204040	100.0	94.44	91.48	88.08	85.86	84.88	76.71	89.47	90.45	91.15	89.95	90.39
RMN_002	99.21	95.45	91.46	89.14	89.44	85.94	81.70	88.02	87.21	87.89	89.44	88.71
RMN_006	93.75	90.96	88.89	85.02	82.11	78.51	83.33	90.20	91.06	90.96	89.95	87.75
RMN_008	97.84	97.39	94.27	96.13	93.06	93.57	85.27	89.49	87.83	88.96	82.72	81.88

strong candidate is RMN_008 (purple) as it has a flatter curve in each metric. However, we expect the future test images to be less noisy as mentioned in the analyzer design. Therefore, RMN_204040 is the final winner. This reinforces the flexibility of the analyzer design.

The best models of ResNet-18 and ResNet-50 are relatively easy to decide. Because RMN_006 (ResNet-18) and RMN_333333 (ResNet-50) have top performance in most metrics and a relatively flat performance curve compared to their rival models.

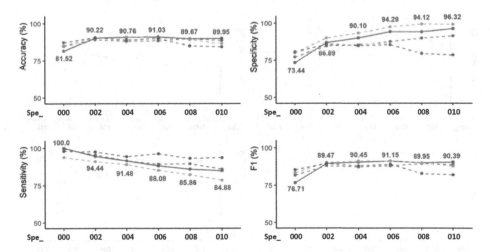

Fig. 5. AlexNet candidate models' performance curves on MT_small: Candidates are RMN_002 (green), RMN_006 (yellow), RMN_008 (purple), and RMN_204040 (red). The scores of the best model (RMN_204040) are listed. (Color figure online)

In the above three cases, the competition for the best model is moderate. However, in the case of VGG16, we observe very close performance curves, especially between RMN_004 and RMN_404020, as shown in Fig. 8. As a tie-breaker, we reference their performance on the trimmed BUSI test set. In Fig. 9, RMN_004 demonstrates a comparable or slightly better performance over RMN_404020 in each metric. Therefore, it is selected as the best model for VGG16.

To conclude, we provide an empirical optimal training scheme that generates a noise trained model with the best performance for each backbone CNN in Table 5. For AlexNet, the best model fine-tunes on a mix-level noisy dataset by combining Spe_002, Spe_006 and Spe_008 at the proportion of (20%, 20%, 40%). For ResNet-50, training on the mix-level noisy dataset consisting of 33% of each of Spe_002, Spe_006 and Spe_008 generates the best model. On the other hand, for ResNet-18 and VGG16, a single-level noisy dataset is all you need. It is Spe_006 and Spe_004 respectively.

Table 5. Candidate and winner models for each backbone CNN.

Backbone CNN	Candidates				Winner
	Stage 1			Stage 2	
AlexNet	RMN_002	RMN_006	RMN_008	RMN_202040	RMN_202040
ResNet-18	RMN_004	RMN_006	RMN_010	RMN_404020	RMN_006
ResNet-50	RMN_002	RMN_006	RMN_008	RMN_333333	RMN_333333
VGG16	RMN_000	RMN_002	RMN_004	RMN_404020	RMN_004

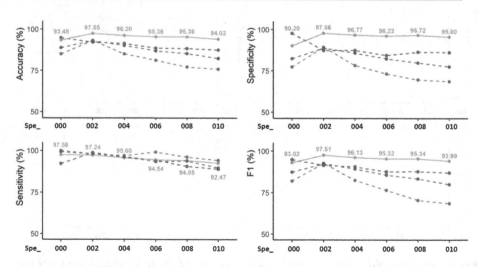

Fig. 6. ResNet-18 candidate models' performance curves on MT_small: Candidates are RMN_004 (green), RMN_006 (yellow), RMN_010 (purple), and RMN_402020 (red). The scores of the best model (RMN_006) are listed. (Color figure online)

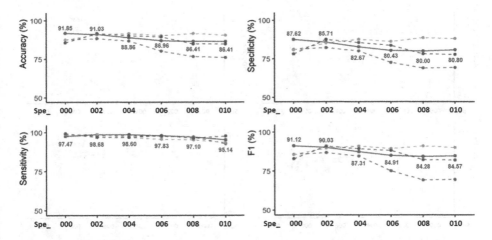

Fig. 7. ResNet-50 candidate models' performance curves on MT_small: Candidates are RMN_002 (green), RMN_006 (yellow), RMN_008 (purple), and RMN_333333 (red). The scores of the best model (RMN_333333) are listed. (Color figure online)

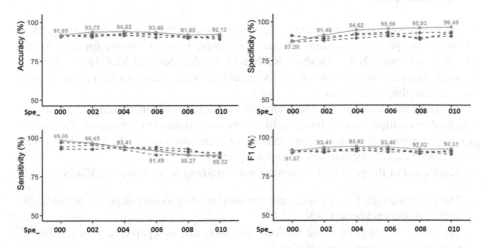

Fig. 8. VGG16 candidate models' performance curves on MT_small: Candidates are RMN_002 (green), RMN_004 (yellow), RMN_000 (purple), and RMN_404020 (red). The scores of the best model (RMN_004) are listed. (Color figure online)

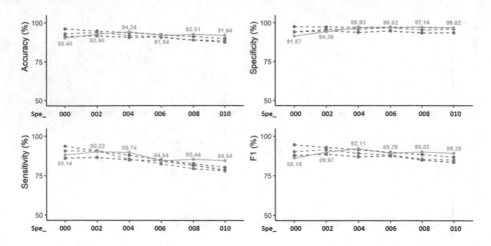

Fig. 9. VGG16 candidate models' performance curves on the trimmed BUSI.

5 Conclusions

In this study, we explore the impact of speckle noise on breast ultrasound image classification. We propose a systematic dual-stage noise training scheme for four widely adopted backbone CNNs: AlexNet, ResNet-18, ResNet-50, and VGG16. To mitigate the medical data scarcity issue and class imbalance issue, we adopt data augmentation and oversampling techniques.

In addition, we present a comprehensive model performance comparison design, which takes multiple aspects into consideration, and a dataset mixer design. Finally, we provide an empirical noise training scheme for each backbone CNN, including single-level noisy dataset selection and the mix proportion.

Highlights of the proposed dual-stage noise training scheme are as follows.

- The performance of single-level noise trained models mainly depends on the architecture of the backbone CNN.
- The mixer is designed to be random, one-shot, and independent. It is a trade-off between effectiveness and efficiency.
- The comprehensive performance comparison strategy is flexible and subject to particular experiments.
- The performance of a mix-level noise trained model is related to the corresponding mixed single-level noise trained models. It usually has a flatter performance curve, which indicates the immunity to noise intensity.

For our future research directions, we plan to expand the studied medical images to more types such as X-ray images, Magnetic Resonance Imaging (MRI) images, Optical Coherence Tomography (OCT) images, etc. Moreover, we would like to design lightweight neural architectures using neural architecture search (NAS) that is specialized for medical image processing. While the shortage of medical data will remain a major obstacle, we also decide to explore the topic of small dataset training. We believe our work will promote the development of CAD systems in medical image processing area. We also hope patients would be provided with more accessible and reliable medical advice in the near future.

Acknowledgements. The research reported in this paper in part was funded by the Philip and Virginia Sproul Professorship at Iowa State University. The computing for this research was supported by HPC@ISU equipment mostly purchased through funding provided by the NSF grants numbers MRI 1726447 and MRI 2018594. All opinions, findings, and conclusions expressed are those of the authors.

References

1. Young, J.: SEER summary staging manual 2000: codes and coding instructions. National Cancer Institute, National Institutes of Health (2001)
2. Wang, Y., Ge, X., Ma, H., Qi, S., Zhang, G., Yao, Y.: Deep learning in medical ultrasound image analysis: a review. IEEE Access **9**, 54310–54324 (2021)
3. Liu, S., et al.: Deep learning in medical ultrasound analysis: a review. Engineering **5**, 261–275 (2019)
4. Deng, J., Dong, W., Socher, R., Li, L., Li, K., Fei-Fei, L.: Imagenet: a large-scale hierarchical image database. In: 2009 IEEE Conference on Computer Vision and Pattern Recognition, pp. 248–255 (2009)
5. Russakovsky, O., et al.: Imagenet large scale visual recognition challenge. Int. J. Comput. Vision **115**, 211–252 (2015)
6. He, K., Zhang, X., Ren, S., Sun, J.: Deep residual learning for image recognition. In: Proceedings of the IEEE Conference on Computer Vision and Pattern Recognition, pp. 770–778 (2016)
7. Bian, Y., Somani, A.: An effective two-stage noise training methodology for classification of breast ultrasound images. In: Proceedings of the 14th International Joint Conference on Knowledge Discovery, Knowledge Engineering and Knowledge Management - KDIR, pp. 83–94 (2022)
8. Kim, H., Cosa-Linan, A., Santhanam, N., Jannesari, M., Maros, M., Ganslandt, T.: Transfer learning for medical image classification: a literature review. BMC Med. Imaging **22**, 1–13 (2022)
9. Ayana, G., Park, J., Jeong, J., Choe, S.: A novel multistage transfer learning for ultrasound breast cancer image classification. Diagnostics **12**, 135 (2022)
10. Wang, X., et al.: UD-MIL: uncertainty-driven deep multiple instance learning for OCT image classification. IEEE J. Biomed. Health Inform. **24**, 3431–3442 (2020)
11. Bhateja, V., Srivastava, A., Singh, G., Singh, J.: A modified speckle suppression algorithm for breast ultrasound images using directional filters. In: ICT and Critical Infrastructure: Proceedings of the 48th Annual Convention of Computer Society of India-Vol II, pp. 219–226 (2014)
12. Li, X., Wang, Y., Zhao, Y., Wei, Y.: Fast speckle noise suppression algorithm in breast ultrasound image using three-dimensional deep learning. Front. Physiol. **13**, 698 (2022)
13. Tan, M., Le, Q.: Efficientnetv2: smaller models and faster training. In: International Conference on Machine Learning, pp. 10096–10106 (2021)
14. Szegedy, C., Vanhoucke, V., Ioffe, S., Shlens, J., Wojna, Z.: Rethinking the inception architecture for computer vision. In: Proceedings of the IEEE Conference on Computer Vision and Pattern Recognition, pp. 2818–2826 (2016)

15. Sezer, A., Sezer, H.: Deep convolutional neural network-based automatic classification of neonatal hip ultrasound images: a novel data augmentation approach with speckle noise reduction. Ultrasound Med. Biol. **46**, 735–749 (2020)
16. Sudharson, S., Kokil, P.: An ensemble of deep neural networks for kidney ultrasound image classification. Comput. Methods Programs Biomed. **197**, 105709 (2020)
17. Dainty, J.: Laser Speckle and Related Phenomena. Springer, Heidelberg (2013). https://doi.org/10.1007/978-3-662-43205-1
18. Al-Dhabyani, W., Gomaa, M., Khaled, H., Fahmy, A.: Dataset of breast ultrasound images. Data Brief **28**, 104863 (2020)
19. Rasham, N., Abbas, H., Abdul Razaq, A., Mohamad, H.: Simulation of speckle noise using image processing techniques. In: Computer Networks and Inventive Communication Technologies, pp. 489–501 (2022)
20. Badawy, S., Mohamed, A., Hefnawy, A., Zidan, H., GadAllah, M., El-Banby, G.: Automatic semantic segmentation of breast tumors in ultrasound images based on combining fuzzy logic and deep learning-a feasibility study. PLoS ONE **16**, e0251899 (2021)
21. Buda, M., Maki, A., Mazurowski, M.: A systematic study of the class imbalance problem in convolutional neural networks. Neural Netw. **106**, 249–259 (2018)
22. Ling, C., Li, C.: Data mining for direct marketing: problems and solutions. In: KDD 1998, pp. 73–79 (1998)
23. Nawaz, W., Ahmed, S., Tahir, A., Khan, H.: Classification of breast cancer histology images using ALEXNET. In: International Conference Image Analysis and Recognition, pp. 869–876 (2018)
24. Masud, M., et al.: Pre-trained convolutional neural networks for breast cancer detection using ultrasound images. ACM Trans. Internet Technol. (TOIT) **21**, 1–17 (2021)
25. Jiang, Y., Chen, L., Zhang, H., Xiao, X.: Breast cancer histopathological image classification using convolutional neural networks with small SE-ResNet module. PLoS ONE **14**, e0214587 (2019)
26. Al-Haija, Q., Adebanjo, A.: Breast cancer diagnosis in histopathological images using ResNet-50 convolutional neural network. In: 2020 IEEE International IOT, Electronics and Mechatronics Conference (IEMTRONICS), pp. 1–7 (2020)
27. Virmani, J., Agarwal, R., et al.: Deep feature extraction and classification of breast ultrasound images. Multimedia Tools Appl. **79**, 27257–27292 (2020)
28. Yap, M., et al.: Breast ultrasound region of interest detection and lesion localisation. Artif. Intell. Med. **107**, 101880 (2020)
29. Moon, W., Lee, Y., Ke, H., Lee, S., Huang, C., Chang, R.: Computer-aided diagnosis of breast ultrasound images using ensemble learning from convolutional neural networks. Comput. Methods Programs Biomed. **190**, 105361 (2020)
30. Jahangeer, G., Rajkumar, T.: Early detection of breast cancer using hybrid of series network and VGG-16. Multimedia Tools Appl. **80**, 7853–7886 (2021)
31. Albashish, D., Al-Sayyed, R., Abdullah, A., Ryalat, M., Almansour, N.: Deep CNN model based on VGG16 for breast cancer classification. In: 2021 International Conference on Information Technology (ICIT), pp. 805–810 (2021)
32. Krizhevsky, A., Sutskever, I., Hinton, G.: Imagenet classification with deep convolutional neural networks. In: Advances in Neural Information Processing Systems, vol. 25 (2012)
33. Simonyan, K., Zisserman, A.: Very deep convolutional networks for large-scale image recognition. arXiv Preprint arXiv:1409.1556 (2014)
34. Taha, A., Hanbury, A.: Metrics for evaluating 3D medical image segmentation: analysis, selection, and tool. BMC Med. Imaging **15**, 1–28 (2015)

A General-Purpose Multi-stage Multi-group Machine Learning Framework for Knowledge Discovery and Decision Support

Eva K. Lee[1,2]([envelope]) [iD], Fan Yuan[2], Barton J. Man[3], and Brent Egan[4,5] [iD]

[1] Center for Operations Research in Medicine and Healthcare, The Data and Analytics Innovation Institute, Atlanta, USA
evalee-gatech@pm.me
[2] Georgia Institute of Technology, Atlanta, USA
[3] The American Orthopedic Society for Sports Medicine, Chicago, USA
[4] American Medical Association, Chicago, USA
brent.egan@ama-assn.org
[5] Medical University of South Carolina, Charleston, USA

Abstract. We present a general-purpose multi-stage, multi-group machine learning framework that incorporates the discriminant analysis via mixed integer programming (DAMIP) classifier with an exact combinatorial branch-and-bound (BB) algorithm and a fast particle swarm optimization (PSO) for feature selection. DAMIP delays making decisions on 'difficult-to-classify' observations by placing them into a reserved judgment region and develops new classification rules in a later stage. Such a design is well-suited for poorly separated data that are difficult to classify without committing a high percentage of misclassification errors. The model misclassification limits, and reserved judgment levels can be fine-tuned to facilitate the efficient management of imbalanced groups. This ensures that the minority groups (with relatively few entities) are treated equally as the majority groups. We tackle four medical problems that involve poorly separated data and imbalanced groups in which traditional classifiers yield low prediction accuracy: (a) multi-site treatment outcome prediction for best practice discovery in cardiovascular disease; and (b) diabetes; (c) early disease diagnosis in predicting subjects into normal cognition, mild cognitive impairment, and Alzheimer's disease groups using neuropsychological tests and blood plasma biomarkers; and (d) uncovering patient characteristics that predict optimal response to intra-articular injections of hyaluronic acid for knee osteoarthritis. The multi-stage BB-PSO/DAMIP returns interpretable predictive results with over 80% blind prediction accuracy. One advantage of our findings is that the features identified are easily interpreted and understood by clinicians as well as patients. All of which can have a significant impact on translating the findings to clinical practice to achieve an improved quality of life and medical outcome. The multiple rules with relatively small subsets of discriminatory features afford flexibility for different sites (and different patient populations) to adopt different policies for implementing the best practice.

Keywords: Multi-stage multi-group machine learning framework · Multi-group classification · Imbalanced data · Discriminant analysis via mixed integer · Program · Multi-site knowledge discovery · Cardiovascular disease · Diabetes ·

© The Author(s), under exclusive license to Springer Nature Switzerland AG 2023
F. Coenen et al. (Eds.): IC3K 2022, CCIS 1842, pp. 71–106, 2023.
https://doi.org/10.1007/978-3-031-43471-6_4

Alzheimer's disease · Mild cognitive impairment · Early diagnosis of dementia ·
Knee osteoarthritis · Injections of hyaluronic acid · Machine learning for
evidence-based practice · Branch-and-bound · Particle swarm optimization

1 Introduction

Mathematical modelling and computational methods have long been cornerstones for advancement of business analytics in industrial, government, and military applications. They are playing key roles in advancing and transforming medicine and healthcare delivery. Multi-source data system modelling and computational big data analytics and technologies play an increasingly important role in modern healthcare enterprises. Many problems can be formulated into mathematical models and can be analyzed using sophisticated machine learning, optimization, decision analysis, and computational techniques. In this paper, we will share some of our successes in early disease diagnosis and treatment outcome prediction in healthcare through innovation in machine learning predictive big data analytics.

Biological and clinical data stored across distributed sites have revolutionized health care advances. A critical component of healthcare involves the extraction and evaluation of terabytes of clinical data from electronic medical records (EMRs), laboratory and imaging systems, and from "omics" databases holding patient genomes, proteomics, metabolomics, nutritional genomics, pharmacogenomics, and toxicogenomics, to glean knowledge of the onset and progression of disease and the effectiveness of treatment strategies.

Using existing EMRs and prospectively collected population health data from research program, machine learning has been applied to identify patterns that predict outcomes and potentially inform and improve clinical care [1–3]. However, many strategies proposed compromise on data quality (e.g., the amount of missing data from frontline workers and their imputation by analysts) or breadth (the number of examined parameters with acceptable missingness) [4–6]. There is also a lack of exploring missing data to better understand their implications to access and societal bias [7] or investigating and interpreting different objectives among different stakeholders. Hence, advances must be made in modeling and analytics to accommodate the enormous quantity and evolving nature of available data, variations in quality and completeness of data, conflicting disease characteristics, and competing clinical objectives [1, 2, 8–11].

To tackle unbalanced class size and missing data, majority under-sampling, minority oversampling, and synthetic minority oversampling techniques (SMOTE) have been commonly employed [12, 13]. However, these approaches pose serious weaknesses [14]. Under-sampling may introduce biased in data or discard useful information that are necessary and important to establish an unbiased classifier. Oversampling may increase the likelihood of overfitting while synthetic patient data alters the actual practice patterns, skews the classifiers, and impedes implementation potential [14]. The failure of IBM Watson's predictive health and evidence-based approach showcases the paramount importance of using real and unbiased data and interoperability across multiple sources [15, 16].

Temporal data mining of longitudinal health data offers invaluable knowledge of health patterns but remains difficult to analyze [8, 17]. This is a particularly important issue when analyzing outcome, health equity, and health conditions for patients with chronic disease, or to uncover earliest onset of certain health conditions. To accommodate evolving data and outcome trends, models must also be dynamic and adaptable. Moreover, to ensure a model is robust, reliable, and generalizable, independent multiple data sources should be used to both train the model and to independently validate its results [18]. The model must also be able to be interpreted by a diverse group of stakeholders for feedback and refinement purposes.

In this paper, we present a multi-stage, multi-group machine learning framework that incorporates discriminant analysis via mixed integer programming (DAMIP) as a classifier with an exact combinatorial branch-and-bound (BB) algorithm and a fast particle swarm optimization (PSO) for feature selection. DAMIP utilizes a reserved judgment region to delay making decisions on 'difficult-to-classify' observations and develops new classification rules in a later stage. Such a design works well for poorly separated data that are difficult to classify without committing a high percentage of misclassification errors. To facilitate efficient management of imbalanced groups, we derive multiple DAMIP variants that enable problem-specific fine tuning on the misclassification limits and reserved judgement levels. This ensures that minority groups with relatively few entities are treated equally as the majority groups.

We apply the framework to four real-life medical problems: (a) multi-site treatment outcome prediction for best practice discovery in cardiovascular disease and (b) diabetes; (c) early disease diagnosis in predicting subjects into normal cognition, mild cognitive impairment, and Alzheimer's disease groups using neuropsychological tests and blood plasma biomarkers; and (d) uncovering patient characteristics that predict optimal response to intra-articular injections of hyaluronic acid for knee osteoarthritis. These medical problems involve poorly separated data and imbalanced groups in which traditional classifiers yield low prediction accuracy. The multi-stage, BB-PSO/DAMIP manages the poorly separable and imbalanced data well and returns interpretable predictive results with over 80% blind prediction accuracy.

2 Optimization-Based Classification Models

Classification is a fundamental concept in machine learning and statistics that involves categorizing or assigning a set of observations or data points into predefined classes or categories based on their characteristics or features. The goal of classification is to develop a model or algorithm that can accurately predict the class or category of new, unseen instances based on patterns and relationships learned from a labeled training dataset.

In the context of machine learning, classification is a supervised learning task, meaning that the training data is labeled with the correct class or category for each instance. The classification model learns from this labeled data to generalize patterns and make predictions on new, unseen instances.

This technology has wide-spread applications including agriculture, energy, finance, marketing and consumer sectors, psychology and behavior science, social science, criminology, electronics, internet-of-things, biology, and healthcare, etc. [19–27].

2.1 A Multi-group Machine Learning Framework

A Multi-group Classifier: Discriminant Analysis via Mixed Integer Program (DAMIP). Let $\mathcal{O}_g$ denote the set of observations in group g, and n_g denote the number of observations in group $g \in \mathcal{G}$. Let π_g be the prior probability of group g and $f_g(x)$ be the conditional probability density function of group g, $g \in \mathcal{G}$ for the data point $x \in \mathbb{R}^m$. Let u_{hgi} represent the binary variable that indicates whether observation i in group g is classified to group h, $h \in \{0\} \cup \mathcal{G}$. Thus, $u_{ggi} = 1$ denotes a correct classification for observation i in group g. Let $\alpha_{hg} \in (0, 1), h, g \in \mathcal{G}, h \neq g$ be the predetermined limit on the misclassifications where the observations of group g are classified to group h. The group assignment decisions of observations that are classified into a reserved judgment region are denoted by group $g = 0$. The multi-group model with a reserved judgement region is formulated as:

$$\max \sum_{g \in \mathcal{G}} \sum_{j \in \mathcal{O}_g} u_{ggj}$$

subject to

$$L_{hgj} = \pi_g f_g(x_j) - \sum_{h \in \mathcal{G}, h \neq g} \lambda_{hg} f_h(x_j), \forall h, g \in \mathcal{G}, j \in \mathcal{O}_g \tag{1}$$

$$y_{gj} - L_{hgj} \leq M(1 - u_{hgj}), \quad \forall h, g \in \mathcal{G}, j \in \mathcal{O}_g \tag{2}$$

$$y_{gj} \leq M(1 - u_{0gj}), \quad \forall g \in \mathcal{G}, j \in \mathcal{O}_g \tag{3}$$

$$y_{gj} - L_{hgj} \geq \varepsilon(1 - u_{hgj}), \quad \forall h, g \in \mathcal{G}, j \in \mathcal{O}_g \tag{4}$$

$$y_{gj} \geq \varepsilon u_{hgj}, \quad \forall h, g \in \mathcal{G}, j \in \mathcal{O}_g \tag{5}$$

$$\sum_{h \in \{0\} \cup \mathcal{G}} u_{hgj} = 1, \quad \forall g \in \mathcal{G}, j \in \mathcal{O}_g \tag{6}$$

$$\sum_{j \in \mathcal{O}_g} u_{hgj} \leq \lfloor \alpha_{hg} n_g \rfloor, \quad \forall h, g \in \mathcal{G}, g \neq h \tag{7}$$

$$u_{hgj} \in \{0, 1\} \quad \forall h \in \{0\} \cup \mathcal{G}, g \in \mathcal{G}, j \in \mathcal{O}_g \tag{8}$$

$$y_{gj} \geq 0, \quad \forall h, g \in \mathcal{G}, j \in \mathcal{O}_g \tag{9}$$

$$\lambda_{hg} \geq 0 \quad \forall h, g \in \mathcal{G}, g \neq h \tag{10}$$

Constraints (1) define the loss functions, constraints (2)–(6) guarantee an observation is uniquely assigned to the group with the maximum value of $L_g(x)$ among all groups, and constraints (7) set the misclassification limits. With the reserved judgment region in place, the mathematical system ensures that a solution that satisfies the pre-set errors always exists.

Feature Selection via Particle Swarm Optimization. Feature selection in machine learning refers to the process of selecting a subset of relevant features (input variables or predictors) from a larger set of available features. The goal of feature selection is to (a) improve the model's performance, (b) reduce overfitting, (c) enhance interpretability, and (d) potentially reduce computational requirements by eliminating irrelevant or redundant features.

Feature selection methods can be categorized into three main types: (a) Filter methods assess the relevance of features based on their statistical properties, such as correlation, mutual information, chi-square test, or variance. They rank or score features independently of any specific machine learning algorithm and select the top-ranked features. Examples of filter methods include Pearson correlation coefficient and information gain. (b) Wrapper methods evaluate feature subsets by training and evaluating the machine learning model on different combinations of features. They use a specific machine learning algorithm as an evaluation criterion and search through the space of possible feature subsets to find the optimal set that maximizes the model's performance. (c) Embedded methods incorporate feature selection as part of the model training process. They select features during the model's training process based on certain criteria, such as regularization techniques like L1 regularization or decision tree-based feature importance (e.g., Lasso and LAR [28, 29]). Embedded methods have the advantage of combining feature selection and model training into a single step, resulting in more efficient and interpretable models.

Feature selection is a crucial step in machine learning as it can significantly impact the model's performance, generalization ability, and interpretability. However, it is also essential to validate the selected features' effectiveness using appropriate evaluation metrics and cross-validation techniques to ensure robustness and avoid overfitting.

Combinatorially, feature selection is intrinsically $\mathcal{NP} - hard$ as there are exponential choices to select among a given set of features. A feature selection algorithm can be described in four steps: subset generation, subset evaluation, stopping criterion, and result validation. Numerous algorithms including branch-and-bound [29, 30], greedy procedure and sequential search [31, 32], and random search [33] have been widely studied.

PSO (both continuous and binary) was originally proposed by Kennedy and Eberhart [34]. PSO solves an optimization problem by iteratively trying to improve a candidate solution in the population of candidate solutions, named particles. A particle moves around in the search space based on its position and a randomly generated velocity. Its movement is influenced by its best-known position (associated with the best objective value) and the best-known position of the particles in its neighbourhood. Let x_i denote the position and v_i denote the velocity of particle i. Let p_i be the best position of particle i achieved thus far. Initially, x_i and v_i for each particle i are randomly generated within predetermined ranges. At each iteration, x_i and v_i are updated by.

$$v_i \leftarrow v_i\omega + (p_i - x_i)c_1 rand() + (p_{n^*(i)} - x_i)c_2 rand()$$

$$x_i \leftarrow x_i + v_i$$

where $p_{n^*(i)}$ is the position in the neighbourhood of particle i that holds the best objective value thus far, $rand()$ is a random number between 0 and 1, and ω, c_1, and c_2 are parameters.

Because of its computational speed, numerous variant PSO-based algorithms have been proposed for feature selection [35–39].

A Fast Modified PSO. The PSO/DAMIP framework uses a modified PSO algorithm for feature selection and the DAMIP model for classification. For particle i, let v_i denote the velocity and x_i represent a binary vector of length m, where m is the number of features. Let x_{ij} denote whether the jth feature is selected in particle i. In each iteration of the modified PSO algorithm, a DAMIP model is solved using the selected features in each particle. Particle i records the current selected features x_i and the best achieved objective function value of DAMIP thus far, denoted by y_i. Then v_i and x_i in the next iteration is determined by a random combination of v_i, x_i, p_i, and $p_{n(i)}$ in the current iteration where $n(i)$ is the set of particles in the neighbourhood of particle i. The von Neumann neighbourhood topology was adopted to construct the particles. The algorithm terminates when (a) the maximum number of iterations is achieved, or (b) the percentage of the number of moving particles is less than a pre-set threshold.

A Combinatorial Exact BB Algorithm. To compare the performance of the feature selection heuristics, we also implemented the state-of-the-art BB solver within DAMIP with an additional constraint to limit the number of features that will be selected during the solution process. We use this exact algorithm to contrast the performance of the modified PSO heuristics.

Figure 1 shows the DAMIP-based multi-group machine learning framework where features are first selected via particle swarm optimization and the branch-and-bound algorithm. The resulting classification rule is subsequently established via the DAMIP classifier.

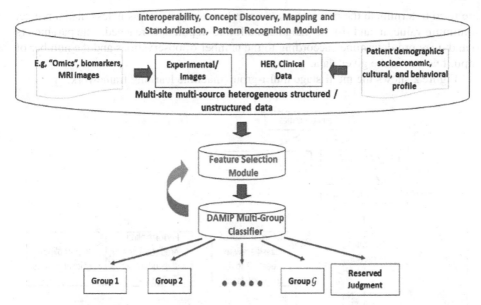

Fig. 1. The DAMIP-based multi-group machine learning framework. Multi-site multi-source data are processed by the "Interoperability, Concept Discovery, Mapping and Standardization, Pattern Recognition Modules" [2, 8, 9, 17]. Features are then selected via particle swarm optimization or the exact branch-and-bound algorithms. The resulting classification rule is subsequently established via the DAMIP classifier.

2.2 A Multi-stage Multi-group Machine Learning Framework

The multi-stage classification model utilizes the reserved judgment region in DAMIP to improve the classification performance. The DAMIP model bisects the data set into an 'easy-to-classify' subset that it classifies to specific groups, and a 'difficult-to-classify' subset that it classifies to a *reserved judgment region*. By delaying the group assignment of the difficult-to-classify subjects, DAMIP classifier can maintain low misclassification errors. In the multi-stage model, the subjects in the reserved judgment region are moved to the next stage where a new feature set is selected and a new DAMIP classifier is developed. In this way, the multi-stage framework constructs a chain of successive classifiers using different subsets of features. The classifier at the ith stage, denoted by f_i, can be represented by a discriminant function $f(x_i, \lambda_i)$, which is determined by the feature subset x_i, and the decision variables λ_i in DAMIP.

More stages do not necessarily produce a better model. At each stage, the framework selects the better of two models: a single-stage model that solves a DAMIP model without a reserved judgment region and a multi-stage model that solves a DAMIP model with a reserved judgment region. The algorithm naturally terminates when there are no observations in the reserved judgment region. As more stages are processed, fewer observations remain for DAMIP, and the constructed model consists of too many successive classifiers. This may result in over-fitting. Hence, two additional stopping criteria are used to terminate the process: (a) the number of observations is less than a pre-set minimum value, n, and (b) the maximum allowed depth, d, is reached. The parameters n and d are pre-determined according to the number of observations and the number of input features in the given data.

Figure 2 shows the multi-stage multi-group machine learning framework.

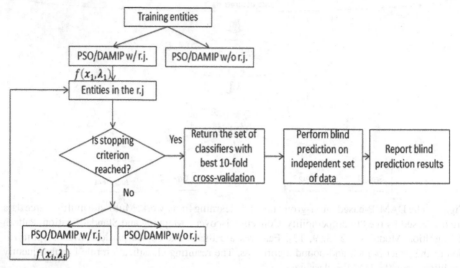

Fig. 2. The multi-stage algorithm selects the better of the two at each stage to continue. Termination can be triggered by the number of stages reached or the size of unclassified entities.

2.3 Balancing Misclassification Levels vs Size of the Reserve Judgement Region

The size of the reserved judgment region is bounded by the misclassification rates specified in constraints (7). Consider the case when we have two imbalance groups, group 1 and group 2 (minority). Figure 3 shows the relationship of the output results with respect to the choice of misclassification rate in the DAMIP model. If the model misclassification rate was low, too many entities would be classified into the reserved judgment region. On the other hand, if the model misclassification rate was set too high, the resulting misclassification of the minority group (group 2 in this example) can be very large.

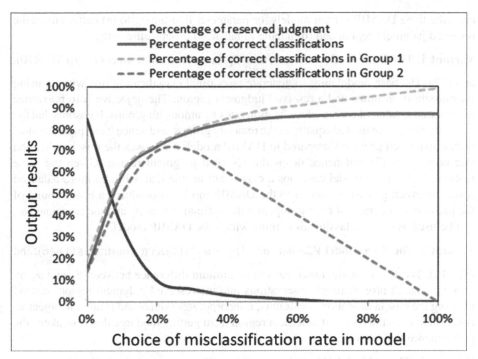

Fig. 3. This figure illustrates the relationship of the output results with respect to the choice of misclassification rate in the DAMIP model for two imbalance groups. If the model misclassification rate is small, too many entities will be classified into the reserved judgment region. If the model misclassification rate is large, the resulting misclassification rate of the minority group (group 2 in this example) can be large.

Problem-specific fine tuning the misclassification constraints enables DAMIP to return good classification results, especially when the groups are unbalanced. Classifiers in a multi-stage model require the ability of balancing misclassifications and 'difficult to classify' observations in order to maximize the prediction accuracy through the multi-stage construct.

For group g, let α_g be the misclassification rate, β_g be the correct classification rate, and γ_g be the 'difficult to classify' rate, i.e., the percentage of observations placed in the reserved judgment region. These three parameters can be defined in DAMIP as follows:

$$\alpha_g = \frac{1}{n_g} \sum_{h \in \mathcal{G}, h \neq g} \sum_{j \in \mathcal{O}_g} u_{hgj} \tag{11}$$

$$\beta_g = \frac{1}{n_g} \sum_{j \in \mathcal{O}_g} u_{ggj} \tag{12}$$

$$\gamma_g = \frac{1}{n_g} \sum_{j \in \mathcal{O}_g} u_{0gj} \tag{13}$$

Recall $\mathcal{O}_g$ is the set of observations of group g and n_g is the size of group g (i.e., $n_g = |\mathcal{O}_g|$). The three parameters satisfy that $\alpha_g + \beta_g + \gamma_g = 1$ for each group g. We describe three DAMIP variant models for parameter fine-tuning to (a) better utilize the reserved judgment region and (b) handle imbalanced groups efficiently.

Variant 1: The Base Model $V1$. $max \min_{g \in \mathcal{G}} \beta_g$, subject to constraints (1)–(6), (8)–(10), and (12). The base model aims to generate an optimal classification rule without using misclassification limits and a reserved judgment region. The objective is to maximize the minimum value of correct classification rates β_g among all groups. It ensures that the minority groups are treated equally as the majority groups, and hence it can perfectly deal with imbalanced groups. Compared to DAMIP model, it removes the misclassification rate constraints (7) and hence drops the reserved judgment region. Given the same feature set, the base model develops a classification rule that achieves more balanced results between groups compared to the DAMIP model. It produces a lower bound of the prediction accuracy of each group, and the optimal values β_g and the associated α_g can be used as the misclassification limits within the DAMIP model.

Variant 2: The β - α Model $V2$. $max \min_{g \in \mathcal{G}} \left(\beta_g - \alpha_g \right)$ subject to constraints (1)–(6), and (8)–(12). The $\beta - \alpha$ model maximizes the minimum difference between β_g and α_g by moving a small proportion of observations into the reserved judgment region. Instead of using the misclassification constraints, it incorporates both α and β into the objective function to keep the reserved judgment region from getting too large that it weakens the performance of the model.

Variant 3: The γ Model $V3$. $max \sum_{g \in \mathcal{G}} \beta_g$ subject to constraints (1)–(6), (8)–(10), (12), and (13), plus the new constraint $\sum_{j \in \mathcal{O}_g} u_{0gj} \leq \lfloor \gamma_g n_g \rfloor$, $\forall g \in \mathcal{G}$. The γ model maximizes the prediction accuracy while limiting the size of the reserved judgment region by adding constraints on the percentage of reserved judgment γ_g for each group g. It provides accurate control of the reserved judgment region to avoid too many stages in the model. The maximum percentage $\overline{\gamma_g}$ for each group g is predetermined according to the size of the problem. Thus the γ model resembles the original DAMIP model except it constrains the reserved judgment region instead of constraining the misclassification rates for each group.

Special Case: Solutions for 2 Groups. For two groups, the DAMIP variant models ($V1$-$V3$) can be solved in polynomial time. The constraints that define $L(x)$ can be written as:

$$L_{1i} = \pi_1 f_1(x_i) - \lambda_{21} f_2(x_i) \quad \forall i \in \mathcal{O}$$

$$L_{2i} = \pi_2 f_2(x_i) - \lambda_{12} f_1(x_i) \quad \forall i \in \mathcal{O},$$

where optimal λ_{12} and λ_{21} are determined in DAMIP. Previously, we proved that the optimal λ_{12} and λ_{21} in a two group DAMIP model that maximizes the total correct classifications can be found by searching on the sorted array f_2/f_1 where f_1 and f_2 are the density functions in constraint (1) of group 1 and 2 respectively [40].

Below, we formally prove the 2-group results for the DAMIP variants. When no reserved judgment region is used in the modified DAMIP model, i.e., the base model, we define a partition p on the sorted array f_2/f_1 such that observations having $f_2(x)/f_1(x) \leq p$ are classified to group 1, and observations having $f_2(x)/f_1(x) > p$ are classified to group 2. By searching on the sorted array f_2/f_1, p* can be found such that the objective function which is the minimum of the correct classifications of the two groups in the base model is maximized. An optimal solution of $(\lambda_{12}, \lambda_{21})$ then can be determined by $\frac{\pi_1 + \lambda_{12}}{\pi_2 + \lambda_{21}} = p^*$.

When a reserved judgment region is used in the DAMIP models, we define two partitions p_1 and p_2 of the sorted array f_2/f_1: observations having $f_2(x)/f_1(x) \leq p_1$ are classified to group 1, observations having $p_1 < f_2(x)/f_1(x) \leq p_2$ are classified to the reserved judgment region, and observations having $f_2(x)/f_1(x) > p_2$ are classified to group 2. By searching on the sorted array f_2/f_1, (p_1^*, p_2^*) can be found such that the objective function is optimized. An optimal solution of $(\lambda_{12}, \lambda_{21})$ then can be determined by $\frac{\pi_1}{\lambda_{21}} = p_1^*$ and $\frac{\lambda_{12}}{\pi_1} = p_2^*$.

The optimal partition may not be unique: any partition $p \in [l_1, l_2)$ results in the same objective function value as $p^* \in [l_1, l_2)$ where l_1 is the maximum value of f_2/f_1 of observations that is less than or equal to p^* and l_2 is the minimum value of f_2/f_1 of observations that is greater than p^*. A proper way of determining p^* when searching on the sorted array is to choose the mid-point $p^* = \frac{l_1 + l_2}{2}$. The complexity of this algorithm is O(nlogn): it takes O(nlogn) to sort the array f_2/f_1, and O(n) to search through the array to find the partition that reaches the optimal objective.

2.4 Applying Multi-stage BB-PSO/DAMIP to Real-World Problems

We tackle four real-world medical problems that challenge existing classifiers where they perform poorly due to imbalanced data and the very mixed nature of the groups (poorly separable). By design, the DAMIP classifier partitions the group space in a non-linear and segmented manner, where observations belonging to the same group could be classified under different conditions (obtained via different stages). This is particularly useful in medical applications. For example, patients with the same outcome could have very diverse sets of lab or treatment results. It is the entire system that one must examine to classify properly.

We apply the multi-stage multi-group machine learning framework (Fig. 2) on four applications: cardiovascular disease, diabetes, Alzheimer's disease, and hyaluronic acid injection for knee osteoarthritis. The cardiovascular and diabetes disease analyses involve over 737 clinical sites of -patient data. They showcase the need for conducting unsupervised learning analyses to uncover the group status prior to carrying out machine learning research, since the data originated from diverse sites with a heterogeneous interpretation of outcome status. The Alzheimer's disease study distinguishes itself from other work as our analyses involve raw neuro-psychological data instead of the overall clinical scores. Furthermore, we couple these low-cost non-invasive exams/tests with the blood plasma biomarkers for comprehensive analyses. The knee osteoarthritis study aims to uncover patient types and health characteristics that would benefit most from intra-articular injections of hyaluronic acid.

Ten-fold cross validation is performed for training and model evaluation. In ten-fold cross validation, the training set is partitioned into ten roughly equal parts. In each run, nine-fold are selected to establish the rule, and the remaining one-fold is then tested, counting how many of them are classified into each group. Through the tn-fold procedure (where each fold is validated exactly once), we obtain an unbiased estimate of the classification accuracy. If the resulting unbiased estimate satisfies some pre-set conditions (e.g., greater than 70% for each group), the classification rule is reported. Blind prediction using this rule is then performed.

Blind prediction is performed on patients that are independent of the training set to gauge the predictive power of the established rule. These patients have never been used in the machine learning feature selection and training analysis. We run each patient through the rule, and it returns the status of the patient. The status is then checked against the clinical status to confirm the accuracy. We contrast the BB-PSO/DAMIP results with eight commonly used classifiers: Bernoulli Naïve Bayes, Decision Tree, Gradient Boosting, K-nearest neighbors, Logistic Regression, Neural Network, Random Forest, and Support Vector Machine (SVM).

3 Results for Disease Diagnosis and Treatment Outcome prediction

3.1 Cardiovascular Disease

The leading cause of death globally is cardiovascular disease (CVD), also known as heart disease. CVD encompasses various conditions affecting the heart and blood vessels, including coronary artery disease, heart attacks, stroke, and heart failure. It is responsible for 17.9 million deaths worldwide each year [41].

Coronary heart disease (CHD) is highly prevalent in the United States and is the leading cause of death. According to the American Heart Association (AHA), it affects approximately 20.1 million adults aged 20 and older [42, 43]. According to the Centers for Disease Control and Prevention (CDC), in 2019, approximately 365,914 deaths were attributed to CHD, accounting for about 13.2% of all deaths in the country.

In our previous work, we tackled 2.7 million patient data from the Care Coordination Institute (CCI). The cohort covers 9,000 physicians from 737+ clinical sites. To perform multi-site best practice discovery, a comprehensive, efficient "pipeline" for extracting, de-identifying, and mapping clinical notes and terms/concepts to standard ontologies was first designed and implemented to establish interoperability for these patients [1, 2, 8, 9, 17]. That prior work also addressed challenges associated with temporal laboratory time series data and unstructured text data and described a novel approach for clustering irregular Multivariate Time Series (MTS).

The analysis herein involves 37,742 CVD patients. Each patient is characterized by 11 raw features including demographics, treatment duration, and co-existing conditions, and 1,757 mapped standardized features described in Systematized Nomenclature of Medicine-Clinical Terms (SNOMED-CT), which includes laboratory tests, diagnosed problems, and medications. These 1,757 standardized features were obtained from 19,800 raw features that were extracted from clinical notes and mapped onto standard ontologies. The treatment duration for each patient was calculated using the elapsed time between diagnosis (indicated by the first prescription of a medication) and the last recorded activity (i.e., procedure, lab, etc.).

Lipids and lipoproteins play important roles in cardiovascular health, but an imbalance or abnormalities in their levels can contribute to the development of CVD [44]. High levels of low-density lipoprotein cholesterol (LDL), often referred to as "bad" cholesterol, are associated with an increased risk of CVD. LDL can build up in the walls of arteries, forming plaques that can lead to atherosclerosis, narrowing of the arteries, and increased risk of heart attacks and strokes. On the other hand, high-density lipoprotein cholesterol (HDL), often called "good" cholesterol, helps remove cholesterol from the bloodstream and has a protective effect against CVD. Triglycerides are another type of lipid that serves as a storage form of energy in the body. Elevated levels of triglycerides in the blood, especially when combined with low levels of HDL, are associated with an increased risk of CVD. High triglyceride levels may contribute to atherosclerosis and increase the risk of developing conditions such as coronary artery disease.

We used HDL, LDL, and Triglyceride measurements to form an MTS containing three time series for each patient. Each of these time series was resampled to quarterly frequency. Gaps in the data were filled by propagating the non-NaN values forward first, and then backward, along each time series. For each of the three types of laboratory measurements, we include only patients with more than three measurements after resampling from the dataset. This produces a data set containing 450 patients. The global alignment kernel (GAK) distance between each pair of corresponding time series was calculated [1, 9, 17, 45]. The pairwise distance between each pair of MTS was then obtained by averaging the three distances for each pair of corresponding univariate time series. Specifically, given two patients, P^1 and P^2, each with m lab measurement time series, their pairwise distance was calculated using the following equation:

$$\text{Distance} \left(P^1, P^2 \right) = \left(\sum_{t=1}^{m} D_{GAK} \left(P_t^1 P_t^2 \right) \right).$$

Clustering to Establish CVD Treatment Outcome Groups. K-medoids clustering performed on the CVD distance matrix partitioned the patients into three groups. Since medoids are actual data points, they can handle any type of distance metric and are not restricted to Euclidean distance like K-means. Furthermore, K-medoids is more robust to outliers since medoids are less sensitive to extreme values than the mean used in K-means. However, it is computationally expensive, especially for large datasets, as it requires calculating pairwise distances between data points. The clinical experts examined the raw laboratory records for each group and associated the cluster characteristics as "Good," "Medium," or "Poor" outcomes (blue, red, or green). We caution that such interpretation by clinical experts is of paramount importance.

Figure 4 shows the raw HDL, LDL, and Triglyceride laboratory records by cluster. The "Poor Outcome" group is well-segregated from the other two groups, showing high variability in HDL and LDL levels, which is a high-risk factor for myocardial infarction. Although the "Good" and "Medium" outcome groups have similar trajectories of cholesterol levels, the "Good" outcome group has slightly higher HDL levels, lower LDL and Triglyceride levels, and shows more consistency in all three types of cholesterol levels. Table 1 shows the patient partition for machine learning training and blind prediction.

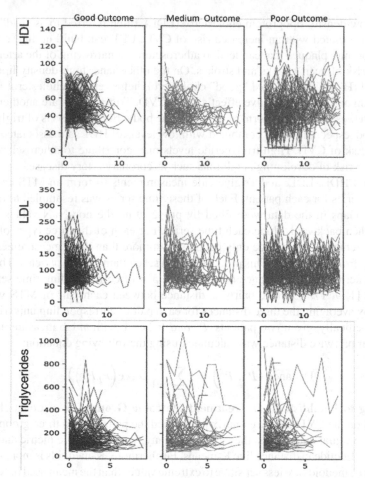

Fig. 4. HDL, LDL, and Triglyceride laboratory records for each patient cluster characterized as "Good," "Medium," or "Poor" outcomes (blue, red, or green) [1]. (Color figure online)

Table 1. Partition of CVD patients for machine learning training and blind prediction [1].

	Total	Good	Medium	Poor
Training	314	60	158	96
Blind set	136	19	75	42
Total	450	79	233	138

Predicting CVD Treatment Outcome Across Multiple Sites. We aim to uncover discriminatory features that can predict good outcomes. This facilitates evidence-based, best practice discovery and dissemination of good clinical practice evidence across different sites.

Table 2. Features selected in top BB-PSO/DAMIP classification rules in predicting CVD Treatment outcome.

Discriminatory feature (chosen from 1,768 features)	Exact combinatorial branch-and-bound search BB/DAMIP					Heuristics particle swarm optimization PSO/DAMIP				
Name of classifier	1	2	3	4	5	1	2	3	4	5
Treatment Length	X	X	X	X	X	X	X	X	X	X
Glucose measurement, urine (procedure)	X			X	X	X	X	X	X	X
Synthetic steroid (substance)			X	X	X		X	X	X	
Acute digestive system disorder (disorder)						X		X		
Inflammatory disorder of upper respiratory tract (disorder)				X		X	X	X	X	X
Calcium channel blocking agent (product)	X	X	X							
Neoplasm by body site (disorder)		X	X							
Diabetic - poor control (finding)						X	X			
Implantation (procedure)						X	X			
Investigations (procedure)						X	X			
Acute disorder of ear (disorder)							X			
Disorder of immune system (navigational concept)					X					
Allergen or pseudo allergen (substance)									X	
Oral form naproxen (product)										X
Electrocardiogram finding (finding)									X	X
Disinfectants and cleansers (product)									X	X
Imaging (procedure)									X	X

Table 2 summarizes the top 5 machine learning results for the CVD patients using DAMIP, coupled with either an exact combinatorial (BB) feature-selection algorithm or the PSO feature-selection heuristic. Each rule (a column) consists of 3–7 discriminatory features. The multiple rules with relatively small subsets of discriminatory features afford flexibility for different sites (and different patient populations) to adopt different policies for implementing the best practice. BB/DAMIP and PSO/DAMIP produce similar results, although results from BB/DAMIP tend to have fewer features than those from PSO/DAMIP.

DAMIP classified patients into "Good Outcome" vs. "Medium" and "Poor" outcome by uncovering a set of discriminatory features that yields a blind prediction accuracy of 88.3% to 97.6%. Figure 5 compares the DAMIP results against the best two results among the eight classifiers. Specifically, Decision Tree and Random Forest yielded 10-fold cross-validation unbiased estimates of 65% and 63% for the "Good Outcome" and 80%–90% for the "Medium" and "Poor" outcome groups respectively. The blind prediction fared worse, with a roughly 50% predictive accuracy for the "Good Outcome" group. The remaining six classifiers similarly suffered from imbalanced data, and the accuracy for "Good Outcome" was uniformly below 40%. In all cases, Randomized Lasso was used for feature selection, and it selected twenty-five discriminatory features. In contrast, the BB-PSO/DAMIP results offer higher accuracy using fewer discriminatory features. Because of the poor separable data, we observed that after the first stage classification, about 46% of "Good" outcome were placed in the reserved judgement region.

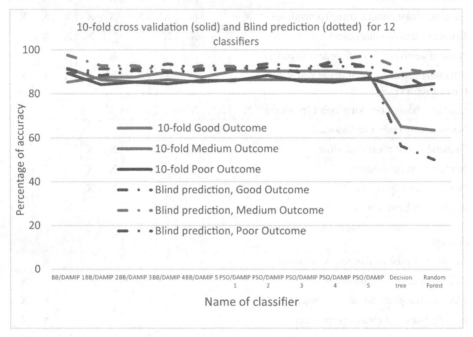

Fig. 5. Comparison of BB-PSO/DAMIP results versus the decision tree and random forest. BB/DAMIP and PSO/DAMIP produce similar results while the results from decision tree and random forest are inferior, especially in the minority "Good Outcome" group.

3.2 Diabetes

Diabetes is among the top ten leading causes of death [46, 47]. In 2021, the International Diabetes Federation reports that 537 million global adult populations are living with diabetes, causing at least $966 billion dollars in health expenditure. In the United States, the American Diabetes Association reports that 37.3 million Americans had diabetes, with estimated 96 million had prediabetes in 2019 [48]. It was estimated that the total cost of diagnosed diabetes was $327 billion which includes $237 billion in direct medical costs and $90 billion in reduced productivity [49].

High blood glucose levels are often observed in diabetes patients and that increase the risk of complications such as stroke, diabetic retinopathy, and glaucoma [50]. Therefore, improvements in its management could have a significant health impact.

Management of diabetes focuses on maintaining blood glucose level within the recommended range. When dietary control and physical activities fail to control the blood glucose level, insulin injection or oral anti-diabetic medications will be used. One of the difficulties in diabetes management is to estimate the treatment effect on patients receiving insulin or drug therapy. Since patients vary in their eating habits, dose response, and treatment compliance, it is difficult for clinicians to determine if a treatment is effective. Clinicians rely on a trial-and-error approach for prescribing drugs and setting their dosage.

The CCI-health database contains 267,666 diabetes patients [2]. Each patient is characterized by 24 features including hospital site, demographics, laboratory tests and results, prescriptions, treatment duration, chronic conditions, blood pressure, number of visits and visit frequencies (Table 3). These variables are considered potential features that may influence treatment outcome. They are used as input for our classification analysis.

Clustering to Establish Diabetes Treatment Outcome Groups. To establish the outcome group status for these diabetes patients, Glycated hemoglobin (HbA1c) lab measurement series throughout the treatment duration were used as indicators of treatment outcome. In our analysis, only patients with 7 or more HbA1c measurements recorded were included. This resulted in 3,875 patients. On each patient's HbA1c measurement series, we performed sliding window with a size of five measurements with equal weights to reduce potential noise. Figure 6 compares a patient's HbA1c data before and after sliding window is performed.

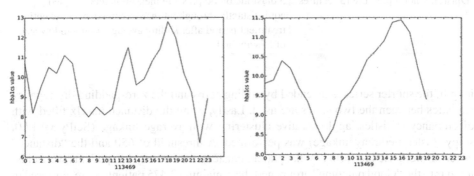

Fig. 6. Patient Glycated hemoglobin (HbA1c), a laboratory measurement (over the entire treatment duration) is used to assess glucose control in diabetes patients, before (left) and after sliding window (right) with size of five measurements and equal weight.

Using the smoothed HbA1c lab measurement series, patients were clustered into two groups: Since each patient has different numbers of records, a method for clustering time series of different lengths is required. Here we compared these measurements based on the method proposed by Caiado et al. [51]: First a periodogram of each patient's smoothed HbA1c measurements was calculated. Next, discrepancy statistics were calculated for each pair of periodograms and used as the distance between each pair of patients. In the case when their recorded measurements are not equal in

Table 3. Name and description of the 24 features for each diabetes patient.

Features used in training classifiers	Description
Treatment duration	Total time elapsed since first prescription of a diabetic medication
Visit frequency	Number of vitals measurements recorded / treatment duration
Diagnoses (6 features)	6 binary variables (true or false) indicating if patient has been diagnosed with the following conditions: hypertension, hyperlipidemia, cardiovascular disease, stroke, emphysema, asthma
Race	Patient race
Gender	Patient gender
Age	Patient age
Height	Patient height measured during first visit
Weight	Patient weight measured during first visit
Provider site	Clinical site that patient receives treatment
Systolic blood pressures (5 features)	5 systolic blood pressure measurements sampled equi-distantly throughout measurements over the entire treatment period after sliding average with window size of 5 is applied
Diastolic blood pressure (5 features)	5 diastolic blood pressure measurements sampled equi-distantly throughout measurements over the entire treatment period after sliding average with window size of 5 is applied

length, the shorter series is extended by adding zeros and the zero-padding discrepancy statistics between the two series are used. Lastly, using the distance matrix filled with discrepancy statistics, agglomerative clustering with average linkage (SciPy v0.17.0, scipy.cluster.hierarchy.linkage) was performed. A threshold of 650 and the "distance" criterion were used to form two flat patient clusters. As a result, 400 patients were clustered into the "Good outcome" group, and the remaining 3,475 patients were clustered in the "Mixed outcome" group. We characterized the two groups as "Good" versus "Mixed" based on the trend of HbA1c lab measurements of patients in each group.

To establish the classification rule, the 3,875 diabetes patient datasets were partitioned into a training set and an independent set for blind prediction using stratified random sampling. The training set consisted of 2,325 patients (60% of the population), and the blind prediction set consisted of 1,550 patients (40% of the population). Table 4 summarizes the number of patients in each set.

Predicting Diabetes Treatment Outcome Across Multiple Sites. Figure 7 contrasts our in-house PSO/DAMIP classification results with eight other classifiers. Uniformly the eight classifiers suffer from group imbalance and tend to place all patients into the

Table 4. Partition of diabetes patients for machine learning training and blind prediction.

	Total	Good Outcome	Mixed Outcome
Training	2,325	2,074	251
Blind set	1,550	1,401	149
Total	3,875	3,475	400

larger "Mixed outcome" group (Red). In contrast, the PSO/DAMIP classifier selects 5 discriminatory features (treatment duration, visit frequency, hyperlipidemia, asthma, provider site) among the 24 features and achieves relatively high classification and blind prediction accuracies for both groups. We remark that the commonly used Pap Smear diagnosis test has an accuracy of roughly 70%.

The "*PSO/DAMIP extended result" (2nd on the graph, the pink diamond point) was obtained by running PSO/DAMIP with 2,205 additional features obtained via mapping of extracted terms in laboratory tests, diagnosed problems, and medications to SNOMED-CT terminologies. With these added features, DAMIP selects 9 features (treatment duration, visit frequency, asthma, + 6 features from mapping: Injection of therapeutic agent (procedure), Oral form levofloxacin (product), Clopidogrel (product). Aspirin (product), Nystatin (product), and Metformin (product)) and improve its prediction accuracies. We observe that instead of selecting "provider site" as one of the discriminatory features, DAMIP selects the type of procedures and medications used instead. Identifying these features facilitates dissemination of best practice and target treatment regime to specific patients among the sites. For the eight classifiers, the results select over 200+ features and improve only marginally on the "Good outcome" group.

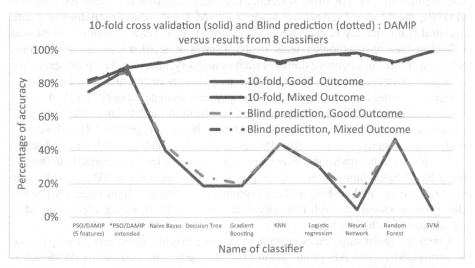

Fig. 7. Comparison of PSO/DAMIP results versus eight other classifiers. PSO/DAMIP produces balanced results for both groups while the other classifiers suffer from imbalanced data with inferior results for the minority "Good Outcome" group.

3.3 Alzheimer's Disease

Dementia refers to a decline in cognitive function and memory severe enough to inter-fere with daily life. It is not a specific disease but rather a syndrome caused by various underlying conditions. Alzheimer's disease (AD) is the most common cause of dementia, accounting for 60–70% of cases. Other causes include vascular dementia, Lewy body dementia, frontotemporal dementia, and others. Dementia is characterized by a signifi-cant impairment in multiple cognitive domains, including memory, thinking, language, judgment, and behavior.

In 2019, Alzheimer's disease (AD) and other forms of dementia ranked as the 7th leading cause of death, affecting over 55 million people worldwide. Some of the highest rates of dementia are found in developed countries with older populations. Globally, 65% of deaths from Alzheimer's and other forms of dementia are among women [52]. Mostly AD occurs in people over 65, although familial AD has an earlier onset.

There is no single test to diagnose Alzheimer's disease definitively. Diagnosis is typically based on medical history, neurological exams, cognitive assessments, and ruling out other possible causes of symptoms. Advanced brain imaging techniques, such as MRI or PET scans, may be used to support the diagnosis. Currently, AD is incurable; drugs are used to manage the symptoms or to prevent or slow the progress of the disease. Currently, Mild cognitive impairment (MCI) is a condition that lies between the normal cognitive decline of aging and the more severe cognitive decline seen in dementia. People with MCI experience noticeable cognitive changes that are greater than expected for their age and education level, but they can still perform their daily activities independently. MCI is considered a transitional stage between normal aging and dementia. Not all individuals with MCI will progress to Alzheimer's disease or another form of dementia; some may remain stable, while others may even improve over time.

Some common steps and tools used in evaluating AD and MCI include a com-plete medical history, cognitive screening tests (e.g., Mini-Mental State Examination (MMSE), the Montreal Cognitive Assessment (MoCA)), neuropsychological exam, structural brain imaging (e.g., MRI, CT), laboratory tests, genetic testing, and clinical evaluation. Neuropsychological tests involve a series of detailed tests and assessments that evaluate various cognitive domains such as memory, attention, language, executive function, and visuospatial skills. These tests provide a more comprehensive evaluation of cognitive strengths and weaknesses. Neuropsychological data can be analyzed statisi-cally to understand MCI patients [53, 54]. Classification models have also been used to analyze neuropsychological data for predicting brain damage [55–58] and whether nondemented elderly patients declined to a diagnosis of dementia or Alzheimer's disease.

In addition to the traditional diagnosis, active research has been carried out investi-gating blood-based biomarkers that can provide information about AD. These include markers such as amyloid-beta and tau proteins, neurofilament light chain (NfL), and other proteins associated with neurodegeneration [59–65]. However, identifying MCI and AD remains challenging.

Using the multi-stage classification model, we classify three groups of patients: the control, MCI, and AD groups, using two data sets: The first one is de-identified neuropsychological test data conducted by Emory Alzheimer's Disease Research Center.

The second one is plasma biomarkers information collected by two independent centers (University of Pennsylvania, Philadelphia; Washington University, St. Louis, MO).

Predictive Analysis Using Neuro-Psychological Data. Neuropsychological tests are commonly used to assess cognitive function and detect changes associated with Alzheimer's disease. The neuropsychological tests conducted in this data set include (a) MMSE: This widely used screening test assesses overall cognitive function. It includes tasks such as orientation, memory recall, attention, language, and visuospatial abilities. (b) Clock Drawing Test: This test assesses visuospatial and executive functions. The individual is asked to draw a clock face and set the hands to a specific time. (c) The Word List Memory tasks by the Consortium to Establish a Registry for Alzheimer's Disease (CERAD): This is used to assess episodic memory, which is often impaired in AD. The CERAD Word List Memory tasks are designed to evaluate an individual's ability to learn (Word List Learning) and recall (Word List Recall) a list of words over several trials.: The individual is presented with a list of ten common words (e.g., apple, chair, house) and asked to remember as many words as possible. They are given multiple trials, usually three, with the same list of words. After each trial, the individual is asked to recall the words they remember. After a short delay, typically around 5 min, the individual is asked to recall the words again, without any additional presentation of the word list. (d) The Geriatric Depression Scale (GDS): This is a widely used screening tool designed to assess depression in older adults. It was specifically developed to address the unique features and manifestations of depression in geriatric populations. The GDS is a self-report questionnaire that consists of a series of questions related to mood, feelings, and other symptoms associated with depression.

Table 5 summarizes the group status of a total of 267 patients. Among the 267 subjects, two-thirds of the subjects in each group are randomly selected as the training set for 10-fold cross-validation, while the remaining subjects are used for blind prediction. The input includes 107 features for each patient, covering 3 features representing age, gender, years of education, 13 features from the MMSE, 15 features from the Clock drawing test, 65 features from the Word List Memory tasks, and 11 features from the GDS.

Table 5. Group information of 267 subjects in the neuropsychological data set [1].

	Total	Control	MCI	AD	MCI or AD
Training	178	72	51	55	106
Blind set	89	36	26	27	53
Total	267	108	77	82	159

464 discriminatory feature sets, each with no more than 10 features satisfy the pre-set conditions of predicting correctly over 80% of the subjects in both 10-fold cross-validation and blind prediction. Table 6 highlights two Pareto best prediction accuracy results. They are associated with multiple feature sets. We include two sets

Table 6. Prediction accuracy of the best feature sets via PSO/DAMIP using Neuro-psychological data against the best performer among 8 other classifiers.

Result label	10-fold Cross-Validation			Blind Prediction		
	Ctrl	MCI	AD	Ctrl	MCI	AD
Using NP data only 1	87.8%	80.0%	88.3%	88.2%	80.6%	90.9%
Using NP data only 2	89.2%	80.0%	86.7%	85.3%	80.6%	90.9%
RandomForest	83.3%	60.8%	45.5%	77.8%	57.7%	48.2%

here for the purpose of explanation: [cClockNumbers4, cClockCenter, GDS6, 'Score for What is the year?', MMSE Total, cWL1Ar, cWL1Ticket, cWL2Ticket, cWLrTotal. cWRyCabin], and [cClockNumbers4, cClockHands4, cClockCenter, 'Score for What is the month?', 'Score for Where are we?', MMSE Total, cWL1Ticket, cWLrTotal, cWRyButter, cWRnVillage].

The overall prediction accuracy of 10-fold cross-validation and blind prediction are over 85%, with the blind prediction accuracy of each group ranging from 80.6% to 90.9%. The features represent the smallest set that offer high-quality results. The prediction accuracy does not improve when more features are selected in the classification model. We highlight the features that most frequently occur in the 464 feature sets in Table 7.

Table 6 also includes the best performer among the eight classifiers. About 54% MCI and 37% of AD were mixed, rendering the poor performance of these classifiers. These comparative results underscore the poorly separable concept and the advantage of a multi-stage approach.

Our analysis offers invaluable clinical knowledge: earliest diagnosis of mild cognitive impairment, which allows early intervention thus lowering the risk of manifestation to AD.

Table 7. Features with the highest occurrences in the 464 discriminatory feature sets [1].

Feature	Test	Occurrences
MMSE Total	MMSE	100.0%
cWLrTotal	Word List	94.4%
cWL1Ticket	Word List	94.2%
cClockCenter	Clock	76.1%
Score for What is the year?	MMSE	59.5%
Score for What is the month?	MMSE	53.4%

The features selected highlight the test modules or specific questions/tasks that are most predictive. One advantage in our findings is that they are easily interpreted and understood by clinicians as well as patients. Thus, these discriminatory features can serve as an early detection tool that family members and providers can use to monitor disease in patients.

Predictive Analysis Using Plasma Biomarker. Table 8 shows the group status of 342 subjects with collected biomarkers. We use the same partition strategy to establish the training set and the blind prediction set. The input includes thirty-one features: gender, age, education years, MMSE, and 10 indicators and 17 analytes (apolipoprotein E, brain natriuretic peptide, cortisol, C-reactive protein, E-selectin, FAS, Gamma-IFN-induced monokine, interleukin (IL)-3, IL-10, IL-12p40, IL-13, IL-15, osteopontin, pancreatic polypeptide, resistin, serum amyloid protein, stem cell factor) that were identified by Hu [59].

Table 8. Group information of 352 subjects in plasma biomarkers data set [1].

	Total	Control	MCI	AD	MCI or AD
Training	250	35	133	82	215
Blind set	102	21	62	19	81
Total	352	56	195	101	296

The PSO/DAMIP framework returns 92 discriminatory feature sets, each with no more than 10 features, that correctly predict with accuracy ranging from 82.9%–91.5% in 10-fold cross-validation and 81% to 94.7% in blind prediction.

Figure 8 presents the best prediction accuracy when plasma biomarkers are included (label "Add plasma biomarkers") and contrasts it against the two best results using neuro-psychological data alone (Table 6). This plasma best result associates with 3 feature sets: -[MMSE, ApoE_1, tTau, Ab42, BNP, Resistin, IGFBP2, tTauG91, LoAbHi-Tau, SAP3],[MMSE, ApoE_1, tTau, Ab42, BNP, SAP, IGFBP2, TauG91, LoAbHiTau], and [MMSE, ApoE_1, tTau, Ab42, IGFBP2, tTauG91, LoAbHiTau, BNP3, Resistin3, SAP3]. Note that the 3 sets share 80% of the selected features.

Table 9 highlights the features that most frequently occur in the 92 feature sets.

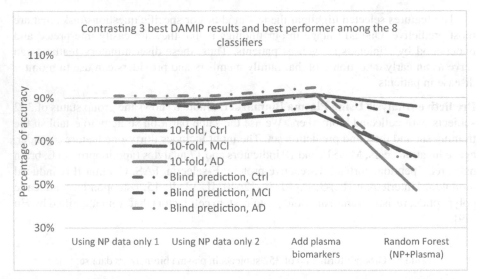

Fig. 8. Prediction accuracy of the best feature sets via PSO/DAMIP when plasma biomarkers are included; and contrasts it against the two best results obtained from neuro-psychological data alone (Table 6). Random Forest is the best performer among the 8 classifiers.

Table 9. Features with the highest occurrences in the 92 discriminatory feature sets [1].

Feature	Occurrences
ApoE_1	100.0%
tTau	100.0%
Ab42	100.0%
IGFBP2	100.0%
tTauG91	100.0%
LoAbHiTau	100.0%
MMSE	100.0%
BNP	59.8%
Resistin	52.2%
SAP3	52.2%

The analyses using two independent patient sets of data illustrate that MMSE can function as a low-cost procedure to be added to annual physical exams for the aged population. It offers good predictive power for the brain's cognition status. Early detection of MCI offers the opportunity for treatment to slow down the onset of AD.

3.4 Knee Osteoarthritis

Osteoarthritis (OA) is the most common form of arthritis. It is a degenerative joint disease or "wear and tear" arthritis. It occurs most frequently in the hands, hips, and knees.

Osteoarthritis of the knee (OA-K) happens when the cartilage in the knee joint breaks down, enabling the bones to rub together. The friction makes the knees hurt, become stiff and sometimes swell. OA-K is a leading cause of arthritis disability. Although it cannot be cured, treatments are available to slow its progress and ease the symptoms.

According to CDC, approximately 46% of people will develop OA-K during their lifetimes. Knee osteoarthritis affects more than 14 million Americans, and its symptoms often lead to physical inabilities, disabilities, and all sorts of inconveniences for patients. It is estimated that knee osteoarthritis is associated with approximately $27 billion in total healthcare costs every year, with about 800,000 knee surgeries performed annually. In a multicenter longitudinal cohort study, it was reported that about one-third of knee replacements may be unnecessary [66].

At least 18% of out-patient visits to military treatment facilities by active-duty personnel are attributed to painful knee disorders. The management of knee pain depends on the diagnosis, inciting activity, underlying medical conditions, body mass, and chronicity. In general, non-operative management is the mainstay of initial treatment and includes rehabilitation, activity modification, weight loss when indicated, shoe orthoses, local modalities, and medication. The oral medication often prescribed is an analgesic, usually with anti-inflammatory properties. Supplements, such as chondroitin sulfate and glucosamine have been shown to have a role. Since 1997, the regimen has expanded to include viscosupplementation. These agents are preparations of hyaluronic acid or their derivatives (HA) which are sterilely injected into the knee. Although research studies have clearly demonstrated that HA improves knee function, the efficacy of this treatment is extremely controversial, however, many clinicians have observed that effects seem to depend on several patient characteristics such as age, weight, gender, severity of the OA, and technical issues such as injection site and placement [67].

The goal of this study is to evaluate which patient population or patient characteristics would benefit most from HA injection. The study uses a prospective, double blinded clinical trial. The multi-stage multi-group machine learning model described in Sect. 2 is used to uncover discriminatory patterns that can predict outcomes. The resulting predictive rule can be implemented as part of a clinical practice guideline for evidence-based intervention. The model enables providers to administer HA products more selectively and effectively to targeted population to maximize cost effectiveness and the percentage of patients who experience a successful HA trial.

Data Collection. The data collected prior to HA injection includes (a) patient demographic data: age, sex, height, weight, BMI (as calculated from height and weight), and smoking history; (b) the Western Ontario and McMaster Universities Osteoarthritis Index [68](WOMAC) as a measure of knee OA symptoms and functioning; (c) the RAND-36 [69] as a measure of general health status; (d) the MARX Knee Activity Rating Scale [70] to assess activity level (running, deceleration, cutting (changing directions while running) and pivoting); (e) patients rated other health conditions using a comorbidity questionnaire [71] and rated quality of life as measured by the EuroQOL EQ-5D [72];

and (f) patient completed Arthritis Self-Efficacy Scale [73], an eight-item instrument that assesses perceived ability to manage arthritis symptoms.

Patients were randomly assigned to receive either Hylan G-F 20 (Synvisc®) [Sanofi Biosurgery, Cambridge, MA, USA], a high molecular weight (MW = 6000 kDa) cross-linked HA product derived from an avian source, or EUFLEXXA® [bioengineered 1% sodium hyaluronate (IA-BioHA); Ferring Pharmaceuticals, Inc., Parsippany, NJ], a medium weight (MW = 2400–2600 kDa) HA product derived from bacterial fermentation.

Patients received injections every 7 days for a total of 3 injections. The primary outcome was treatment responder status defined a priori by improvement in the Western Ontario and McMaster Universities Osteoarthritis Index (WOMAC) Pain Scale [74, 75] between baseline and 3-month assessments. Patients whose Pain scores decreased by 20% or more compared with their baseline scores were classified as treatment responders and those whose scores did not meet this criterion were classified as non-responders.

Predicting Response to Intra-articular Injections of Hyaluronic Acid. We analyze the HA data to uncover patient and treatment factors that predict optimal response to intra-articular injections of hyaluronic acid for knee osteoarthritis. The treatment responder six months after final injection is measured by 'WOMACP20," Treatment Responder Status Using 20% Reduction in WOMAC Pain Scale. Recovery status is assessed via the KOOS Scale. The machine learning model determines which patient variables lead to the best outcomes of HA. We also analyze each of the two types of injections to gauge their similarities and differences in treatment outcome characteristics.

Table 10 shows the number of patients in the training set and the blind prediction set for predicting reinjection status. In this analysis, for every attribute in which there is any missing data, an associated binary attribute is created to capture if data is missing or not for this field. The number of attributes at three time-points: (a) baseline screening before first injection, (b) prior to second injection (prefix: T0), and (c) six months after final injection (prefix: T5) are 27, 483, and 1215 respectively. Table 11 shows the training set and blind prediction statistics used for predicting treatment responder status and recovery status.

Table 10. Training set and blind prediction set characteristics for predicting reinjection status.

Training set			Blind Prediction Set		
Total	No reinjection	Reinjection	Total	No reinjection	Reinjection
150	111	39	53	40	13

We summarize herein the best predictive rules for each of the analyses. Table 12 shows the prediction accuracy for no-reinjection versus re-injection using attributes collected up to the three stated time-points.

For the baseline results, factors that appear to be critical includes "Weight", "Currently Smoke Cigarettes" and "Smoking: Number per day". Baseline prediction results are comparable to Pap Smear test accuracy (~70%).

Table 11. Training set and blind prediction set characteristics for predicting treatment responder status and recovery status.

Training set			Blind Prediction Set		
Total	Non-Responder	Responder	Total	Non-Responder	Responder
71	34	37	70	41	29
Synvisc					
40	18	22	36	19	17
Euflexxa					
35	21	14	30	17	13

We can obtain high accuracy in predicting success for patients using screening and T0 attributes alone (86% blind predictive accuracy). This is very promising for identifying patients early (just after the first injection) who should be targeted for HA intervention (with expected success outcome). The discriminatory features selected includes the Marx Activity Scale "T0MarxCuttingSymptomFree", "T0MarxCutting", effectiveness of exercise "T0ExerciseEffective", confidence in the injector "T0ConfidenceInjector", and other medications "T0MedicationXEffective."

Including attributes until T5 significantly increases the accuracy for predicting the reinjection group (from 71% to 89%). However, early attributes include "T0PhysicalTherapyEffective", "T0MedicationXEffective," and overall health "T0EQRateHealth" continue to appear among the selected features.

Table 12. Best predictive rule for re-injection status when using attributes (a) baseline screening before first injection, (b) prior to 2nd injection, (c) 6 months after final injection respectively.

Input attributes	10-fold cross validation		blind prediction	
	No-reinjection	Re-injection	No-reinjection	Re-injection
Baseline screening	71%	71%	72%	71%
Prior to 2nd injection	89%	74%	86%	71%
6 months after final injection	84%	83%	81%	89%

Figure 9 show the 10-fold cross validation and blind prediction accuracies for predicting treatment responder status and recovery status for patients injected with Synvisc and Euflexxa, respectively. Specifically, for each HA, four columns are included: PSO/DAMIP results for predicting treatment responder and recovery respectively versus the best results from the 8 commonly used classifiers, RandomForest. Our PSO/DAMIP framework selected 3–8 discriminatory features whereas RandomForest uses over 40 features with poor results. Although the size of the two groups is rather balanced, the challenge here is due to the highly inseparable data thus making it difficult to classify using traditional approaches. Multi-stage approach allows partitioning of patients from the same group via different rules (associated with different features).

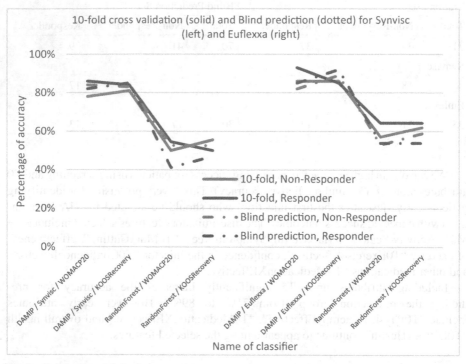

Fig. 9. Comparison of the best DAMIP classification rules for predicting treatment responder status and recovery status using Synvisc (left) and Euflexxa (right) against the RandomForest approach.

Our study shows that early predictors can be used to determine the group of patients who benefit the most from HA injection. A more detailed analysis comparing the two HA and discussion on the predictors is reported in Lee et al. 2023 [76].

4　Discussions

Medical decisions are intrinsically complex. They affect the health and clinical care of individuals and can also influence or facilitate health policy development. Recent technological innovation in prevention, diagnosis, and treatment have assisted in preventing illness, prolonging life, and promoting health. However, they also add new dimensions and extra complexity to the medical decision-making process. With the advent in human genome sequencing, microarrays, "omics," and discovery of biomarkers, and the adoption of Electronic Health Records, large-scale biological and clinical data are frequently generated. This data offers invaluable evidence for mining best practice and cost-effective clinical care and uncovering gaps that need to be closed. However, the exploding data stream means that more parameters, variables, and effects must be considered to determine the best course of action. Since medical decisions have substantial consequences and involve uncertainties and trade-offs, decision makers must balance the potential harm and benefit of their chosen interventions.

Computational methods such as mathematical programming, simulation, machine learning and classification, and optimization have found broad applications in medicine and healthcare to assist in determining the best decision(s), understanding the alternatives, and estimating the impact of each option. In particular, machine learning has become ubiquitous and is routinely employed to decipher data and identify patterns that can predict health and treatment outcomes that potentially inform and improve clinical care. However, effective handling of imbalanced data, tackling the computational complexity of multi-group classifiers, empirical experimentation on managing missing data, and robustness remain major challenges and key research focuses of investigators in the field of classification. It remains a grand challenge to establish a classifier in which all these critical properties co-exist simultaneously for optimal predictive effect. Our recent work on discriminant analysis via mixed integer programming (DAMIP) offers all these features in a single modeling framework [1].

In this paper, we present a general-purpose multi-stage, multi-group machine learning framework. The informatics-driven framework incorporates (a) particle swarm optimization and an exact branch-and-bound algorithm for feature selection and (b) discriminant analysis via mixed integer programming as its multi-group classifier. By utilizing a reserved judgment region, DAMIP delays making decisions on 'difficult-to-classify' observations and develops new classification rules at later stages. Geometrically, DAMIP partitions the group space where a group can be comprised of several disconnected partitions. Such a design works well for poorly separated data that are difficult to classify without committing a high percentage of misclassification errors. It is also well-suited for medical data (e.g., patients may achieve the same outcome through different clinical and decision pathways, thus belonging to the same group status even though they are characterized by different classification rules). The variant DAMIP models facilitate problem-specific fine-tuning to determine conducive misclassification limits and reserved judgement levels for efficient management of imbalanced groups. By design, DAMIP classifier ensures that minority groups with relatively few entities are treated equally as the majority groups.

We tackle four real-world medical problems using our multi-stage machine learning design: (a) multi-site treatment outcome prediction for best practice discovery in cardiovascular disease; and (b) diabetes; (c) early disease diagnosis in predicting subjects into normal, mild cognitive impairment, and Alzheimer's disease groups using neuropsychological tests and blood plasma biomarkers; and (d) uncovering patient characteristics that predict optimal response to intra-articular injections of hyaluronic acid for treatment of knee osteoarthritis.

These problems all involve poorly separated data, with inter-group mixed over 40% rendering challenging for classification. Three of the applications (except the knee osteoarthritis) also involve imbalanced groups in which traditional single-stage classifiers yield low prediction accuracy. The multi-stage PSO/DAMIP handles the poorly separable and imbalanced data well and returns interpretable predictive results with over 80% blind prediction accuracy. This is promising since the frequently used Pap Smear test has an accuracy of roughly 70%. Specifically multi-stage classifiers return feature sets consisting of 3–10 discriminatory features that offer actionable knowledge for establishing clinical practice guidelines for implementation in practice.

For the multi-site cardiovascular and diabetes studies, the ability to uncover best practices that pinpoints a specific clinical process, treatment regimen and duration, and drug types helps to establish improved clinical practice guidelines for adoption by other sites. This accelerates patient-centered, evidence-based care. Our findings reveal that the best practice uncovered was only carried out at fewer than 5% of the patient population among the 737 clinical sites. This offers an excellent opportunity for knowledge sharing and rapid learning, speeding dissemination, and implementation of best practice among all sites. The features identified allow physicians to (a) practice evidence-based treatment tailored to improve quality of life and health of patients; (b) allocate limited time and resources for best usage and results; (c) improve community health; (d) practice knowledge sharing and rapid learning across sites; and (e) close the health disparity gap by evidence-based practice.

Improving quality of life and health of patients through evidence-based best practice that result in good outcome and reduce complications is of paramount importance. We performed simulation to estimate potential improvement using the uncovered best practices. Simulation results show that best practice implementation can lead to 31% reduction in complication and 52% reduction in cost for CVD patients. This translates to over $300 million in return on investment (ROI) when only half of the 37,742 CVD patients comply. In a similar token, diabetes increases the risk of severe complications such as stroke, diabetic retinopathy, and glaucoma. Therefore, improvements in its management could have a significant health impact. Simulation results reveal that the best practice will reduce 81% complication and 43% costs. Over the 267,666 diabetes patients, the ROI can be very significant (about $5.5 billion) when half of the patients comply. This underscores the importance of evidence-based best practice and rapid knowledge dissemination. It also reveals the steep healthcare cost incurred by suboptimal care. For Alzheimer's disease, an early diagnosis of MCI can lead to proactive treatment that can slow down or prevent the onset of Alzheimer's. The features selected highlight the test modules and specific questions/tasks that are most predictive. These non-invasive neuropsychological tests can be added to the annual physical examination. They can serve as a low-cost early detection tool for family members and providers to monitor as they care for the elderly population. Alzheimer's is one of the most expensive diseases in America, costing more than cancer and heart disease combined. Over 6 million Americans are currently living with Alzheimer's disease, which costs an estimate of $321 billion in 2022. The disease takes an extraordinary emotional toll on the family and incurs an estimated $271 billion in unpaid caregiving.

For knee osteoarthritis, we are able to uncover patient characteristics that predict optimal response to intra-articular injections of hyaluronic acid. The discriminatory features selected offer evidence of efficacy that can be predicted based on the health baseline (with 70% accuracy) and characteristics obtained after the first injection. Being able to pinpoint which patient groups can benefit most from the injection helps targeted treatment and improve treatment and recovery outcomes. With one-third of knee replacements reported to be unnecessary, an effective non-invasive HA injection can make a significant difference to the quality of life of these patients.

One advantage in our findings is that the features identified are easily interpreted and understood by clinicians as well as patients. All of which can have a significant impact on translating the findings to clinical practice to achieve improved quality of life and medical outcome. The multiple rules with relatively small subsets of discriminatory features afford flexibility for different sites (and different patient populations) to adopt different policies for implementing the best practice.

In our applications, the imbalanced data is compounded further by the fact that they are poorly separable, with 30%-51% of intergroup mixing. After the first stage classification, about 35%-46% of the minority group were placed in the reserved judgement region. These data underscore the poorly separable concept and the advantage of a multi-stage approach,

Much of previous work on classification models investigates two-group discrimination. Multi-group classification is less often considered due to the tendency of generalizations of two-group models to produce misclassification rates that are higher than desirable. Indeed, producing good multi-group rules is generally more difficult. The original DAMIP multi-group model was established by Gallagher, Lee, and Patterson [40]. A linear-programming approximation was introduced to provide a rapid solution capability [77]. The study presented herein materializes the multi-stage construct by integrating both an exact combinatorial branch-and-bound algorithm and a fast heuristic for feature selection along with a systematic multi-group classifier schema, with a set of problem-specific, fine-tuning models to guide its practical usage.

Theoretically, DAMIP is a discrete support vector machine and has been proven to be $\mathcal{NP} - complete$ when the number of groups is greater than two. Its classifier is *universally strongly consistent*. A classifier is called universally consistent if its error probability converges to the Bayes-risk as the size of the training data grows for all possible distributions of the random variable pair of the observation vector and its class. Hence DAMIP has desirable solution characteristics for machine learning purposes.

Computationally, DAMIP is the first multi-group, multi-stage classification model that simultaneously includes a reserved judgment capability and the ability to constrain misclassification rates within a single model. Further, Constraints (1) reduce the problem dimension by transforming the features from their original space to the group space.

The resulting multi-stage multi-group machine learning framework remains computationally intractable. Although each iteration of feature selection can be achieved rapidly when heuristics are employed, the wrapper design evaluation via DAMIP is computationally intensive. For our applications, the solution time to establish the final classification rules can take days of CPU time in a cloud environment [1, 9]. Nonetheless, the high quality of the blind predictive results is promising and usable for clinical stakeholders who must carefully make critical decisions. In addition, many of the predictive rules developed do not require frequent refinement or re-training, rather they only need periodic updates. The blind prediction process takes only nanoseconds, allowing for real-time decision support. We are currently developing new hypergraphic theoretical and computational results to efficiently solve these intractable instances [78].

Acknowledgements. A portion of the results from this project (the machine learning advances, and the results obtained for cardiovascular disease and diabetes) received the first runner-up prize at the 2019 Caterpillar and INFORMS Innovative Applications in Analytics Award. This work is partially supported by grants from the National Science Foundation (IIP-1361532), and the American Orthopedic Society for Sports Medicine. Findings and conclusions in this paper are those of the authors and do not necessarily reflect the views of the National Science Foundation and the American Orthopedic Society for Sports Medicine. The authors would like to acknowledge the participation of Zhuonan Li in this project. The authors also thank Dr. Allan Levey, Dr. Felicia Goldstein, and Dr. William Hu of Emory Alzheimer's Disease Research Center for their collaboration and clinical advice. The authors extend their deepest respect and gratitude to the late Dr. Barton J. Mann PhD, with whom we collaborated on the knee osteoarthritis research, and to Dr. Captain Marlene DeMaio for her clinical guidance and collaboration on the project. We thank the anonymous reviewers for their useful comments.

References

1. Lee, E.K., Egan, B.M.: A multi-stage multi-group classification model: applications to knowledge discovery for evidence-based patient-centered care. In: Proceedings of the 14th International Joint Conference on Knowledge Discovery, Knowledge Engineering and Knowledge Management, vol. 1, pp. 95–108 (2022). KDIR. ISBN 978-989-758-614-9. ISSN 2184-3228
2. Lee, E.K., Wang, Y., Hagen, M.S., Wei, X., Davis, R.A., Egan, B.M.: Machine learning: multi-site evidence-based best practice discovery. In: Pardalos, P.M., Conca, P., Giuffrida, G., Nicosia, G. (eds.) MOD 2016. LNCS, vol. 10122, pp. 1–15. Springer, Cham (2016). https://doi.org/10.1007/978-3-319-51469-7_1
3. Rose, S.: Machine learning for prediction in electronic health data. JAMA Netw. Open **1**(4) (2018). https://doi.org/10.1001/jamanetworkopen.2018.1404
4. Marlin, B.M., Zemel, R.S., Roweis, S.T., Slaney, M.: Recommender systems: missing data and statistical model estimation. In: IJCAI International Joint Conference on Artificial Intelligence (2011). https://doi.org/10.5591/978-1-57735-516-8/IJCAI11-447
5. McDermott, M.B.A., Yan, T., Naumann, T., Hunt, N., Suresh, H., Szolovits, P., Ghassemi, M.: Semi-supervised biomedical translation with cycle Wasserstein regression GaNs. In: 32nd AAAI Conference on Artificial Intelligence, AAAI 2018 (2018). https://doi.org/10.1609/aaai.v32i1.11890
6. Mohan, K., Pearl, J., Tian, J.: Graphical models for inference with missing data. In: Advances in Neural Information Processing Systems (2013)
7. Rajkomar, A., Hardt, M., Howell, M.D., Corrado, G., Chin, M.H.: Ensuring fairness in machine learning to advance health equity. Ann. Internal Med. **169**(12) (2018). https://doi.org/10.7326/M18-1990
8. Lee, E.K., Wang, Y., He, Y., Egan, B.M.: An efficient, robust, and customizable information extraction and pre-processing pipeline for electronic health records. In: IC3K 2019 - Proceedings of the 11th International Joint Conference on Knowledge Discovery, Knowledge Engineering and Knowledge Management, vol. 1 (2019). https://doi.org/10.5220/0008071303100321
9. Lee, E.K., Egan, B.M.: Free text to standardized concepts to clinical decisions. In: Wang, J. (ed.) Encyclopedia of Data Science and Machine Learning. IGI Global (2022)
10. Lee, E.K., Yuan, F., Hirsh, D.A., Mallory, M.D., Simon, H.K.: A clinical decision tool for predicting patient care characteristics: patients returning within 72 hours in the emergency department. In: AMIA Annual Symposium Proceedings/AMIA Symposium. AMIA Symposium 2012 (2012)

11. Suresh, H., et al.: Proceedings of Machine Learning for Healthcare 2017 Clinical Intervention Prediction and Understanding with Deep Neural Networks. Ml4H, 68 (2017)
12. Basha, S.J., Madala, S.R., Vivek, K., Kumar, E.S., Ammannamma, T.: A review on imbalanced data classification techniques. In: 2022 International Conference on Advanced Computing Technologies and Applications (ICACTA), pp. 1–6 (2022). https://doi.org/10.1109/ICACTA 54488.2022.9753392
13. Fujiwara, K., et al.: Over- and under-sampling approach for extremely imbalanced and small minority data problem in health record analysis. Front. Public Health **8**, 178 (2020). https://doi.org/10.3389/fpubh.2020.00178
14. Gao, L., Zhang, L., Liu, C., Wu, S.: Handling imbalanced medical image data: a deep-learning-based one-class classification approach. Artif. Intell. Med. **108** (2020). https://doi.org/10.1016/j.artmed.2020.101935
15. O'Leary, L.: How IBM's Watson Went From the Future of Health Care to Sold Off for Parts. https://slate.com/technology/2022/01/ibm-watson-health-failure-artificial-intellige nce.html. Accessed 22 Jan 2023
16. Sweeney, E.: Experts say IBM Watson's flaws are rooted in data collection and interoperability. https://www.fiercehealthcare.com/analytics/ibm-watson-s-flaws-trace-back-to-data-collection-interoperability. Accessed 23 Jan 2023
17. Lee, E.K., Li, Z., Wang, Y., Hagen, M.S., Davis, R., Egan, B.M.: Multi-site best practice discovery: from free text to standardized concepts to clinical decisions. In: 2021 IEEE International Conference on Bioinformatics and Biomedicine (BIBM), pp. 2766–2773 (2021). https://doi.org/10.1109/BIBM52615.2021.9669414
18. Ghassemi, M., Naumann, T., Schulam, P., Beam, A.L., Chen, I.Y., Ranganath, R.: A review of challenges and opportunities in machine learning for health. In: AMIA Joint Summits on Translational Science Proceedings. AMIA Joint Summits on Translational Science, 2020 (2020)
19. Cui, L., Yang, S., Chen, F., Ming, Z., Lu, N., Qin, J.: A survey on application of machine learning for Internet of Things. Int. J. Mach. Learn. Cybern. **9**(8) (2018). https://doi.org/10.1007/s13042-018-0834-5
20. Dixon, M.F., Halperin, I., Bilokon, P.: Machine learning in finance: from theory to practice. In: Machine Learning in Finance: From Theory to Practice (2020). https://doi.org/10.1007/978-3-030-41068-1
21. Hayward, K.J., Maas, M.M.: Artificial intelligence and crime: a primer for criminologists. Crime Media Cult. **17**(2) (2021). https://doi.org/10.1177/1741659020917434
22. Lei, Y., Yang, B., Jiang, X., Jia, F., Li, N., Nandi, A.K.: Applications of machine learning to machine fault diagnosis: a review and roadmap. Mech. Syst. Signal Process. **138** (2020). https://doi.org/10.1016/j.ymssp.2019.106587
23. Myszczynska, M.A., et al.: Applications of machine learning to diagnosis and treatment of neurodegenerative diseases. Nat. Rev. Neurol. **16**(8) (2020). https://doi.org/10.1038/s41582-020-0377-8
24. Narciso, D.A.C., Martins, F.G.: Application of machine learning tools for energy efficiency in industry: a review. Energy Rep. **6** (2020). https://doi.org/10.1016/j.egyr.2020.04.035
25. Qu, K., Guo, F., Liu, X., Lin, Y., Zou, Q.: Application of machine learning in microbiology. Front. Microbiol. **10**(Apr) (2019). https://doi.org/10.3389/fmicb.2019.00827
26. Yarkoni, T., Westfall, J.: Choosing prediction over explanation in psychology: lessons from machine learning. Perspect. Psychol. Sci. **12**(6) (2017). https://doi.org/10.1177/174569161 7693393
27. Zhao, S., et al.: Application of machine learning in intelligent fish aquaculture: a review. Aquaculture **540** (2021). https://doi.org/10.1016/j.aquaculture.2021.736724
28. Efron, B., et al.: Least angle regression. Ann. Stat. **32**(2) (2004). https://doi.org/10.1214/009 053604000000067

29. Tibshirani, R.: Regression shrinkage and selection via the lasso: a retrospective. J. Roy. Stat. Soc. Ser. B Stat. Methodol. **73**(3) (2011). https://doi.org/10.1111/j.1467-9868.2011.00771.x
30. Hocking, R.R., Leslie, R.N.: Selection of the best subset in regression analysis. Technometrics **9**(4) (1967). https://doi.org/10.1080/00401706.1967.10490502
31. Pudil, P., Novovičová, J., Kittler, J.: Floating search methods in feature selection. Pattern Recognit. Lett. **15**(11) (1994). https://doi.org/10.1016/0167-8655(94)90127-9
32. Silva, A.P.D., Stam, A.: Second order mathematical programming formulations for discriminant analysis. Eur. J. Oper. Res. **72**(1) (1994). https://doi.org/10.1016/0377-2217(94)903 24-7
33. Siedlecki, W., Sklansky, J.: A note on genetic algorithms for large-scale feature selection. Pattern Recognit. Lett. **10**(5) (1989). https://doi.org/10.1016/0167-8655(89)90037-8
34. Kennedy, J., Eberhart, R.C.: Discrete binary version of the particle swarm algorithm. In: Proceedings of the IEEE International Conference on Systems, Man and Cybernetics, vol. 5 (1997). https://doi.org/10.1109/icsmc.1997.637339
35. Agrafiotis, D.K., Cedeño, W.: Feature selection for structure-activity correlation using binary particle swarms. J. Med. Chem. **45**(5) (2002). https://doi.org/10.1021/jm0104668
36. Correa, E.S., Freitas, A.A., Johnson, C.G.: A new discrete particle swarm algorithm applied to attribute selection in a bioinformatics data set. In: GECCO 2006 - Genetic and Evolutionary Computation Conference, vol. 1 (2006). https://doi.org/10.1145/1143997.1144003
37. Hu, Y., Zhang, Y., Gong, D.: Multiobjective particle swarm optimization for feature selection with fuzzy cost. IEEE Trans. Cybern. **51**(2) (2021). https://doi.org/10.1109/TCYB.2020.301 5756
38. Jain, N.K., Nangia, U., Jain, J.: A review of particle swarm optimization. J. Inst. Eng. (India): Ser. B **99**(4) (2018). https://doi.org/10.1007/s40031-018-0323-y
39. Monteiro, S.T., Kosugi, Y.: Particle swarms for feature extraction of hyperspectral data. IEICE Trans. Inf. Syst. **E90-D**(7) (2007). https://doi.org/10.1093/ietisy/e90-d.7.1038
40. Gallagher, R.J., Lee, E.K., Patterson, D.A.: Constrained discriminant analysis via 0/1 mixed integer programming. Ann. Oper. Res. **74** (1997). https://doi.org/10.1023/a:1018943025993
41. World Health Organization. Cardiovascular diseases (2022). https://www.who.int/health-top ics/cardiovascular-diseases#tab=tab_1. Accessed 23 Jan 2023
42. Tsao, C.W., et al.: Heart disease and stroke statistics-2022 update: a report from the American heart association. Circulation **145**(8), e153–e639 (2022). https://doi.org/10.1161/CIR.000000 0000001052. Epub 2022 Jan 26. Erratum in: Circulation. 2022 Sep 6;146(10):e141. PMID: 35078371
43. Cardiovascular diseases affect nearly half of American adults, statistics show. American Heart Association News (2019). https://www.heart.org/en/news/2019/01/31/cardiovascular-diseases-affect-nearly-half-of-american-adults-statistics-show
44. Gordon, T., Castelli, W.P., Hjortland, M.C., Kannel, W.B., Dawber, T.R.: High density lipoprotein as a protective factor against coronary heart disease. The Framingham study. Am. J. Med. **62**(5) (1977). https://doi.org/10.1016/0002-9343(77)90874-9
45. Nwegbu, N., Tirunagari, S., Windridge, D.: A novel kernel based approach to arbitrary length symbolic data with application to type 2 diabetes risk. Sci. Rep. **12**(1) (2022). https://doi.org/ 10.1038/s41598-022-08757-1
46. Ogurtsova, K., et al.: IDF diabetes atlas: global estimates for the prevalence of diabetes for 2015 and 2040. Diabetes Res. Clin. Pract. **128** (2017)
47. Riddle, M.C., Herman, W.H.: The cost of diabetes care—an elephant in the room. Diabetes Care **41**, 929–932 (2018)
48. American Diabetes Association. Statistics About Diabetes (2022). https://diabetes.org/about-us/statistics/about-diabetes

49. American Diabetes Association. Economic Costs of Diabetes in the U.S. in 2017. Diabetes Care **41**(5), 917–928 (2018). https://doi.org/10.2337/dci18-0007. PMID 29567642; PMCID PMC5911784
50. Nathan, D.M., et al.: Diabetes control and complications trial/epidemiology of diabetes interventions and complications (DCCT/EDIC) study research group. Intensive diabetes treatment and cardiovascular disease in patients with type 1 diabetes. N. Engl. J. Med. **353**(25), 2643–2653 (2005). https://doi.org/10.1056/NEJMoa052187. PMID 16371630; PMCID PMC2637991
51. Caiado, J., Crato, N., Peña, D.: Comparison of times series with unequal length in the frequency domain. Commun. Stat. Simul. Comput.® **38**(3), 527–540 (2009)
52. World Health Organization. The top 10 causes of death (2022). https://www.who.int/news-room/fact-sheets/detail/the-top-10-causes-of-death. Accessed 24 Jan 2023
53. Kluger, A., Ferris, S.H., Golomb, J., Mittelman, M.S., Reisberg, B.: Neuropsychological prediction of decline to dementia in nondemented elderly. J. Geriatr. Psychiatry Neurol. **12**(4) (1999). https://doi.org/10.1177/089198879901200402
54. Lopez, O.L., et al.: Neuropsychological characteristics of mild cognitive impairment subgroups. J. Neurol. Neurosurg. Psychiatry **77**(2) (2006). https://doi.org/10.1136/jnnp.2004.045567
55. Lee, E.K., Wu, T.L.: Classification and disease prediction via mathematical programming. In: Springer Optimization and Its Applications, vol. 26 (2009). https://doi.org/10.1007/978-0-387-09770-1_12
56. Lee, E.K., Wu, T.L., Goldstein, F., Levey, A.: Predictive model for early detection of mild cognitive impairment and Alzheimer's disease. Fields Inst. Commun. **63** (2012). https://doi.org/10.1007/978-1-4614-4133-5_4
57. Stuss, D.T., Trites, R.L.: Classification of neurological status using multiple discriminant function analysis of neuropsychological test scores. J. Consult. Clin. Psychol. **45**(1) (1977). https://doi.org/10.1037/0022-006X.45.1.145
58. Tabert, M.H., et al.: Neuropsychological prediction of conversion to Alzheimer disease in patients with mild cognitive impairment. Arch. Gen. Psychiatry **63**(8) (2006). https://doi.org/10.1001/archpsyc.63.8.916
59. Hu, W.T., et al.: Plasma multianalyte profiling in mild cognitive impairment and Alzheimer Disease. Neurology **79**(9) (2012). https://doi.org/10.1212/WNL.0b013e318266fa70
60. Hu, W.T., et al.: CSF complement 3 and factor H are staging biomarkers in Alzheimer's disease. Acta Neuropathol. Commun. **4** (2016). https://doi.org/10.1186/s40478-016-0277-8
61. Palmqvist, S., et al.: Discriminative accuracy of plasma phospho-tau217 for Alzheimer disease vs other neurodegenerative disorders. JAMA J. Am. Med. Assoc. **324**(8) (2020). https://doi.org/10.1001/jama.2020.12134
62. Ray, S., et al.: Classification and prediction of clinical Alzheimer's diagnosis based on plasma signaling proteins. Nat. Med. **13**(11) (2007). https://doi.org/10.1038/nm1653
63. Reddy, M.M., et al.: Identification of candidate IgG biomarkers for Alzheimer's disease via combinatorial library screening. Cell **144**(1) (2011). https://doi.org/10.1016/j.cell.2010.11.054
64. Rocha de Paula, M.R., Gómez Ravetti, M., Berretta, R., Moscato, P.: Differences in abundances of cell-signalling proteins in blood reveal novel biomarkers for early detection of clinical Alzheimer's disease. PLoS ONE **6**(3) (2011). https://doi.org/10.1371/journal.pone.0017481
65. Schindler, S.E., Bateman, R.J.: Combining blood-based biomarkers to predict risk for Alzheimer's disease dementia. Nat. Aging **1**(1) (2021). https://doi.org/10.1038/s43587-020-00008-0

66. Riddle, D.L., Jiranek, W.A., Hayes, C.W.: Use of a validated algorithm to judge the appropriateness of total knee arthroplasty in the united states: a multicenter longitudinal cohort study. Arthritis Rheumatol. **66**(8), 2134–2143 (2014)
67. Mora, J.C., Przkora, R., Cruz-Almeida, Y.: Knee osteoarthritis: pathophysiology and current treatment modalities. J. Pain Res. **11**, 2189–2196 (2018). https://doi.org/10.2147/JPR.S15 4002. PMID: 30323653; PMCID: PMC6179584.
68. Bellamy, N.: WOMAC Osteoarthritis Index User Guide. Version V. Brisbane, Australia (2002)
69. Hays, R.D., Sherbourne, C.D., Mazel, R.M.: The RAND 36-item health survey 1.0. Health Econ. **2**(3), 217–227 (1993)
70. Marx, R.G., Stump, T.J., Jones, E.C., Wickiewicz, T.L., Warren, R.F.: Development and evaluation of an activity rating scale for disorders of the knee. Am. J. Sports Med. **29**, 213–218 (2001)
71. Sangha, O., Stucki, G., Liang, M.H., Fossel, A.H., Katz, J.N.: The self-administered comorbidity questionnaire: a new method to assess comorbidity for clinical and health services research. Arthritis Rheum. **49**, 156–163 (2003)
72. Brooks, R.: EuroQol: the current state of play. Health Policy **37**(1), 53–72 (1996)
73. Lorig, K., Chastain, R.L., Ung, E., Shoor, S., Holman, H.R.: Development and evaluation of a scale to measure perceived self-efficacy in people with arthritis. Arthritis Rheum. **32**, 37–44 (1989)
74. Ebrahimzadeh, M.H., Makhmalbaf, H., Birjandinejad, A., Keshtan, F.G., Hoseini, H.A., Mazloumi, S.M.: The western Ontario and Mcmaster universities osteoarthritis index (WOMAC) in Persian speaking patients with knee osteoarthritis. Arch. Bone Jt. Surg. **2**(1), 57–62 (2014). PMID 25207315; PMCID PMC4151432
75. Hochberg, M.C., Altman, R.D., Brandt, K.D., Moskowitz, R.W.: Design and conduct of clinical trials in osteoarthritis: preliminary recommendations from a task force of the osteoarthritis research society. J. Rheumatol. **24**, 792–794 (1997)
76. Lee, E.K., Mann, B.J., DeMaio, M.: Prediction of responses to intra-articular injections of Hyaluronic acid for knee osteoarthritis. Preprint (2023)
77. Lee, E.K., Gallagher, R.J., Patterson, D.A.: A linear programming approach to discriminant analysis with a reserved-judgment region. INFORMS J. Comput. **15**(1) (2003). https://doi.org/10.1287/ijoc.15.1.23.15158
78. Shapoval, A., Lee, E.K.: Generalizing 0–1 conflict hypergraphs and mixed conflict graphs: mixed conflict hypergraphs in discrete optimization. J. Glob. Optim. **80**(4) (2021). https://doi.org/10.1007/s10898-021-01012-3

Comparative Assessment of Deep End-To-End, Deep Hybrid and Deep Ensemble Learning Architectures for Breast Cancer Histological Classification

Hasnae Zerouaoui[1] (iD) and Ali Idri[1,2]([envelope]) (iD)

[1] Mohammed VI Polytechnic University, Benguerir, Morocco
Hasnae.zerouaoui@um6p.ma, ali.idri@um5.ac.ma
[2] Software Project Management Research Team, ENSIAS, Mohammed V University in Rabat, Rabat, Morocco

Abstract. Breast cancer (BC) is considered one of the major public health issues and a leading cause of death among women in the world. Its early diagnosis using histological imaging modalities can significantly help to increase the chances of survival rate by choosing the adequate treatment. This research work is a comparative study that assesses and compares the performances of: (1) seven deep end-to-end architectures using seven deep learning models including VGG16, VGG19, ResNet 50, MobileNet V2, Inception V3, Inception ResNet V2 and DenseNet 201, (2) a deep hybrid architectures combining the deep learning model DenseNet 201 for feature extraction and MLP for classification and (3) a deep end-to-end heterogeneous ensembles of seven deep learning models used as base learners including VGG16, VGG19, ResNet50, Inception V3, Inception ResNet V2, Xception, and MobileNet V2 and combined with weighted voting over a hematoxylin and eosin (H&E)-stained pathological images. The experiments were conducted using the public BreakHis dataset, 5-fold cross validation method, four metrics of performances, the Scott Knott statistical test and the Borda Count voting method. The results showed that the deep end-to-end architecture DenseNet 201 is outperforming the others architectures with an accuracy value of 94,9%, 94,4%, 93,1%, 93,1% and 98,07% for the MF 40X,100X, 200X and 400X respectively, The comparison of the deep end-to-end, hybrid and end-to-end ensemble learning architectures proved the potential of the deep learning model DenseNet 201 for both feature extraction and classification since it gave the best results and outperformed the others.

Keywords: Deep learning · Machine learning · Ensemble learning · Computer vision · Breast cancer · Whole slide images · Digital pathology

1 Introduction

Breast cancer (BC) is the world's fifth leading cause of death and the second leading cause of death in women [1]. Early detection and diagnosis of this disease are critical for lowering the disease's morbidity rates for women. Moreover, as the number of BC

F. Coenen et al. (Eds.): IC3K 2022, CCIS 1842, pp. 107–124, 2023.
https://doi.org/10.1007/978-3-031-43471-6_5

patients grows, it becomes more difficult for radiologists and pathologists to accurately handle the diagnosis process in a limited amount of time [2]. Medical imaging analysis remains among the most promising research areas, since it enables the diagnosis of a variety of cancer diseases, including BC. Undoubtedly, for BC diagnosis, various imaging modalities, particularly mammography, magnetic resonance imaging, and pathological modalities such as histological and cytological images, have been used [3]. Since there is an increase of using medical images especially the pathological images which remain a gold standard for BC diagnosis, more attention has been paid to computer vision, deep learning (DL) and machine learning (ML) to help experts in interpreting the medical images [3]. In general, the use of DL techniques as feature extractors instead of classical image feature extraction (FE) techniques positively impacted the performance of classical ML architectures [4]. In this context, previous studies designed and compared end-to-end DL architectures with deep hybrid architectures that combine the strengths of DL techniques for FE and classical ML models for classification [5–10]. For instance:

- In the study [9], the authors compared the results of: (1) the hybrid architectures designed using the deep learning models VGG16 and AlexNet for feature extraction where the features are concatenated to one vector and classified using SVM classifier, and (2) the end-to-end architecture using the AlexNet model for a binary classification using the histological BreakHis dataset. Results showed that the end-to-end architecture using the AlexNet model outperformed the hybrid ones with an accuracy of 90.96%, 90.58%, 91.37% and 91.30% for the MF 40X, 100X, 200X and 400X respectively.
- The study [8] collected 3771 histological images and tested a designed hybrid architecture with end-to-end architectures from state of the art. The proposed architecture is designed using the Inception V3 DL models for feature extraction and the LSTM (long short-term memory) classifier for a binary classification. Results showed the potential of the hybrid architecture since it achieved an accuracy value of 91.3% and outperformed the state-of-the-art end-to-end architectures such as inception V3, VGG16 and ResNet 50 when using histological imaging modalities for BC diagnosis.
- The study [10] compared: (1) a proposed architecture using fully connected layer for feature extraction and Bi-LSTM (bidirectional long short term memory) for classification, and (2) an end-to-end architecture using AlexNet for binary histological BC classification using the CIFAR-10 dataset. Results showed the potential of the designed hybrid architectures since it outperformed the end-to-end with an accuracy of 91.90%.

However, we identified five major limitations in [8–10]: (1) lack of use of data augmentation for data processing, (2) comparison of only one designed end-to-end architecture and one hybrid architecture, (3) lack of a clear and rigorous empirical design process which prevents replications, (4) lack of use of statistical methods to evaluate the obtained results and (6) lack of evaluation single end-to-end or hybrid architectures with deep ensemble learning architectures.

In a previous work [11], deep end-to-end ensembles were developed using seven pretrained DL models: VGG16, VGG19 [12], ResNet50 [13], Inception V3 [14], Inception ResNet V2 [15], Xception [16], and MobileNet V2 [17] and constructed based on accuracy using majority and weighted voting. Results showed the effectiveness of deep end-to-end ensemble learning techniques for binary BC pathological classification. The results showed that the ensembles designed with weighted voting method exceeded the others with an accuracy value reaching 93.8%, 93.4%, 93.3%, and 91.8% through the BreakHis dataset's four magnification factors (MFs): 40X, 100X, 200X, and 400X respectively. In order to compare the results of the study [11], and to elevate the burdens of the previous related works, a comparative assessment is conducted which aims at: (1) designing and evaluating the performance of seven end-to-end architectures using seven DL models (DenseNet 201 [18], InceptionV3, InceptionReseNetV2, MobileNetV2, ResNet50, VGG16, and VGG19) for binary BC classification, (2) comparing the obtained results with the best performing deep hybrid architectures developed and evaluated in the study [19] using DenseNet 201 for FE and MLP for classification over the same dataset, and (3) comparing the best designed deep end-to-end ensemble learning model using seven DL models as base learners and combined using weighted voting [11]developed and evaluated on the same dataset.

All the experiment evaluations used four performance criteria (accuracy, precision, recall, and F1-score), the SK statistical test and Borda Count voting method to rank the compared deep architectures. Note that the SK test [20] and Borda Count [21] has been widely used to compare and cluster multiple ML models in different fields such as software engineering [7] and medicine [24].

Furthermore, the comparative assessment discusses three research questions (RQs):

(RQ1): What is the overall performance of the deep end to end developed architectures in a BC binary classification?
(RQ2): Is there any deep end-to-end architecture which distinctly outperformed the others when used in BC histological classification?
(RQ3): Which deep architecture outperforms the other for histological BC classification?

The main contributions of comparative assessment are the following:

1. Designing seven end-to-end architectures using seven DL techniques for FE and classification: VGG16, VGG19, DenseNet201, Inception ResNet V2, Inception V3, ResNet 50 and MobileNet V2 for BC binary classification.
2. Evaluating the end-to-end architectures over a hematoxylin and eosin (H&E)-stained pathological imaging dataset.
3. Comparing the performances of the seven end-to-end architectures with a deep hybrid architecture and a deep end-to-end ensemble learning architectures using SK test and Borda Count voting method.

The rest of this paper is organized as follow. Section 2 presents the Material and methods which includes the definition of transfer learning and deep learning, the empirical methodology followed in this research, the dataset used to evaluate the designed models and the abbreviation. Section 3 reports and discusses the empirical results. Section 4 presents the threats of validity of the study. Section 5 outlines conclusions and future works.

2   Material and Methods

This section presents: (1) the deep learning concept and transfer learning strategy, (2) the empirical configuration and the empirical design, (3) the dataset used, and (4) the abbreviations followed for this study.

2.1   Deep Learning and Transfer Learning

In this subsection, transfer learning and deep learning are introduced.

Deep Learning: The field of DL is a new frontier in ML research. It is composed of many hidden layers of artificial neural networks and focuses on two fundamental aspects: nonlinear processing in multiple layers or stages and supervised or unsupervised learning. A nonlinear processing in many layers' algorithm is one in which the current layer uses the output of the previous layer as input [25]. DL has resulted in incredible advancements in fields such as computer vision, natural language processing, and speech recognition. One of the applications of DL is image classification. There are several types of DL architectures: recurrent neural networks (RNN), autoencoders, convolutional neural networks (CNN), multi-layer perceptron's (MLP), and generative adversarial networks (GANs).

In this study, we focus on the use of CNN architectures since we are dealing with an image classification problem. It should be noted that the image classification problems can be solved using DL and TF. In fact, several cutting-edge discoveries in image categorization are based on TFs solutions.

Transfer Learning: Transfer learning (TF) is a technique that transfers a model's knowledge from a related source task to a second related task, optimizing the model by allowing for faster progress and better performance than training from scratch [18]. As a result of the high computational cost of training deep learning models, it is common practice, particularly in computer vision, to use transfer learning with pre-trained models. The TF technique can be applied in two ways:

1- *TF for Fine Tuning*

The core principle is to unfreeze a few of the DL model's top convolutional layers and jointly train both the unfrozen layer and the newly added classifier to adjust the model to the classification problem by changing some parameters such as the learning rate, number of epochs, and regularization parameters. This enables to fine tune the higher-order feature representations to make them more relevant for the task [26]. This method produces accurate results and is commonly used to design end-to-end architectures when having a larger dataset and limited computation time.

2- *TF for Feature Extraction*

The major objective is to retain and freeze the pre-trained DL model's in its original form to produce an entirely novel dataset called the feature vectors dataset, and then use its outputs to feed the classifier [27]. This method produces better and faster results, and it is commonly used to design deep hybrid architectures with small datasets and limited computation time.

2.2 Experiment Configuration and Design

To evaluate the seven deep end-to-end architectures based on DL models for FE and classification; and compare the obtained results with the best performing deep hybrid architecture of the study [19], and the best performing deep end-to-end ensemble learning architectures of the study [11], many concepts and techniques were used such as transfer learning for fine-tunning and for FE, seven DL models (DenseNet 201, Inception V3, Inception ResNet V2, MobileNet V2, ResNet 50, VGG16, and VGG19), the MLP classifier and the ensemble learning strategy using the weighted combination method. To evaluate the performances of the developed architectures we adopted four performance measures [3]: accuracy, precision, recall and F1-score and used 5-fold cross validation since it gives less biased results compared to data splitting [28]. For the statistical evaluation SK test and Borda Count voting were adopted. As for the training, the seven DL models were finetuned using transfer learning technique [29] by downloading the pre-trained models on the ImageNet dataset that contains 1.2 million images for training, 50,00 for validation and 10.000 for testing and 1000 class [12].We froze the last and updated the top layers using the same layers for the seven DL models, which includes a fully connected layer with the RELU activation, followed by a dropout layer with a probability of 0.5 and an output layer for the binary classification instead of the 1000 of ImageNet. For the parameter tunning the batch size was set to 32 and the number of epochs to 200, the ADAM optimizer was adopted with an adaptive learning rate that was initially initialized to 0.0001 and the L2 reguilazer [30]. The methodology followed to carry the experimental study is similar to the design of the studies [8, 9] and consists of five steps:

1. Assess the accuracy of each variant of the seven end-to-end architectures (VGG16, VGG19, DenseNet 201, MobileNet V2, ResNet 50, Inception V3, Inception ResNet V2) tested on the histological BreakHis dataset four MFs (40X, 100X, 200X and 400X)
2. Clustering the seven end-to-end architectures using the SK test based on accuracy and identify the best SK cluster over the pathological dataset.
3. Rank the end-to-end architectures belonging to the best SK cluster of step 2 using the Borda Count voting method based on accuracy, precision, recall and F1-score to identify the best performing method.
4. Clustering the deep end-to-end architectures belonging to the best SK cluster with the best performing deep hybrid architectures [19] and the best performing deep end-to-end ensemble learning model [11] using SK test based on accuracy and identify the best SK clusters.
5. Rank the models belonging to the best SK cluster of step 4 over the BreakHis (40X, 100X, 200X, 400X) dataset using Borda Count voting system based on the four performance measures. Select the top performing designed method.

In order to distinguish the difference between a deep end-to-end and a deep hybrid architecture, Fig. 1 illustrate the main steps to design both architectures.

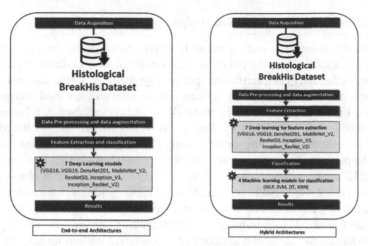

Fig. 1. Steps of designing deep end-to-end architecture and a deep hybrid architecture

2.3 Data Preparation

In this study the histological BreakHis dataset which is composed of 7,909 breast micro-scopic images generated from breast tissue biopsy slides and acquired from 82 patients with various MFs (40X, 100X, 200X, and 400X) was used. In order to prepare the images, three image pre-processing techniques were used: (1) intensity normalization to normalize input images to the standard normal distribution using min-max normaliza-tion [3], (2) Contrast Limited Adaptive Histogram Equalization (CLAHE) to improve the contrast [23], and (3) data augmentation [34] to increase and balance the benign and malignant images of the BreakHis dataset. Therefore, the total number of samples for both datasets was increased by 2 times.

2.4 Abbreviation

In this sub section the abbreviation used to represent the deep end-to-end, deep hybrid and deep end-to-end ensemble learning architectures.

Abbreviation for the End-to-End Architectures
We abbreviate the name of each variant of DL techniques as demonstrated in Table 1.

Abbreviation for the Deep Hybrid Architectures
The abbreviation naming rule used for the hybrid architectures is [19]:

Classifier Deep Learning Architecture

The deep hybrid architecture used for this study is MDEN (MLP for classification and DenseNet 201 for FE).

Abbreviation for the Deep End-to-End Ensemble Learning Architectures
The abbreviation naming rule used for the deep end-to-end ensemble learning architec-tures is the same used in the study [11]:

Table 1. Abbreviations of the deep end-to-end architectures

DL techniques	Abbreviation
VGG16	VGG16
VGG19	VGG19
Inception V3	INV3
ResNet 50	RES50
Inception ResNet V2	INRES
DenseNet 201	DENS
MobileNet V2	MOB

EnWV: Ensemble of size n combined with the weighted voting combination method.

The deep end-to-end ensemble learning model used in this study is E7WV an ensemble of seven DL models used as base learners and the weighted voting combination rule.

3 Results and Discussions

This section presents and discusses the results of the empirical evaluations of the comparative assessment of the deep end-to-end, hybrid and end-to-end ensemble learning architectures over the histological BreakHis dataset four MFs. First, the performances of the seven deep end-to-end architectures are evaluated in terms of accuracy (RQ1). Thereafter, the end-to-end architectures are clustered using the SK test based on accuracy and the architectures belonging to the best SK cluster are ranked using the Borda Count voting methods based on the four-performance metrics: accuracy, precision, recall and F1-score (RQ2). Hereafter, the obtained results of the end-to-end architectures were compared with the best performing deep hybrid architectures of the study [19] and the best performing deep end-to-end ensemble learning architectures [11] to identify which designed architecture performed better (RQ3).

3.1 Overall Performance of the Deep End-to-End Architectures

We firstly present and discuss the performances of each deep end-to-end architecture over the histological BreakHis dataset which contains histopathological images with various magnification factors MFs including 40X, 100X, 200X, and 400X. Table 2 and Fig. 2 summarizes the validation accuracy values.

It is observable that:

- The best accuracy values of VGG16, VGG19, Inception V3, DenseNet 201, Inception ResNet V2 and MobileNet V2 were obtained when the number of epochs is higher than almost 25, except for ResNet50 (number of epoch higher than almost 100) regardless the MFs values: 40X,100X,200X and 400X.

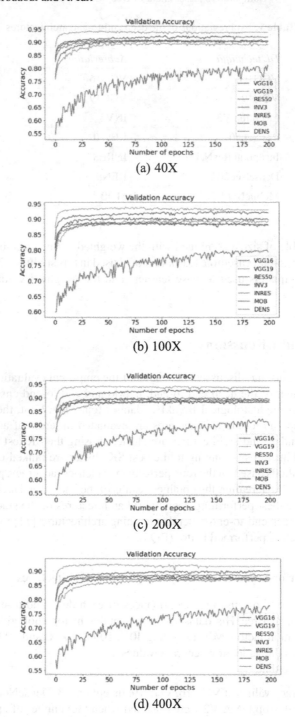

Fig. 2. Accuracy values vs number of epochs of the deep end-to-end architectures over the BreakHis dataset.

- The best accuracy values of VGG16, Inception V3, DenseNet 201 and Inception ResNet V2 were achieved with MF 40X with a value of 91.46%, 91.53% 94.9% and 91.61% respectively, for VGG19 the best accuracy value was achieved using MF 100X with a value of 90.36%; and for ResNet 50 and MobileNet V2 the best accuracy values was achieved using MF 200X with a value of 82.8% and 93.8% respectively.
- All the seven architectures get the worst accuracy values when using images with MF 400X.
- ResNet 50 underperformed compared to the six remaining models with the best accuracy value reaching 82.8% with MF 200X and the worst accuracy value 78.99 with MF 400X.
- DenseNet 201 outperformed compared to the six remaining models using the MF 40X, 100X and 400X with an accuracy value reaching 94.9%, 94.4% and 93.1 respectively.
- MobileNet V2 outperformed compared to the remaining six end-to-end architectures when using the MF 200X with an accuracy value of 93.8%.

Table 2. Accuracy values of the deep end-to-end architectures over the BreakHis dataset

MF	VGG16 (%)	VGG19 (%)	ResNet50 (%)	Inception V3 (%)	Inception ResNet V2 (%)	MobileNet V2 (%)	DenseNet 201 (%)
40X	91.46	90.33	81.79	91.53	91.61	93.4	94.90
100X	91.09	90.36	80.59	89.77	89.77	90.95	94.40
200X	90.61	89.57	82.80	89.68	90.79	93.80	93.10
400X	88.18	88.02	78.99	89.23	89.68	91.00	93.10

3.2 Performance Comparison of Deep end-to-end Architectures

In order to address RQ2, SK statistical test based on accuracy was used to evaluate the predictive capabilities of the designed end-to-end architectures and Borda Count voting method based on the four performance measures to rank them over each dataset. Note that the SK test consists of grouping the architectures with no significant difference between their accuracy values by clustering the seven end-to-end architectures into overlapping free clusters. The architectures belonging to the same cluster have similar predictive capability and the best cluster contains the architectures that have the highest value of accuracy. Figure 3 illustrates the SK test diagram results based on accuracy over the four MFs of the histological BreakHis dataset. Three clusters were identified for each MF and the portioning of the seven end-to-end architectures is the same regardless the MF value. It is observed that the four MFs SK best clusters contain the two end-to-end architectures DenseNet 201 and MobileNet V2, the second clusters include the four architectures: VGG16, VGG19, Inception V3 and Inception ResNet V2 and the worst clusters contain ResNet 50. This implies that the performances in term of accuracy were not influenced by the image characteristics.

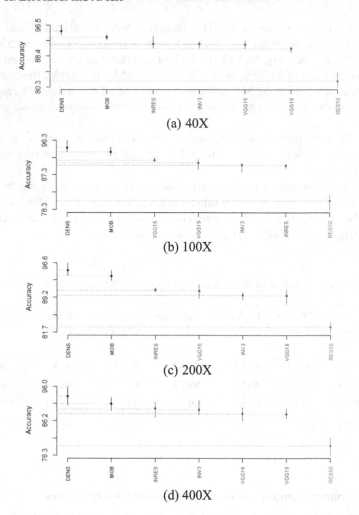

Fig. 3. Results of SK test for the end-to-end architecture over the histological BreakHis dataset.

Table 3. Borda count ranking fort the end-to-end and hybrid architectures of the best SK cluster over the BreakHis dataset.

Rank	40X	100X	200X	400X
1	DENS	DENS	DENS	DENS
2	MOB	MOB	MOB	MOB

Table 3 shows the Borda Count ranking of the two deep end-to-end architectures belonging to the best SK clusters over the histological BreakHis dataset based on the four-performance metrics. Table A1 of the Appendix describes the validation precision, recall and F1-score value of the seven DL models over the four MFs of the BreakHis dataset. As can be seen, DenseNet 201 was ranked first and outperformed MobileNet V2 regardless the MF used.

3.3 Comparison of Deep end-to-end, Hybrid and End-to-end Ensemble Learning Architectures

RQ3 aims at comparing the performances of the deep end-to-end, deep hybrid and deep end-to-end ensemble learning architectures. To this aim: (1) the results of the study [19] proposing deep hybrid architectures were summarized and presented, (2) the mains outcomes of the study [11] proposing deep end-to-end ensemble learning models are summarized and presented and (4) SK test is used based on the accuracy values of the three deep architectures to cluster the ones that have the same predictive capabilities, and Borda Count voting method is used based on the four-performance metrics to rank the architectures belonging to the best SK clusters.

Performances of the Deep Hybrid Architectures
In a previous research work [19] twenty-eight deep hybrid architectures were designed combining seven DL techniques for FE (DenseNet 201, Inception V3, Inception Res Net V2, MobileNet V2, ResNet 50, VGG16 and VGG19), and four classifiers (MLP, SVM, DT and KNN) over the BreakHis pathological dataset. According to the results, the accuracy outcomes of the designed deep hybrid architectures were significantly affected by the DL techniques used for FE and the four ML classifiers. As regard, the deep hybrid architecture MDEN (DenseNet 201 for FE and MLP for classification) almost gave the best results with an accuracy value of 92.61%, 92%, 93.93%, 91.73% over the four MFs 40X, 100X, 200X, 400X respectively. Table A2 presents the validation accuracy, precision, recall and F1-score of the MDEN architecture over the four MFs.

Performances of the Deep end-to-end Ensemble Learning
In a previous research work [11] six deep end-to-end ensemble learning architectures were designed using top 2, 3, 4, 5, 6 and 7 DL models for both FE and classification and combined with two combination methods (hard and weighted voting) evaluated on the BreakHis dataset. The outcomes of the study showed the performance of the proposed with the best performing designed ensemble is the one designed with weighted voting and top 7 DL models with an accuracy value reaching 93.8%, 93.4%, 93.3%, and 91.8% over the four MFs 40X, 100X, 200X, 400X respectively. Table A3 presents the validation accuracy, precision, recall and F1-score of the deep ensemble E7WV over the BreakHis dataset.

Comparison of the Deep Architectures
To compare the deep end-to-end, hybrid and ensemble learning architectures, we selected the two best ranked deep end-to-end architectures (DenseNet 201 and MobileNet V2), the deep hybrid architecture MDEN (DenseNet 201 for FE and MLP for classification) and the deep end-to-end ensemble learning model E7WV. Figure 4 shows the SK test results based on accuracy over the histological BreakHis dataset. The SK test results show 2clusters for MF 40X and 1 cluster for the MFs 100X, 200X and 400X. This

implies that the accuracy performances were not affected by the type of architectures used for the classification.

Moreover, it can be observed that:

- For MF 40X, the best SK cluster contains 1 end-to end architecture which is DenseNet 201 and that the last SK cluster contains the remaining architectures.
- For MF 100X, 200X and 400X, the best SK cluster contains the three deep architectures including the two selected end-to-end architectures DenseNet 201 and MobileNet V2, the deep hybrid architecture MDEN and the deep end-to-end ensemble learning architecture E7WV.

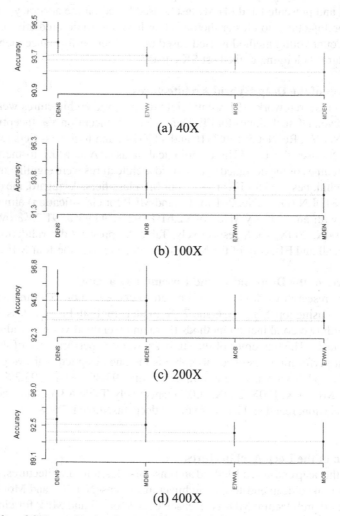

(a) 40X

(b) 100X

(c) 200X

(d) 400X

Fig. 4. Results of SK test for the deep end-to-end, hybrid and end-to-end ensemble learning architecture over the histological BreakHis dataset four MFs (40X, 100X, 200X and 400X).

To distinguish the best performing architectures, we ranked the architectures belonging to the best SK cluster as described in Table 4, using the Borda Count voting method. The results show that:

- The deep end -to-end architecture DenseNet 201 is ranked four times first (for the MF 40X, 100X, 200X and 400X).
- The deep end-to-end architecture MobileNet V2 is ranked second for the MF 100X, third for the MF 200X and furth for the MF 400X.
- The deep hybrid architecture MDEN is ranked second for the MF 200X and 400X and fourth for the MF 100X.
- The deep end-to-end ensemble learning architecture E7WV is ranked third for the MF 100X and 400X and fourth for the MF 200X.

Table 4. Borda count ranking fort the end-to-end and hybrid architectures of the best SK cluster over the BreakHis dataset.

Rank	40X	Rank	100X	Rank	200X	Rank	400X
1	DENS	1	DENS	1	DENS	1	DENS
2	–	2	MOB	2	MDEN	2	MDEN
3	–	2	E7WV	3	MOB	3	E7WV
4	–	3	MDEN	4	E7WV	4	MOB

To select the best performing architectures regardless the MF, we count the number of occurrences of the architectures (DenseNet 201, MobileNet V2, MDEN and E7WV). In case of a tie, we refer to the Borda Count ranking. As can be seen in Table 5, the best performing architecture is the end-to-end architecture DenseNet 201, since it appears 4 times in the best SK cluster and was ranked 4 times first. The following architecture is the deep hybrid architecture MDEN, it appears 3 times in the best SK cluster and was ranked 2 times second and one time third. The third architectures are both the deep end-to-end ensemble learning E7WV and the end-to-end architecture MobileNet V2 since it appeared 3 times in the best SK cluster and was ranked second, third and fourth.

To summarize, when using a hematoxylin and eosin (H&E)-stained histological BreakHis dataset, it is recommended to use the end-to-end architecture DenseNet 201 since it always appears in the best SK cluster and was always ranked first based on accuracy, precision, recall and F1-score for the four MF 40X, 100X, 200X and 400X. The end-to-end DenseNet 201 architecture achieved an accuracy of 94,9%, 94,4%, 93,1% and 93,1 for the MF 40X, 100X, 200X and 400X respectively. The performance of the end-to-end DenseNet 201 is highly related to the design of the dense block of its architecture that enables to learn discriminative features from images, reduce the vanishing gradient problem and provide a robust features propagation. The results of this comparative study advocate the use of the DL architecture of DenseNet for both feature extraction and classification [35].

Table 5. Appearance in the best SK cluster and Borda Count ranking over the BreakHis dataset.

Architecture	Appearance in the best SK cluster	Borda count ranking
DenseNet 201	4	4 times first Rank
MobileNet V2	3	1 time second 1 time third 1 time fourth
MDEN	3	2 times second 1 time third 1 time third rank
E7WV	3	1 time second 1 time third 1 time forth

4 Threats of Validity

The threats to this paper's validity with respect to external and internal validity are.

Internal Validity: For the validation of the deep architectures, 5-fold cross validation was used with four performance measures to evaluate the performances. All the deep architectures were trained using transfer learning for both FE and classification since the dataset used is not voluminous compared to the ImageNet dataset [36].

External Validity: In this study we focused on the histological pathological BC images since it is the gold stander for BC diagnosis. Regardless of that, we cannot generalize the obtained results for all the pathological images type and all histological images of other cancers. However, a good perspective for this study is to retest the proposed deep architectures using other pathological modalities and a private dataset.

5 Conclusion and Future Work

This paper presents and discusses the results of an empirical comparative study of deep end-to-end, deep hybrid and deep end-to-end ensemble learning architectures in order to study the impact of the DL models for FE and classification and whether to design ensemble learning models using end-to-end DL models. The developed deep end-to-end architecture were designed using seven DL techniques for FE and classification (DenseNet201, MobileNetV2, ReseNet50, InceptionV3, InceptionReseNetV2, VGG16 and VGG19) to classify the histopathological BreakHis. The Results showed that the accuracy results of the deep end-to-end architectures DenseNet 201 positively influenced the classification results since it outperformed the other architectures and reached an accuracy of 94,9%, 94,4%, 93,1% and 93,1 for the MF 40X, 100X, 200X and 400X respectively. The use of the DL model DenseNet 201 outperformed the ensemble learning and the hybrid architectures therefore it is highly recommended to be used in the digital pathological workflow to help the pathologist confirm their diagnoses.

Ongoing works intend to investigate the tradeoff performance and interpretability using DL models and unstructured medical datasets.

Acknowledgement. This work was conducted under the research project "Machine Learning based Breast Cancer Diagnosis and Treatment", 2020–2023. The authors would like to thank the Moroccan Ministry of Higher Education and Scientific Research, Digital Development Agency (ADD), CNRST, and UM6P for their support.
    This study was funded by Mohammed VI polytechnic university at Ben Guerir Morocco.
    Compliance with ethical standards
    Conflicts of interest/competing interests Not applicable.
    Code availability not applicable

Appendix A: Deep Architectures four Performance Measures Validation Results

Table A1. Accuracy, precision, recall and F1-score values of the deep end-to-end architectures over the BreakHis dataset.

MF	End-to-end architecture	Accuracy (%)	Precision (%)	Recall (%)	F1-Score (%)
40X	VGG16	91.46	90.15	93.14	91.60
	VGG19	90.33	88.99	92.04	90.49
	RES50	81.79	78.39	88.25	82.87
	INV3	91.53	91.02	92.19	91.59
	INRES	91.61	90.68	92.77	91.71
	MOB	93.40	92.60	94.50	93.50
	DENS	94.90	94.70	95.20	94.90
100X	VGG16	91.09	89.59	93.04	91.26
	VGG19	90.36	89.39	91.65	90.49
	RES50	80.59	76.87	87.61	81.87
	INV3	89.77	88.61	91.30	89.91
	INRES	89.77	88.38	91.58	89.95
	MOB	90.95	89.49	92.83	91.12
	DENS	94.40	93.20	95.80	94.40

(*continued*)

Table A1. (*continued*)

MF	End-to-end architecture	Accuracy (%)	Precision (%)	Recall (%)	F1-Score (%)
200X	VGG16	90.61	90.14	91.36	90.72
	VGG19	89.57	88.06	91.64	89.80
	RES50	82.80	81.29	85.50	83.30
	INV3	89.68	88.56	91.29	89.86
	INRES	90.79	89.89	92.00	90.93
	MOB	93.80	92.70	95.10	93.90
	DENS	93.10	91.40	95.10	93.20
400X	VGG16	88.18	86.65	90.34	88.38
	VGG19	88.02	86.31	90.42	88.27
	RES50	78.99	79.73	77.68	78.610
	INV3	89.23	89.23	89.29	89.20
	INRES	89.68	87.52	92.61	89.97
	MOB	91.00	90.00	92.20	91.10
	DENS	93.10	91.4	95.10	93.20

Table A2. Accuracy, precision, recall and F1-score values of the MDEN deep hybrid architecture over the BreakHis dataset.

MF	Accuracy (%)	Precision (%)	Recall (%)	F1-Score (%)
40X	92.61	91.52	94.09	92.75
100X	92.00	91.41	93.13	92.23
200X	93.93	93.10	94.97	93.98
400X	91.73	90.30	93.66	91.91

Table A3. Accuracy, precision, recall and F1-score values of the E7WV deep ensemble learning architecture over the BreakHis dataset.

MF	Accuracy (%)	Precision (%)	Recall (%)	F1-Score (%)
40X	93.80	90.90	97.20	93.90
100X	93.10	90.10	96.90	93.40
200X	93.30	92.50	94.40	93.40
400X	91.80	89.10	95.70	92.20

References

1. Sung, H., et al.: Global cancer statistics 2020: globocan estimates of incidence and mortality worldwide for 36 cancers in 185 countries. CA. Cancer J. Clin. **71**(3), 209–249 (2021)
2. Zhang, G., Wang, W., Moon, J., Pack, J.K., Jeon, S.I.: A review of breast tissue classification in mammograms. In: Proceedings of the 2011 ACM Symposium on Research in Applied Computation RACS 2011, pp. 232–237 (2011)
3. Zerouaoui, H., Idri, A.: Reviewing machine learning and image processing based decision-making systems for breast cancer imaging. J. Med. Syst. **45**(1), 8 (2021)
4. Gao, F., et al.: SD-CNN: a shallow-deep CNN for improved breast cancer diagnosis. Comput. Med. Imaging Graph. **70**, 53–62 (2018)
5. Almajalid, R., Shan, J., Du, Y., Zhang, M.: Development of a deep-learning-based method for breast ultrasound image segmentation. In: 2018 17th IEEE International Conference on Machine Learning and Applications (ICMLA), ICMLA 2018, pp. 1103–1108 (2019)
6. Khamparia, A., Bharati, S., Podder, P., Gupta, D.: Diagnosis of breast cancer based on modern mammography using hybrid transfer learning. Multidimens. Syst. Signal Process. **32**(2), 747–765 (2021)
7. Alkhaleefah, M., Wu, C.C.: A hybrid CNN and RBF-based SVM approach for breast cancer classification in mammograms. In: 2018 IEEE International Conference on Systems, Man, and Cybernetics SMC 2018, pp. 894–899 (2019)
8. Yan, R., et al.: Breast cancer histopathological image classification using a hybrid deep neural network. Methods **173**(February), 52–60 (2020)
9. Deniz, E., Şengür, A., Kadiroğlu, Z., Guo, Y., Bajaj, V., Budak, U.: Transfer learning based histopathologic image classification for breast cancer detection. Heal. Inf. Sci. Syst. **6**(1), 1–7 (2018)
10. Budak, Ü., Cömert, Z., Najat, Z., Şengür, A., Çıbuk, M.: Computer-aided diagnosis system combining FCN and Bi-LSTM model for efficient breast cancer detection from histopathological images. Appl. Soft Comput. J. **85**, 105765 (2019)
11. Zerouaoui, H., Idri, A., El Alaoui, O.: Assessing the impact of deep end-to-end architectures in ensemble learning for histopathological breast cancer classification. In: International Jt. Conference Knowledge Discovery Knowl. Eng. Knowl. Manag. IC3K -Proc., vol. 1, pp. 109–118 (2022)
12. Russakovsky, O., et al.: ImageNet large scale visual recognition challenge. Int. J. Comput. Vis. **115**(3), 211–252 (2015)
13. He, K., Sun, J.: Deep Residual Learning for Image Recognition (2016)
14. Szegedy, C., Vanhoucke, V., Ioffe, S., Shlens, J., Wojna, Z.: Rethinking the inception architecture for computer vision. In: Proceedings of the IEEE Conference on Computer Vision and Pattern Recognition, pp. 2818–2826 (2016)
15. Szegedy, C., Ioffe, S., Vanhoucke, V., Alemi, A.: Inception-v4, inception-resnet and the impact of residual connections on learning. In: Proceedings of the AAAI Conference on Artificial Intelligence, vol. 31, no. 1 (2017)
16. Chollet, F.: Xception: deep learning with depthwise separable convolutions. In: Proceedings -30th IEEE Conference on Computer Vision and Pattern Recognition, CVPR 2017, pp. 1251–1258 (2017)
17. Sandler, M., Howard, A., Zhu, M., Zhmoginov, A., Chen, L.C.: Mobilenetv2: inverted residuals and linear bottlenecks. In: Proceedings of the IEEE Conference on Computer Vision and Pattern Recognition, pp. 4510–4520 (2018)
18. Yu, X., Zeng, N., Liu, S., Dong, Y.: Utilization of DenseNet201 for diagnosis of breast abnormality. Mach. Vis. Appl. **30**(7), 1135–1144 (2019)

19. Zerouaoui, H., Idri, A.: Biomedical signal processing and control deep hybrid architectures for binary classification of medical breast cancer images. Biomed. Signal Process. Control **71**, PB, 103226 (2022)
20. Worsley, A.K.J.: A non-parametric extension of a cluster analysis method by Scott and Knott published by. Int. Biometric Soc. Stable **33**(3), 532–535 (2009). http://www.jstor.org/stable/2529369
21. García-Lapresta, J.L., Martínez-Panero, M.: Borda count versus approval voting: a fuzzy approach. Public Choice **112**(1), 167–184 (2002)
22. Mittas, N., Angelis, L.: Ranking and clustering software cost estimation models through a multiple comparisons algorithm. IEEE Trans. Softw. Eng. **39**(4), 537–551 (2013)
23. Mittas, N., Mamalikidis, I., Angelis, L.: A framework for comparing multiple cost estimation methods using an automated visualization toolkit. Inf. Softw. Technol. **57**(1), 310–328 (2015)
24. Idri, A., Bouchra, E.O., Hosni, M., Abnane, I.: Assessing the impact of parameters tuning in ensemble based breast Cancer classification. Health Technol. (Berl) **10**(5), 1239–1255 (2020)
25. Ibrahim, A., et al.: Artificial intelligence in digital breast pathology: techniques and applications. Breast **49**(December), 267–273 (2020)
26. Saikia, A.R., Bora, K., Mahanta, L.B., Das, A.K.: Comparative assessment of CNN architectures for classification of breast FNAC images. Tissue Cell **57**, 8–14 (2019)
27. Hameed, Z., Zahia, S., Garcia-Zapirain, B., Aguirre, J.J., Vanegas, A.M.: Breast cancer histopathology image classification using an ensemble of deep learning models. Sensors (Switzerland) **20**(16), 1–17 (2020)
28. Xu, Y., Goodacre, R.: On splitting training and validation set : a comparative study of cross - validation, bootstrap and systematic sampling for estimating the generalization performance of supervised learning. J. Anal. Test. **2**(3), 249–262 (2018)
29. Xiao, T., Liu, L., Li, K., Qin, W., Yu, S., Li, Z.: Comparison of transferred deep neural networks in ultrasonic breast masses discrimination. Biomed Res. Int. (2018)
30. Ying, X.: An overview of overfitting and its solutions. J. Phys. Conf. Ser. **1168**, 22022 (2019)
31. Idri, A., Hosni, M., Abran, A.: Improved estimation of software development effort using classical and fuzzy analogy ensembles. Appl. Soft Comput. J. **49**, 990–1019 (2016)
32. Kharel, N., Alsadoon, A., Prasad, P.W., Elchouemi, A.: Early diagnosis of breast cancer using contrast limited adaptive histogram equalization (CLAHE) and morphology methods. In: 2017 8th International Conference on Information and Communication Systems (ICICS), pp. 120–124. IEEE (2017)
33. Makandar, A., Halalli, B.: Breast cancer image enhancement using median filter and clahe. Int. J. Sci. Eng. Res. **6**(4), 462–465 (2015)
34. Perez, L., Wang, J.: The Effectiveness of Data Augmentation in Image Classification using Deep Learning (2017)
35. Zhou, T., Ye, X., Lu, X., Zheng, X., Qiu, S., Liu, Y.: Review article dense convolutional network and its application in medical image analysis. Biomed. Res. Int. (2022)
36. Carneiro, G., Nascimento, J., Bradley, A.P.: Deep learning models for classifying mammogram exams containing unregistered multi-view images and segmentation maps of lesions. Deep Learn. Med. Image Analy. 321–339 (2017)

Knowledge Engineering and Ontology Development

CIE: A Cloud-Based Information Extraction System for Named Entity Recognition in AWS, Azure, and Medical Domain

Philippe Tamla(✉)📧, Benedict Hartmann📧, Nhan Nguyen📧,
Calvin Kramer📧, Florian Freund📧, and Matthias Hemmje📧

Faculty of Mathematics and Computer Science, University of Hagen, 58097 Hagen,
Germany
{philippe.tamla,florian.freund,matthias.hemmje}@fernuni-hagen.de,
bha443@proton.me

Abstract. This research introduces an extended Information Extraction system for Named Entity Recognition (NER) that allows machine learning (ML) practitioners and medical domain experts to customize and develop their own models using transformers and a range of Cloud resources. Our system provides support for the entire process of managing Cloud resources, including hardware, computing, storage, and training services for NER models.

The paper discusses the design and development of two prototypes that target the AWS and Azure Cloud, which were evaluated by experts using the cognitive walkthrough methodology. Additionally, the paper presents quantitative evaluation results that showcase the promising performance of our NER model training approach in the medical domain, outperforming existing approaches.

Keywords: Natural language processing · Named entity recognition · Medical expert systems · Clinical decision support · Micro service architecture · Cloud computing · Cloud-based resources

1 Introduction and Motivation

With the evolution of modern text analysis, developing **Machine Learning (ML)**-based models to support standard **Information Extraction (IE)** tasks such as **Named Entity Recognition (NER)** remains a challenge for many users. Medical domain experts, in particular, face difficulties due to *"the abundance of unstructured textual data found in electronic medical records"* [33]. Unstructured data, such as text, pictures, videos, and audios are computationally opaque and challenging to query and process [52]. Furthermore, NER model training for medical usage suffers from the lack of appropriate training data (gold-standards) [29,40]. Creating gold-standards requires not only *"expertise in the respective domain ... and linguistic expertise"* [45], but also proficiency in

F. Coenen et al. (Eds.): IC3K 2022, CCIS 1842, pp. 127–148, 2023.
https://doi.org/10.1007/978-3-031-43471-6_6

programming languages like Java or Python, as unstructured data lack predefined or fixed rules to govern their content [8]. Training a NER model using an ML approach requires utilizing various technologies to successfully set up and run a series of **Natural Language Processing (NLP)** pipelines, such as data annotation and cleaning, as pre-processing steps of NER to guarantee a better performance of the trained model. Users without software engineering and ML experience may struggle with such preprocessing procedures [61]. Additionally, there are challenges related to storage resources and computing power when training NER models using ML, as NER often requires large amounts of gold-standards, which can take up significant amounts of space. NER also requires significant preprocessing steps that operate on data, such as tokenization, stemming, and stop-word removal. This can be computationally expensive and may require significant amounts of storage. Recent approaches for NER are making use of efficient algorithms, pre-trained models (such as transformers), and distributed computing resources originating from the Cloud. However, managing these resources to support NER in a Cloud environment remains a challenge for both novice users and ML experts. NER models must be able to handle large amounts of data and scale to meet the demands of a growing user base, while being efficient and effective.

2   State of the Art in Science and Technology

2.1   Named Entity Recognition

The first NLP frameworks featuring NER originated in the early 19901990ss [14] and many more NLP frameworks have been developed in various programming languages since then. NER is a sub-discipline of NLP and is an important technique used in **Clinical Decision Support Systems (CDSSs)** to extract knowledge from domain-specific, unstructured texts [23,38,44,57]. Medical notes are often generated when healthcare experts (such as clinicians or radiologists) are documenting treatments, trials or clinical tests during patient examinations or medical research in a **Electronic Health Record (EHR)** [30]. These notes are often written in medical free text documents, while having an unstructured nature and being difficult to extract [41]. Furthermore, healthcare experts generally face the problem of **Information Overload (IO)** [4] because *"the rapidly growing production of healthcare information"* can easily lead to an ever-increasing amount of information which can easily affect *"all actors of the healthcare system ... threatening to impede the adoption of evidence-based practice"* [31]. NER is a well-known IE used to address IO as it can extract unstructured data from free text documents. *"Medical named entity recognition (MNER) is an area in which medical named entities are recognized from medical texts, such as diseases, drugs, surgery reports, anatomical parts, and examination documents"* [67]. MNER can efficiently *"identify all occurrences of specific clinically relevant types of Named Entities (NEs) in the given unstructured clinical report. Using the named entity information, one can then analyze, aggregate,* *and mine for insightful patterns."* [33]. The extracted data can then be easily converted into coded (useful) information [42] and applied, for instance, to support **Information Retrieval (IR)** in a CDSS [44].

2.2 ML and Deep Learning in Named Entity Recognition

The evolution of ML and **Deep Learning (DL)** has made a major impact in many fields especially and including in the research area of **Human Activity Recognition (HAR)** and made our lives very simple. DL algorithms consist of multiple layers of artificial neural networks, which enables them to learn complex relationships and more nuanced patterns between inputs and outputs. This allows DL algorithms to outperform other ML algorithms that rely on a single layer of computation. Many established NER frameworks based on various programming languages (Java, Python) and featuring DL are already provided as open-source and can be used to develop and experiment on NER models. Well-known frameworks for NER include spaCy, TensorFlow, OpenNLP, NLTK, Stanza, AllenNLP, Stanza by Stanford University, Flair, Keras, BERT, PyTorch, ELMo). TensorFlow (from Google), PyTorch and ELMo have helped to extract medical texts and develop clinical NER tools such as ClinicalBERT [26], C-ELMo [69], ChemBERTa [13], BioBert NER [34,55]. Transformers are a type of neural network architecture that have been widely used to develop pre-trained models for NLP-related tasks. They were first introduced in a 2017 paper by Google researchers, "Attention Is All You Need", and have become very popular in many standard DL frameworks. Transformers are a type of DL architecture that uses self-attention mechanisms to process and understand the relationships between words in a sentence. This allows transformers to effectively capture context and semantic meaning, which is critical for NER. Incorporating transformers into NER frameworks leverages the powerful NLP capabilities of these models to improve the accuracy and performance of NER tasks. Additionally, the use of pre-trained transformers can save time and resources as it allows users to fine-tune existing models instead of training new ones from scratch. Transformers can optimize NER model training in a number of ways. A popular method is to use transformer-based architectures like BERT [60], RoBERTa [39], and GPT-2 [54] as pre-trained models, and fine-tune them on NER task-specific data. This technique enables comparison of the performance of different pre-trained NER models through fine-tuning. Devlin et al., point out the impact of hyperparameters on the performance of fine-tuned BERT-based NER models. Although optimal values are generally task-specific, they recommend using batch sizes of 16 or 32, learning rates (Adam) of 5e-5, 3e-5, or 2e-5, a dropout probability of 0.1, and 2 to 4 epochs of training [17]. Tai et al., tested the effects of other hyperparameters on variants of BERT fine-tuned on biomedical data. Their results show that the size of feed-forward and hidden layers affect the performance of fine-tuned NER models as well [60].

The hyperparameters that can be adjusted are dependent on the specific transformer and framework being utilized. For instance, in spaCy, the hyperparameters can be fine-tuned through a configuration file, following Thinc's configuration system[1]. In Keras, model-related hyperparameters are either passed to the constructor or to a model builder function. Training-related hyperparameters, such as the learning rate, can be subsequently set through the compile method of a concrete model instance[2]. Alternatively, a transformer-based architecture can be used as the backbone of an NER model, with additional layers added for sequence labeling, such as a **Conditional Random Fields (CRFs)** layer. However, transformers require significant computational resources, including substantial memory and processing power for storing the model, pre-processing and post-processing data, and model training.

2.3   Cloud Resource Management for Named Entity Recognition

Resource management and cost on the Cloud for model training is an important consideration as the Cloud can be more cost-effective and flexible than traditional on-premise infrastructure, but it also requires careful management to avoid unexpected costs. [51] present a comprehensive examination of the state of the art techniques for effective resource management and cost on the Cloud. Some key factors include: a) selecting the appropriate instance type (e.g. CPU, memory, TPU) based on your workload and size of your data, b) considering the size of your data, the frequency of access, and the retrieval time requirements when choosing a Cloud storage solution, c) monitoring your resource utilization and applying auto-scaling and auto-termination of resources to avoid over-provisioning and wasting resources, d) making use of pre-trained models to reduce the time and cost during training instead of training everything from scratch, e) applying cost optimization tools offered by Cloud providers (like AWS Cost Explorer, Google Cloud Billing) to monitor your usage and identify areas where you can reduce costs. Existing approach for Cloud resource management propose solutions for cost-awareness based on the Cloud resources [11], the quality of service requirements of applications, and the resource utilization of Cloud systems [5]. In [15] a framework based on multi-objective resource management for cost optimization and performance in the Cloud was introduced. This framework includes an online resource prediction system, that automatically *"anticipates resource utilization of the servers and balances the load accordingly"*, facilitating power saving, using minimization of the number of active servers, VM migrations, and maximizing the resource utilization.

Cloud computing resources can be used to support NER activities with advanced technologies such as transformers in several ways. Cloud instances such as **Central Processing Units (CPUs)**, **Tensor Processing Units (TPUs)** and **Graphics Processing Units (GPUs)** are often employed for Model Training, providing the necessary computational power for complex matrix operations required by transformers. CPUs are commonly used for smaller-scale ML models or pre-processing and data preparation tasks prior to training models on more powerful hardware. TPUs are specialized for ML workloads and developing

---

[1] https://spacy.io/api/data-formats#config.
[2] https://keras.io/api/models/model_training_apis/.

matrix operations used in DL, providing significantly higher performance compared to traditional CPUs for large-scale ML models. GPUs, originally designed for high-performance graphics computations, provide higher parallel processing compared to traditional CPUs and have been utilized for optimizing NER systems based on parallel processing and DL algorithms [12,47,58]. Once NER models are trained, they can be deployed and customized in real-time using various Cloud Computing resources to perform NER tasks at scale. **Virtual Machines (VMs)** can be configured with specialized hardware such as GPUs and TPUs to dynamically scale computing resources up or down based on the number of training jobs or the size of the data being processed. This accelerates the training of ML models. VMs can also serve at running grid search algorithms [24] or ensemble methods [9] that use hyperparameters to optimze the NER model performance. **Containers** allow the deployment of NER models in a lightweight and isolated environment, providing increased portability and scalability. They can be easily deployed and managed using platforms such as Docker and Kubernetes. Cloud storage resources (like Amazon S3, Google Cloud Storage [6]) provide a scalable, secure, and easily accessible solution for storing NER models and optimization data (like training and validation data) in the Cloud. **API-based access** is another method that can be used for hosting trained models as APIs, providing an easy access and integration of the NER functionalities into applications and services, without the need for any local installations. Established Cloud APIs (like Amazon SageMaker[3], Google Healthcare Natural Language API[4], Microsoft Azure ML API[5]) were used for serving NER models in different domains including healthcare [37], news articles [27] and finance [2]. Other popular Cloud resources used for NER model training are Cloud Functions and Serverless Architectures. They enable the deployment and optimization of models without the need for server management.

Many research approaches were proposed in the literature to support NER using Cloud Computing [7,10,46,50]. However, their main goal was primarily to improve the scalability and flexibility of the training process [10,46,50], while handling other aspects such as data privacy [7], usability [10], or service management [50]. In each of these projects, one single standard NER framework was chosen to experiment on trained models in the chosen Cloud environment. None of these proposed solutions were designed to integrate multiple standard NER frameworks which can bring multiple advantages for the end-user. Providing multiple standard NER frameworks in a Cloud environment can, first, increase the flexibility for users to choose the best framework suiting their particular needs. Second, users will have the ability to handle a wider range of NER tasks and being able to integrate their system with other cloud-based services more easily. This also brings scalability in handling large-scale NER projects. Domain experts can benefit from a tool that can enable an integration of established NER frameworks in the Cloud. For instance, clinicians in the medical domain will be

---

[3] https://aws.amazon.com/amazon/sagemaker.

[4] https://cloud.google.com/healthcare-api/docs/concepts/nlp?hl=de.

[5] https://learn.microsoft.com/en-us/rest/api/azureml/.

able to easily *select* and *compare* well-established NER frameworks, which will improve the accuracy in extracting relevant information from medical records.

2.4 Named Entity Recognition Frameworks

There is a large number of open-source NER frameworks and several papers have tried to compare them when used in different domains. Atdağ and Labatut compared various NER tools extracting biographical texts in Wikipedia [3]. Formal and social media texts were used in this research to compare the performance of the selected NLP frameworks. It was shown that standard toolkits like OpenNLP generally performed better on formal texts (like news articles) compared to more specialized tools (like Twitter NLP) that work well on social media texts. Weiying et al. found that the *"selection of the right NLP library is critical in developing an NLP-based application as it affects the accuracy of analysis tasks"* in their work, benchmarking NLP toolkits for Enterprise Applications [66]. In that research, CoreNLP and spaCy produced higher accuracy compared to other standard NLP frameworks, while spaCy is significantly faster than CoreNLP. SpaCy is an open-source platform for NER that provides a transformer-based model integrated within its framework and a comprehensive API that can be utilized for deployment in the Cloud. It was considered in [59] as *"a better and accurate Custom NER system"*. *"The spaCy-transformers framework provides the spaCy interface to combine pre-trained representations from transformer-based language models and its own NLP models via Hugging Face's transformers"* [28]. Being primarily a Python library, spaCy also provides a Cython-based extension [56] that can be used for performance-critical parts of the library, making it faster than other NLP frameworks relying on pure Python implementation support. Additionally, spaCy supports the programming languages R and Java Script via its spacy-js package[6]. Finally, spaCy supports two main data formats for model training, SpaCy JSON format, a JSON-based format used by the SpaCy NER library, and ConLL-2003, which is a tab-separated file format used by many NER frameworks [61]. CoreNLP is primarily a Java-based framework supporting various NLP tasks, such as tokenization, part-of-speech tagging, NER, sentiment analysis. This framework provides a number of pre-trained models for different natural spoken languages, including English, Arabic, Chinese, French, German, Italian, Japanese, Portuguese, and Spanish. CoreNLP support CoreNLP data format and can be also integrated with other programming languages (Python, Perl, Ruby, PHP, Java Script) through its integrated APIs[7]. As shown, multiple aspects can influence the performance of NER frameworks (such as target domain, programming languages, data formats, built-in NLP libraries), which make the comparison of standard frameworks very challenging. Also, the advances in ML and DL are leading to the development of new tools, making the selection of an efficient, easy-to-use NER framework time consuming and difficult for both data scientists and domain experts. A framework-independent

---

[6] https://spacy.io/universe/project/spacy-js.
[7] https://stanfordnlp.github.io/CoreNLP/api.html.

easy-to-use toolkit for NER is proposed by Florian et al. [20] to address this problem. Through an integration of their system in a knowledge management system, the authors aim at enabling data scientists and domain experts (like medical experts) to easily *select* and *compare* multiple NER frameworks before training new models to satisfy their need. A remaining challenge is however to enable utilizing Cloud infrastructures and resources that will provide access to cutting-edge NER frameworks (with advanced technologies like transformers), making it easier to compare them in a single application while supporting much more NLP-related tasks and use cases.

2.5   Related Research Projects

Many scientific research projects were also proposed in the literature to enable domain experts and non-ML experts to develop new NER models using ML. Dernoncourt et al. introduced "NeuroNER", where non-ML experts can easily annotate **NEs** using a graphical web-based user interface and use them to train their models [16]. Li et al. proposed an easy-to-use toolkit for various NLP tasks with DL support for NER [36]. DL, a very popular sub discipline of ML, *"has attracted significant attention due to its success in various domains"* and successful application in NER [36]. More and more standard NER frameworks (such as spaCy, Spark NLP, Flair, Stanza) have already included DL as a standard feature in their NLP toolset [35]. **Artificial Intelligence for Hospitals, Healthcare & Humanity (AI4H3)** proposes an **Information System (IS)** called KlinSH-EP [21], which is based on a **Knowledge Management System (KMS)**, called **Content and Knowledge Management Ecosystem Portal (KM-EP)**. KM-EP was developed at the University of Hagen in the Faculty of Mathematics and Computer Science at the Chair of Multimedia and Internet Applications[8] and the associated FTK e.V. Research Institute for Telecommunications and Cooperation (FTK) and was already used successfully to address the challenges of IO using NER in many research projects. One of them is the **Horizon 2020 (H2020)** project **Metaplat** [65]. It was built with KM-EP to manage a large amount of data in the domain of genomic research and to provide the software infrastructure for knowledge management. SenseCare [18] is an H2020 project in the medical domain. It was also built on top of KM-EP and tries *"to capture, analyze, and store information on emotional outputs in the aim of providing effective tools for caregivers and medical professionals to provide more holistic care to people with dementia"*. Another related project is **Recommendation Rationalisation (RecomRatio)** [63]. It aims to support medical experts making medical decisions by providing evidence-based textual arguments in the medical literature. Evidence is collected from relevant corpora, to make the evidence for or against specific treatments explicit in a knowledge base. Nawroth utilizes NLP, NER, and ML in his work [45] to make emerging knowledge from those corpora available for evidence-based medical argumentation Use Cases (UCs). Like Metaplat and SenseCare, RecomRatio relies

---

[8] http://www.lgmmia.fernuni-hagen.de/en.html.

on KM-EP to implement this knowledge base. Closely related to this research is **Stanford Named Entity Recognition and Classification (SNERC)**, which is also based on KM-EP. This tool aims at empowering domain experts to train and customize their own NER models and use them to support automatic document classification [61]. The recent evaluation of SNERC [62] showed it to be an effective solution for users to develop NER models for document classification. The evaluation also revealed a need for support for different data formats and integration with standard NLP frameworks for advanced users like data scientists and ML experts. To optimize SNERC and enable NER in the Cloud, we will develop a new system called Cloud-based Information Extraction (CIE). This system will be built using the established architecture of SNERC and KM-EP, with a focus on understanding user stereotypes, capabilities, and needs. The goal is to create a successful Cloud-based NER system that meets the unique requirements of users.

This section introduced the latest technologies, techniques, and tools related to this research work and the relevant research projects that inspired the development of our CIE system. The motivation for CIE's development is linked to various research projects. The following section details the modeling approach for CIE, including the use case diagram, component diagram, and Model-View-Controller (MVC)-based system architecture. Additionally, we will present the implementation and evaluation of two prototypes of CIE for managing Cloud resources to enable NER model training in AWS and Azure. These prototypes were evaluated using GERNERMED corpus [19], containing 8599 annotated records of medical NEs such as drugs, routes, strength, frequency, duration, form, and dosage in the German language. This evaluation allowed for the measurement of the prototypes' accuracy in identifying and categorizing these NEs within the medical domain.

3   CIE Modeling and Implementation

The modeling of CIE is based on User Centered Design (UCD) [32], a well-established approach for software design including four main phases [64]. First, "use context" specifies which users will use the product, and why. Second, "user requirements" aims at identifying any business requirements or user goals that must be met for the product to be successful. Third, "design solutions" is based on the product goals and requirements. This phase starts an iterative process of product design and development. Finally, "design evaluation" can be based on usability testing to enable product designers to get users' feedback for the product at every stage of UCD. Our **context of use** is driven by our goal of creating a system for data scientists and medical experts to effectively train and tailor NER models to their specific domain. The CIE **use cases**, shown in Fig. 1, expand upon the initial SNERC use case [62] by utilizing Cloud resources and transformers for model training. Using the existing SNERC features (outlined with fine solid lines), users can set parameters for managing their domain corpus prior to training, such as data cleaning, automatic corpus annotation,training and

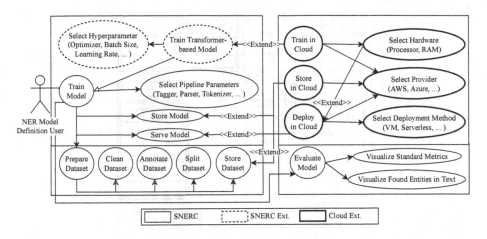

Fig. 1. CIE UML Use Cases Diagram.

testing set generation, and model training. We have added features for transformer-based model training, allowing users to customize various hyper-parameters (e.g. batch size, learning rates, hidden layers) and pipeline parame-ters (e.g. tokenizer, tagger). Standard NER frameworks like spaCy already pro-vide APIs[9] to customize such parameters during model training. In addition, cloud-based model training and deployment, marked in bold, is supported. This includes the selection of a Cloud provider, hardware components, and deploy-ment of trained models using strategies such as serverless, container, or VM. Figure 2 displays our component model for implementing the extended SNERC use case diagram. This includes added features for customizing pipelines and hyperparameters, as well as cloud-based model training. The new Hyperparam-eter and Pipeline Parameter classes, outlined with dashed lines, were added to the existing NER Model Definition Manager. These classes store all configura-tion data for pipelines and hyperparameters. To support cloud-based training and deployment, we introduced the Cloud Definition Manager, Cloud Deploy-ment Handler and Cloud Deployment Manager. Cloud-specific configurations relevant to training are set via the Cloud Definition Manager and stored in the Cloud Training Config class. Deployment-specific configurations are set via the same component but stored in the Cloud Deployment Definition class. Based on a Cloud Deployment Definition, the Cloud Deployment Handler deploys a model by calling an external Deployment Service of a Cloud vendor. The Cloud Deployment Manager oversees all deployed models providing features for mon-itoring, running jobs, stopping, restarting, and deleting deployments. Deploy-ments are internally represented as instances of the Cloud Deployment class. All new components are integrated into the overall system architecture along-side the existing SNERC components. The Cloud Definition Manager and Cloud Deployment Manager serve as controllers to support various view elements for

---

[9] https://spacy.io/universe/category/apis.

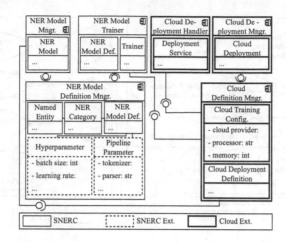

Fig. 2. CIE UML Component Diagram.

editing and viewing parameters for cloud-based model training and deployment. At the lowest level, the service layer, a new web-service, the Cloud Deployment Handler Service, is added. The service is used to deploy trained NER models via well-known Cloud vendors such as AWS or Azure. Cloud-based training is supported by an updated version of the NER Model Trainer Service. Compute Service, Storage Service and Deployment Service represent the built-in services that are generally provided by established vendors (such as AWS or Azure) to train, deploy and store ML models using Cloud resources. The next section summarizes the implementation and evaluation of two CIE prototypes launched in the AWS and Azure Cloud.

3.1   CIE AWS Implementation

The CIE AWS prototype was developed in [25] to cover a subset of the use cases shown in Fig. 1, including training transformer-based models, selecting hyperparameters, training and serving models, storing and splitting datasets, and visualizing standard metrics. The Cloud-related use cases covered by the prototype include storing data in the cloud, selecting compute resource components, and deploying models in the cloud. The model consists of several CIE components, which are depicted in Fig. 2. These components include the NER Model Definition Manager, Cloud Training Config Manager, and Cloud Deployment Manager.

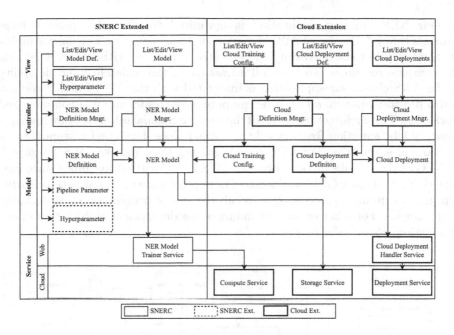

Fig. 3. CIE MVC-based Architecture.

Modeling. [25] implements a subset of the proposed CIE architecture components and is aligned with the Cloud extension architecture shown in Fig. 3, following the same MVC pattern and component allocation.

Implementation. We used spaCy as our NER framework to implement our system, as it uses the Hugging Face Transformers library, which provides a range of pre-trained transformer-based models [68]. The deployment architecture can be seen in Fig. 4, where the shaded box is developed using Python Flask[10], a lightweight Web framework that simplifies the process of building and packaging microservice web applications [70], making them easy to manage and deploy in a containerized environment. The Training Config Manager, Model Definition Manager, and Cloud Deployment Manager are realized as a training job controller that facilitates the inception and configuration of NER model definitions and Cloud Training Configurations. The Manager components are integrated into the Controller component through various classes. NER Model Definition and Cloud Training Configuration are also implemented as separate configuration classes. Users can configure compute resources and job parameters through the Web-based **Graphical User Interface (GUI)**, which then get saved in the configuration classes. The training corpus is split and uploaded to the AWS S3[11] storage service. The jobs run as a container task on AWS and execute spaCy training based on the provided configuration and the uploaded training corpus.

---

[10] https://flask.palletsprojects.com/en/2.2.x/.
[11] https://aws.amazon.com/s3/.

Our NER training application is optimized to efficiently process large datasets through the use of AWS dynamic load balancing [1]. This allows multiple training jobs to be queued up and executed in parallel, without overwhelming the compute resources. To take full advantage of the scalability and flexibility of the AWS cloud, our application is integrated with the AWS Batch[12] service, which provides on-demand scalable compute resources for running containerized workloads. This architecture removes the need for manual infrastructure management. A Job Definition Registry acts as a stand-alone database for keeping track of training executions. For CPU-based training jobs, we use AWS Fargate[13], while GPU-based jobs are executed on AWS EC2[14] virtual machines since Fargate doesn't support GPU workloads. Training jobs are executed within Docker containers running Python scripts to call the spaCy training on these compute environments. For a better understanding of the deployment architecture of our application, please refer to Fig. 4.

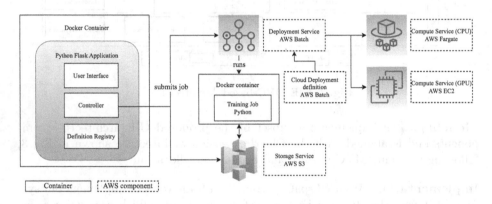

Fig. 4. CIE AWS: Deployment architecture.

The web application is also packaged in a Docker container, providing isolation and portability, and making it independent of a specific runtime platform. This also enhances security since only the required libraries are present on the system, and only the necessary application port is exposed. Additionally, containers conform to a largely standardized compute format, such as the Open Container Initiative [22], making them independent of specific Cloud providers. Using specialized services such as SageMaker can lead to increased vendor lock and dependency on the offered service, since certain functionality may be dictated or discontinued. SageMaker supports a limited number of frameworks and actions, making it unsuitable for some use cases. For instance, it currently does not support the spaCy framework. The AWS Batch service manages the complete lifecycle of the compute resources, including provisioning, execution, and

---

[12] https://aws.amazon.com/batch/.

[13] https://aws.amazon.com/fargate/.

[14] https://aws.amazon.com/ec2/.

tearing down container runtime environments. This creates a clear separation of concerns between the Deployment Service and other components.

Evaluation and Discussion. We utilize the application to train GERN-ERMED [19], a corpus of 8599 annotated medical records in the German language. This corpus includes entities such as drug, route, strength, frequency, duration, form, and dosage. We conduct training on a single g4dn instance of an AWS EC2 virtual machine, which features a single NVIDIA T4 GPU and 15GB of GPU memory. Our initial experiment focuses on assessing the execution time of training, along with the Precision (P), Recall (R), and F score (F), while varying independent variables such as number of CPU cores, batch size, window size, and the spaCy mixed precision setting. The Precision is the proportion of true positives out of all predicted positives. Recall is the proportion of true positives out of all actual positives. The F-Score combines P and R on a scale of 1 (perfect) to 0 (worst) [43]. For training our custom model, we used the pre-trained Roberta [39] model with the Adam optimizer and linear warmup scheduler. The training process was terminated after 1600 steps without improvement or 20,000 iterations of the entire training set. Table 1 displays the results of our first experiment. By utilizing the mixed precision setting, which is applicable to tensor processing units, we were able to reduce the execution time by 9.4%. However, increasing the number of CPU cores led to a significantly longer training process with slightly worse scores, compared to executing with the same settings on 1 CPU.

Table 1. AWS experiment 1: Model Training using pre-trained Roberta model [39].

CPU Cores	Batch Size	mixed precision	Window Size	Duration (minutes)	Precision	Recall	F-Score	GPU RAM	Cost
1	128	false	128	85	0.849	0.836	0.842*	<5GB	0.83$
1	128	true	128	77	0.84	0.835	0.837	<5GB	0.75$
1	256	true	256	76	0.835	0.827	0.831	<5GB	0.74$
1	512	true	128	51*	0.832	0.824	0.828	<5GB	0.49$
4	512	true	128	119	0.838	0.836	0.837	>5GB	1.16$

The second batch of training jobs utilizes the Bert Base Uncased model [17], demonstrating the ability to use various pre-trained transformer models in the application and compare their performance. Certain pre-trained transformers may be better suited for specific tasks. In this batch, the learning rate and training data split were adjusted to observe their effect on the model score. Additionally, mixed precision setting remained enabled, and all trainings used 4 CPUs and 1 GPU, with a batch size of 1024. The window size is set to 128. Table 2 shows the results of the training jobs, indicating that the Roberta model outperforms the Bert model slightly on this training set.

We conducted a comparative analysis of our training results with those of a previous study [19]. This study employed comparable methodologies, such as the spaCy framework, Adam optimizer, and a learning rate of 0.001 on an i7-8665U CPU. We achieved an F-score of 0.842, which is better than the previous study's results as shown in Table 3. However, our execution time is significantly higher. It's worth noting that we did not exhaustively explore all possible training configurations, so there may be more potential for improving both the score and execution time.

Table 2. AWS experiment 2: Model training using Bert Base Uncased model [17].

Learn Rate	Training Split	Duration (minutes)	Epochs	Precision	Recall	F-Score	Cost
5e-5	0.3	44	54	0.838	0.814	0.826	0.43$
10e-5	0.3	44	54	0.831	0.824	0.827	0.43$
15e-5	0.3	34*	41	0.827	0.815	0.821	0.33$
5e-5	0.2	55	61	0.831	0.823	0.827	0.53$
5e-5	0.25	55	65	0.832	0.826	0.829*	0.53$

Table 3. AWS experiment 3: Comparison of CIE AWS model training with GERNERMED scores [19].

Training approach	Processor	Duration minutes	P	R	F
AWS CIE implementation	GPU	85	0.849	0.836	0.842
GERNER-MED [19]	CPU	10	0.823	0.8079	0.8254

To evaluate the GUI features of the application, we conducted a second assessment using cognitive walkthrough methodology [53]. This evaluation was carried out with one NER PhD student and two data scientist experts - including a senior data scientist/PostDoc and an experienced NLP/Python programmer. The evaluation revealed some functional deficiencies in the GUI, including the requirement for retraining of models, compute profile recommendations, and extended model configuration capabilities. These issues will be tackled in future work to optimize the application's performance.

In the next section, we present our second CIE prototype implementation for the Azure Cloud.

3.2   CIE Azure Implementation

This application [48], following the use cases illustrated in Fig. 1, is designed to support NER experts and medical domain experts.

Modeling. Our system follows the CIE architecture shown in Fig. 3. Features include refining the spaCy model, configuring Cloud resources, and training models on the Azure Cloud.

Implementation. Figure 5 illustrates the deployment architecture of our system. The shaded boxes represent the Web application components that are wrapped inside Docker containers. Our frontend uses ReactJS[15], and the backend is built with FastAPI[16]. The backend of our system plays a crucial role as it manages the logic of the GUI and establishes connections to other Azure components enclosed within dash-borders. The application's GUI allows users to upload and select a domain corpus and manage (fine-tune) spaCy parameters. It includes List/Edit/View Corpus and List/Edit/View spaCy Configuration components respectively, as outlined in Fig. 3. The Controller layer consists of the Corpus Manager for processing corpora and the NER Model Definition Manager for processing the spaCy configuration. The domain corpora are stored in the Azure Blob Storage[17] using the Storage Service of Azure Cloud. The Cloud Training Config Manager manages the compute clusters through the Azure Machine Learning SDK for Python[18]. The Cloud Deployment Manager can send requests to the Deployment Service, which then uses the Azure Machine Learning Pipeline[19] to execute model training. The Storage Service manages the spaCy configuration file and corpora, and the Compute Service handles the pipeline and training process. The trained models are saved to Azure Blob Storage and the model's metadata is saved to Cloud Training Config.

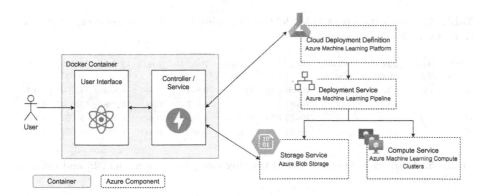

Fig. 5. CIE Azure: Deployment architecture.

---

[15] https://reactjs.org/framework.

[16] https://fastapi.tiangolo.com.

[17] https://learn.microsoft.com/en-us/azure/storage/blobs/storage-blobs-introduction.

[18] https://learn.microsoft.com/en-us/python/api/overview/azure/ml/?view=azure-ml-py.

[19] https://learn.microsoft.com/en-us/azure/machine-learning/concept-ml-pipelines.

Evaluation and Discussion. In our first evaluation experiment, we trained NER models on the GERNERMED corpus [19] using two different virtual machines. The first machine type, Standard NC6, is powered by NVIDIA Tesla K80 GPUs [49] and has 8 GB GPU memory at 1.20$/hour. The second type, Standard NV6, is powered by NVIDIA Tesla M60 GPUs [46] and has 12 GB GPU memory at 0.9 $/hour. In the first experiment, we trained different batch sizes [128, 256] using various transformer models to evaluate performance and execution time. We used the GERNERMED corpus with Adam optimizer and two transformer models: BERT uncased model [17] and RoBERTa [39]. The models were trained on the two compute clusters mentioned above, and the results are presented in Table 4. The shortest training time was 137 min, while the longest training time was up to 4 h. The models trained with RoBERTa outperformed those trained with BERT using the same configuration parameters. Additionally, the training process using the virtual machine Standard_NC6 with 8 GB GPU memory took significantly longer than the models trained on Standard_ NV6 with 12 GB GPU memory.

In our second experiment, we have focused on the impact of learning rates on model performance. All models are trained on a Standard_NC6 virtual machine with a batch size of 128. The RoBERTa transformer model is used due to its good performance in the previous experiment. The results are presented in Table 5, indicating that the learning rate parameter affects both the performance and the execution time of NER models. The experiment shows that the model with a learning rate of 3e-5 provides the best results but also takes the longest time to train.

Table 4. Azure experiment 1: Model training using Bert Base Uncased model [17] and Roberta model [39].

CPU Cores	Batch Size	mixed precision	Window Size	Model	Duration (minutes)	Precision	Recall	F-Score	GPU RAM	Cost
6	128	false	128	Ro-BERTa	137	0.844	0.844	0.844	12 GB	0.90$
6	128	false	128	BERT	150	0.837	0.84	0.838	12 GB	0.90$
6	256	false	256	Ro-BERTa	240	0.861	0.843	0.852	8 GB	1.20$
6	256	false	256	BERT	172	0.852	0.843	0.847	8 GB	1.20$

Table 5. Azure experiment 2: Model training using Roberta model [39] and different learning rates.

CPU Cores	Batch Size	Learn Rate	Window Size	Transformer model	Duration (minutes)	Precision	Recall	F-Score	GPU RAM	Cost
6	128	3e-5	128	Ro-BERTa	207	0.845	0.856	0.850	8 GB	1.20$
6	128	5e-5	128	Ro-BERTa	93	0.851	0.842	0.846	8 GB	1.20$
6	128	10e-5	128	Ro-BERTa	169	0.855	0.849	0.852	8 GB	1.20$

Table 6 compares our experimental results with the GERNERMED study [19], both of which utilized the spaCy framework for training. However, our implementation fine-tunes the model by adjusting the learning rate to 5e-5, instead of the default value of 1e-3 from spaCy, and using RoBERTa as a transformer model for the spaCy pipeline, running on GPU. In contrast, GERNERMED's model was trained on a CPU machine using the default configuration of spaCy. Our model outperforms GERNERMED's by achieving a 4.5% score improvement in F1-Score, as shown in Table 6. However, there is a significant difference in execution time between the two training methods.

As with the cognitive walkthrough evaluation described in Sect. 3.1, the GUI of this implementation was also reviewed by the same group of NER experts. The evaluation revealed weaknesses in the system's features and user experience, such as insufficient descriptions, missing information, and incorrect component headers. Future work should focus on addressing these issues and incorporating suggested improvements to enhance user support.

Table 6. Azure experiment 3: Comparison of CIE Azure model training with GERNERMED scores [19].

Training Approach	Processor	Optimizer	Learn Rate	Transformer model	Duration (minutes)	P	R	F
Azure CIE implementation	GPU	Adam	5e-5	Ro-BERTa	240	0.861	0.843	0.852
GER-NER-MED [19]	CPU	Adam	1e-3	None	10	0.823	0.808	0.815

4   Final Discussion and Conclusion

In this paper, we presented a Cloud-based IE system that helps both novice users and ML experts to train and manage NER models in their domain. Our system was developed using UCD methodology, which allowed us to identify and address the challenges of building such a system. We developed the features of our system using use case diagrams, components diagram, and an overall architecture based on the MVC pattern. We then developed two prototypes of our system for the AWS and Azure Cloud platforms, which were evaluated quantitatively using medical data. Our first prototype, CIE AWS, showed promising results in terms of model performance, demonstrating that the need for powerful hardware like GPUs can be eliminated with advanced Cloud resource management features. However, the cognitive evaluation of its GUI revealed some functional deficiencies, which require future work to improve. These include retraining models and extended support for Cloud resource management and framework settings. Our second prototype, CIE Azure, allows for user groups to fine-tune and train NER models using different hyperparameters and transformer models in the Azure Cloud. Its quantitative evaluation showed good performance of models trained by this implementation, and we suggested integrating CIE Azure into the KM-EP platform for future work. However, the cognitive evaluation of this prototype also revealed weaknesses in the GUI, which are related to the system's features and user experience.

In conclusion, our Cloud-based CIE system provides a user-friendly and scalable environment for NER model training and management in different domains. Our UCD-based approach allowed us to address the challenges of building such a system and develop prototypes for two popular Cloud platforms. Our evaluation results demonstrate the potential of our system and highlight the areas for future work to improve its functionality and user experience.

References

1. Agrawal, N.: Dynamic load balancing assisted optimized access control mechanism for edge-fog-cloud network in internet of things environment. Concurr. Comput. Pract. Exp. **33**(21), e6440 (2021)
2. Alzazah, F., Cheng, X., Gao, X.: Predict market movements based on the sentiment of financial video news sites. In: 2022 IEEE 16th International Conference on Semantic Computing (ICSC), pp. 103–110. IEEE (2022)
3. Atdağ, S., Labatut, V.: A comparison of named entity recognition tools applied to biographical texts. In: 2nd International Conference on Systems and Computer Science, pp. 228–233 (2013). https://doi.org/10.1109/IcConSCS.2013.6632052
4. Bawden, D., Robinson, L.: The dark side of information: overload, anxiety and other paradoxes and pathologies. J. Inf. Sci. **35**(2), 180–191 (2009)
5. Beloglazov, A., Buyya, R.: Energy efficient resource management in virtualized cloud data centers. In: 2010 10th IEEE/ACM International Conference on Cluster, Cloud and Grid Computing, pp. 826–831. IEEE (2010)
6. Bisong, E.: Google cloud storage (GCS). In: Bisong, E. (ed.) Building Machine Learning and Deep Learning Models on Google Cloud Platform, pp. 25–33. Apress, Berkeley (2019). https://doi.org/10.1007/978-1-4842-4470-8_4
7. Blohm, M., Dukino, C., Kintz, M., Kochanowski, M., Koetter, F., Renner, T.: Towards a privacy compliant cloud architecture for natural language processing platforms. In: ICEIS (1), pp. 454–461 (2019)
8. Boulton, D., Hammersley, M.: Analysis of unstructured data. Data Collect. Anal. **2**, 243–259 (2006)
9. Canale, L., Lisena, P., Troncy, R.: A novel ensemble method for named entity recognition and disambiguation based on neural network. In: Vrandečić, D., et al. (eds.) ISWC 2018. LNCS, vol. 11136, pp. 91–107. Springer, Cham (2018). https://doi.org/10.1007/978-3-030-00671-6_6
10. Chard, K., Russell, M., Lussier, Y.A., Mendonça, E.A., Silverstein, J.C.: A cloud-based approach to medical NLP. In: AMIA Annual Symposium Proceedings, vol. 2011, p. 207. American Medical Informatics Association (2011)
11. Chard, R., Chard, K., Bubendorfer, K., Lacinski, L., Madduri, R., Foster, I.: Cost-aware cloud provisioning. In: 11th International Conference on e-Science, pp. 136–144. IEEE (2015)
12. Chen, H., Lin, Z., Ding, G., Lou, J., Zhang, Y., Karlsson, B.: GRN: gated relation network to enhance convolutional neural network for named entity recognition. In: Proceedings of the AAAI Conference on Artificial Intelligence, vol. 33, pp. 6236–6243 (2019)

13. Chithrananda, S., Grand, G., Ramsundar, B.: Chemberta: large-scale self-supervised pretraining for molecular property prediction. arXiv preprint arXiv:2010.09885 (2020)
14. Cunningham, H., Tablan, V., Roberts, A., Bontcheva, K.: Getting more out of biomedical documents with GATE's full lifecycle open source text analytics. PLoS Comput. Biol. **9**(2), e1002854 (2013)
15. Dai, W., Chen, H., Wang, W., Chen, X.: RMORM: a framework of multi-objective optimization resource management in clouds. In: Ninth World Congress on Services, pp. 488–494. IEEE (2013)
16. Dernoncourt, F., Lee, J.Y., Szolovits, P.: NeuroNER: an easy-to-use program for named-entity recognition based on neural networks (2017)
17. Devlin, J., Chang, M.W., Lee, K., Toutanova, K.: Bert: pre-training of deep bidirectional transformers for language understanding. arXiv preprint arXiv:1810.04805 (2018)
18. Donovan, R., et al.: SenseCare: Using automatic emotional analysis to provide effective tools for supporting. In: 2018 IEEE International Conference on Bioinformatics and Biomedicine (BIBM), pp. 2682–2687 (2018)
19. Frei, J., Kramer, F.: Gernermed - an open German medical NER model (2021). https://arxiv.org/abs/2109.12104
20. Freund, F., Tamla, P., Reis, T., Hemmje, M., Kevitt, P.M.: FIT4NER - towards a framework-independent toolkit for named entity recognition. CERC, CERC (2023)
21. FTK: Artificial Intelligence for Hospitals, Healthcare & Humanity (AI4H3). R&D White Paper, Dortmund, Germany (2020)
22. Fu, S., Liu, J., Chu, X., Hu, Y.: Toward a standard interface for cloud providers: the container as the narrow waist. IEEE Internet Comput. **20**(2), 66–71 (2016)
23. Gavrilov, D., Gusev, A., Korsakov, I., Novitsky, R., Serova, L.: Feature extraction method from electronic health records in Russia. In: Conference of Open Innovations Association, FRUCT, pp. 497–500. FRUCT Oy (2020)
24. Habib, M.S., Kalita, J.: Scalable biomedical named entity recognition: investigation of a database-supported SVM approach. Int. J. Bioinform. Res. Appl. **6**(2), 191–208 (2010)
25. Hartmann, B.: Development of an application for the configuration of cloud resources to support NER model training with the spacy framework in the AWS cloud (2023, unpublished). Coursework at University of Hagen
26. Huang, K., Altosaar, J., Ranganath, R.: Clinicalbert: modeling clinical notes and predicting hospital readmission. arXiv preprint arXiv:1904.05342 (2019)
27. Jalbani, A., Memon, M., Memon, M., Depar, S., Koondhar, M.: A study of news recommender system using natural language cloud computing services. Sinh Univ. Res. J. **50**(2), 249–254 (2018)
28. Jiang, H., Hua, Y., Beeferman, D., Roy, D.: Annotating the tweebank corpus on named entity recognition and building NLP models for social media analysis. arXiv preprint arXiv:2201.07281 (2022)
29. Jonnagaddala, J., Chang, N.W., Jue, T.R., Dai, H.J.: Recognition and normalization of disease mentions in pubmed abstracts. In: Proceedings of the Fifth BioCreative Challenge Evaluation Workshop, Sevilla, Spain, pp. 9–11 (2015)
30. Juhn, Y., Liu, H.: Artificial intelligence approaches using natural language processing to advance EHR-based clinical research. J. Allergy Clin. Immunol. **145**(2), 463–469 (2020). https://doi.org/10.1016/j.jaci.2019.12.897
31. Klerings, I., Weinhandl, A.S., Thaler, K.J.: Information overload in healthcare: too much of a good thing? Z. Evid. Fortbild. Qual. Gesundhwes. **109**(4–5), 285–290 (2015)

32. Kling, R.: The organizational context of user-centered software designs. MIS Q. 41–52 (1977)
33. Kundeti, S.R., Vijayananda, J., Mujjiga, S., Kalyan, M.: Clinical named entity recognition: challenges and opportunities. In: 2016 IEEE International Conference on Big Data (Big Data), pp. 1937–1945. IEEE (2016)
34. Lee, J., et al.: Biobert: a pre-trained biomedical language representation model for biomedical text mining. Bioinformatics **36**(4), 1234–1240 (2020)
35. Li, J., Sun, A., Han, J., Li, C.: A survey on deep learning for named entity recognition. IEEE Trans. Knowl. Data Eng. **34**(1), 50–70 (2020)
36. Li, J., Sun, A., Han, J., Li, C.: A survey on deep learning for named entity recognition. IEEE Trans. Knowl. Data Eng. **34**(1), 50–70 (2022). https://doi.org/10.1109/TKDE.2020.2981314
37. Lin, B.Y., et al.: Triggerner: learning with entity triggers as explanations for named entity recognition. arXiv preprint arXiv:2004.07493 (2020)
38. Liu, N., Hu, Q., Xu, H., Xu, X., Chen, M.: Med-BERT: a pre-training framework for medical records named entity recognition. IEEE Trans. Ind. Inform. **18**(8), 5600–5608 (2021). https://doi.org/10.1109/TII.2021.3131180
39. Liu, Y., et al.: Roberta: a robustly optimized BERT pretraining approach. arXiv preprint arXiv:1907.11692 (2019)
40. Makino, T., Ohta, Y., Tsujii, J., et al.: Tuning support vector machines for biomedical named entity recognition. In: Proceedings of the ACL-02 Workshop on Natural Language Processing in the Biomedical Domain, pp. 1–8 (2002)
41. Mao, W., Chu, W.W.: Free-text medical document retrieval via phrase-based vector space model. In: Proceedings of the AMIA Symposium, p. 489. American Medical Informatics Association (2002)
42. Meystre, S., Haug, P.J.: Automation of a problem list using natural language processing. BMC Med. Inform. Decis. Mak. **5**(1), 30 (2005). https://doi.org/10.1186/1472-6947-5-30
43. Moosavi, N.S., Strube, M.: Which coreference evaluation metric do you trust? A proposal for a link-based entity aware metric. In: Proceedings of the 54th Annual Meeting of the Association for Computational Linguistics (Volume 1: Long Papers), Berlin, Germany, pp. 632–642. Association for Computational Linguistics (2016). https://doi.org/10.18653/v1/P16-1060. https://aclanthology.org/P16-1060
44. Nawroth, C.: Emerging named entity recognition supporting medical argumentation. In: KEOD, p. 9 (2020)
45. Nawroth, C.: Supporting information retrieval of emerging knowledge and argumentation. Ph.D. thesis, FernUniversität in Hagen, Hagen (2020)
46. Nawroth, C., Schmedding, M., Brocks, H., Kaufmann, M., Fuchs, M., Hemmje, M.: Towards cloud-based knowledge capturing based on natural language processing. Procedia Comput. Sci. **68**, 206–216 (2015)
47. Nguyen, L.T., Nguyen, D.Q.: Phonlp: a joint multi-task learning model for Vietnamese part-of-speech tagging, named entity recognition and dependency parsing. arXiv preprint arXiv:2101.01476 (2021)
48. Nguyen, N.: Development of an application for the configuration of cloud resources to support NER model training with the spacy framework in the azure cloud (2023, unpublished). Coursework at University of Hagen
49. NVIDIA: NVIDIA tesla-M60. https://images.nvidia.com/content/tesla/pdf/188417-Tesla-M60-DS-A4-fnl-Web.pdf
50. Pais, S., Cordeiro, J., Jamil, M.L.: NLP-based platform as a service: a brief review. J. Big Data **9**(1), 54 (2022). https://doi.org/10.1186/s40537-022-00603-5

51. Parikh, S.M.: A survey on cloud computing resource allocation techniques. In: 2013 Nirma University International Conference on Engineering (NUiCONE), pp. 1–5. IEEE (2013)

52. Patil, N., Patil, A.S., Pawar, B.: Issues and challenges in Marathi named entity recognition. Int. J. Nat. Lang. Comput. (IJNLC) **5**(1), 15–30 (2016)

53. Polson, P.G., Lewis, C., Rieman, J., Wharton, C.: Cognitive walkthroughs: a method for theory-based evaluation of user interfaces. Int. J. Man Mach. Stud. **36**(5), 741–773 (1992)

54. Qu, Y., Liu, P., Song, W., Liu, L., Cheng, M.: A text generation and prediction system: pre-training on new corpora using BERT and GPT-2. In: 2020 IEEE 10th International Conference on Electronics Information and Emergency Communication (ICEIEC), pp. 323–326. IEEE (2020)

55. Ruas, P., Lamurias, A., Couto, F.M.: LasigeBioTM team at CLEF2020 ChEMU evaluation lab: named entity recognition and event extraction from chemical reactions described in patents using BioBERT NER and RE. In: CLEF (Working Notes) (2020)

56. Saabith, A.S., Vinothraj, T., Fareez, M.: Popular python libraries and their application domains. Int. J. Adv. Eng. Res. Dev. **7**(11) (2020)

57. Savova, G.K., et al.: Mayo clinical text analysis and knowledge extraction system (cTAKES): architecture, component evaluation and applications. J. Am. Med. Inform. Assoc. **17**(5), 507–513 (2010)

58. Sharma, R., Morwal, S., Agarwal, B., Chandra, R., Khan, M.S.: A deep neural network-based model for named entity recognition for Hindi language. Neural Comput. Appl. **32**, 16191–16203 (2020)

59. Shelar, H., Kaur, G., Heda, N., Agrawal, P.: Named entity recognition approaches and their comparison for custom NER model. Sci. Technol. Libr. **39**(3), 324–337 (2020)

60. Tai, W., Kung, H., Dong, X.L., Comiter, M., Kuo, C.F.: exBERT: extending pre-trained models with domain-specific vocabulary under constrained training resources. In: Findings of the Association for Computational Linguistics: EMNLP 2020, pp. 1433–1439 (2020)

61. Tamla, P., Freund, F., Hemmje, M.: Supporting named entity recognition and document classification for effective text retrieval. In: The Role of Gamification in Software Development Lifecycle, p. 24. IntechOpen (2021). https://doi.org/10.5772/intechopen.95076

62. Tamla, P., Freund, F., Hemmje, M., Mc Kevitt, P.M.: Evaluation of a system for named entity recognition in a knowledge management ecosystem. In: Proceedings of the 14th International Joint Conference on Knowledge Discovery, Knowledge Engineering and Knowledge Management - KEOD, pp. 19–31. INSTICC, SciTePress (2022). https://doi.org/10.5220/0011374000003335

63. Bielefeld University: RATIO: Rationalizing Recommendations (RecomRatio) (2017). http://ratio.sc.cit-ec.uni-bielefeld.de/projects/recomratio/

64. Vredenburg, K., Mao, J.Y., Smith, P.W., Carey, T.: A survey of user-centered design practice. In: Proceedings of the SIGCHI Conference on Human Factors in Computing Systems, pp. 471–478 (2002)

65. Vu, B., et al.: A metagenomic content and knowledge management ecosystem platform. In: 2019 IEEE International Conference on Bioinformatics and Biomedicine (BIBM), pp. 1–8. IEEE (2019)

66. Weiying, K., Pham, D.N., Eftekharypour, Y., Pheng, A.J.: Benchmarking NLP toolkits for enterprise application. In: Nayak, A.C., Sharma, A. (eds.) PRICAI

2019. LNCS (LNAI), vol. 11672, pp. 289–294. Springer, Cham (2019). https://doi.org/10.1007/978-3-030-29894-4_24

67. Wen, C., Chen, T., Jia, X., Zhu, J.: Medical named entity recognition from un-labelled medical records based on pre-trained language models and domain dictionary. Data Intell. **3**(3), 402–417 (2021)

68. Wolf, T., et al.: Transformers: state-of-the-art natural language processing. In: Proceedings of the 2020 Conference on Empirical Methods in Natural Language Processing: System Demonstrations, pp. 38–45 (2020)

69. Zhou, Y., et al.: Clinical named entity recognition using contextualized token representations. arXiv preprint arXiv:2106.12608 (2021)

70. Ziade, T.: Python Microservices Development: Build, test, deploy, and scale microservices in Python. Packt Publishing Ltd (2017)

From Natural Language Texts to RDF Triples: A Novel Approach to Generating e-Commerce Knowledge Graphs

André Gomes Regino[1]([ORCID]) , Rodrigo Oliveira Caus[2], Victor Hochgreb[2] ,
and Julio Cesar dos Reis[1,3]

[1] Institute of Computing, University of Campinas (Unicamp), São Paulo, Brazil
andre.regino@students.ic.unicamp.br, jreis@ic.unicamp.br
[2] GoBots, Campinas, São Paulo, Brazil
{rodrigo.caus,victor}@gobots.com.br
[3] Nucleus of Informatics Applied to Education, University of Campinas, Campinas,
SP, Brazil

Abstract. The use of Knowledge Graphs (KGs) has gained traction in various software systems to improve data handling. E-commerce platforms, for example, have leveraged KGs to perform a range of tasks, including advertisement and product recommendation. However, generating accurate, trustworthy, and scalable RDF triples for populating KGs remains a challenging and error-prone task, especially given the lack of accurate and complete data. This article presents the QART framework, a natural language processing-based approach for generating RDF triples from e-commerce product Q&A. Our QART framework leverages templates to extract entities and intents and generates summarized sentences useful to populate KGs. Our experimental results demonstrate results concerning how we fine-tuned and used few-shots prompts in models such as T5, PTT5, GPT Neo and Bloom in an e-commerce dataset for the summarization task. Our evaluations identified key challenges in building the framework. Our contribution paves the way for the development of automatic mechanisms for text-to-triple transformation in e-commerce systems.

Keywords: Knowledge graphs · Natural language understanding ·
Text-to-Text transformations · Text-to-Triples · E-commerce

1 Introduction

Retail commerce has recently undergone a digital transformation, with several services previously offered in person now being conducted online. Consequently,

This study was financed by the National Council for Scientific and Technological Development - Brazil (CNPq) process number 140213/2021-0. In addition, this research was partially funded by the São Paulo Research Foundation (FAPESP) (grants #2022/13694-0 and #2022/15816-5). The opinions expressed in this work do not necessarily reflect those of the funding agencies.

F. Coenen et al. (Eds.): IC3K 2022, CCIS 1842, pp. 149–174, 2023.
https://doi.org/10.1007/978-3-031-43471-6_7

e-commerce has become the primary mode of product sales, increasing the volume of data associated with product visits, abandoned carts, purchases, and other relevant information. To improve user experience, researchers have directed their efforts towards exploring innovative techniques, including eye-tracking [30], recommendation systems [25], and chatbots [29]. In this context, Knowledge Graphs (KGs) have emerged as a popular and effective approach for representing knowledge.

Due to their evolutionary nature, KGs require constant updates as the knowledge they represent often changes over time. For example, in KGs related to biomedicine, new mutations are added and existing drugs are modified to reflect the evolving nature of the domain. In the context of e-commerce, significant changes also occur over time. For example, products may change their availability or compatibility with other products. Given this, there is a need for solutions that can provide KGs that are as credible as possible within e-commerce platforms.

Populating Knowledge Graphs (KGs) with accurate and dependable information can be complex. Manual input by domain experts often results in inconsistencies and is time-consuming. There are various available methods to tackle this challenge, such as knowledge base completion, knowledge base population, and ontology learning [2,3,12]. Knowledge base completion is designed to create new facts in KGs from existing knowledge [13,27]. On the other hand, knowledge base population and ontology learning from texts aim to extract knowledge from natural language texts and incorporate it into KGs. This approach is useful for identifying components in text and transforming them into triples, including entities, stopwords and actions.

NNatural Language Processing (NLP) techniques have been utilized and integrated to create text-to-triple conversions that accurately reflect the author's intended meaning [15]. Knowledge Graphs and Large Language Models (LLMs) are currently being combined to produce more effective textual outputs [5,9]. In e-commerce, such a conversion can aid customers in making informed decisions and influence their purchasing behavior. However, the challenge of automatically transforming natural language text from e-commerce platforms into valid RDF (Resource Description Framework) triple knowledge persists.

This article presents the QART (Question and Answer to RDF Triples Framework), a framework aimed at generating structured representations (RDF triples) from natural language texts that express facts in an e-commerce context. The primary objective is to construct RDF triples and populate a Knowledge Graph (KG) based on natural language texts from e-commerce customers. In this approach, RDF triples construction is based on previous NL questions answered by customers regarding sold products. The users' new questions use the knowledge stored in the KG to answer facts about the product, including its compatibility and specifications.

The framework is organized in three steps, composed of: 1) Automatic extraction of intents and entities relevant to the e-commerce context; 2) transformation of the original text into a summarized text, without abbreviations, with shorter and direct sentences. They must be suitable to be transformed into triples in the next step; 3) generation of RDF triples from the summarized text and adding them to an existing KG in place.

In this study, we present an extended and refined version of our preliminary investigation available in [21]. In the current study, we present several significant improvements. First, we improved the related work review by including additional studies addressing how to transform texts into RDF triples. This allows us a more comprehensive literature review and a deeper understanding of the state of the art. Second, we improved the framework methodology presentation, which now clearly differentiates between what occurs at design time and its functioning at run time. This helps the understanding of our proposal in transforming NL text into RDF triples. Third, in step two, we have explored the concept of templates for text summarization. We found that the templates can be very useful and be relevant as input examples for the refinement of language models. Now, we included novel experiments (cf. Sect. 5) using text generative models [6,8,19,24] to create summarized texts, which are transformed into triples. This provides a more comprehensive evaluation of our approach including further results. Finally, we improved the discussion of our findings and challenges to provide more insights and suggestions for future research directions.

The remaining of this article is organized as follows: Sect. 2 discusses the related work. Section 3 presents our proposed framework, its formalization and an application scenario with a practical example. Section 4 and Sect. 5 report on the evaluations performed to assess key steps of our framework. Section 6 discusses our findings and open research challenges to advance the development of QART in distinct research directions. Section 7 draws conclusion remarks.

2   Related Work

Comprehending and organizing information from natural language texts has been a persistent challenge in computer science and linguistics. With the introduction of formal structures like ontologies, which provide a semantic framework for representing knowledge, various tools have been developed to construct ontologies and RDF triples with greater precision.

The first of these technologies is FRED [12]. It utilizes various NLP techniques to convert multilingual texts into OWL and RDF graphs. The tool performs Named Entity Recognition (NER) to identify relevant parts of the text that can be converted into graph resources and Entity Linking (EL) to link existing resources in the graph with external resources in larger, more established graphs like DBpedia. It also uses Discourse Representation Structures (DRSs), a first-order logic language used for the initial representation of processed text.

Akter and Rahman [1] discussed two methods for extracting triples from not only NL generated texts, but any kind of raw text. *Syntactic parsing* - the first method - uses a tool named UDPipe [28] to identify the root of a sentence and the various subjects and objects connected to it, with each of these forming a part of the triples. This method was not able to identify compound objects. *The semantic role extraction* - the second method - uses a frame parser of the

Senna framework [10]. Senna outputs large chunks of text as subject and object arguments, which is a bad aspect of the semantic parser. The authors restricted some words by their type to reduce the length of subject and object (*e.g.* relative pronouns like 'which'). In addition, the authors created a small human-annotated gold-standard dataset to evaluate their tool. Their results achieved 34% and 46% of precision and recall measure, respectively in each method.

Lodifier [4] developed one of the first software tools to transform NL text into triples. The input text is first processed through the Wikifier Named Entity Recognition system (NER) to identify and map relevant entities onto DBpedia URIs. The relationships between these entities (the predicates) are then detected using the C&C statistical parser and the Boxer semantics construction toolkit, which generates Discourse Representation Structures (DRS). Subsequently, the text is lemmatized and individual words are disambiguated through the use of a Word Sense Disambiguation tool named UKB, enabling the creation of WordNet mappings. In this approach, the resulting data is explored to construct a RDF graph. This is subsequently enriched through the incorporation of both DBpedia URIs, linking the entities within the graph to the Linked Open Data cloud. The authors evaluated *Lodifier* in a comparison task, verifying if two newspaper articles talks about the same topic [4].

Seq2RDF [15] presents a machine learning model for generating RDF triples from text using DBpedia as a training dataset. The model leverages the encoder-decoder architecture of neural networks to form triples. Unlike FRED [12], this tool does not employ multiple text processing techniques but instead focuses on training a sequence-to-sequence model. One of the drawbacks of Seq2RDF is that it can not produce multiple triples per sentence.

Martinez-Rodriguez *et al.* [17] introduced a methodology to produce triples from unstructured text, irrespective of the language used. The first step focuses on feature extraction using the popular Stanford CoreNLP tool. It involves tokenizing and segmenting text to avoid splitting compound words. However, the authors encountered a challenge in identifying errors in sentences that contain grammatical and spacing errors, a problem we also face when handling e-commerce texts using QART. The second step is entity extraction, which involves identifying text entities by linking them to large datasets like DBpedia. Here, the text "Barack Obama" in a passage on international politics is linked to the corresponding resource in DBpedia. The next step is relation extraction, where the tool utilizes OpenIE to identify predicates of triples. Nonetheless, there are limitations as not all rules and standards are recognized. Finally, the representation step generates RDF triples. The tool proposed by Martinez-Rodriguez *et al.* only deals with named entities in the object, leaving out the generation of RDF triples with literals in the object.

Rossanez and dos Reis [23] have developed a semi-automatic tool that constructs Knowledge Graphs using scientific texts of a particular domain, namely Alzheimer's disease. The texts are simplified to eliminate redundancy, repetition, and abbreviations before being processed by the tool. The tool uses Semantic Role Labeling (SRE) to extract all triples from the sentences. These triples are connected to a public domain ontology of the Alzheimer's disease domain. In contrast, the QART framework generates KGs and associates them with an existing ontology. The triplifying process in the QART framework uses SRE to generate triples. However, instead of SRE, we employ a combination of templates and text generative models based on templates to summarize the text.

Our framework, inspired by Seq2RDF [15], builds a KG and maps it with an existing ontology similar to Rossanez and dos Reis [23], and FRED [12]. Unlike previous approaches, our solution trains neural network models using templates. In contrast to using only Semantic Role Labeling, our framework combines templates and text generation models to generate triples from NL texts. To the best of our knowledge, we are the first proposal to transform NL texts into RDF triples in a Q&A e-commerce context.

3   Framework QART

TIn this section, we introduce QART, a framework that can be used to convert natural language written texts into RDF triples. Our framework takes a set of e-commerce questions and answers, $D = \{d_1, d_2, ..., d_n\}$, as input and generates a set of triples, $T = \{t_1, t_2, ..., t_n\}$, related to the input data. The triples in T can then be added to an existing Knowledge Graph (KG), which is a directed graph consisting of nodes representing real-world entities, such as the "Eiffel Tower" and edges representing relationships between entities. Each RDF triple, t, consists of a subject (s), a predicate (p), and an object (o), and can be represented as $t = (s, p, o)$.

The methodology for converting NL texts into RDF triples is presented in Fig. 1. The framework consists of three main parts, each represented by a box labeled A to C in the middle of the figure. We provide a detailed description of each step in the following subsections. Subsection 3.1 explains the processing and field selection, Subsect. 3.2 describes the text-to-text transformations, and Subsect. 3.3 outlines our RDF tripling method from the summarized text. Algorithm 1 encodes all the steps of our framework. We also provide the corresponding lines in Algorithm 1 for each step.

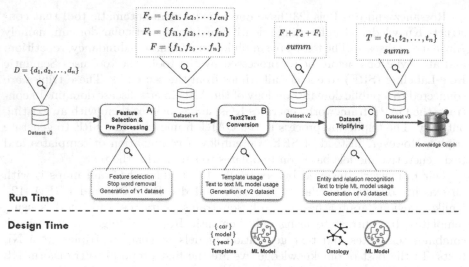

Fig. 1. QART Framework composed of three steps (rectangles in the middle of this Figure); a description of each step (rectangles in the bottom of this Figure); the content of each input/output dataset (rectangles in the top of this Figure); and other input data produced at design time (bottom of this Figure). D represents all the fields from v_0. F, F_i, F_e are the fields from dataset v_0, their intents and entities, respectively. *summ* is the summarized text and T is the set of produced triples. [21].

Algorithm 1. Transforming NL texts from a set of question and answers about products into RDF triples.

Require: D

1: $F \leftarrow chooseFields(D)$
2: $F \leftarrow preprocessFields(F)$
3: $F_e \leftarrow identifyEntities(F)$
4: $F_i \leftarrow identifyIntents(F)$
5: **if** $F \neq \emptyset$ **then**
6:     $v_1 \leftarrow F \cup F_e \cup F_i$
7:     $summ \leftarrow getSummary(v_1)$
8:     $v_2 \leftarrow mergeColumns(v_1) \cup summ$
9:     $v_3 \leftarrow triplifyDataset(v_2)$
10:     **if** $v_3 \neq \emptyset$ **then**
11:         **return** $v_3.t$
12:     **end if**
13: **end if**

To illustrate our methodology, we provide a specific example of a triple generated by processing a natural language question from an e-commerce Q&A. In particular, the used NL text relates to a user question about the compatibility between a product sold by a store (p_1) and an item possessed by the consumer (*ci*). From now on, we name it the "consumer item". Figure 2 shows an instantiated version of Fig. 1, describing how QART generates a triple from the questions and the answers asked about a product (in the example, we explore the product "Motorcycle Battery 5 ah").

3.1   Step A: Field Selection and Pre-processing

Our system takes as input a dataset (v_0) comprising all customer interactions in an e-commerce setting, including product evaluations, account creations, purchases, questions, and answers (shown in the blue rectangle in Fig. 2). D represents the set of all fields present in v_0. For the purpose of this example, Fig. 2 only presents part of the whole v_0 dataset. We consider, for instance, a pair of question and answering in NL text such as question: "Does this motorcycle battery fit on my CG 150 Titan KS?" along with the answer "Yes, the products are compatible" and the purchase of the motorcycle battery made by the customer (original text translated to English language by the authors).

Using the content of dataset v_0 as input, Algorithm 1 asks the user for the dataset fields to be used to construct the triples (line 2 of Algorithm 1). The contents of the selected fields undergo a pre-processing step (line 3 of Algorithm 1) to eliminate any noisy data that does not contribute to the meaning of the text or the triple construction in later steps. Noisy data may include stop-words, abbreviations, greetings, and punctuation.

Algorithm 1 starts by filling F with pre-processed selected fields from v_0 and identifying entities and intents from these fields in lines 1 to 4. Intents represent the types of actions mentioned in one or more sentences. In an e-commerce context, there are user sentences that refer to purchase intent ("I would like to buy two units of this shoe"), product availability intent ("Do you have it in blue?"), and shipping intent ("What is the shipping value to São Paulo?"). Identifying intents is crucial in determining the type of triples t generated and stored in the KG in step C of QART, such as purchase or availability.

Entities are pieces of information in sentences that are affected by the intents. In an e-commerce scenario, entities may include product specifications, such as size, weight, model, year of manufacture, and voltage, among others. The QART framework uses entities as resources of the triples in step C (s and o of each t). The set of all chosen fields $F = \{f_1, f_2, ...f_n\}$, the entities from these fields $F_e = \{f_{e1}, f_{e2}, ..., f_{en}\}$ and the intents from the fields $F_i = \{f_{i1}, f_{i2}, ..., f_{in}\}$ forms the dataset v_1.

In this section, we use a running example illustrated in Fig. 2. The v_0 dataset has several fields, but the user (e.g., an ontology maintainer) defines at runtime that only the title, the question, and the answer fields are necessary for the triple generation task ($F = \{$"$ProductName$", "$Question$", "$Answer$"$\}$) (line 1 of Algorithm 1). Figure 2 (green rectangle) shows these three attributes related to the "*Motorcycle Battery 5 ah*" product (p_1). From these three attributes, the framework proceeds to the task of finding important parts in the text: the entities and intents. Figure 2 presents that the identified intent of the text is "compatibility" and the entities are "car name", "model", and "year". Together with the three original fields ("Product Name", "Question", "Answer"), these fields form the v_1 dataset (green rectangle).

In the QART framework, questions asked by clients are classified into two categories based on their intent: stable and mutable. Stable intent questions have responses that remain relatively constant over time, while mutable intent questions can have responses that vary frequently. For example, in the e-commerce domain, product specification, and compatibility are stable intent questions, while product availability and shipping options are mutable intent questions. Categorizing questions based on their intent is crucial in defining the scope of knowledge addressed by the resulting KG. Stable intent questions lead to stable triples in the KG, while mutable intent questions generate triples that can change over time. A different approach is needed to address mutable intent questions, such as using Temporal Knowledge Graphs [22]. Step A of the QART framework deals with triples arising from stable intents and performs this categorization.

3.2   Step B: Text2Text Conversion

The second rectangle in the center of Fig. 1 represents Step B, which takes v_1 as input. In this step, QART generates a concise and informative text (v_2) by summarizing the most relevant fields from v_1. The rationale is that generating triples from summarized, condensed, and factual texts can be something positive, facilitating the generation of triples in Step C.

Algorithm 1 uses line 7 to select fields from the v_1 dataset and condense them into a single field labeled *summ*. The resulting v_2 dataset includes two fields: the complete text that comprises questions, answers, intents, and entities gathered from the v_1 dataset, and a summarized version represented by the *summ* field (line 8 of Algorithm 1).

To summarize the text, the QART framework uses templates and pre-trained machine learning models, text generation models specifically. The use of templates is based on filling the summarized texts *summ* with entities F_e. Choosing the appropriate template for each *summ* is based on the F_i intent found in the question/answer pair. The templates serve as input to a machine learning model that are trained to generate the summarized text. At run time, the framework uses the chosen machine learning model to perform the text to text transformation. The template filling, model training and model evaluation are performed during design time (cf. Fig. 1). Section 5 describes our experiments to identify the model that better fits the framework process.

Using the example from Fig. 2, the summarized column contains text capable of briefly expressing the content of the columns referring to the title, question, and answer of the motorcycle battery product (field "Summarized Text", red rectangle of Fig. 2). For this text-to-text transformation, the framework generates *summ* "The Motorcycle Battery 5 ah is compatible with CG 150 Titan KS 2004/2005", summarizing that the product p_1 entitled "Motorcycle Battery 5 ah" is compatible with the customer item *ci* "CG" model "Titan KS" with the year "2004/2005". The v_2 dataset is filled with all these fields (and their intents) and *summ*. In summary, from the v_1 dataset, we have a v_2 filled with

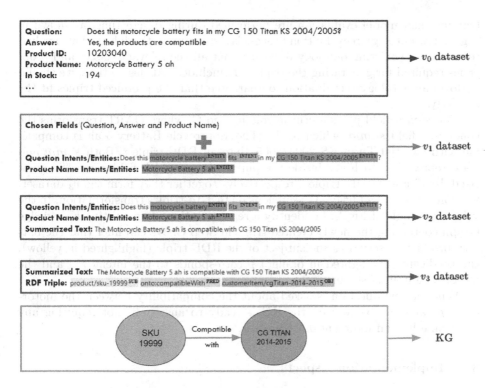

Fig. 2. Example of QART functioning examplified with the use of one product and one related question and answer. The blue rectangle illustrates the v_0 dataset; the green rectangle represents v_1 dataset, the red rectangle represents v_2 dataset and the pink illustrates v_3 dataset. The yellow rectangle indicates the resulting triple t that is added to the existing KG [21]. (Color figure online)

summarized texts suitable to be transformed into a triple in the next step. Step B is where the original texts are transformed into a "factual text', easier to be addressed as a RDF triple and added to a KG.

3.3   Step C: Text Triplifying

The dataset v_2 serves as an input to Step C, which is the dataset triplifying. This transforms the summarized facts *summ*, into triples t (line 9 of Algorithm 1). The fact *summ* must contain statements with intent of the stable type, described in Sect. 3.1.

The triplifying task is addressed using the Semantic Role Labeling (SRL) technique [16], which identifies subject, predicate, and object of the summarized facts *summ* and machine learning text to triple transformation. This generates the dataset v_3. Triples, part of the v_3 dataset, are returned by the algorithm to be added in the KG. At run time, the framework uses the chosen machine learning model and the SRL to generate triples. The ontology reevaluation, model training, and model evaluation are performed during design time, as shown in Fig. 1. The ontology reevaluation process is a step our methodology that involves reviewing the existing ontology to ensure that all the relevant classes and properties required for generating the triples are included. At design time, we should perform an ontology reevaluation to guarantee that the produced triples fit the ontology.

The *summ* field plays a crucial role in step C, where QART transforms the condensed field *summ*, which reads "The Motorcycle Battery 5 ah is compatible with CG 150 Titan KS 2004/2005" into an RDF triple t. Both *summ* and t are represented in Fig. 2 inside the pink rectangle, with field name "Summarized Text" and "RDF Triple", respectively. Together they form the v_3 dataset. Section 6 presents additional discussions on text-to-triples transformation. In the yellow rectangle of Fig. 2, we identify a representation of an existing Knowledge Graph containing the newly created triple in Step C. We can infer that the battery product p_1 serves as the subject of the RDF triple (highlighted in yellow), the predicate (highlighted in orange) p corresponds to the intent f_{i1}, and the motorcycle item ci serves as the object o.

When a new question is asked about the compatibility between the motorcycle p_1 and the battery c_i, the KG is ready to answer it, not requiring any additional human intervention to answer.

3.4   Implementation Aspects

For Step A, the framework uses RASA [26], a conversational AI platform to identify the intents (F_i) and entities (F_e) of the chosen attributes after preprocessing (green rectangle in Fig. 2). Through the use of a word embeddings model, RASA identifies the intention expressed by a given input phrase. In this case, the question asked by the client. To identify entities, we use models based on Conditional Random Fields [14].

For Step B, the generation of *summ* is achieved using templates and machine learning models. Table 1 shows template examples. All templates use the same entities, and there is more than one template for each intent. The choice to create more than one template per intent is motivated by introducing linguistic variability in step B. We understand that the more diverse the templates are in linguistic terms, the lower the chance of bias. Table 1 presents that an intent is capable of generating numerous summarized texts with linguistic variability. The four templates by each template have the same meaning, using different words.

Templates can be used to fine-tune text generation models (such as GPT 2 [18] or T5 [20]), create a large volume of data, and form artificial datasets. Section 5 presents further aspects regarding experimental evaluation using text generation models.

For Step C, QART processes *sum* using Semantic Role Labeling from IBM Watson [11] and the resulting triples are in n-triples format[1].

---

[1] https://www.w3.org/TR/n-triples.

4   Evaluating Template-Based Text Summarization

This section evaluates part of step B of the QART, which transforms a text composed of the question and answer into a summarized text. We measure the quality of the sentences generated using templates based on the number of correctly identified intents and entities. The entities and intents identified by evaluators are compared with those detected by QART. We utilize real compatibility questions and answers from a Brazilian e-commerce platform. The templates' quality directly impacts the quality of the summarized texts and the triples generated in the last phase of the framework. These summarized texts represent stable facts, as discussed in Sect. 3.1, that are transformed into triples in subsequent steps of the framework. In this evaluation, we focus on compatibility Q&A, an example of a stable type of intent.

4.1   Setup and Procedures

As our first step, we created a dataset that contains questions asked about the products by the customer and answers from the attendant. Through step 2 of QART we generated summarized texts using templates. The summarized text should succinctly express the question's intent, the entities, and the answer's intent. For instance, in a query with a compatibility objective, the answer must confirm or deny the compatibility between the product p_1 and the consumer's item ci, thereby revealing its intent.

We gathered a dataset of 3737 questions with different intent types from the top ten stores on the marketplace platform. These questions were asked between January and February 2022. Subsequently, we randomly selected 20 questions and corresponding answers from each of these ten stores, which led to a total of 200 real-life examples of e-commerce questions asked by customers who are GoBots users. The dataset containing these 200 examples should contain examples whose question intent was of the compatibility type, which is the focus of this experimental evaluation. In Sect. 6, we will explore the challenges associated with addressing other types of intents.

Along with the creation of the evaluation dataset, we also generated a set of templates (see Table 1). These templates were paired with each of the 200 sentences from the evaluation dataset to produce a summarized sentence. Each

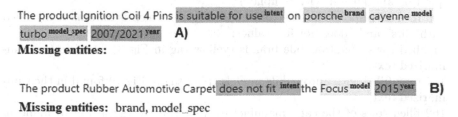

Fig. 3. Two examples of summarized texts and their intents and entities [21]. (Color figure online)

template has a specific response intent (column 1 in Table 1) and related content (column 2 in Table 1). The content includes placeholders (enclosed in square brackets) where the entities are inserted to generate the final summarized text.

Table 1. List of all templates used in the evaluation. The first column represents the answer intent. The second column shows the templates, four for each type of answer intent [21].

Intent	Template
fits	The product [PROD] is compatible with [BRAND] [MODEL] [MODEL_SPEC] [YEAR]
	This product [PROD] fits in [BRAND] [MODEL] [MODEL_SPEC] [YEAR]
	The car [BRAND] [MODEL] [MODEL_SPEC] [YEAR] is compatible with [PROD]
	The product [PROD] is suitable for use in [BRAND] [MODEL] [MODEL_SPEC] [YEAR].
no fit	The product [PROD] is incompatible with [BRAND] [MODEL] [MODEL_SPEC] [YEAR]
	The product [PROD] does not fit in [BRAND] [MODEL] [MODEL_SPEC] [YEAR]
	The car [BRAND] [MODEL] [MODEL_SPEC] [YEAR] is incompatible with [PROD]
	The product [PROD] is not suitable for use in [BRAND] [MODEL] [MODEL_SPEC] [YEAR]

There are four templates for each response intent type, resulting in a total of eight templates. The intention "fits" refers to affirmative responses regarding the compatibility between the consumer's item and the product; and "does not fit" refers to products and consumer items that are not compatible. Once the response intent is identified, one of the four templates available for that intent is chosen randomly to generate the summarized sentence. The dataset with 200 summarized texts is generated by processing the dataset used in this evaluation containing 200 compatibility questions and answers with the dataset containing the eight templates.

Figure 3 shows two examples of summarized texts and fields used for the evaluation. The example (A in Fig. 3) states that the consumer item fits the product (intent). Each entity of the consumer item is identified by different colors. The example (B in Fig. 3) presents a "does not fit" intent, two entities from the consumer item (model and year) and two missing entities in the summarized text. The v2 evaluation dataset generated by QART contains the following data:

- 200 rows of summarized texts, based on the combination of product title, question and answer with templates;
- 200 rows of response intents (red tag in Fig. 3), which is automatically filled with "fits" and "does not fit" values;
- 41 filled rows of automobile brands (yellow tag in Fig. 3) found in the summarized text;
- 187 rows filled with automobile models (pink tag in Fig. 3) found in the summarized text;
- 162 filled rows of the car's manufacture year (purple tag in Fig. 3) found in the summarized text;

Each of the entities has values less than 200 due to the QART framework not being able to find such entities in the summarized text; observe the missing entities from the example B in Fig. 3. It is part of this assessment to determine how many of these missing fields were erroneously unidentified; and fields that were identified as a particular entity but belonged to a different entity classification.

Gold Standard. This evaluation was only possible due to the comparison against a gold standard dataset created a priori. The gold standard was composed of 200 sets of questions and answers, 200 intent classification ("fits", "does not fit", "not a compatibility question") and 508 annotated entities ("brand", "model", and "year"). To identify the intent of the answers and the four different entities in each pair, we enlisted six independent evaluators who possessed prior experience in Artificial Intelligence. Each evaluator analyzed a random set of intents and entities.

4.2   Results

The accuracy, precision, and recall of QART in comparison to the gold standard are presented through the results shown in Table 2 for intent classification and Table 3 for entity discovery.

Table 2. Results of a comparison between the intents in the gold standard and the predicted values from QART, as assessed by a set of evaluators, for a Brazilian e-commerce platform. The comparison is presented in terms of three categories: fits, does not fit, and no compatibility. The table clearly shows the number of compatibility assessments falling into each category, including the total number of assessments made. The data used in this table is taken from [21].

		Gold Standard			
		fits	does not fit	no compatibility	Total
QART	fits	135	7	5	147
	does not fit	4	44	5	53
	Total	139	51	10	200

Table 2 presents the intersection between the QART results and the annotated results in the gold standard, divided into "fits" and "does not fit" columns and "fits", "does not fit" and "is not a compatibility question" rows. Each cell shows the sum of the intersection between the results, indicating how many cases the QART correctly identified the intent of the answer. The analysis of the table reveals that the QART correctly identified 135 cases in which the consumer item fits the product, and 44 cases in which the framework correctly detected incompatibility between ci and p (i.e., "does not fit"). The True Positive and True

Negative cases showed that the QART obtained 179 out of 200 compatibility intentions (89.5%).

Among the 10.5% of erroneously categorized cases, according to Table 2, we have 4 cases (2%) in which the QART incorrectly categorized the intention of the response as "does not fit", classified as False Negative cases. The opposite situation occurs in another 7 cases (3.5%), erroneously categorizing intent as "fits", classified as False Positive cases.

The third column of Table 2 represents the remaining cases with classification errors made by the framework (5%). The framework incorrectly classified ten questions with other intentions (such as thanks, shipping, and availability) as compatibility questions. Based on the results presented in Table 2, Eq. 1 and Eq. 2 illustrate the weighted precision and recall.

The members of Eq. 1 are, respectively, the precision of "fits" cases (P_F), the precision of "does not fit" (P_{NF}) and the precision of "not compatibility question" (P_{NC}). The recall is calculated by Eq. 2 with three weighted recalls (R_F, R_{NF}, and R_{NC}). The weighted average is used instead of a simple average because the three classes (F, NF, and NC) are not balanced.

$$Precision_W = P_F + P_{NF} + P_{NC} = 85.00\% \tag{1}$$

$$Recall_W = R_F + R_{NF} + R_{NC} = 89.5\% \tag{2}$$

The accuracy results of the QART in identifying the three entities are presented in Table 3. Based on Eq. 3, the QART accurately identified 516 entities (86%) out of the 600 entities (200 brands, 200 models, and 200 years) in the gold standard. Each of the 200 summarized texts contained 0 to 3 entities, and the QART correctly identified all three entities in 135 cases (67.5%). There were 50 cases (25%) in which two entities were correctly identified, 11 cases (5.5%) in which only one entity was correctly identified, and 4 cases (2%) in which no entity was correctly identified.

$$Accuracy = \frac{TP + TN}{AllOccurrences} = \frac{516}{600} = 86\% \tag{3}$$

Table 3. Results of the comparison between 3 entities (brand, model and year) in gold standard and predicted values from QART [21].

	Brand	Model	Year	Total
Total	183	168	165	516
%	91,5	84,0	82,5	86,0

Figure 4 shows two real-world examples of triples generated from the *summ* text of this evaluation.

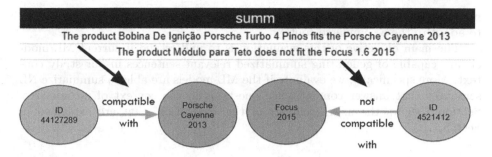

Fig. 4. Example of two triples created from *summ* texts. The first triple shows a compatible product and the second triple an incompatible product [21].

4.3   Discussion

We understand that high precision and recall in intent results and high accuracy in entity results indicate good quality in the generated templates. The first observation is that only 5% of questions were incorrectly categorized as compatibility questions, demonstrating the framework's ability to correctly identify intent. The second finding is that the framework can classify responses as "fits" or "does not fit" with an 85% accuracy rate, in addition to identifying compatibility intent.

The third observation concerns the entities. The entity with the highest accuracy was brand, with 91.5%, whereas the one with the lowest accuracy was the year, with 82.5%. We believe this discrepancy is due to the nature of each field, with the brand being a simple text field and the year being more complex due to differences in syntax and semantics. The year field can have different representations, such as "1994" and "94", with varying separators (e.g., "/", "-"), ranges ("1994 to 1998"), and may be confused with other car features ("1.8", "180 horsepower").

The fourth finding refers to the positive result of the accuracy of 86% of correctly identified entities and 92.5% of cases with two or more correctly identified entities. Some products and cars have very specific compatibilities, serving only a particular model, brand, and year. Thus, the more the proposal can identify all the entities of a compatibility phrase, the more assertive its answer can be. Identifying no entity in the question and answer makes the correct answer impossible. There is no way to detect that the product is compatible with a consumer item without specificity.

5   Evaluating Automatic Text-to-Text Transformation

In this evaluation, we explored the generated summarized texts (template-based) from the experimental evaluation described in Sect. 4. In particular, we investigate how the templates are used as fine-tuning and prompt parameters to improve the effectiveness of four different text-to-text machine learning (ML) models (described at Subsect. 5.1). It allowed us to evaluate the models' ability to adapt to the e-commerce context.

The main objective of this evaluation is to understand if current ML models are capable of generating summarized relevant sentences in our study context. More specifically, we evaluate if the ML models are able to summarize NL sentences that answer compatibility questions in the context of e-commerce. Section 5 shows the main elements of this evaluation, that are explained in Sect. 5.1.

5.1 Setup and Procedures

This evaluation adopted four text-to-text transformation models: T5-small [19], PTT5 [8], GPT-Neo [6], and Bloom [24]. These models were selected because they have been shown to be effective in NL processing tasks, specially in text generation. We aimed to evaluate their effectiveness in our specific task in the e-commerce scenario. We categorized the four models in two majors groups: T5-family and GPT-family. The T5-family represents the models based on the T5 model from Google. They are finetuned using our dataset. The GPT-family represents the models based on GPT-3, that are not easily finetuned. Instead, we adopt the few-shot prompting to summarize our dataset.

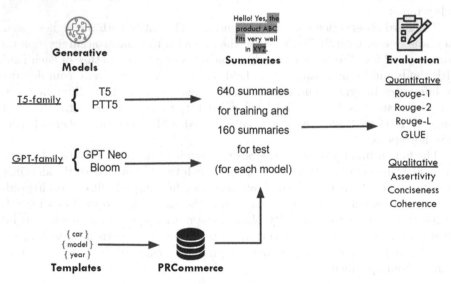

Fig. 5. The five main elements of the current evaluation: (1) the templates, representing the main source of data for the dataset; (2) the EcommercePR, containing the natural language text used in the evaluation; (3) the four text generative models, categorized in two main groups (T5-family and GPT-family); (4) the generated summaries and (5) the evaluation metrics.

We chose T5 for our evaluation because this allows us to understand the results obtained when using a multilingual model in our Portuguese dataset. We chose PTT5 in order to understand how a pre-trained model with a Portuguese dataset would perform with our dataset, compared to a multilingual and bigger model, as is the case with T5. We chose GPT Neo to understand how a model that uses prompts, with characteristics similar to GPT-3, would perform with our dataset. Unlike GPT-3, GPT-Neo is open source. And the final choice, Bloom, was chosen because it is the most current model among the four, released in 2022. Table 4 presents relevant characteristic of each model.

Table 4. Models used on this evaluation. The lines represent each of the four text generation models and the columns represent each characteristic of the models.

Model	Architecture	Parameters	Dataset	Vocab. Size	Training Data
T5-small	Encoder-Decoder	60 million	C4	32,000 tokens	Multi-domain text
PTT5	Encoder-Decoder	220 million	BrWac	60,000 tokens	Multi-domain text
GPT-Neo	Transformer	2.7 billion	The Pile	50,257 tokens	Large and diverse text corpus
Bloom	Transformer	176 billion		50,264 tokens	Large and diverse text corpus

To train these models, we used the *EcommercePR* dataset, a dataset generated from our first evaluation present in Sect. 4. The *EcommercePR* consists of two columns and 800 rows. The first column contains a product name, a question, and an answer, whereas the second column contains the summarized version of the first column, produced using the templates. The 800 rows consist of compatibility question and answers of ten different Brazilian automobile stores.

Table 5 shows a random row of the *EcommercePR* dataset. We highlight some characteristics of NL written texts by including the greeting in the question (*"Bom dia"* is the Portuguese translation of "good morning"); and the grammar error in the answer (*"nao"* instead of *"não"* is the Portuguese translation of the "no" negative word).

First, the *EcommercePR* dataset was used to train two text-to-text transformation models, T5-small and PTT5. In order to train the models, we first split the dataset into training and testing sets, with an 80/20 proportion. We chose to fine-tuning the models using this dataset because this allows the models to learn from the domain-specific data. This must improve their effectiveness on the task at hand [7]. The T5-small and PTT5 models were fine-tuned on the training set of *EcommercePR*, with the aim of generating accurate and concise summaries of the product-related questions. The fine-tuning process involved repeatedly presenting the models with the training data and adjusting the model's parameters to minimize the error between the generated summaries and the actual summaries in the dataset.

In addition, we evaluated the effectiveness of GPT Neo and Bloom (categorized as GPT-family). Instead of fine-tuning the entire model, we chose to use few-shot prompts [7] to train the models due to their relatively large sizes. To create few-shot prompts, we randomly selected a few examples from the support set and used them to generate prompts for the models. The support set - a small subset of the original training data - is used to help the algorithm learn to generalize from a few examples. We opted for few-shot prompts instead of fine-tuning the entire model because it was easier and faster to train [7].

After the models were fine-tuned (T5-family) and summarized in few-shots (GPT-family), they were assessed on the testing set of *EcommercePR* to assess their ability to generalize to new data. Subsection 4.2 presents the results of the evaluation and compares the effectiveness of the four models. We found which model achieved better results on the specific task of summarizing product-related questions.

To evaluate the results, we use four quantitative metrics and three qualitative metrics. The quantitative metrics are: Rouge-1, which measures the overlap of unigrams between the generated summary and the reference summary; Rouge-2, which measures the overlap of bigrams between the generated summary and the reference summary; Rouge-L, which measures the longest common subsequence between the generated summary and the reference summary and BLEU, which measures the n-gram overlap between the generated summary and the reference summary. The results shows the median of F-measures for each metric and ranges from 0 to 1, where values closer to 1 represents more similar summaries. The qualitative metrics are: assertivity, conciseness and coherence.

We used Hugging Face platform[2] to fine-tune, prompt and evaluate each model because it offers a wide range of functions for working with text data.

5.2 Results

We showcase the outcomes achieved through our conducted procedures (cf. Fig. 5). Our presentation includes both quantitative and qualitative analysis. The quantitative analysis presents the use of summarization metrics such as

Table 5. One of the eight hundred examples in EcommercePR dataset. The columns product, question and answer are condensed in a single column at the model training step of the evaluation. The text is written in Portuguese natural language and presents a real-world example.

Feature	Content
Product	Junta Deslizante Câmbio Kombi 1.6 1977/96
Question	Bom dia sebe me dizer se serve no golf 2001 Sr 1.6
Answer	Nao serve
Summary	Junta Deslizante Câmbio Kombi 1.6 1977/96 não serve no golf 2001

---

[2] https://huggingface.co/models.

Rouge and BLEU, whereas the qualitative analysis consists of examples of summaries created by each model.

Quantitative Analysis. We evaluated the effectiveness of the four text-to-text ML models: T5, PTT5, GPT Neo, and Bloom, using 800 templates as a resource to improve their fine-tuning and prompt parameters. We used a test dataset consisting of product-related questions and evaluated their ability to provide accurate answers. We measured the effectiveness of each model using four metrics: Rouge-1, Rouge-2, Rouge-L, and BLEU.

Table 6 shows the results of our evaluation. Our results show that PTT5 achieved the second lowest score on all four metrics, with Rouge-1, Rouge-2, Rouge-L, and BLEU scores of 0.683, 0.656, 0.682, and 0.38, respectively. GPT Neo and Bloom performed better, achieving high scores on all four metrics; GPT Neo achieving Rouge-1, Rouge-2, Rouge-L, and BLEU scores of 0.784, 0.672, 0.797, and 0.61, respectively.

Bloom achieving Rouge-1, Rouge-2, Rouge-L, and BLEU scores of 0.802, 0.722, 0.777, and 0.65, respectively. T5 performed the worst, achieving the lowest scores on all four metrics, with Rouge-1, Rouge-2, Rouge-L, and BLEU scores of 0.283, 0.145, 0.265, and 0.05, respectively.

Table 6. Evaluation metrics for the four evaluated models. The values represent the median of the f-measure. Values closer to 1 represent more similar summaries produced by each model.

Model	Rouge-1	Rouge-2	Rouge-L	BLEU
T5	0.283	0.145	0.265	0.05
PTT5	0.683	0.656	0.682	0.38
GPT Neo	0.784	0.672	**0.797**	0.61
Bloom	**0.802**	**0.722**	0.777	**0.65**

Qualitative Analysis. The aim of our study is to uncover key aspects of the summarized texts created by each evaluated ML model. We collected two texts and their corresponding summarized versions to explore and understand the information retention, conciseness and coherence. By using a combination of these analyses, we provide a more detailed and nuanced evaluation of the summaries produced by each model. We aim to gain insights into the strengths and weaknesses of each approach.

Table 7. Generated summaries by each generative model, divided in two examples. The fist column represents the IDs and the second the correspondent text. The first line from each example represents the original Portuguese text, composed by the product name, the compatibility question and answer; the second line represents the gold standard summarized text; lines three to six represent each text generative model: T5 Small, PTT5, GPT Neo and Bloom [21].

Example #1	
ID	Texts
Original	Lente Espelho Retrovisor Cristal Omega 92/93/94/ Dir Ou Esq A lente Serve no omega gls 93 no retrovisor eletrico Sim, serve
GS	Lente Espelho Retrovisor Cristal Omega 92/93/94/ Dir Ou Esq serve no omega gls 9
T5	Lente Espelho Retrovisor Cristal Omega 92/93/94/ Dir Ou Esq lente Serve no omega gls 93 no retrovisor eletrico
PTT5	Lente Espelho Retrovisor Cristal Omega 92/93/94/ Dir
GPT	A lente Espelho Retrovisor Cristal Omega 92/93/94/ Dir Ou Esq não serve no omega gls 93 no retrovisor eletrico
Bloom	A Lente Espelho Retrovisor Cristal Omega 92/93/94/ Dir Ou Esq serve no omega gls 93
Example #2	
ID	Texts
Original	Kit Central Multimídia Mp5 Câmera Moldura Fiesta Ecosport Oie! Serve no fiesta 2003 modelo 2004? Não tem comandos no volante. Infelizmente não é compatível com o seu carro este kit
GS	Kit Central Multimídia Mp5 Câmera Moldura Fiesta Ecosport não é compatível com fiesta 2003 modelo 2004
T5	kit central multimdia Mp5 Câmera Moldura Fiesta Ecosport no é compatvel com seu carro .
PTT5	Kit Central Multimídia Mp5 Câmera Moldura Fiesta Ecosport
GPT	O Kit Central Multimídia Mp5 Câmera Moldura Fiesta Ecosport não é compatível com fiesta 2003/2004
Bloom	O Kit Central Multimídia Mp5 Câmera Moldura Fiesta Ecosport não é compatível com fiesta 2003/2004

Table 7 shows the original text (before summarization), the gold standard summarized text (from the *EcommercePR* dataset) and the summarized texts produced by each text generation model; all of them written in Portuguese natural language text. The original text (ID Original) is composed by three lines: the first line contains the title of the product (a rearview mirror lens from example 1 and a multimedia kit from example 2); a compatibility question about the product (if it fits in a Omega GLS 93 car in example 1 and if it fits in a Fiesta 2003 in example 2); and the compatibility answer (it fits the car in example 1 and it does not fit the car in example 2). The second line (ID GS acronym for Gold Standard) describes the compatibility in a summarized sentence.

From the third to the sixth lines (IDs T5, PTT5, GPT and Bloom), we identify important aspects of the summarized texts:

- **Assertivity:** the goal is to analyze whether the summary correctly identified the compatibility. **Example #1:** T5 and Bloom correctly identified that the product and the car are compatible. PTT5 could not identify the compatibility and GPT wrongly identified it as not compatible. **Example #2:** T5, GPT and Bloom correctly identified that the product and the car are not compatible. PTT5 could not identify the compatibility.
- **Conciseness:** the goal is to analyze whether the generated summary is concise. **Example #1:** The original text has 23 words. The GS text (line two) has 16 words, a 30.4% reduction, which is our expected results for the models. T5 is presented the least aggressive reduction, resulting in a text with 20 words (13%), followed by GPT, which reduced the text to a 19 words (17.3%) and by Bloom with a text composed by 17 words (26.09%). On the other hard, PTT5 presented the most aggressive reduction, resulting in 9 words (60.8%). **Example #2:** The original text has 30 words. The GS text presented 16 words (46.67%). T5 reduced to a 14-word text (53.33%); PTT5 reduced to a 8-word text (73.33%) whereas GPT and Bloom reduced to 15-word texts (50%), respectively.
- **Coherence:** the goal is to verify which models produced complete and error-proof phrases. **Example #1 and Example #2:** T5, GPT and Bloom produced complete phrases, composed by subjects, verbs and objects. PTT5 cut the phrase, avoiding to add compatibility verbs (fits, compatible with) and car references.

5.3   Discussion

The present results concerned the evaluation using several models, where the results are expressed in the form of F-measure values for each model, as measured by four evaluation metrics. We highlight that the higher the F-measure value, the better the effectiveness of the model, as it indicates a higher degree between the generated summary and the reference summary.

Looking at the Rouge-1 metric, we observe that T5 achieved the lowest score of 0.283, whereas Bloom achieved the highest score of 0.802. This suggests that Bloom was able to generate summaries that contained more of the important words from the original text.

For the Rouge-2 metric, Bloom again achieved the highest score of 0.722, whereas T5 had the lowest score of 0.145. This suggests that Bloom was able to capture relevant phrases and sentence structures from the original text better than the other models.

For the Rouge-L metric, GPT Neo had the highest score of 0.777; T5 had the lowest score of 0.265. This suggests that GPT Neo was able to generate summaries that were more similar in structure to the reference summary.

Finally, for the BLEU metric, Bloom achieved the highest score of 0.65; T5 achieved the lowest score of 0.05. This suggests that Bloom was able to generate summaries that were more similar in phrasing to the reference summary.

Overall, the results suggest that Bloom performed the best among the four models, achieving the highest scores in three out of the four metrics. However, it is worth noting that the explored evaluation metrics may not capture all aspects of a good summary. Other factors such as readability, coherence, and relevance to the original text should also be considered when evaluating the quality of the summaries.

Our evaluation of the summarizations in qualitative terms (Table 7) revealed that the models differed in their ability to accurately identify the compatibility of the product with the car. T5 and Bloom showed better results in identifying compatibility in Example #1; T5, GPT and Bloom showed better results in Example #2. PTT5, on the other hand, struggled to identify compatibility in both examples. In terms of conciseness, we found that all models achieved a reduction in the number of words in the summarized texts, with the expected reduction of around 30% in most cases. The level of aggressiveness in the reduction varied across models, with PTT5 being the most aggressive and T5 was the least aggressive. Regarding coherence, we observed that T5, GPT and Bloom were able to produce complete and error-proof phrases; PTT5 cut the phrase and omitted important information.

As a final aspect, our study discovered the relevance of considering multiple aspects of summary quality when evaluating text generation models.

6   Overall Discussion and Challenges

This section discusses key aspects of the QART framework and presents the main challenges involved in further building it.

The majority of newly generated information is commonly shared as NL text online. The pace of generating and publishing such texts has significantly increased compared to the creation and expansion rate of KGs. The ideation and development of adequate software tools such the QART to create KGs based on that NL texts paves the way for the growth of a more semantic Web.

We developed the QART framework as the combination of a series of NL processing and NL understanding techniques and tools with KG creation and population. Our hypothesis is that the addition of intermediary steps between the input NL texts and the RDF triples, such as the text summarization, can produce better results, such as better triples. We provided two evaluations to investigate and demonstrate that these intermediary steps (Step A and Step B in our framework) fit in the QART process and produce meaningful outcome.

In our first evaluation (cf. Sect. 4), we demonstrated that the framework can identify relevant intents and entities of Q&A from e-commerce texts. We showed that the correct identification of such data can fit in the construction of templates.

We hypothesized that the templates can be used as training data to text generation models – our second evaluation (cf. Sect. 5). In this phase, our results showed that both GPT Neo and Bloom achieved high scores on all four metrics, indicating that few-shot prompts can be an effective way to train large language models on domain-specific datasets, such as the e-commerce. Furthermore, using few-shot prompts is a more efficient way of training language models than fine-tuning the entire model.

In our current study, we faced research challenges that are source of future work, as follows:

Text Interpretation in Natural Language. The interpretation of natural language poses significant challenges, like difficulty reading and identifying terms. This obstacle is present in all three stages of the framework presented in Fig. 1, owing to inherent features of NL texts, such as colloquialisms, regionalisms, and abbreviations.

Step A is mainly affected by grammatical errors that can hamper the identification of subjects and objects of the sentences (entities) and the classification of actions (intentions). For instance, if the model or year of the motorcycle were to be written with grammatical errors (such as "Titan SKS" and "2040" instead of "2004"), the subsequent steps would be affected.

The subsequent steps of the framework, where text-to-text and text-to-triple transformation takes place, face challenges in processing texts that contain ambiguities, sarcasm, and irony. If the text about the question in Sect. 3 was a product criticism instead of a compatibility question - with the use of sarcasm and irony - it would have a negative impact on the pipeline.

Portuguese Language and Size of Dataset. In our study, we utilized natural language (NL) questions, answers, and product titles extracted from major e-commerce platforms in Brazil in the Portuguese language. To summarize the text in Step B of our framework (cf. Fig. 1), we experimented with multilingual and fine-tuned models. However, as a future research direction, we plan to train models specifically on Portuguese language datasets. To achieve this, we aim to build a more extensive dataset in the e-commerce domain.

Structure of Existing KG. Step C generates the v_3 dataset that contains the summarized text *summ* and the triple t associated with it. This triple should be inserted into an existing KG to add more knowledge. Ensuring that the generated triples are compatible with the existing ontology is an important challenge in integrating the new knowledge into the existing knowledge graph. It requires careful consideration of the ontology structure and the entities and relationships already defined. In addition, it is essential to ensure that the new instances conform to the class definitions and have the necessary properties and attributes. Figure 6 illustrates the existing KG structure for the running example of Sect. 3. In red, we have the classes and, in green, the instances of these classes. A triple with compatibility intent generated by the QART must conform to this knowledge representation. In some cases, it may be necessary to extend the ontology to accommodate new classes and relationships that are not already defined. This can be a challenging task, particularly if the ontology is complex and has many interrelated classes and relationships.

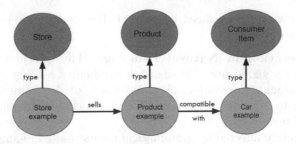

Fig. 6. Synthetic representation of a KG that is prepared to store knowledge about compatibility between $prod_1$ and c_i. The red circles refer to the classes Store, Product and Consumer Item. The green circles refers to examples of instances from the 3 classes [21]. (Color figure online)

7 Conclusion

Using NL texts to automatically discover meaningful data and fill semantic-enhanced structures, such as KG, is a promising task. Much data is lost for not being further processed, such as questions and answers about products in an e-commerce context. This investigation proposed the QART framework to generate RDF triples with a pipeline composed of entity and intent detection, text-to-text transformation, and text-to-triples generation. We described the framework and the challenges in its further development. Our study provided an illustrative example to describe the advancements of our solution to generate RDF triples. In particular, we evaluated using templates for text summarization as a critical step in our solution. We found that they can be useful as training data for machine learning models, given the high accuracy, precision, and recall achieved. We also evaluate using text generative models to produce summarized texts using the templates as input. The text generative models show a strong adaptation to the e-commerce context and exhibited notable effectiveness, attaining a high level of accuracy with f-measures of 0.8 for the Rouge-1 metric and 0.65 for the Bleu metric in a given model. Future work involves the development of an interactive software tool that guides the users throughout the process, such as a data engineer who fills a KG with relevant data based on our framework.

References

1. Akter, Y.A., Rahman, M.A.: Extracting RDF triples from raw text. In: 2019 1st International Conference on Advances in Science, Engineering and Robotics Technology (ICASERT), pp. 1–4. IEEE (2019)
2. Ao, J., Dinakaran, S., Yang, H., Wright, D., Chirkova, R.: Trustworthy knowledge graph population from texts for domain query answering. In: 2021 IEEE International Conference on Big Data (Big Data), pp. 4590–4599. IEEE (2021)
3. Asgari-Bidhendi, M., Janfada, B., Minaei-Bidgoli, B.: FarsBase-KBP: a knowledge base population system for the Persian knowledge graph. J. Web Semant. **68**, 100638 (2021)

4. Augenstein, I., Padó, S., Rudolph, S.: LODifier: generating linked data from unstructured text. In: Simperl, E., Cimiano, P., Polleres, A., Corcho, O., Presutti, V. (eds.) ESWC 2012. LNCS, vol. 7295, pp. 210–224. Springer, Heidelberg (2012). https://doi.org/10.1007/978-3-642-30284-8_21

5. Bi, Z., Cheng, S., Zhang, N., Liang, X., Xiong, F., Chen, H.: Relphormer: relational graph transformer for knowledge graph representation. arXiv preprint arXiv:2205.10852 (2022)

6. Black, S., Leo, G., Wang, P., Leahy, C., Biderman, S.: GPT-Neo: Large Scale Autoregressive Language Modeling with Mesh-Tensorflow (2021). https://doi.org/10.5281/zenodo.5297715

7. Brown, T., et al.: Language models are few-shot learners. Adv. Neural. Inf. Process. Syst. **33**, 1877–1901 (2020)

8. Carmo, D., Piau, M., Campiotti, I., Nogueira, R., Lotufo, R.: PTT5: pretraining and validating the T5 model on Brazilian Portuguese data. arXiv preprint arXiv:2008.09144 (2020)

9. Colon-Hernandez, P., Havasi, C., Alonso, J., Huggins, M., Breazeal, C.: Combining pre-trained language models and structured knowledge. arXiv preprint arXiv:2101.12294 (2021)

10. Daiber, J., Jakob, M., Hokamp, C., Mendes, P.N.: Improving efficiency and accuracy in multilingual entity extraction. In: Proceedings of the 9th International Conference on Semantic Systems, pp. 121–124 (2013)

11. Ferrucci, D.A.: Introduction to "this is Watson". IBM J. Res. Dev. **56**(3.4), 1:1–1:15 (2012). https://doi.org/10.1147/JRD.2012.2184356

12. Gangemi, A., Presutti, V., Reforgiato Recupero, D., Nuzzolese, A.G., Draicchio, F., Mongiovì, M.: Semantic web machine reading with FRED. Semant. Web **8**(6), 873–893 (2017)

13. Kadlec, R., Bajgar, O., Kleindienst, J.: Knowledge base completion: baselines strike back. In: Proceedings of the 2nd Workshop on Representation Learning for NLP, pp. 69–74 (2017)

14. Lafferty, J., McCallum, A., Pereira, F.C.: Conditional random fields: probabilistic models for segmenting and labeling sequence data (2001)

15. Liu, Y., Zhang, T., Liang, Z., Ji, H., McGuinness, D.L.: Seq2RDF: an end-to-end application for deriving triples from natural language text. In: CEUR Workshop Proceedings, vol. 2180. CEUR-WS (2018)

16. Màrquez, L., Carreras, X., Litkowski, K.C., Stevenson, S.: Semantic role labeling: an introduction to the special issue (2008)

17. Martinez-Rodriguez, J.L., Lopez-Arevalo, I., Rios-Alvarado, A.B., Hernandez, J., Aldana-Bobadilla, E.: Extraction of RDF statements from text. In: Villazón-Terrazas, B., Hidalgo-Delgado, Y. (eds.) KGSWC 2019. CCIS, vol. 1029, pp. 87–101. Springer, Cham (2019). https://doi.org/10.1007/978-3-030-21395-4_7

18. Radford, A., Wu, J., Child, R., Luan, D., Amodei, D., Sutskever, I., et al.: Language models are unsupervised multitask learners (2019)

19. Raffel, C., et al.: Exploring the limits of transfer learning with a unified text-to-text transformer. J. Mach. Learn. Res. **21**(140), 1–67 (2020). http://jmlr.org/papers/v21/20-074.html

20. Raffel, C., et al.: Exploring the limits of transfer learning with a unified text-to-text transformer. J. Mach. Learn. Res. **21**, 1–67 (2020)

21. Regino, A.G., Caus, R.O., Hochgreb, V., dos Reis, J.C.: QART: a framework to transform natural language questions and answers into RDF triples. In: Aveiro, D., Dietz, J.L.G., Filipe, J. (eds.) Proceedings of the 14th International Joint Conference on Knowledge Discovery, Knowledge Engineering and Knowledge Management, IC3K 2022, Volume 2: KEOD, Valletta, Malta, 24–26 October 2022, pp. 55–65. SCITEPRESS (2022). https://doi.org/10.5220/0011529200003335

22. Rossanez, A., Reis, J., Torres, R.D.S.: Representing scientific literature evolution via temporal knowledge graphs. In: CEUR Workshop Proceedings (2020)

23. Rossanez, A., dos Reis, J.C.: Generating knowledge graphs from scientific literature of degenerative diseases. In: SEPDA@ ISWC, pp. 12–23 (2019)

24. Scao, T.L., et al.: Bloom: a 176B-parameter open-access multilingual language model. arXiv preprint arXiv:2211.05100 (2022)

25. Shaikh, S., Rathi, S., Janrao, P.: Recommendation system in e-commerce websites: a graph based approached. In: 2017 IEEE 7th International Advance Computing Conference (IACC), pp. 931–934. IEEE (2017)

26. Sharma, R.K., Joshi, M.: An analytical study and review of open source chatbot framework, rasa. Int. J. Eng. Res. **9**, 1011–1014 (2020)

27. Shi, B., Weninger, T.: Open-world knowledge graph completion. In: Proceedings of the AAAI Conference on Artificial Intelligence, vol. 32 (2018)

28. Straka, M., Hajic, J., Straková, J.: UDPipe: trainable pipeline for processing CoNLL-U files performing tokenization, morphological analysis, POS tagging and parsing. In: Proceedings of the Tenth International Conference on Language Resources and Evaluation (LREC 2016), pp. 4290–4297 (2016)

29. Vegesna, A., Jain, P., Porwal, D.: Ontology based chatbot (for e-commerce website). In. J. Comput. Appl. **179**(14), 51–55 (2018)

30. Wong, W., Bartels, M., Chrobot, N.: Practical eye tracking of the ecommerce website user experience. In: Stephanidis, C., Antona, M. (eds.) UAHCI 2014. LNCS, vol. 8516, pp. 109–118. Springer, Cham (2014). https://doi.org/10.1007/978-3-319-07509-9_11

Situational Question Answering over Commonsense Knowledge Using Memory Nets

Joerg Deigmoeller[1]([✉]), Pavel Smirnov[1], Julian Eggert[1], Chao Wang[1], and Johane Takeuchi[2]

[1] Honda Research Institute Europe, Carl-Legien-Straße 30, 63073 Offenbach am Main, Germany
{joerg.deigmoeller,pavel.smirnov,julian.eggert,chao.wang}@honda-ri.de
[2] Honda Research Institute Japan, 8-1 Honcho, Wako, Saitama 351-0114, Japan
johane.takeuchi@jp.honda-ri.com

Abstract. In this paper we extend the idea of Embodied Question Answering (EQA), which is a rather novel research direction. EQA provides a way to evaluate the behavior and reasoning of a mobile robotic platform based by a well defined question answering problem. The task is to respond to requests by exploring the environment for required information. Questions are usually related to object properties or object conditions. To enforce a robotic agent to answer questions beyond object properties or conditions, we deal with Situational Question Answering (SQA). The difference to EQA is that SQA requires context-relevant commonsense reasoning. We show the SQA performance of a knowledge graph complemented by inference mechanisms with transparent, human-understandable explanations. In particular, we combine a set of facts with basic knowledge about the world, a situational memory and commonsense understanding. As simple interface between natural language input and the knowledge graph, we propose a Semantics Abstraction Layer (SAL). The SAL is designed in a way that reasoning functions can be executed hierarchically to allow for modular processing chains. We evaluate our system on a set of object related questions first (similar to EQA) and, second, on a set of questions that requires commonsense information about tools, actions and objects. For the latter evaluation, we compared our method against human performance, which is simulated by a mental exercise, similar to the urn problem. The human answers are drawn from a distribution based on real annotated data including 20 subjects.

Keywords: Situational question answering · Knowledge representation and reasoning · Natural language understanding · Commonsense

1 Introduction

The ultimate goal of our work is to enable an Intelligent Agent (IA) to interact cooperatively with humans on a shared understanding for a given situation.

As this is a quite high goal, we approach the problem by continuously refining an agent's knowledge base by incorporation of new facts, extracted either from commonsense knowledge sources, perception in the environment or knowledge provided by the user. To focus on the high level interaction first, we use the VirtualHome simulator [26] with an agent acting in a realistic home environment. This idea is similar to Embodied Question Answering (EQA, [6]), which gets greater attention in recent years. Here, an environment related question is raised to an agent and the task is to explore the surrounding until it finds the required information (usually using visual recognition) to answer the question. The main difference to our work is that the reasoning is not embedded into an end-to-end deep neural network, but in a knowledge engine that combines world knowledge with environment information into a single graph representation. This allows for transparent explanation of internal reasoning steps, inserting new information on the fly and compact inferences. Another difference is that we leave the recognition task out of scope for this paper and focus on the reasoning in certain situations, given that the environment information is delivered by our simulator framework. In this paper we put focus on the agent's knowledge engine system, which provides two main functions: continuously store and retrieve complex structured and unstructured information about the environment and infer additional context relevant knowledge in situations. Our previous work [11, 12] introduces the idea of Memory Net (MemNet), which provides a conceptual basis for a knowledge engine that facilitates an agent to act in a physical environment.

As a means to share knowledge with a user and measure the reasoning performance, we attached a natural language understanding to the knowledge engine. Given an environment setting in the simulator and a dedicated set of questions and answers, we can enforce the agent to utilize and show its reasoning capabilities. Our focus is that the agent makes sense out of a situation it is in, by using its gained contextual knowledge and making this process transparent. We call this approach Situational Question Answering (SQA).

Enabling an agent for situational reasoning requires a semantic understanding of the context, which goes beyond natural language understanding only. It requires a close interplay between language and semantic concepts, stored and updated in a large network. Observations also need to be embedded in such a network to include all available information at once for inference. Further, we are convinced that each observed object should be differentiated by its role, depending on the context. For example, an object could be manipulated or it could be used for manipulating another object (tool), which makes a big difference for an acting agent. The idea of context dependent roles is also known from linguistics, called verb semantics [2]. Each participant plays a different role, where the context mainly relies on the action that is performed. The most important roles for our setting are the agent itself, the object and the tool that contribute to an action.

The novelty we present in this paper, especially in relation to EQA, constitutes in two parts. First, the detailed distinction between different action participants (object, tool, subject, location) and their tight linkage to the language understanding. In our work, we call such context definitions *action patterns* which provide the key structure for situational reasoning. The action patterns have been extracted from commonsense knowledge for question answering. Second, the embedding of observations and action patterns into a large semantic network, combined with commonsense information. We show both novelties on the task of situational question answering.

In the reminder of this paper, we present our work in the area of EQA and focus on a knowledge representation that requires situational aspects for the embodied agent. In Sect. 3, we explain the different components of the system and show how they interact to gain information for a situation. Finally, we evaluate the system on two sets of question-answer pairs in Sect. 4 and conclude the paper in Sect. 5.

2   Related Work

The domain of Embodied Question Answering (EQA) has rapidly grown in recent years, which combines agents in simulated home environments [20,26] with question answering. EQA [6,10,35], sometimes also called Interactive Question Answering (IQA) [15], focuses on raising questions related to the environment, followed by an exploration step of the agent to gather required information for the answer. Usually, there is no memory to answer future questions from past observations. EQA provides a great direction for researchers interested in combining language grounding in robotics [31] and question answering [24] using a well defined performance measure. Even though the relation to SQA might be obvious, the questions differ significantly in the scientific direction, which enforces more consideration of commonsense knowledge. The focus in SQA is less on dedicated object information, but rather on the embedding of objects in everyday contexts.

Closest to our idea is the work of [30]. The difference to EQA, which usually use deep neural networks, is the usage of a scene graph for reasoning and storing information. They call their approach K-EQA (Knowledge-based Embodied Question Answering) and additionally couple their scene graph with semi-structured data from ConceptNet. The performance is estimated by comparing the question answering task with and without visual recognition (scripted scene information). The question set is automatically generated from selected link types in ConceptNet. Even if the idea is a great contribution, using the same data source for question and answer generation gives no real insights into the performance of the system. Further, the reasoning is performed on triplet information like ('Sports equipment', 'ReceivesAction', 'purchased at a sporting goods store'), which is questionable that such text snippets provide any machine interpretable meaning. As already described in the introduction, our approach further splits such snippets like 'purchased at a sporting goods store' into clear roles of 'purchased' is the action and 'sporting goods store' is the location where the action takes place. Making these types explicit enables an agent for a better semantic understanding and embedding into the context. We also combine commonsense and scene graph information into a single knowledge graph, which provides a strong connection between semantic types and observations.

A fine-grained description of actions and their participants is also known from knowledge representations in robotics [25, 32]. The goal is a manipulation task, where missing information is inferred for successful execution [4]. The required knowledge is usually demonstrated by humans or scripted and not extracted from external knowledge sources. Language interaction is not in focus, especially not for resolving situations on a high level, including ambiguities coming from language.

We think that SQA provides a novel direction to bring the domains of question answering, commonsense knowledge and robotics closer together to finally enable a natural interaction with agents, either in simulation or in real.

3   System Overview

The overall system consists of components, which are described below in detail. The Knowledge Engine (KE) is the central part (see Fig. 1) and connects all other components. The components provide an interface to the KE as well as to the outer world by either natural language (Semantic Parsing), inspection of internal reasoning (Explainable AI) or insertion of externally gathered knowledge (Knowledge Insertion). The successful interaction between all modules enables the system to deal with SQA through reasoning, language understanding and commonsense.

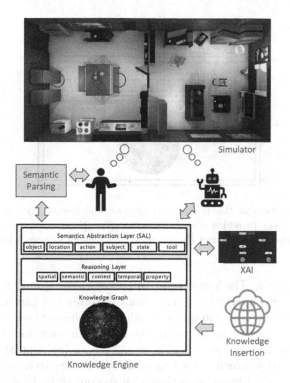

Fig. 1. [7] Overall system sketch with the knowledge engine as core component. The simulated environment and the semantic parsing allows for situational question answering using externally gathered knowledge. The XAI facilitates tracing of the reasoning steps in the knowledge engine.

3.1 Knowledge Engine

The Knowledge Engine is layered in three parts (see Fig. 2), the knowledge graph, the reasoning layer, and the Semantics Abstraction Layer (SAL). Such a layering allows for modular access of the Knowledge Engine, where the SAL provides the highest and most abstract layer. Its interface consists of independent and orthogonal access functions, which scales well by executing nested calls. This is close to the idea of Inductive Functional Programming [9] and provides a good basis for learning applications on top.

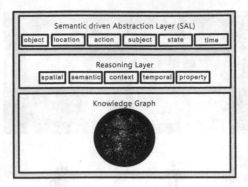

Fig. 2. Different layers of the knowledge engine. The lowest layer is the knowledge graph. The mid layer provides several reasoning functions on the underlying graph. The top layer allows for accessing the graph content using semantic types.

Knowledge Graph. The lowest layer is the knowledge graph, which is according to the MemNet representation [12]. MemNet consists of four main hierarchies that are motivated by verb semantics [2], which has already been described in the introduction. The hierarchies represent the most high-level roles that contribute to an action, which are objects, subjects and states (see Fig. 3). An exception is the state hierarchy, which is used to attach properties to an action, object or agent. Every specialization of an action, that has one or multiple objects or subjects attached, builds an *action pattern*. Objects and subjects can, off course, get an additional role depending on the context. As an example, a *knife* is no longer a simple object, but rather a tool if it contributes to the action *cut* (cf. Sect. 3). In the same way, a *table* can become a location in the action *putting*, while the table is still a simple object. Or an agent can become an actor or recipient in an action *bring*, and so on. The action patterns in MemNet are created trough inheritance or even multiple inheritance if required. More details are described in our previous publications [11,12].

Action patterns are the core of situational reasoning, for example if we are interested in objects that are usually related to the action *cutting*, what objects are used for *cutting* or which agent applied which tool for a certain action. For our work we focus on actors, locations and objects/tools, as they cover most obvious everyday interactions. As initial hierarchy, we use WordNet [14] and import it into MemNet. For simplicity, we assign all nouns to the object column and all verbs to the action column.

Instances that are in the simulator (agents, rooms, objects) are inserted into the knowledge graph as specializations of object or subject concepts. For each instance, we identified the correct concept in the graph and enriched the specialization with geometric information, either position or shape, as will be explained in Sect. 3.4.

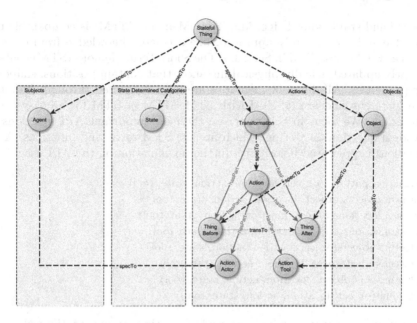

Fig. 3. Memory Nets representation as described in [12]. The distinction into four main columns allows for a detailed description of situational relations with the action as central connection. The assumption is that situations are constituted by an agent (left column), that executes a certain action (third column from left) on an object (column to the right) by using a tool (object that becomes a specific semantic meaning in an action context). The object undergoes a transformation through the action, which is expressed by the distinction between a specialized object before and after the execution.

Reasoning Layer. On next higher level is the reasoning layer, which provides methods to find concepts through different access points, like single semantic association, action pattern contexts or spatial relations. Single association is a straightforward search along the inheritance hierarchy in MemNet. Action pattern contexts include a multiple hierarchy search, usually along action, object and tool hierarchies. Finally, spatial relations are identified by associations like *on* or *in*, which is independent of hierarchies and a search in pure geometric space. Spatial reasoning is based on simple geometric interpretations based on 2D shapes and points.

Semantics Abstraction Layer. The highest level of the KE is the Semantics Abstraction Layer, as already introduced before as SAL. The interface focuses on abstract functions operating on the concept types: objects, locations, actions, states and tools. All concept types can be accessed via getting and setting functions, either by specifying an utterance or a unique graph node ID. Such an abstraction does not require any deep understanding of the previous layers and simplifies operating on the graph. Concepts can be stored in three different memories in the graph. One is the Long Term Memory (LTM), which contains approved and stable knowledge. Mid Term Memory (MTM) is comparable new knowledge and not yet fully approved, like extracted knowledge from external sources as will be described in Sect. 3.3. The Short Term Memory (STM) contains frequently updated, usually physical instances that contain positions, shapes or other properties. All different memories are fully connected through the inheritance hierarchy and are labelled with LTM, MTM or STM for an easy access in the graph. We focus in this paper on the most important API functions for situational question answering, which are the STM retrieving functions. A list of functions is presented below with further explanation on the API usage:

```
get_action_patterns(object, location, action, state, tool)
get_stm_objects(object, location, action, state, tool)
get_stm_locations(object, location, action, state, tool)
get_stm_actions(object, location, action, state, tool)
get_stm_subjects(object,location, action, state, tool)
get_stm_states(object, location, action, state, tool)
get_stm_tools(object, location, action, state, tool)
get_count(object, location, action, state, tool)
```

For every concept type, which are used as function arguments, there also exist getting and setting functions. If a function is called, with one or more arguments, the internal inference first enters the graph by matching concepts in either LTM, MTM or STM. Starting from there, the inference continues exploring the graph for specializations, i.e. child concepts, until it finally hits matching instances. That means, we could access a *banana* instance in multiple ways. Either by direct reference

```
get_stm_objects (object="banana")
```

or by circumscribing with properties

```
get_stm_objects (object="fruit", state="yellow").
```

or by using an action pattern containing an under-specified object (*something that is yellow*) and the action *eat*:

```
get_stm_objects (object="something", state="yellow", action="eat").
```

A special type of states are spatial keys, which are currently limited to *in* and *on* or *close*. Nevertheless, most spatial references in natural language make use of one of these three indicators. As an example, all objects on a table could be accessed by calling

```
get_stm_objects (state="on", location="table").
```

In the same way, if we have context information extracted from external knowledge sources, tools that are used to *cut* a *bread* could be accessed by

```
get_stm_tools (action="cut", object="bread").
```

The functions always return concept IDs, which again can be forwarded to any function as argument, so that we can create nested calls. With a comparably low number of functions, we get a quite large flexibility by executing different functions in a sequence. This is an important feature for natural language to graph query mapping, which will be discuss in the next section.

3.2 Semantic Parsing

To map natural language requests into SAL calls, we apply a semantic parsing, that is close to our previous work [13]. In a first step, we analyze the incoming user request by the syntactic parser spaCy [18], which returns the text as a graph, encoding the grammatical structure of the sentence (see Fig. 4, left). This graph contains valuable information about what and in which sequence the SAL has to be accessed, which goes beyond usual intent and slot recognition known from natural language understanding in chat-bot systems [19]. The tree structure of the sentence helps in identifying sub-clauses and can group them into semantically closed sub-contexts. As an example, if we look at "where is something to drink", we can identify the pattern "where is [object]" on a high level (see Fig. 4). We map this pattern to the function get_stm_locations. Further, on a next level, the [object] is again specified by the sub-clause "something to drink" which is reflected in the branch to the right of the syntactic tree in Fig. 4. The graph gives us all information we need to map this sub-clause to the function get_stm_objects, where the arguments are "something" for the object and "drink" for the action.

Pursuing this idea, we applied a set of rules to map words (tagged as parts-of-speech) and the dependency tree to a sequence of SAL calls. The advantage here is that this is a generic mapping, because it relies on the syntactic tree of a sentence.

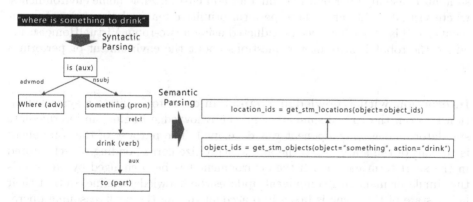

Fig. 4. Processing of natural language input starting from syntactic parsing and analysis of the sentence tree structure (left-hand side). The semantic parsing (right-hand side) translates the sentence structure into calls on the Semantic Abstraction Layer which resolves the meaning of words from the Knowledge Engine.

3.3 Knowledge Extraction

For the reasoning on action patterns, we require contextual information about which object or tool can be used for a certain action. Such knowledge is neither available out of the box nor is it straightforward to extract from external sources. To our knowledge, there are only a few sources containing commonsense information that might be useful for robotic agents [16]. We used ConceptNet [27] for our KE, probably the most comprehensive and most widely used database. We are specifically interested in extracting action patterns containing tool-action-object triplets like knife-cut-orange. We again use the syntactic parser of spaCy [18] to analyze text phrases with the relation *used_for* in ConceptNet. The tool is given by the start node of an *used_for* relation. The end node usually contains phrases like "cutting an orange into pieces". We finally extract the action ("cut") and the object ("orange") using the syntactic parser. More details and an analysis of the extraction precision can be found in [22] and [21]. Altogether, we extracted 5887 action patterns and inserted them into the KE.

As the extracted information is on text level only, we apply a Word Sense Disambiguation (WSD) [5] for identifying the correct synset in the KE. We used the state-of-the-art method CONSEC [3], which solves the task by phrasing the WSD as a text extraction problem. The method is based on the pre-trained Transformer model DEBERTA [17], which was fine-tuned using the annotated SEMCOR data [23].

3.4 Virtual Simulation

Virtual environments allow to save lots of time and costs for conducting experiments and rapid prototyping. Projects like VirtualHome [26], AI2-THOR [20], Habitat-Sim [29], ProcTHOR [8] show that the scientific community has a huge interest in developing and using of virtual simulations for robotic tasks. Virtual simulators usually offer multiple different and customizable home environments, where virtual agents are able to perform primitive manipulation tasks. Experiments for this paper have been conducted using a two-room VirtualHome scene, where the robot has to answer questions about the environment or perform a task.

Interaction with Knowledge Engine. In order to facilitate a synchronization between the virtual simulator and the Knowledge Engine, an intermediate simulator-managing component was developed. The purpose of the component is to control the state of a scene and synchronize corresponding objects stored in the short-term memory. If the environment has been changed by an agent's the simulator-managing component updates the knowledge engine, so that their latest state of the scene is taken into account during the next reasoning operations.

Pre-simulation of complex execution tasks is another purpose of the simulator-managing component. Execution tasks that are forwarded to an agent might be simple (e.g. "go forward", "turn left", etc.) or a consist out of combination of multiple atomic actions. In case of invalid tasks (e.g. "put chair on a bottle"), the failure should be immediately reported to the knowledge engine or user. In a scene-graph level the agent is able to pre-simulate desired tasks sequence before starting any real execution. In case, a pre-simulation was successful, the agent is able to analyze the posterior state of the environment, then execute the desired sequence in real and update corresponding objects in short-term memory. If a pre-simulation fails, then the agent does not need to revert the environment to the original state, rather just to restart with a previous scene graph state. Pre-simulations are performed in another (headless) instance of the VirtualHome simulator, that runs in parallel to the main instance. Orchestration between two running instances of the VirtualHome simulator provided by the simulator-managing component.

3.5 XAI

The eXplainable AI (XAI) field deals with interfaces that help expert users to understand on which assumptions a system draws a conclusion [1,28,33]. Here we propose an interface to give expert users a better understanding of the internal reasoning processes and data in real-time. The visualization of the XAI is close to the SAL calls combined with the knowledge graph content. We implemented a web-based graphical user interface (GUI), that combines different modes and a chat-box to communicate with the system using natural language. There are three targets of the XAI interface: 1) send commands to the system and receive feedback from the agent, 2) visualize the reasoning process of the agent and 3) supervise the current status and execution of the agent.

The first mode is the graph mode, as shown in Fig. 5. It splits the reasoning processes and returned query results into a structured visualization. First, we have the chat-box that forwards the natural language input to the Semantic Parsing. The Semantic Parsing extracts the values "something" and "drink" as object and action input arguments (white element in Fig. 5. The horizontal bars depict the function calls that are also coming from the Semantic Parsing, reading from top to bottom. First, objects are accessed by get_stm_objects with the previously gathered arguments. The return values, which are shown as red circles, are forwarded to the next function get_locations, because the user asked for a location (Where is ...") of an object ("something to drink"). The final output are the locations in the objects, which is actually the answer to the question.

As second mode, we have the camera mode (see Fig. 6, which shows a video stream of the VirtualHome simulation embedded in the web GUI. The video stream allows to supervise the translation from natural language instructions to the physical world. This can include two instruction types, execution on one hand-side (*"bring* [object] *to* [location]" or *"go to* [location]") or highlighting objects in the environment in case of question answering (*"Where is [object]"*, *"What is in/on* [location]", *"How many* [object] *are on/in* [location]?" or *"Is there a/an* [object] *on/in the* [location]?). The object and location highlighted in the camera mode are the same instance candidates that are visible in the graph mode (cf. red circles in Fig. 5).

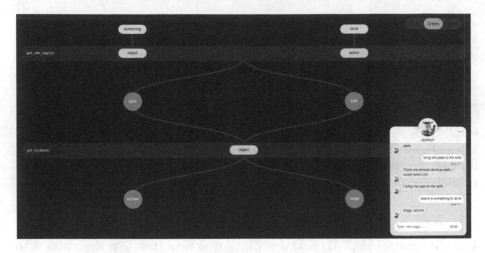

Fig. 5. The graph mode of the XAI interface. Bottom right is the chat-box that forwards text input ("where is something to drink") to queries on the Knowledge Engine. The horizontal bars show the SAL function calls with their arguments (green elements). The top red circles are instances returned by the first function (get_stm_objects) and forwarded as argument to the second function (get_locations). The lower instances are the final answer to the question, which is also returned as text in the chat-box. (Color figure online)

Fig. 6. The camera mode of the XAI interface. This is an alternative visualization to the graph mode and shows the mapping of the user input into the physical world. Here the agent executed the action that results from the instruction "bring the book to the kitchen". In the same way as instances are marked in the graph mode by red circles, related instances are highlighted by a boundary box in the simulation. (Color figure online)

Overall, the XAI is a great inspection tool to track the whole processing chain from Semantic Parsing, over identifying candidates in the knowledge graph, the mapping into physical environment and the final response of the system in natural language [34]. For interested reader, [34] gives a deeper insight into our XAI interface.

4 Evaluation

To evaluate our system, we split our experiments into two parts. First, we measure the performance on instance questions referring to object conditions, like their location, quantity or existence. This includes similar questions as for EQA [6,10,30,35], with the difference that we drop the recognition part and assume that all instance information is already in our knowledge graph. In the second part, we clearly distinct from EQA by asking questions that require commonsense information about usual relations between tools, actions and objects. While the latter evaluation requires human annotation, the first experiment can be performed with auto-generated questions and answers.

4.1 Instance Question Answering

For evaluating the question-answering performance of the Knowledge Engine we generated a Question-Answer (QA) data-set using the same data sources (scene-graph, taxonomic, commonsense) as we put into knowledge-engine. The data-set is targeted to stress the knowledge engine by hundreds realistic questions about the particular scene simulated in VirtualHome. As mentioned in [7], we performed the evaluation in a two-room environment instead of multiple environments. The validity of generated questions, as well correctness as expected answers have been validated manually using 3D-renders of the scene. In the ideal case the knowledge engine is expected to reach 100% performance, otherwise mismatches would clearly outline the problems either in the generated benchmark or in reasoning of the engine.

In [7] we presented an aggregated knowledge-engine performance over a set, where questions have been grouped by intents and presence/absence of commonsense knowledge. Such a grouping was an inspiration from question types described in state-of-the-art [6,10,30,35]. In comparison to the existing work, we added the semantic types tool, location and action stored as action patterns in the KE, which are extracted from commonsense knowledge. This allowed us to increase the variations in phrasing questions and to enforce the system to show its capabilities related to situational understanding.

While the aforementioned questions grouping provided the overall performance evaluation of the knowledge engine, it did not provide enough insights for a fine-grained analysis. To localize all the problematic cases, we advanced the benchmark by several improvements. First, all the answers were supplied with debug information, which lists all facts, why an answer is considered to be

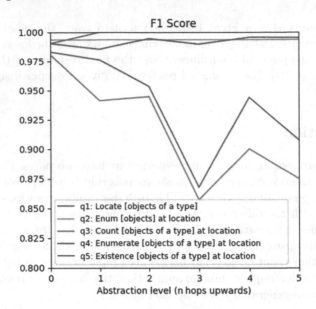

Fig. 7. Performance per question type and level of abstraction (instance questions only).

correct. The "reason" is tremendously helpful during manual inspection of mismatches between returned answers and expected ground-truths. Second, questions are now grouped by question type and not only by intent, as it was before. The grouping by type isolates a certain type of reasoning involved into answering questions, which allows to localize reasoning problems rapidly. Third, auto-generated questions are also separated by abstraction level - a number of hops upwards from the requested instance class. This step allows to evaluate, how a mismatch the lower levels of abstraction (e.g. instance level) affects the performance of question-answering on a higher level. Detecting and solving a problem on the lowest possible level prevents problem propagation to all upper layers.

Table 1. Overview of question types used for the instance questions.

Intent	Question Template	Amount	Precision
Locating	Where is [object of type X]?	107	0.95
Enumerating	What is in/on [location]?	12	1.0
	Which [objects of type X] are at the [location]?	312	0.98
Counting	How many [object of a type X] are on/in [location]?	312	0.94
Check	Is there [object of a type X] on/in the [location]?	312	0.98
Total		1055	0.96

Table 1 demonstrates question types, their amount and averaged performance for all abstraction layers per question type. From the table it can be clearly seen that the KE reaches a high performance (94–100%) for each question type. Figure 7 demonstrates the averaged performance (F1 score) per question type depending on abstraction level. From the figure a performance drop down to 85% could be seen for counting and locating questions. This can be explained by a decreasing amount of questions on higher abstraction levels. An error on lower level (being e.g. 1 incorrect of 100 questions) would contribute much stronger on higher levels (being e.g. 1 incorrect out of 10 questions). Errors on 0-level can be explained by a difference in spatial reasoning of the knowledge engine and the benchmark. For example, a frying pan has a handle, which is geometrically located outside of a kitchen stove and finally leads to different reasoning results for answer generation and KE reasoning.

4.2 Action Pattern Question Answering

To go beyond instance question answering, which can be understood as a KE unit test, we gathered human annotated data that requires commonsense understanding. In total, we compiled a set of 109 action pattern questions that are related to our virtualHome environment and asked 20 subjects to answer them. More specifically, we asked questions about which tool, present in the environment, might be useful to execute a certain action on another object. For example, "What can I use to drink coffee?" might result in the answers cup, water glass and wine glass. The subjects were asked to pick any candidate from the list of 47 object/tool types and order them from most to least applicable. The number of answer candidates should be minimum three for each question. Finally, we ordered the candidates by the number of subject votes, which gives an arbitrary length of answers, depending on the selected tools by the subjects. Answer candidates that have less than 3 overall votes are assumed to be outliers and have been removed from the annotated set. In comparison to the first experiment, where the answers had an equally distributed relevance, they now have an order, where front candidates fit well to a situation and candidates ranked to the end have lower relevance. Anyhow, all answer candidates should be somewhat applicable in a situation.

We compared the human annotated answers to the tool answers of our system. This could be understood as a kind of measuring the shared understanding between human and machine through imagination. It has to be considered that the human answers are subjective and gives varying candidates and rankings, depending on personal preferences. Therefore, we compared the KE answers with two different baselines. One is a fairly simple one, using the most frequent subject answers (see Sect. 4.2) and the second is an emulated human performance (see Sect. 4.2).

For the evaluation, we introduced a new measure called *match score*. First, because we think the match score reflects well the shared understanding for tool candidates, humans and systems have in mind for a given question. Second, this measure allows to introduce a human performance emulation easily, which is not straightforward using the F1 score.

The match score is based on set theory, where $R \cap S$ is the intersection between the reference answer set R and the system answer set S. If there is any intersection between the two sets, having $|R \cap S| > 0$, we count this as a match $p = 1$. If there is no intersection ($|R \cap S| = \emptyset$) we count a negative match as $n = 1$. The overall match score can be finally computed for n questions by $M = \sum_{i=1}^{n} /(\sum_i p_i + \sum_j n_j)$. To inspect the correct rank of answers, we compute M for an increasing answer set size from 1–10 for R and S (cf. Fig. 8).

Baseline 1 - Most Frequent Subject Answers. For this baseline, we computed a single list of tool candidates, that is given as standard answer to all questions, independent of the situation. We ranked the candidates based on their frequency in the overall set, which gives "plate" as first candidate (513 votes), "kitchen counter" as second 493 (votes), "dish bowl" as third (486), "knife" as fourth (435) and so on. Even if this approach is simple, it is a quite reasonable strategy in terms of choosing a correct answer if the system is question agnostic.

Baseline 2 - Human Performance Emulation. For comparison with the knowledge engine, the best human performance can be determined by the following mental exercise, similar to the urn problem[1]. Asking the question q to further participants, we assume that they guess, drawing their responses statistically from the same distribution as the human annotated data $\hat{p}_m^q$, gathered by the 109 questions. If they are allowed to give n options as answers, they guess n times. This guess has to be compared to the first m most frequent responses given by $\hat{p}_1^q, ..., \hat{p}_m^q$.

The matching score is then calculated as follows: The probability that they successfully "guess" one of the target tools (a tool that is among first m in $\hat{p}_r^q$) is

$$\hat{p}_{1..m}^q := \sum_{r=1}^{m} \hat{p}_r^q \ . \tag{1}$$

Alternatively, if they did not guess one of the target tools with the first guess, but are allowed to guess a second time, the probability to guess one of the target tools gets:

$$\left(1 - \hat{p}_{1..m}^q\right) \hat{p}_{1..m}^q \ . \tag{2}$$

This continues analogously for the m guesses, so that in total, the probability to have a match is

$$\sum_{s=0}^{m-1} \left(1 - \hat{p}_{1..m}^q\right)^s \hat{p}_{1..m}^q$$

$$= \hat{p}_{1..m}^q \frac{1 - \left(1 - \hat{p}_{1..m}^q\right)^m}{1 - \left(1 - \hat{p}_{1..m}^q\right)}$$

$$= 1 - \left(1 - \hat{p}_{1..m}^q\right)^m \tag{3}$$

---

[1] https://en.wikipedia.org/wiki/Urn_problem.

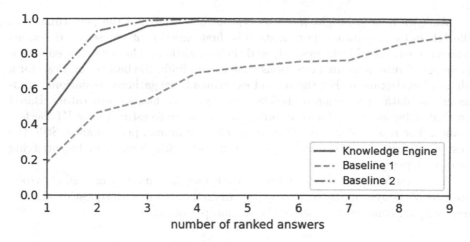

Fig. 8. Match score comparing the Knowledge Engine against the lower baseline 1 (most frequent user answers) and the upper baseline 2 (emulated human performance). The match score increases with larger number of candidates and saturates for the Knowledge Engine at four answer candidates.

Comparison of Results. We compared the KE performance against the two, previously introduced baselines (see Fig. 8). The lower limit should be the most frequent subject answers, as described in Sect. 4.2. Even if this might be trivial and does not consider the context of a question, it is already a quite good strategy to take the statistically most frequent candidates into account. Nevertheless, the KE performance is significantly above the lower baseline curve. The upper baseline is the human performance emulation curve (Sect. 4.2), that considers the full context and is hard to outperform. Even though, we are able to get close with our KE performance. After increasing the number of answer candidates to four, the KE nearly matches the human performance. Greater number of candidates, off course includes at least one matching candidate with the human annotated data. We can also observe that the KE provides best results at a length of three returned answers.

5 Conclusion

We proposed Situational Question Answering (SQA), which is a new direction based on Embodied Question Answering with the addition of situational reasoning. The main intention is to enforce an agent to show its abilities to reason on all day situations and infer contextually related items in its environment.

For SQA, we used a Knowledge Engine (KE), which is a knowledge graph based on MemNet with reasoning methods on top, that can be accessed through a Semantic Abstraction Layer (SAL).

We gave a deep insight into the type of questions and the performance of the KE in two separate experiments. The first experiment focuses on questions related to simulated instances only and their conditions. There we showed with a large set of auto-generated questions that we can fulfill the basic operations for a physical environment. For the second experiment, we gathered situational commonsense data in a action-tool-object context from human annotators. Based on that data, we created a lower and upper baseline to estimate the KE performance. The results show the KE is quite close to human performance. Still, the best matching candidates are at position 2 and 3, which may not be satisfying from user perspective.

As an outlook, we would like feed back user information in case of wrong answers of the system. By this, we expect to further improve the question answering task and come even closer to the human performance.

References

1. Arrieta, A., et al.: Explainable artificial intelligence (XAI): concepts, taxonomies, opportunities and challenges toward responsible AI. Inf. Fusion **58**, 82–115 (2020)
2. Baker, C., Fillmore, C., Lowe, J.: The Berkeley FrameNet project. In: Proceedings of the COLING-ACL (1998)
3. Barba, E., Procopio, L., Navigli, R.: ConSeC: word sense disambiguation as continuous sense comprehension. In: Conference on Empirical Methods in Natural Language Processing (2021)
4. Beetz, M., Bessler, D., Haidu, A., Pomarlan, M., Bozcuoglu, A.K., Bartels, G.: Know rob 2.0 - a 2nd generation knowledge processing framework for cognition-enabled robotic agents. In: International Conference on Robotics and Automation (2018)
5. Bevilacqua, M., Pasini, T., Raganato, A., Navigli, R.: Recent trends in word sense disambiguation: a survey. In: International Joint Conference on Artificial Intelligence (2021)
6. Das, A., Datta, S., Gkioxari, G., S. Lee, D.P., Batra, D.: Embodied question answering (2017). https://arxiv.org/abs/1711.11543. Accessed 11 July 2022
7. Deigmoeller, J., Smirnov, P., Losing, V., Wang, C., Takeuchi, J., Eggert, J.: Situational question answering using memory nets. In: Aveiro, D., Dietz, J.L.G., Filipe, J. (eds.) Proceedings of the 14th International Joint Conference on Knowledge Discovery, Knowledge Engineering and Knowledge Management, IC3K 2022, Volume 2: KEOD, Valletta, Malta, 24–26 October 2022, pp. 169–176. SCITEPRESS (2022)
8. Deitke, M., et al.: Procthor: large-scale embodied AI using procedural generation. arXiv preprint arXiv:2206.06994 (2022)
9. Diaconu, A.: Learning functional programs with function invention and reuse (2020). https://arxiv.org/abs/2011.08881. Accessed 27 Jan 2023
10. Duan, J., Yu, S., Tan, H.L., Zhu, H., Tan, C.: A survey of embodied AI: from simulators to research tasks (2022). https://arxiv.org/abs/2103.04918. Accessed 27 Jan 2023
11. Eggert, J., Deigmoeller, J., Fischer, L., Richter, A.: Memory nets: knowledge representation for intelligent agent operations in real world. In: 11th International Conference on Knowledge Engineering and Ontology Development. SCITEPRESS (2019)

12. Eggert, J., Deigmoeller, J., Fischer, L., Richter, A.: Action representation for intelligent agents using memory nets. In: Communications in Computer and Information Science. SPRINGER (2020)
13. Eggert, J., Takeuchi, J.: Graph based pattern classification for NLU and slot filling: approach and analysis. In: 6th International Conference on Natural Language Processing and Information Retrieval (2022)
14. Fellbaum, C.: WordNet: An Electronic Lexical Database. Bradford Books (1998)
15. Gordon, D., Kembhavi, A., Rastegari, M., Redmon, J., Fox, D., Farhadi, A.: IQA: visual question answering in interactive environments (2018). https://arxiv.org/abs/1712.03316. Accessed 27 Jan 2023
16. Gupta, R., Kochenderfer, M.: Common sense data acquisition for indoor mobile robots. In: Proceedings of the Nineteenth National Conference on Artificial Intelligence (2004)
17. He, P., Liu, X., Gao, J., Chen, W.: DeBERTa: decoding-enhanced BERT with disentangled attention. In: Conference on Learning Representations (2021)
18. Honnibal, M., Montani, I.: spaCy 2: natural language understanding with Bloom embeddings, convolutional neural networks and incremental parsing (2017). https://sentometrics-research.com/publication/72. Accessed 27 Jan 2023
19. Jiao, A.: An intelligent chatbot system based on entity extraction using RASA NLU and neural network. J. Phys. Conf. Ser. (2020)
20. Kolve, E., et al.: AI2-THOR: an interactive 3D environment for visual AI (2019). https://arxiv.org/abs/1712.05474. Accessed 27 Jan 2023
21. Losing, V., Eggert, J.: Extraction of common physical properties of everyday objects from structured sources. In: 6th International Conference on Natural Language Processing and Information Retrieval (2022)
22. Losing, V., Fischer, L., Deigmoeller, J.: Extraction of common-sense relations from procedural task instructions using BERT. In: Proceedings of the 11th Global Wordnet Conference (2021)
23. Miller, G.A., Chodorow, M., Landes, S., Leacock, C., Thomas, R.G.: Using a semantic concordance for sense identification. In: Human Language Technology: Proceedings of a Workshop held at Plainsboro (1994)
24. Pandya, H.A., Bhatt, B.S.: Question answering survey: directions, challenges, datasets, evaluation matrices (2019). https://arxiv.org/abs/2112.03572. Accessed 27 Jan 2023
25. Paulius, D., Sun, Y.: A survey of knowledge representation in service robotics. In: Robotics and Autonomous Systems (2018)
26. Puig, X., et al.: VirtualHome: simulating household activities via programs. In: Conference on Computer Vision and Pattern Recognition (2018)
27. Speer, R., Chin, J., Havasi, C.: Conceptnet 5.5: an open multilingual graph of general knowledge. In: Proceedings of AAAI-31 (2017)
28. Spinner, T., Schlegel, U., Schäfer, H., El-Assady, M.: explainer: a visual analytics framework for interactive and explainable machine learning. IEEE Trans. Vis. Comput. Graph. **26**(1), 1064–1074 (2019)
29. Szot, A., et al.: Habitat 2.0: training home assistants to rearrange their habitat. In: Advances in Neural Information Processing Systems (NeurIPS) (2021)
30. Tan, S., Ge, M., Guo, D., Liu, H., Sun, F.: Knowledge-based embodied question answering (2021). https://arxiv.org/abs/2109.07872. Accessed 27 Jan 2023
31. Tangiuchi, T., et al.: Survey on frontiers of language and robotics. https://arxiv.org/abs/2112.03572. Accessed 27 Jan 2023

32. Thosar, M., Zug, S., Skaria, A.M., Jain, A.: A review of knowledge bases for service robots in household environments. In: 6th International Workshop on Artificial Intelligence and Cognition (2018)

33. Tjoa, E., Guan, C.: A survey on explainable artificial intelligence (XAI): toward medical XAI. IEEE Trans. Neural Netw. Learn. Syst. **32**(11), 4793–4813 (2020)

34. Wang, C., Deigmoeller, J.: A user interface for sense-making of the reasoning process while interacting with robots. In: International Conference of Human-Computer Interaction (2023)

35. Yu, L., Chen, X., Gkioxari, G., Bansal, M., Berg, T.L., Batra, D.: Multi-target embodied question answering (2019). https://arxiv.org/abs/1904.04686. Accessed 27 Jan 2023

Archives Metadata Text Information Extraction into CIDOC-CRM

Davide Varagnolo[1,3], Dora Melo[2,3](✉) [iD], Irene Pimenta Rodrigues[1,3] [iD],
Rui Rodrigues[4,5] [iD], and Paula Couto[4,5] [iD]

[1] Department of Informatics, University of Évora, Évora, Portugal
d.varagnolo@studenti.unipi.it, ipr@uevora.pt
[2] Polytechnic of Coimbra, Coimbra Business School—ISCAC, Coimbra, Portugal
dmelo@iscac.pt
[3] NOVA Laboratory for Computer Science and Informatics, NOVA LINCS, Caparica, Portugal
[4] Department of Mathematics, FCT NOVA, Caparica, Portugal
{rapr,mpcc}@fct.unl.pt
[5] Center for Mathematics and Applications (CMA), FCT NOVA, Caparica, Portugal

Abstract. This paper presents an Information Extraction approach to extract
events and entities from ISAD(G) elements with semi-structured text descriptions. Natural Language processing is done by using two methodologies: the
ANNIE system, by defining proper Gazetteers and Jape rules to process the text
and extract the intended information; and a reduced Portuguese BERT Language
model that is fine-tuned for Semantic Role Labelling. The evaluation of the Information Extraction processes is done in a sample of 1000 records, for each type of
information, and a corresponding dataset is manually built for each type of information considered, baptism events and passport requisitions. The CIDOC-CRM
knowledge base is automatically populated with newly linked events and entities,
using several automatic information extraction processes. The use of SPARQL
queries to explore the information represented in CIDOC-CRM, obtained from
the migration of DigitArq records and extracted from text descriptions, allows
new ways of visualising the archival records and retrieving information from different sources, including archives digital repositories.

Keywords: Natural language processing · Knowledge representation ·
Knowledge discovery · Semantic web · Archives linked data semantic
representation

1 Introduction

The research project EPISA (Entity and Property Inference for Semantic Archives), in
which the current work was developed, involves the Portuguese National Archives -
Torre do Tombo, archival experts, and Information and Computer Science researchers.

This work is financed by National Funds through FCT - Foundation for Science and Technology
I.P., within the scope of the projects UIDP/04516/2020 (NOVA Laboratory for Computer Science
and Informatics) and UIDB/00297/2020 (Center for Mathematics and Applications).

F. Coenen et al. (Eds.): IC3K 2022, CCIS 1842, pp. 195–216, 2023.
https://doi.org/10.1007/978-3-031-43471-6_9

The general purpose of the project is to represent archival information on a linked data model, by designing a prototype as an open-source knowledge platform. One of the project's main tasks is the semantic migration task, consisting of extracting and representing the relevant entities and their properties from the records in the current DigitArq [22], the Portuguese National archive system. This platform uses well-established description standards, where the archival records metadata has a scheme that supports the recommendations of ISAD(G) (General International Standard Archival Description) [7] and ISAAR(CPF) (International Standard Archival Authority Record for Corporate Bodies, Persons and Families) [26] with a hierarchical structure adapted to the nature of archival assets.

The migration process was performed by developing an automatic semantic migration prototype [19], based on Knowledge Discovery from Digital Archive metadata to populate an ontology in CIDOC-CRM. The data model and descriptive vocabulary were built using the CIDOC-CRM (Conceptual Reference Model) standard [8,17,19]. This ontology was primarily developed for museums by the International Committee for Documentation (CIDOC) of the International Council of Museums (ICOM) [6,16]. A set of Description Mapping Rules, modelling the information in a CIDOC-CRM representation, was developed to support the semantic migration process.

DigitArq information is structured in a set of fields and their values, which comprises atomic values or descriptions. The atomic values, of fields such as 'Reference code', the 'Title', or the 'Recipient', do not require further interpretation, and the migration process is accomplished by applying the corresponding Description Mapping Rules. Description fields, such as 'Scope and content' and 'Archival and Custodial History', characterized by having additional information about their unit, are written in text format with a structure that can be recognized, by applying Natural Language Processing (NLP) tools. The recognition output is a feature value list that will be the input for the additional ontology Population.

It is intended to extract, from the description fields, information that is considered relevant, such as passport requisitions, baptism activities, birth events, inventories due to death, incorporation of documents between archives, institutions, persons, and places involved in those activities. In this work, two approaches for information extraction were implemented: one uses ANNIE (A Nearly-New Information Extraction System)[1] system, from GATE environment[2], and the other one uses a reduced Portuguese BERT (Bidirectional Encoder Representations from Transformers) [3] Language model that is fine-tuned for Semantic Role Labelling. The dataset for the fine-tuning of BERT is built with the results of the ANNIE Information extraction implementation, which are validated by a dataset manually built. The Portuguese language is a low-resource language, with only a few datasets available for Named Entity Recognition or Semantic Role Labelling. The use of the ANNIE Information Extraction results, the tagged text, allowed the creation of a Semantic Role Labelling dataset automatically that can be used to fine-tune BERT.

The main results of this paper include, first, an evaluation of the two approaches for the automatic extraction of information about events and entities, such as persons,

---

[1] https://gate.ac.uk/sale/tao/splitch6.html#chap:annie.

[2] https://gate.ac.uk/.

locations, dates, relationships, baptisms, births, etc.; and second, the exploration of this information to show that the CIDOC-CRM archive metadata representations supply a new organization of the archives information. In a relational database, the archives material is the information unit, in CIDOC-CRM, the events and entities are the information unit and they are linked together by properties, giving rise to new ways to naturally explore the information as can be seen in Sect. 6.

The remainder of this paper is organized as follows. Section 2 presents related work on methods for automatic ontology population and information extraction from text. An overview of the Archives metadata information and its representation in CIDOC-CRM is provided in Sect. 3. In Sect. 4, the proposed approach for extracting events and entities from semi-structured text is presented. Section 5 details the evaluation of the extraction information process. Section 6 highlights the advantages of the new information representation, by presenting the exploration of the CIDOC-CRM knowledge base, using SPARQL queries. Finally, in Sect. 7, conclusions and future work are drawn.

2 Related Work

Automatic ontology population methods extract entities and relations from knowledge sources such as databases, web pages, text documents, etc. [9–11,21]. The extraction process of data, from text to populate ontologies, uses Natural Language Processing techniques (NLP), namely Part-of-Speech Tagging, Syntactic Parsing, Semantic Analysis, and Machine Learning Classifiers based on language models, e.g., bag-of-words or word embedding, such as Word2Vec, GloVe, BERT, etc. [2,9–12,15,21].

Current approaches [14,15,20,27] on text information extraction use Natural Languages Processing task-oriented tools, such as Named Entity Recognition or Semantic Role Labelling. Some of these approaches are Ontology-Based Information Extraction (OBIE) [9,12,14,23,27], which extract knowledge from text to represent it into semantic web ontologies.

Common methods for information extraction from text include the use of Information Extraction tools, such as ANNIE, or the use of Language Models, such as BERT, with fine-tuning on the specific task, e.g. Named Entity Recognition or Semantic Role Labeling [28].

ANNIE is an Information Extraction tool that is a component of the GATE environment. This tool uses a natural language pipeline that includes linguistic information, Gazetteers, and the possibility of using Pattern Matching Rules (Jape rules) to activate actions to mark text according to a set of tags for Named Entity Recognition or Semantic Labelling Role.

The language model BERT can be fine-tuned for Semantic Role Labelling through Transfer Learning, which involves fine-tuning a pre-trained model on a specific task, e.g., it involves training BERT on a corpus of text annotated with semantic roles. This allows BERT to learn the language-specific patterns associated with the task, which can then be used to identify roles in text.

In the proposed approach presented in this paper, the two methods, ANNIE and BERT, are used for the task of Information Extraction from semi-structured text descriptions. The fine-tuning of BERT on tasks, such as Named Entity Recognition or Semantic

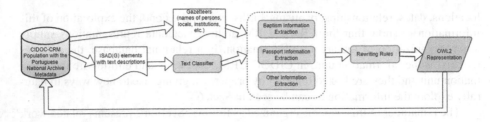

Fig. 1. Architecture of the Events and Entities Ontology Population.

Role Labeling, requires the annotation of a large sample of texts, to avoid manual tagging, the results of ANNIE are used as the dataset to fine-tune a pre-trained BERT with Portuguese texts.

3   Overview of Archives Metadata Representation in CIDOC-CRM

The information that can be extracted from the Archives Metadata, ISAD(G) elements, is presented in natural language texts and depending on the type of the archive material has different subjects. For instance, some archives materials are documents describing passport requisitions, others are baptism registrations or inventories due to death. The information that can be founded in those documents is about activities such as baptisms, births, passport requisitions, and events such as institutions, persons, dates, and places.

The mapping rules to represent the information extracted from the archives' metadata, in the CIDOC-CRM ontology, are presented in Subsect. 3.2.

Texts can be classified according to the type of activities and entities they describe. To determine the type of information conveyed by a text, an automatic text classifier is used. For each type of text, a different information extraction process was defined taking into account the semi-structured scheme of the specific type of text.

The information extraction processes are defined using the ANNIE tool of the GATE environment, see Subsect. 4.1. And, an extraction process using the results of ANNIE and the language model BERT is explained in Subsect. 4.2.

The architecture of the process for events and entities extraction from text and the population of the CIDOC-CRM ontology is presented in Fig. 1. This process consists of 3 phases. First, a classifier decides the type of text that is going to be processed and some of the document OWL representation such as the reference code is saved to be used in the last phase. Next, the text information is extracted using the process for the specific type of text. Finally, the extracted entities and their roles are represented in the CIDOC-CRM ontology using the OWL rewriting rules (mapping rules).

3.1   Extracted Information from ISAD(G) Elements

The information of interest to be extracted from ISDA(G) elements depends mostly on the subject of the record. Therefore, this work focuses especially on passport and baptism records, and the information that can be extracted from text ISAD(G) elements, such as the 'title' or the 'Scope and content'. Passport and baptism records provide relevant information about family relationships and events, as well as the names of persons participating in these events, and also the date of the events. The availability of this information will provide the target audience with new and different visualizations of the information, as well as new and different searches. From both equally, passport and baptism records, it is possible to extract the following information:

Recipient - Name of the person that requested the passport or was baptized.
Father Name - Name of the father of the recipient.
Mother Name - Name of the mother of the recipient.
Production Date - Date of the passport emission or the baptism event, given by the ISAD(G) 'date range' element.

From baptism records, it is possible to extract the following additional information:

Grandparents Names - At most the name of all the grandparents of the recipient.
Godparents Names - The names of the two godparents of the recipient.
Date of Birth - Date of birth of the recipient.

From passports records, in particular, it is possible to extract the following information:

Place of Birth - Local, Parish and County Names in Portugal of the birth's place of the recipient.
Age - Age of the recipient.
Literacy - Normally the annotation is: 'can write' or 'cannot write'.
Marital Status - The recipient's marital state: 'married', 'single', 'widow' or 'divorced'.
Occupation - The recipient's occupation, such as 'farmer', 'domestic', 'mason', 'tailor', 'student', etc.
Place of Destination - The country or a country and a town to where the recipient is going.

As an illustrative example, consider two DigitArq records, the passport requisition of 'José Augusto Teixeira'[3] and the baptism registration of 'Ana'[4]. From the information of interest to be extracted and identified above, the ISAD(G) 'Scope and content' element provides most of the information about the recipient. For instance, the 'Scope and content' of the passport record provides information such as parents' names, age, occupation, literacy, marital status, and travel destination of the applicant, and the 'Scope and content' of the baptism record provides the parents' names, grandparents' names, godparents' names and the birth date of the baptized person, see Table 1 for further details.

As can be observed from the examples, the written information contained in the 'Scope and content' has an intentional scheme in mind, with the aim of facilitating the recording of information by archivists, as well as by anyone who wishes to consult it. Regarding the passport and baptism records, the schemes displayed in the 'Scope and content' element are used to develop a method to extract the intended information, see Sect. 4 for further details.

---

[3] http://digitarq.adbgc.arquivos.pt/details?id=1298186.
[4] https://pesquisa.adporto.arquivos.pt/details?id=1374658.

Table 1. The ISAD(G) 'Scope and content' element of Illustrative Examples.

Âmbito e Conteúdo (PT)	Scope and Content
The passport requisition of 'José Augusto Teixeira'.	
Registo n.° 228 - f.28	Registration n.° 228 - f.28
Filho de: José Maria Teixeira e de Ana da Anunciação Gamboa;	Son of: José Maria Teixeira and Ana da Anunciação Gamboa;
Natural de: Ligares-Ligares-Freixo de Espada á Cinta;	Born in: Ligares-Ligares-Freixo de Espada á Cinta;
Idade: 14 anos;	Age: 14 years old;
Literacia: sabe escrever;	Literacy: can write;
Estado Civil: solteiro(a);	Marital Status: single;
Profissão: Estudante;	Occupation: Student;
Destino: Brasil.	Destination: Brazil
The baptism registration of 'Ana'.	
Pais: António Joaquim de Araújo Bessa e de Guiomar Rosa da Silva	Parents: António Joaquim de Araújo Bessa and de Guiomar Rosa da Silva
Avos maternos: Caetano Francisco da Silva e Clara Joaquina Rosa sa Silva	Maternal parents: Caetano Francisco da Silva and Clara Joaquina Rosa sa Silva
Avós paternos: José Ferreira de Araújo e Maria Pereira	Paternal parents: José Ferreira de Araújo and Maria Pereira
Padrinhos: António Teixeira Bezerra e Ana (sic)	Godparents: António Teixeira Bezerra and Ana (sic)
Data de nascimento: 8 de Maio de 1812	Date of birth: 8th May 1812

3.2 CIDOC-CRM Representation of the Events and Entities Extracted

Predefined mapping rules are used to represent information in CIDOC-CRM ontology [19,24]. In particular, the representation of an activity such as a passport requisition must be modelled in the target ontology, CIDOC-CRM, defining how the information is linked to the document information, see Subsect. 3.1.

Figure 2 presents the CIDOC-CRM representation of the information that can be found in a text describing a passport requisition.

A document representation ('$E_3$1 Document') can have activities ('E_7 Activity') linked by the property 'P_{129} is about'. A passport requisition is represented as a CIDOC-CRM activity ('E_7 Activity') with the type 'passport'. Activities can be linked: to dates, the passport emission date; to locals, destiny place; to a person, the person that made the requisition; etc. The text can describe the date of birth and the parents, in CIDOC births are represented by the class ('E_{67} Birth'), and are linked to the document by the property 'P_{67} refers to'. The information related to a birth such as parents is represented by properties such as 'P_{96} by mother' and 'P_{97} by father'.

The CIDOC-CRM representation of the information extracted from the text in the ISAD(G) element 'Scope and content', is automatically obtained by using a set o migration rules that map the entities and relations extracted into CIDOC-CRM classes and properties.

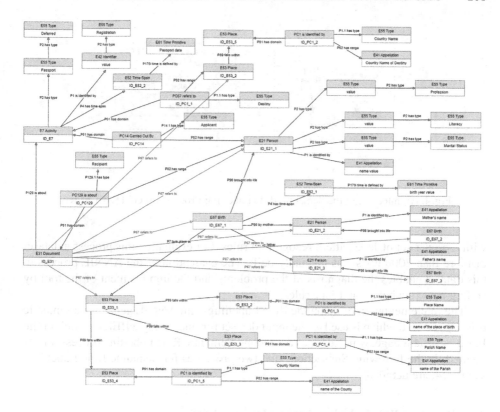

Fig. 2. CIDOC-CRM Representation of a Passport Requisition Activity.

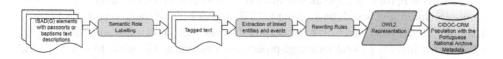

Fig. 3. Architecture of the Extraction Process from Semi-structured Text.

4 The Extraction of Events and Entities from Semi-structured Text

The Information Extraction process consists of: firstly, the text in ISAD(G) elements is marked by the Semantic Role Labelling process producing a new tagged text; then, a process for extracting linked data from tagged text is applied and a set of related structures are generated; and finally, the resulting structures are used as the input of the process that populates the CIDOC-CRM ontology with the information extracted from the text. The architecture of the Information Extraction process is presented in Fig. 3.

The Semantic Role Labelling task was initially implemented using a Natural Language Processing tool from the GATE environment, the extraction information system ANNIE, which was configured for the domain vocabulary of the proposed work and

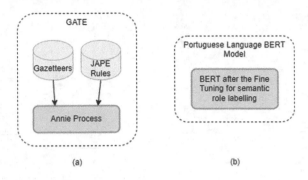

Fig. 4. Architecture of the Semantic Role Labelling Process: (a) GATE (b) BERT.

with a proper set of Jape pattern recognition rules. For evaluating this process a dataset of more than 2000 texts was manually built. The evaluation of the ANNIE process in this dataset enables the diagnosis of the problems and the improvement of the tool by adding new vocabulary and Jape rules.

The implementation of Semantic Role Labelling with ANNIE generates a semantic role-tagged text, which is used as the input dataset for fine-tuning a BERT model for the Portuguese language, which defines the second Semantic Role Labelling process implemented. In the following Subsections, the two processes for Semantic Role Labelling, see Fig. 4, are detailed.

4.1 Semantic Role Labelling Process Using GATE

As mentioned before, an implementation of the Information Extraction process from the semi-structured text was defined using GATE, a Java suite of tools to perform Natural Language Processing tasks over the corpus. In Gate, the tasks are managed by applications that include several language-processing resources. The main tool is ANNIE, which is composed of a pipeline comprising a tokenizer, a gazetteer, a sentence splitter, a part-of-speech tagger, a named entities transducer, and a coreference tagger. To configure ANNIE for the proposed Information Extraction task, gazetteers and Jape rules were defined, see Fig. 4(a).

Since some of the written baptism and passport texts follow a semi-structured scheme, see Table 1, it is possible to define a corresponding methodology, using ANNIE system, for extracting information based on this scheme. Therefore, each Information Extraction task, baptism or passport texts, is implemented by defining new rules for two modules:

Gazetteer - Designed, originally, to comprise the definition of a geographical dictionary or a directory used in conjunction with a map or atlas, in this work, are used as entity dictionaries to tag text words, in ANNIE, within the Named Entity Recognition task.

Jape Rules - Named Entity Extraction can be performed by applying the technique Named Entity Transducer, based on Finite State Transducer composed of rules. The

ANNIE application allows the creation and modification of rules, by using Jape[5] (Java Annotation Pattern Engine). A group of pattern/action rules composes each phase of the Jape grammar. These phases constitute a cascade of finite state transducers over annotations and run sequentially. An annotation pattern description is represented on the left-hand-side (LHS) of the rules and annotation manipulation statements are defined on the right-hand-side (RHS).

Consider, as an illustrative example, the text of the 'Scope and content' of the passport record presented in Table 1. As mentioned before, a predefined structure scheme is identified in the written text and it is common to other passport records. For instance:

- The parents' names of the applicant
  {Filho de}: {father} e {mother}
- The applicant's occupation
  {Profissão}: {occupation}

The entity extraction process can be facilitated by defining rules matching this kind of structured text. The patterns identified and the application of the corresponding Jape rules are sufficient to perform the extraction process and there is no need to apply additional Named Entity Recognition techniques.

The first-degree relatives and the places mentioned in the texts are tagged with the Gazetter processing. After the Sentence Splitter and the POS Tagger are processed, the Jape rules are applied and the names of the parents, birthplaces, parishes, and counties are tagged. In regards to the other text classification, specialized rules are defined to cover different patterns and make it possible to extract the relevant information. For instance, the following Jape rules represent the way to extract the father's name, the mother's name, and the occupation of the applicant, from the text, classified as 'passport'.

```
Rule: Parents Priority: 100
({Token.string ==~ "[Ff]ilho"}
{Token.string == "de"} {Token.string == ":"}):start
({Person.kind == fullName}):father
({Token.string == "e"}|({Token.string == "e"}
{Token.string == "de"})):and
({Person.kind == fullName}):mother
-->
:father.Recipient = {field= "Father", recipient = "1" },
:mother.Recipient = {field= "Mother", recipient = "1" }

Rule: Profession Priority: 100
({Token.string ==~ "[Pp]rofisso"}
{Token.string == ":"}):start
(({Token.category == NN}|
{Token.category == NNP})+):occupation
-->
:occupation.Recipient = {field= "Occupation", recipient = "1" }
```

The output of each extraction task is a file with the input text tagged.

---

[5] https://gate.ac.uk/sale/tao/splitch8.html.

4.2   Semantic Role Token Labelling Process Using BERT

BERT [3] is a Transformer Neural Network [25] with a bidirectional context well integrated. The use of feed-forward neural networks instead of recurrent ones allows for much better parallelization. Bert is a Transformer Encoder, therefore, is composed of several transformer encoder blocks. In the BERT training, each BERT's input is one sentence or a pair of sentences. Each sentence is converted to a sequence of tokens using a Tokenizer. Each word is converted into one or more tokens since, in BERT, tokens are more meaningful when they correspond to frequent words, suffixes or prefixes. Before a sequence of words is given as input to the transformer, each token is converted to a vector of floats with a fixed length, called the embedding. Each Bert's encoder block transforms each token embedding according to the context, i.e., the embedding sequence. The output of BERT, for each example, is then a sequence of fixed-size vectors.

BERT is pre-trained on two tasks:

- Some percentage (e.g. 10%) of the words in a sentence are masked and BERT tries to predict them.
- Two sentences, A and B, are given and BERT must decide if B is the sentence that follows A.

Two network layers (in parallel) are added to BERT in order to train it on these tasks.

In the implementation of Semantic Role Labeling, with BERT, a small-size Bert, Bert-Tiny, was trained for the Portuguese language. In this reduced BERT model, the embedding length is 128 and only two encoder blocks are used. The Portuguese Corpus used contained only 340 million words, this is a small Corpus for training the more usual size BERT model. This is the first reason to use the reduced-size BERT.

For the Semantic Role Labeling task, one untrained layer of neurons was added to the end, and then the new model was trained for the token classification task. The training dataset was obtained by using the output of the ANNIE Semantic Role Labeling process in a sample with 1600 records, only the records from the ANNIE sample that achieve 100% accuracy and 100% recall were used. This tagged text was converted into BERT tokens with the appropriated semantic role label.

For instance and regarding the illustrative example of the baptism record, see Table 1, the tagged text:

Pais:*O* António*FTHB* Joaquim*FTHI* de*FTHI* Araújo*FTHI* Bessa*FTHI* e de Guiomar*MTHB* Rosa*MTHI* da*MTHI* Silva*MTHI*

Avos*O* maternos:*O* Caetano*GFMB* Francisco*GFMI* da*GFMI* Silva*GFMI* e Clara*GMMB* Joaquina*GMMI* Rosa*GMMI* sa*GMMI* Silva*GMMI*

Avós*O* paternos:*O* José*GFFB* Ferreira*GFFI* de*GFFI* Araújo*GFFI* e Maria*GMFB* Pereira*GMFI*

Padrinhos:*O* António*GP1B* Teixeira*GP1I* Bezerra*GP1I* e Ana*GP1B* (sic)*GP2I*

Data*O* de*O* nascimento:*O* 8*DOBB* de*DOBI* Maio*DOBI* de*DOBI* 1812*DOBI* is converted into:

Pais:*O* António***FTHB*** Joaquim***FTHI*** de***FTHI*** Araújo***FTHI*** Bessa***FTHI*** e*O*
de*O* Gui***MTHB*** ##o***MTHI*** ##mar***MTHI*** Rosa***MTHI*** da***MTHI*** Silva***MTHI***
Av*O* ##os*O* ma*O* ##ter*O* ##nos*O* :*O* Caetano***GFMB*** Francisco***GFMI*** da***GFMI***
Silva***GFMI*** e*O* Clara***GMMB*** Jo***GMMI*** ##a***GMMI*** ##quin***GMMI*** ##a***GMMI***
Rosa***GMMI*** sa***GMMI*** Silva***GMMI***
Av*O* ##ó*O* ##s*O* p*O* ##at*O* ##ern*O* ##os*O* :*O* José***GFFB*** Ferreira***GFFI***
de***GFFI*** Araújo***GFFI*** e*O* Maria***GMFB*** Pereira***GMFI***
Padr*O* ##inhos*O* :*O* António***GP1B*** Teixeira***GP1I*** Be***GP1I*** ##zer***GP1I*** ##ra***GP1I***
e*O* Ana***GP2B*** (***GP2I*** si***GP2I*** ##c***GP2I***)***GP2I***
Da*O* ##ta*O* de*O* nascimento*O* :*O* 8***DOBB*** de***DOBI*** Maio***DOBI*** de***DOBI***
18***DOBI*** ##12***DOBI***

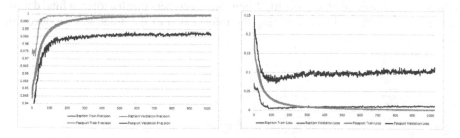

Fig. 5. Precision and Loss BERT Results for Baptism and Passport Dataset.

Given the relatively small number of available classified examples, the dataset was divided into 10 folds and cross-validation was used to train and evaluate the developed system in the Semantic Role Token Labeling task. Each round one fold was used for testing and the others for training and validation. The reported results are for run 4. In Fig. 5, the run 4 results are presented for the metrics Precision and Loss for the Baptism and Passport train and validation datasets. As can be seen in these figures, the best model is obtained with the 256 epochs in both datasets. In the test dataset with the model obtained with run 4 and 256 epochs, for the baptism domain, the precision is 97.7% and recall is 92.6%, and for the passport domain, the precision is 98.9% and recall is 97.8%. These preliminary results are very encouraging to continue to improve the proposed BERT model fine-tuned with the Passport and Baptism datasets.

5   Evaluation of the Extraction Process

In this Section, the evaluation of the two information extraction processes, ANNIE and BERT, is presented.

The evaluation process is done individually for each topic considered, i.e., for each different information extraction, such as baptism or passport descriptions. A set of 1000 records was randomly selected from DigitArq, for each process classification type, and assigned the information accordingly classified with the topic. For each set of records, the corresponding information was used to manually build a dataset, namely a CSV file. Additionally, the information represented in CIDOC-CRM and retrieved through SPARQL queries from each set of records are used to build another dataset, also a CSV file, with the same structure as the dataset manually built.

5.1 Dataset

The DigitArq records are worked by 3 researchers, who independently and individually define a dataset for each topic considered. Each researcher decides which information is adequate to extract from the records and therefore manually creates the corresponding dataset. The resulting dataset file, a CVS file, is organized into a set of columns, each one identified by the corresponding attribute, and a set of rows, each one corresponding to the values of each DigitArq record. When the researchers finish a topic, a final dataset for the topic is obtained by combining the information of the 3 datasets produced by them.

URL	Referência	Nome	Data de Emissão	Pai	Mãe	Naturalidade	Idade	Literacia	Estado Civil	Profissão	Destino
http://digitarq	PT/ADBGC/AC/GCI	António	3/15/1906	João Gonçalves	Eufémia Maria	Maçaira-Vale de Janeiro-Vinhais	30 anos	não sabe escrever	Solteiro(a)	Jornaleiro	Rio de Janeiro - Brasil
http://digitarq	PT/ADBGC/AC/GCI	Manoel	3/15/1906	JFrancisco Pires	Bernarda Luiza	Vale de Janeiro-Vale de Janeiro	45 anos	não sabe escrever	Casado(a)	Jornaleiro	Rio de Janeiro - Brasil
http://digitarq	PT/ADBGC/AC/GCI	José Augusto	3/16/1906	António Augusto	Maria Filá	Pinheiro Velho-Pinheiro Novo-V	22 anos	sabe escrever	Solteiro(a)	Agricultor	Rio de Janeiro - Brasil
http://digitarq	PT/ADBGC/AC/GCI	Francisco Cândido	3/16/1906	pai incógnito	Felisbina de Jesus	Rebordãos-Rebordãos-Bragança	20 anos	sabe escrever	Solteiro(a)	Empregado Comerc	Manaus - Brasil
http://digitarq	PT/ADBGC/AC/GCI	Arnaldo Carneiro de Carvalho	3/16/1906	João Carneiro de C	Maria dos Santos Gouveia	Freixial-Freixial-Vila Flor	25 anos	não sabe escrever	Solteiro(a)	Proprietário	Brasil
http://digitarq	PT/ADBGC/AC/GCI	José Maria	8/17/1906	João Baptista	Maria da Cruz	Quintela-Paçó-Vinhais	31 anos	sabe escrever	Casado(a)	Agricultor	Rio de Janeiro - Brasil
http://digitarq	PT/ADBGC/AC/GCI	António Januário	9/17/1906	João Baptista	Joanna Baptista	Quintela-Paçó-Vinhais	29 anos	não sabe escrever	Casado(a)	Jornaleiro	Rio de Janeiro - Brasil
http://digitarq	PT/ADBGC/AC/GCI	Cenerlano José	3/19/1906	Domingos Gonçal	Margarida Paris	Quintela-Paçó-Vinhais	35 anos	não sabe escrever	Casado(a)	Agricultor	Rio de Janeiro - Brasil
http://digitarq	PT/ADBGC/AC/GCI	Benedicta Diegues	3/20/1906	Manuel Carlos Ole	Francisca da Silva	Moimenta-Moimenta-Vinhais	64 anos	não sabe escrever	Casado(a)	Agricultora	Rio de Janeiro - Brasil

Fig. 6. A sample from the Dataset of Passport Requisitions.

Figure 6 presents a part of the dataset for the topic 'passport'. Note that some of the records have empty values, which means that the corresponding ISAD(G) elements, such as 'Scope and content' or 'title', do not have that information. The information presented in the ISAD(G) elements may depend on how the Archives are used. The National Portuguese Archive is composed of District and Institutions archives, with their own organization and orientations on how to display and update digital information. For instance, some information like 'literacy', 'occupation', or 'marital status' may not be displayed in the passport record by all archives.

5.2 Evaluation Methodology and Results

Precision and Recall are the metrics used as the evaluation methodology. The dataset retrieved, using SPARQL queries, from the information represented in CIDOC-CRM of each set of records is interpreted as follows: in each dataset row, the non-empty value of an attribute is correct if it matches the corresponding row and column value of the manually built dataset; otherwise, it is considered incorrect. Therefore, the definition of Precision and Recall formulas are:

$$\text{Precision} = \frac{\text{number of correct values}}{\text{number of correct values} + \text{number of incorrect values}} \tag{1}$$

$$\text{Recall} = \frac{\text{number of correct values}}{\text{number of non-empty values in the Manual dataset}} \tag{2}$$

The quality of the values extracted is measured by Precision and the quantity of the information extracted is given by Recall.

The improvement of Information Extraction processes is done through the information provided by the dataset annotations, which allows developers to identify pattern errors in Natural Language Processing rules. The manually built dataset is used to evaluate and test the adequacy of new versions of the extraction processes.

5.3   Evaluation of the ANNIE Extraction Process

ANNIE Information Extraction specialised processes are still under development. New versions to improve precision and recall, or to include new topics that need manually created datasets, new CIDOC-CRM representations, and new Jape rules are being built. Although, the preliminary evaluation of the Information Extraction process shows promising results. Extracting information, such as dates, entities, birth events, baptism activities or passport requisition activities, with the correct roles assigned to the persons who participated in those events, as well as places, see Fig. 9 for more details, from baptism and passport descriptions achieved a precision of 97.7% and recall of 91.7%. When considering just the baptism information, a precision of 97.7% and a recall of 94.7% is achieved. Figure 7 presents the results for the different semantic roles in the baptism material metadata for 1000 examples. In this Figure, the Recipient, the name of the person that was baptised, and the date of baptism are presented in all of the 1000 samples. The roles of grandfather and grandmother from the mother's side have 586 samples and the proposed implementation with ANNIE obtained a precision of 99.4% and a recall of 91% for the grandfather from the mother's side. Figure 8 presents the results, precision and recall, for each role's passport role labelling process. The analysis of these results allows us to diagnose the problems in the proposed implementation and correct them in future versions.

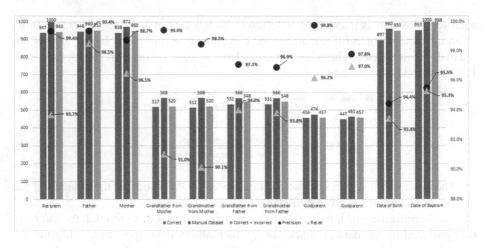

Fig. 7. Evaluation results of a sample of 1000 baptism records.

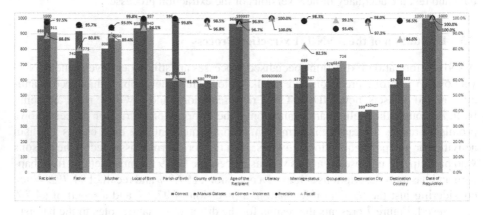

Fig. 8. Evaluation results of a sample of 1000 passports records.

5.4   Evaluation of the BERT Extraction Process

To evaluate the BERT model fine-tuned to Semantic Role Labelling, it is not enough to look at the BERT results since the results are obtained for well-tagged tokens. In this task, it is necessary to obtain the results for well-tagged words. So, when words are braked into sets of tokens, the words must be recovered from those tokens and the final word tag must be decided from the set of tags of the tokens. A preliminary algorithm to build words and decide the correct tag was defined, by assigning the most frequent category tag in the word tokens to the tag of the word, see Table 2 with examples of some problems that occurred.

The results, with a first naive approach for word tagging, are presented in Fig. 10(a) for the Baptism dataset and Fig. 10(b) for the Passport dataset. The results show that the proposed word tag recovery algorithm must be improved since the results for word tags are much lower than those for tokens tagged. Another aspect in the lower results

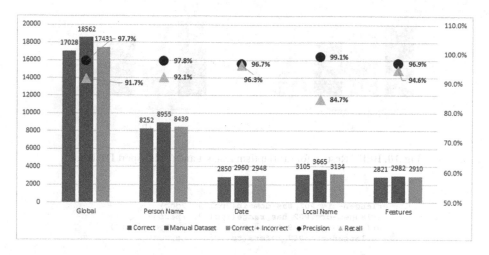

Fig. 9. Evaluation results of a sample of the total 2000 records.

Table 2. Word Tag Recovery Examples.

Word	Tokens	Tagged Tokens	Word tag	Problems
Rosa	Rosa	Rosa\MTHI	\ MTHI	no problem
Guiomar	Gui ##o ##mar	Gui\ MTHB ##o\ MTHI ##mar\ MTHI	\ MTHB	transform the \ MTHI into \ MTHB
Guiomar	Gui ##o ##mar	Gui\ MTHB ##o\ O ##mar\ MTHI	\ MTHB	transform the \ O into \ MTHI

for word tagged to decrease is that the tag 'O' (no category) is not evaluated, and most of the words in a text are tagged as 'O'.

6 Exploration of the Extracted Information

The representation of the Portuguese Archives material metadata in CIDOC-CRM ontology provides archive users with more powerful and expressive searches to explore the information [1,4,5,13].

OWL representation allows writing logic inference rules to obtain new relations linking the new extracted entities to the already known entities enabling searches with simpler expressions.

Consider Semantic Web Rule Language (SWRL)[6] rules such as the following ones [24].

---

[6] https://www.w3.org/Submission/SWRL/.

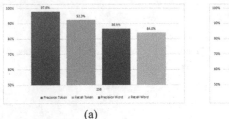
(a)

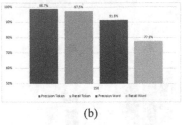
(b)

Fig. 10. BERT Results for (a) Baptism Dataset and (b) Passport Dataset.

```
R1: erlangen-crm:P01_has_domain(?pc129, ?doc)
  ^ erlangen-crm:P02_has_range(?pc129, ?person)
  ^ erlangen-crm:P129.1_has_type(?pc129, 'Recipient')
  -> erlangen-crm:P67_refers_to(?doc, ?person)


R2: erlangen-crm:P67_refers_to(?doc, ?person)
  ^ erlangen-crm:P96_brougth_into_life(?person, ?birth)
  ^ erlangen-crm:P7_took_place_at(?birth,?local)
  -> erlangen-crm:P67_refers_to(?doc, ?local)
     ^ erlangen-crm:P67_refers_to(?doc, ?birth)
```

With rule R1, it is inferred that a person, the recipient of a document, is referred to by the document.

With rule R2 it is inferred that the birth and its place are referred to in the document where a person linked to a birth event is referred to.

With these rules, to search for places referred to in a document, it is enough to search for the relation 'P$_{67}$_refers_to', instead of searching for the different paths in the graph linking a document with a place.

Places can be linked to activities, such as baptisms or passport requisitions, or to entities, such as institutions. For instance, the ISAD(G) element 'Scope and content' of documents of type baptisms or passport requisitions, see Tables 1, allows the extraction of the birthplace of the document recipient, and eventually the birthplaces of other persons, such as the parents of the recipient.

In CIDOC-CRM, dates are ('E$_{52}$ Time-span') class entities. Dates are linked to events or activities by 'P$_4$_has_time' property, see Fig. 11 where a document production event ('E$_{12}$ Production') is linked to a date, a ('E$_{52}$ Time-span') instance. The information extraction process obtains dates associated with activities in the text. The ISAD(G) 'Date Range' element contains the archival material production date and this information is represented as in Fig. 11. In this Figure, according to archives modelling in CIDOC-CRM [19], a 'E$_{31}$ Document', representing the archive material metadata, is linked to an object ('E$_{22}$ Human Made Object'), the archive material. The archive material ('E$_{22}$ Human Made Object') may have a production event ('E$_{12}$ Production') linked by property 'P$_{108i}$ was produced by'.

The date of a document production can be used in searches to give temporal context to entities such as places. When a place name is referred to in a document, it is reasonable to assume that, at the date of the document production, the place name was of common use.

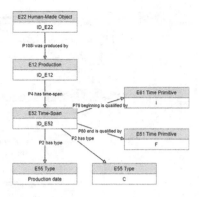

Fig. 11. CIDOC-CRM representation of the document production [24].

An archive user can use Query 1 [24] to know the locals and parishes of the Portuguese county 'Bragança'[7] that were mentioned in documents produced between 1900 and 1910.

Query 1: *Which are the locals and their parishes located in the county 'Bragança', between 1900 and 1910?*

A Graph representation based on the CIDOC-CRM archives representation can be built for this query, in order to obtain the SPARQL query, see Fig. 12.

This graph representation is used to generate the SPARQL query below, by following the graph paths (proprieties) between the classes.

```
PREFIX rdf: <http://www.w3.org/1999/02/22-rdf-syntax-ns#>
PREFIX owl: <http://www.w3.org/2002/07/owl#>
PREFIX rdfs: <http://www.w3.org/2000/01/rdf-schema#>
PREFIX xsd: <http://www.w3.org/2001/XMLSchema#>
PREFIX cidoc: <http://erlangen-crm.org/200717/>

SELECT ?local ?parish
WHERE{
    ?doc cidoc:P70_documents ?hmObj .
    ?hmObj cidoc:P108i_was_produced_by ?prod .
    ?prod cidoc:P4_has_time-span ?t1 .
    ?t1 cidoc:P79_beginning_is_qualified_by ?ti .
    ?t1 cidoc:P80_end_is_qualified_by ?tf .
    ?ti rdfs:label ?ti_datetime .
    ?tf rdfs:label ?tf_datetime .
    BIND(year(xsd:dateTime(?ti_date_time)) AS ?yeari) .
    BIND(year(xsd:dateTime(?tf_date_time)) AS ?yearf) .
    filter(?yeari >= 1900 && 1910 >= ?yearf) .

    ?doc cidoc:P67_refers_to ?loc .
    ?loc cidoc:P89_falls_within ?local0 .
    ?loc cidoc:P89_falls_within ?local1 .
    ?loc cidoc:P89_falls_within ?local2 .

    ?pc0 cidoc:P01_has_domain ?local0 .
    ?pc0 cidoc:P1.1_has_type ?type0 .
    filter(?type0 = "County Name") .
    ?pc0 cidoc:P02_has_range ?localApp0 .
```

---

[7] Bragança is a Portuguese town.

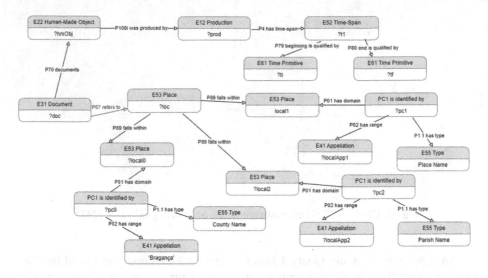

Fig. 12. Graph Representation of Query 1 [24].

```
            ?localApp0 rdfs:label ?local0 .
            filter(?local0="Bragana") .

            ?pc1 cidoc:P01_has_domain ?local1 .
            ?pc1 cidoc:P1.1_has_type ?type1 .
            filter(?type0 = "Place Name") .
            ?pc1 cidoc:P02_has_range ?localApp1 .
            ?localApp1 rdfs:label ?local .

            ?pc2 cidoc:P01_has_domain ?local2 .
            ?pc2 cidoc:P1.1_has_type ?type2 .
            filter(?type2 = "Parish Name") .
            ?pc2 cidoc:P02_has_range ?localApp2 .
            ?localApp2 rdfs:label ?parish .
        }
```

The answer to this query is a set of pairs with a Local's name and its Parish's name. Each Local's name and its Parish's name were mentioned in an ISAD(G) element of a Portuguese National Archives document that was produced at a date between 1900 to 1910.

Varying the date range in query 1, the set of pairs of names may be different, since local, parish, and county names may change over the years due to political and administrative decisions. For sociologists or historians, these queries may be helpful to study the nomenclature evolution in the administrative organization of Portugal regions.

The CIDOC-CRM archives representation enables queries that relate the information extracted from different types of documents, and use aggregation to obtain information that was not possible to obtain in the relational database DigitArq.

Query 2 [24] is an example of a query that uses information extracted from the Portuguese Catholic Church Archives, referring to baptisms and marriages, and from the Portuguese Civil Administration Archives, on passport requisitions, testaments, mar-

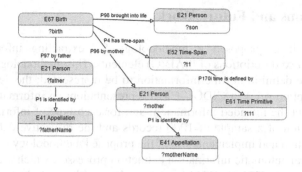

Fig. 13. Graph Representation of Query 2 [24].

riages or divorces. In those documents, persons are often associated with their birth date and their parents. To count the children, it is necessary to use the aggregate function.

Query 2: *What is the number of children per couple, between 1800 and 1850?*

Query 2 Graph representation based on the CIDOC-CRM archives representation is presented in Fig. 13. This graph representation is used to generate the SPARQL query below.

```
PREFIX rdf: <http://www.w3.org/1999/02/22-rdf-syntax-ns#>
PREFIX owl: <http://www.w3.org/2002/07/owl#>
PREFIX rdfs: <http://www.w3.org/2000/01/rdf-schema#>
PREFIX xsd: <http://www.w3.org/2001/XMLSchema#>
PREFIX cidoc: <http://erlangen-crm.org/200717/>

SELECT ?motherName ?fatherName
       (count(?son) as ?numberSons)
WHERE{
    ?birth cidoc:P98_brought_into_life ?son .
    ?birth cidoc:P97_from_father ?father .
    ?father cidoc:P1_is_identified_by ?fatherName.
    ?birth cidoc:P96_by_mother ?mother .
    ?mother cidoc:P1_is_identified_by ?motherName.
    ?birth cidoc:P4_has_time-span ?t1 .
    ?t1 cidoc:P170i_time_is_defined_by ?t11 .
    ?t11 rdfs:label ?t1_datetime .
    BIND(year(?t1_datetime) AS ?year).
    filter(?year >= 1800 && 1850 >= ?year)
}
group by ?motherName ?fatherName
order by desc(?numberSons)
```

The answer to this query is a set of the mother's name, the father's name, and the number of children born between 1800 and 1850.

The result of query 2 gives a good idea of the number of children per couple over a period of time and can be important for demographers that want to collect and analyse data from the Portuguese National Archives.

In [18], a subset of CIDOC-CRM representation of DigitArq records from Bragança District Archive, and two SPARQL query is available.

7   Conclusions and Future Work

In this paper, it is proposed a methodology for extracting information from semi-structured text descriptions of ISAD(G) elements. This methodology is composed of five steps: the definition of the information to be represented; the definition of the mapping description rules in CIDOC-CRM representation; an information extraction process to extract the intended information; and for each type of information considered, the definition of a sample of 1000 records and the respective dataset manually built. The definition and implementation of the proposed methodology led to the development of several automatic information extraction processes, which are used to automatically populate the CIDOC-CRM knowledge base with new linked events and entities and thereafter be evaluated.

The Information Extraction process was done using two methodologies: the ANNIE system, by defining Jape rules and vocabularies, and BERT fine-tuned on the Semantic Role Tokens Labelling. The Information Extraction tool built with ANNIE system achieves a precision of 97.7% and a recall of 91.7% in a test dataset. The BERT model Information Extraction tool achieves a precision of 88% and a recall of 84% in a test dataset when evaluating the semantic role tagging of words. Those results are lower than the ones obtained with ANNIE but show that the investment in improving the BERT model can achieve good results. The improvements on the BERT model include training the BERT language model in the texts of the archive's metadata, creating new loss functions to penalize incorrect token tag sequences, and enlarging the training dataset with more manually built datasets.

The new CIDOC-CRM representation of the information allows exploring and retrieving information that, in the original representation - DigitArq, the relational database, was not easily available. Instead of only using DigitArq public access by a portal with a simple and advanced search that does not include SQL queries, this new representation allows the use of tools, such as SPARQL or DLQuery, for new visualisations of the archival records and the retrieval of information collected in different records from different archives. To highlight these new ways of exploring and retrieving two queries examples were presented. The use of SPARQL or DLQueries over linked data can be quite difficult and complex, besides the language syntax, the information representation structure is also needed to be known by those who wish to explore such knowledge bases. To facilitate this process, in future work, it is intended to develop a friendly interface to automatically generate the SPARQL queries over CIDOC-CRM population from user natural language queries.

References

1. Alma'aitah, W., Talib, A.Z., Osman, M.A.: Opportunities and challenges in enhancing access to metadata of cultural heritage collections: a survey. Artif. Intell. Rev. **53**(5), 3621–3646 (2020)
2. di Buono, M.P., Monteleone, M., Elia, A.: How to populate ontologies. In: Métais, E., Roche, M., Teisseire, M. (eds.) NLDB 2014. LNCS, vol. 8455, pp. 55–58. Springer, Cham (2014). https://doi.org/10.1007/978-3-319-07983-7_8

3. Devlin, J., Chang, M.W., Lee, K., Toutanova, K.: BERT: pre-training of deep bidirectional transformers for language understanding. In: Proceedings of the 2019 Conference of the North American Chapter of the Association for Computational Linguistics: Human Language Technologies, Volume 1 (Long and Short Papers), Minneapolis, Minnesota, pp. 4171–4186. Association for Computational Linguistics (2019). https://doi.org/10.18653/v1/N19-1423. https://aclanthology.org/N19-1423

4. Francart, T.: Sparnatural - Javascript SPARQL Query Builder (2022). https://sparnatural.eu/

5. Hennicke, S.: Representation of archival user needs using CIDOC CRM. In: Conference Proceedings TPDL: International Conference on Theory and Practice of Digital Libraries, Selected Workshops, Valletta, Malta (2013)

6. ICOM/CIDOC: Definition of the CIDOC Conceptual Reference Model. ICOM/CRM Special Interest Group, 7.0.1 edn. (2020)

7. International Council on Archives: ISAD(G): general international standard archival description, 2nd edn. Springer Nature BV (2011)

8. Koch, I., Freitas, N., Ribeiro, C., Lopes, C.T., da Silva, J.R.: Knowledge graph implementation of archival descriptions through CIDOC-CRM. In: Doucet, A., Isaac, A., Golub, K., Aalberg, T., Jatowt, A. (eds.) TPDL 2019. LNCS, vol. 11799, pp. 99–106. Springer, Cham (2019). https://doi.org/10.1007/978-3-030-30760-8_8

9. Kordjamshidi, P., Moens, M.F.: Global machine learning for spatial ontology population. J. Web Semant. **30**, 3–21 (2015)

10. Leshcheva, I., Begler, A.: A method of semi-automated ontology population from multiple semi-structured data sources. J. Inf. Sci. **48**(2), 223–236 (2020)

11. Lubani, M., Noah, S.A.M., Mahmud, R.: Ontology population: approaches and design aspects. J. Inf. Sci. **45**(4), 502–515 (2019)

12. Makki, J.: Ontoprima: a prototype for automating ontology population. Int. J. Web/Semant. Technol. (IJWesT) **8** (2017)

13. Marlet, O., Francart, T., Markhoff, B., Rodier, X.: OpenArchaeo for usable semantic interoperability. In: ODOCH 2019 @CAiSE 2019, Rome, Italy (2019). https://hal.archives-ouvertes.fr/hal-02389929

14. Martínez-Rodríguez, J., Hogan, A., López-Arévalo, I.: Information extraction meets the semantic web: a survey. Semant. Web **11**(2), 255–335 (2020). https://doi.org/10.3233/SW-180333

15. Maynard, D., Li, Y., Peters, W.: NLP techniques for term extraction and ontology population (2008)

16. Meghini, C., Doerr, M.: A first-order logic expression of the CIDOC conceptual reference model. Int. J. Metadata Semant. Ontol. **13**(2), 131–149 (2018)

17. Melo, D., Rodrigues, I.P., Koch, I.: Knowledge discovery from ISAD, digital archive data, into ArchOnto, a CIDOC-CRM based linked model. In: Proceedings of the 12th International Joint Conference on Knowledge Discovery, KEOD, vol. 2, pp. 197–204. INSTICC, SciTePress (2020)

18. Melo, D., Rodrigues, I.P., Varagnolo, D.: Portuguese examples (semantic migration) (2022). https://doi.org/10.17632/t2cx9stwfb.1

19. Melo, D., Rodrigues, I.P., Varagnolo, D.: A strategy for archives metadata representation on CIDOC-CRM and knowledge discovery. Semant. Web 1–32 (2022). https://doi.org/10.3233/SW-222798

20. Niklaus, C., Cetto, M., Freitas, A., Handschuh, S.: A survey on open information extraction. CoRR abs/1806.05599 (2018). http://arxiv.org/abs/1806.05599

21. Petasis, G., Karkaletsis, V., Paliouras, G., Krithara, A., Zavitsanos, E.: Knowledge-Driven Multimedia Information Extraction and Ontology Evolution: Bridging the Semantic Gap. Springer, Heidelberg (2011). https://doi.org/10.1007/978-3-642-20795-2

22. Ramalho, J.C., Ferreira, J.C.: DigitArq: creating and managing a digital archive. In: Building Digital Bridges: Linking Cultures, Commerce and Science: 8th ICCC/IFIP International Conference on Electronic Publishing held in Brasília - ELPUB 2004, Brazil (2004)
23. Stoilos, G., Wartak, S., Juric, D., Moore, J., Khodadadi, M.: An ontology-based interactive system for understanding user queries. In: Hitzler, P., et al. (eds.) ESWC 2019. LNCS, vol. 11503, pp. 330–345. Springer, Cham (2019). https://doi.org/10.1007/978-3-030-21348-0_22
24. Varagnolo., D., Antas., G., Ramos., M., Amaral., S., Melo., D., Rodrigues., I.P.: Evaluating and exploring text fields information extraction into CIDOC-CRM. In: Proceedings of the 14th International Joint Conference on Knowledge Discovery, Knowledge Engineering and Knowledge Management - KEOD, pp. 177–184. INSTICC, SciTePress (2022). https://doi.org/10.5220/0011550700003335
25. Vaswani, A., et al.: Attention is all you need. In: Guyon, I., Luxburg, U.V., Bengio, S., Wallach, H., Fergus, R., Vishwanathan, S., Garnett, R. (eds.) Advances in Neural Information Processing Systems, vol. 30. Curran Associates, Inc. (2017). https://proceedings.neurips.cc/paper/2017/file/3f5ee243547dee91fbd053c1c4a845aa-Paper.pdf
26. Vitali, S.: Authority control of creators and the second edition of ISAAR (CPF), international standard archival authority record for corporate bodies, persons, and families. Cat. Classif. Q. 38(3–4), 185–199 (2004)
27. Wimalasuriya, D.C., Dou, D.: Ontology-based information extraction: an introduction and a survey of current approaches. J. Inf. Sci. 36(3), 306–323 (2010)
28. Zhang, Z., et al.: Semantics-aware BERT for language understanding. In: Proceedings of the AAAI Conference on Artificial Intelligence, vol. 34 n°05, pp. 9628–9635 (2020)

Evolution of Computational Ontologies: Assessing Development Processes Using Metrics

Achim Reiz[✉] and Kurt Sandkuhl

Rostock University, 18051 Rostock, Germany
{achim.reiz,kurt.sandkuhl}@uni-rostock.de

Abstract. Ontologies serve as a bridge between humans and computers. They encode domain knowledge to connect federated data sources or infer tacit knowledge. While the technology used in ontologies is widely adopted and can be considered mature, much has still to be learned about their evolution and development, as understanding ontology evolution could help ensure better quality control and provide knowledge engineers with helpful modeling and selection guidelines.

This paper examines the evolution of computational ontologies using ontology metrics. The authors hypothesize that ontologies follow a similar development pattern. This assumption is broken down into five hypotheses and tested against historical metric data from 69 dormant ontologies and 7,053 versions. The research proved that the development processes of ontologies are highly diverse. While a slight majority of ontologies confirm some of the hypotheses, accepting them as a general rule is not possible. Further, the data revealed that most ontologies have disruptive change events for most measured attributes. These disruptive events are examined regarding their occurrences, combinations, and sizes.

Keywords: Ontology metrics · NEOntometrics · Ontology evolution · Ontology evaluation · Owl · Rdf

1 Introduction

Software needs to evolve over time to meet customers' changing requirements and needs. Computational ontologies are no exception to this rule. Noy and Klein identified three main reasons for ontology evolution: (1) A change in the domain (in the world the ontology captures), (2) a change in the conceptualization, implying a changing view on the modeled domain, and (3) a change in the explicit specification, thus changes in the underlying ontology representation [1].

Domains and conceptualizations frequently change, requiring corresponding electronic representations to develop and evolve. Although the frequency and intensity of these changes may vary, an ontology must adapt to some degree to remain relevant and practical. A dormant artifact is unlikely to conform to evolving requirements and may hinder progress in the domain [2].

Detecting dormant ontologies is reasonably straightforward, as analyzing the publishing dates of new versions and detecting missing activity is sufficient. However,

F. Coenen et al. (Eds.): IC3K 2022, CCIS 1842, pp. 217–238, 2023.
https://doi.org/10.1007/978-3-031-43471-6_10

knowledge engineers and developers could benefit from knowing an ontology's different lifecycle stages before it reaches life's end. This information could allow them to make better development decisions and select artifact that best fits their needs.

This study investigates whether ontology metrics on OWL and RDF ontologies can be used to identify these lifecycle stages. Previous research has proposed stereotypical development processes in ontologies and software development, from the development start to end-of-life. This work tests these assumptions numerically using historical metric data from various research communities, including computer science, bioinformatics, and agricultural science.

The results show that the development processes are highly heterogeneous. While many ontologies share a standard development process, there is a great variety in their evolution, and generally applicable rules do not apply. The analysis further reveals the existence of disruptive changes that drastically change one attribute or more.

This paper is structured as follows: The next section gathers the relevant state of the art in ontology evolution research. Afterward, we derive hypotheses for ontology evolution, followed by the presentation of the dataset and the applied preprocessing. The hypotheses are tested in Sect. 5. Section 6 examines the unexpected occurrences of disruptive changes, followed by a discussion and conclusion of the research.

The paper is an extended version of *"Debunking the Stereotypical Development process"* [3], first published in the 14th edition of the *International Conference on Knowledge Engineering and Ontology Development (KEOD)*. The novelty in this paper is an analysis of the often occurring disruptive changes in Sect. 6.

2 Related Work

Evolution in the context of computational ontologies is mainly understood managing changes throughout the lifetime of an ontology. Stojanovic defines ontology evolution as the *"...timely adaptation of an ontology to the arisen changes and the consistent propagation of these changes to dependent artifacts"* [4]. Numerous studies have explored the identification of changes and their impacts using various methods and levels of granularity. Zablith et al. conducted a thorough literature review on the different perspectives of ontology evolution and change. The review begins with detecting the need for change, followed by its implementation and assessment [5].

Our research primarily concerns the broader perspective of the ontology life cycle rather than managing the minor, regular modifications that occur during ontology development. We are particularly interested in studies that examine the (stereotypical) ontology evolution process from the initial formulation of axioms to the end of the ontology's lifespan when it becomes dormant.

Mihindukulasooriya et al. [6] investigated the evolution of four vocabularies - FOAF, PROV-O, DBPedia, and Schema.org. Their research focused on the numerical development of classes and properties in each published version. The findings highlight the growing size of all the ontologies and the lack of adherence to formal theoretical evolution frameworks.

Ashraf et al. [7] introduced a framework for analyzing ontology usage (Table 1), which introduced various stages of a development lifecycle, such as *engineering, evaluation, population, evolution,* and *usage analysis.* The *evaluation, population,* and *evolution* stages overlap and allow for reiteration. The authors of this paper utilize this cycle primarily to support their presented usage analysis.

Table 1. The ontology development cycle according to Ashraf et al. [7], table from [3].

#	Example	Description
A.1	Engineering	Ontology is developed from scratch according to the given requirements
A.2	Evaluation	Assessment of how well the ontology fits the purpose
A.3	Population	Population of the ontology
A.4	Evolution	Adoption to changes
A.5	Usage Analysis	Ontology usage analysis

Malone and Stevens [2] evaluated change activities in bio-ontologies, which are measured through the addition, deletion, or modification of classes. The authors identified the ontology lifecycle as consisting of five stages: *initial, expanding, refining, optimizing/mature,* and *dormant.* Based on their analysis of 43 ontologies, they provided recommendations for managing community-led development efforts (Table 2).

Table 2. Ontology lifecycle according to Malone and Stevens [2], table from [3].

#	Example	Description
B.1	Initial	State of flux. Hierarchy is not yet settled, coverage not yet sufficient. Many additions, changes, and deletions
B.2	Expanding	Expanding of the domain of interest. Heavy adding of new classes, fairly high level of deletions
B.3	Refining	Low levels of addition and deletion, high level of changes
B.4	Mature	Very low or no level of deletion, some addition or changes
B.5	Dormant	Little or no recent activity

One perspective on computational ontologies is to consider them as pieces of software. Although there is relatively little research on the ontology-specific lifecycle, the field of software evolution has seen considerable progress in recent years. Two papers had an especially significant impact:

Rajlich and Bennet [8] proposed the staged model for the software lifecycle, which is very close in its assumption to the one proposed by Malone and Stevens. This model also has five stages with declining change activity and increasing maturity but with the addition of a release cycle: New versions of the same software can trigger a new iteration of the lifecycle (Table 3).

Table 3. Staged model for software lifecycle by Rajlich and Bennet [8], table from [3].

#	Example	Description
C.1	Initial	First functional version
C.2	Evolution	Extend capabilities to meet users' needs
C.3	Servicing	Simple functional changes and minor defect repairs
C.4	Phaseout	No more servicing, still generating revenue
C.5	Closedown	Withdrawing the system from the market

Lehmann first published his laws of software evolution in 1974 and continuously refined them over the past years. Today, it contains eight fundamentals on the evolutionary behavior of software that depend on or interact with the real world [9]. Lehmann's laws probably had the most significant impact on software evolution research (Table 4).

Table 4. Lehman's laws of software evolution (newest version, from [9]), table from [3].

#	Example	Description
D.I	Continuing change	Systems must adapt continuously to remain satisfactory
D.II	Increasing complexity	As systems evolve, the complexity increases – unless work is done to maintain or reduce it
D.III	Self-regulation	The software evolution process is self-regulating regarding its attributes, with a distribution that is close to normal
D.IV	Conversation and organiz. stability	The average effective activity rate is invariant over the lifetime of the product
D.V	Conservation of familiarity	During the active life of a system, the average content remains invariant
D.VI	Continuing growth	The functional content must continually increase over the lifetime to maintain user satisfaction
D.VII	Declining quality	Unless rigorously adapted to changes in the operational environment, the quality will appear to be declining
D.VIII	Feedback system	Evolution is a multilevel, multiloop, multiagent feedback system

Herraiz et al. [10] conducted a study on the validity of Lehmann's laws of software evolution for open-source software. While some laws, such as D.I and D.VI, were confirmed, others, particularly D.II and D.IV, were mainly invalidated. The validity of other laws fell somewhere in between, with some acceptance and rejection.

3 Hypotheses on Ontology Evolution

In the previous section, we discussed research studies on the evolution of software and ontology artifacts. Based on these studies, we have formulated five hypotheses on how these artifacts evolve over their lifetime. The hypotheses are then linked with ontology metrics and tested against a sizeable metric dataset. The hypotheses and their respective ontology metrics are presented in Table 5.

The initial hypothesis (**H1**) proposes that ontologies will expand in size over the course of their existence, offering a more detailed and extensive representation of their respective domains. This assumption is determined by analyzing the growth of the number of axioms present in the ontology.

The second hypothesis (**H2**) postulates that as an ontology matures, its change activity decreases. While it is supported by B, C, and implicitly by A, it contradicts D.IV. We expect to observe this trend through two measurements: Firstly, by measuring the total number of commits. We anticipate fewer commits towards the end of the lifecycle, indicating reduced activity. Secondly, we measure the size of new versions, determining the percentual axiom change that occurred.

The third hypothesis (**H3**) focuses on the initial stages of ontology development rather than the end of its lifecycle. It proposes that the ontology structure, as indicated by sub-classes and properties on classes, is typically developed before the population of classes with individuals.

Table 5. Hypotheses on ontology evolution, table from [3].

#	Hypothesis	Supported by	Measured By
H1	Ontologies grow during their lifetime	B, C.2, D.VI	Axioms
H2	The level of change decreases over time	(A), B.3–5, C.3–5	Commits, Axioms
H3	The instances (or individuals) are introduced after the initial design	A.3	Sub-classes, Individuals, Property Assertions
H4	Ontology complexity increases with rising maturity	(B.III), D.II	Complexity Measures, Relationship Diversity
H5	A stereotypical development lifecycle can be identified	A, B, C	Diverse

Hypothesis four (**H4**) suggests that the ontology complexity increases over their lifetime. However, measuring ontology complexity is challenging as it can have multiple dimensions. Yang et al. proposed two complexity metrics for the gene ontology, i.e., average relationships per concept and average paths per concept, and we selected the latter for our analysis. However, the gene ontology relies heavily on hierarchical relationships, and these metrics only consider relationships that convey hierarchical meanings [11]. To account for other relationship types, we also include the relationship diversity metric proposed in the OntoQA framework [12], which measures the ratio of non-inheritance and inheritance relationships. While there are other dimensions of complexity, such as concept inclusions or object property characteristics, we focus on these more general metrics, which should apply to a broader range of ontologies.

The hypotheses assume that ontologies have a typical development process and exhibit stereotypical behavior. The last hypothesis (**H5**) generalizes the findings and looks at the bigger picture. It tests whether we can identify joint developments in an ontology or group of ontologies over time. So while the former hypothesis targets specific assumptions out of the lifecycle, H5 takes a broader perspective and considers various data detailed in Sect. 5.5.

4 Dataset Preparation and Analysis

The data for this analysis was obtained from the NEOntometrics application [13], developed by the same authors as this paper. It allows analyzing ontology evolvement using git-based ontology repositories and measures several structural attributes. They include simple ones, like the depth of the graph, the number of classes, or the count of disjoint object properties. However, we also implemented various metrics based on frameworks proposed in the literature. Examples are the OntoQA framework by Tartir et al. [14] and the OQual measurements by Gangemi et al. [15], also used in this paper. The application webpage[1] provides further information on the capabilities and architecture of the metric calculation software.

Figure 1 presents the data pipeline, which starts with accessing metric data through the GraphQL endpoint of NEOntometrics (1), followed by an initial validation check. Ontologies that did not have logical axioms were excluded from further consideration (2). This filtering removed empty ontologies or those that contained only annotations or a wholly customized vocabulary. After the query and validity check, the dataset comprised 159 git-based ontology repositories containing 6,764 ontology files and 56,263 ontology commits (thus, ontology versions).

Next, we applied filters to the data, starting with those related to our specific research questions. Since our focus was on the entire lifecycle of ontologies, we needed to identify those that had reached the end of their development process. To do this, we considered ontologies that had not been active for the last 200 days as dormant. This filtering step resulted in 6,016 ontology files and 31,439 versions.

Additionally, since this research focuses on the evolutionary aspects of ontology development, only ontologies with a significant history can be considered relevant. To ensure this, we set the minimum threshold value for the number of versions to 40 (*result: 77 ontology files, 11,998 versions*). Further irrelevant are isolated or "toy" without a significant user base, which excluded ontologies with only one author (*result: 69 ontology files, 10,810 versions*).

The final filtering step removed reversed commits (4). At times, the data show that metrics are being reversed (*changeOfCommit0* $==$ *changeOfCommit 1 + changeOfCommit2*). For instance, these reversals can occur if one reverses the new commit and

---

[1] http://neontometrics.com

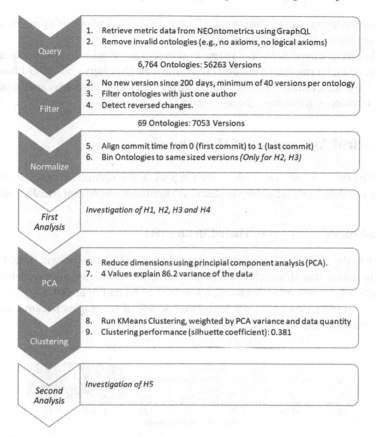

Fig. 1. Data preparation and processing pipeline [3].

recommits the old one. However, this kind of behavior also occurs during merging operations. After this last filter (4), the data set ready for analysis consisted of 69 ontologies with 7053 versions out of 30 repositories.

The dates of the ontology commits in the dataset have a wide range, with some being recently published while others have not had any activity for several years. In order to standardize the time frames and make them comparable, we normalized the dates (5.) by assigning a numerical value ranging from 0 (representing the first commit) to 1 (representing the last commit of the ontology).

At last, two analyses regard the commit count and time during the ontology lifetime (H2, H3). To prevent the disproportionate effect of ontologies with rich version history, we proportionally thinned the commit times to around 40 for these hypotheses to ensure all ontologies are represented equally (6.).

The data preprocessing for answering H1-H4 is finished with the last data preparation step. Subsequently, the processing steps for H5 are described in Subsect. 5.5. The analysis is implemented using Jupyter Notebooks. The source code and ontology metric data are provided online for further exploration[2].

The dataset contains a diverse range of dormant ontologies from various application domains, including the biomedical (e.g., the Cell Ontology and OBO Phenotype), food ontology, agriculture ontology, Italian cultural heritage ontology, and information processing ontology for robots, among others.

5 Empirical Assessment of Hypotheses

Given the hypotheses and metrics described in Sect. 3, this section analyzes the ontology metric data to determine whether the stated assumptions can be empirically validated.

5.1 Ontologies Grow During Their Lifetime (H1)

According to the first hypothesis, ontologies tend to increase in size over time. Our data analysis indicates that this statement is true for most of the ontologies in our study. Specifically, when comparing the median size of the first half of an ontology's life to the median size of the second half, we found that 86.9% of ontologies became larger and only 13% became smaller.

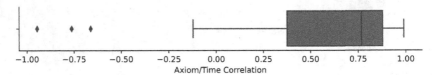

Fig. 2. Distribution of correlation of axioms and time (Pearson) of the ontology files [3].

However, our analysis also shows that the relationship between ontology size and time is not uniform across all ontologies. The boxplot in Fig. 2 illustrates that while half of the ontologies exhibit a strong positive correlation between axiom growth and time, this correlation is less prominent for the second half, and three of the ontologies even demonstrate a robust negative growth trend.

Consequently, we cannot fully confirm H1, as 30.4% of the ontologies in our study have a Pearson correlation value of less than 0.5. Thus, while it is generally true that most ontologies tend to become more extensive over time, this cannot be established as a universal rule.

5.2 The Level of Change Decreases over Time (H2)

The hypothesis (H2) suggests that ontology maturity is inversely related to change activity. To test this hypothesis, we analyzed the frequency and size of commits over time.

---

[2] https://doi.org/10.5281/zenodo.7681423

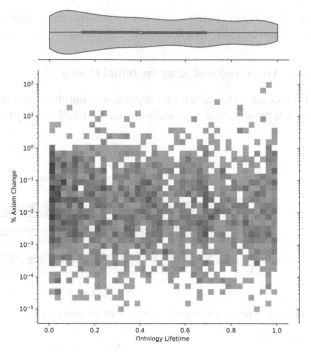

Fig. 3. Development of axioms over the ontology lifetime in percentage (log scale) [3].

The elevated violin plot in Fig. 3 presents the change activity in the ontologies, with the width of the graph representing the number of commits at different stages of the ontology's life cycle. The plot shows that the majority of commits occur at the initial stages of the ontology's development. Within the violin plot, a boxplot indicates that more than half of the ontological changes occur before they reach 40% of their lifetime.

Nevertheless, the size of the changes does not exhibit significant variation. The bivariate histogram below the violin plot illustrates that the magnitude of the changes is not notably different across the ontology's lifespan. The plot depicts the commit count in a given value range as a function of the percentage of increase or decrease in axioms, with darker colors indicating higher frequencies. Notably, the plot reveals that the size of changes varies widely, but there is little difference in their magnitude throughout the ontology's lifespan.

Upon closer examination of the ontology files, it becomes apparent that the data is too heterogeneous to confirm the hypothesis as a universal principle. Out of the 69 analyzed ontologies, it was found that 34 of them had a higher number of changes in the last third of their lifetime compared to the first or second third. Similarly, when comparing the size of the mean change, it was observed that 48 ontologies exhibited more extensive changes in the last third compared to the first or second third.

Similar to H1, H2 cannot be fully confirmed based on the analysis. Although the data indicates that most of the changes and the most significant changes occur at the beginning of ontology development, the rest of the lifecycle does not show a clear pattern of decreasing change activity. Therefore, we cannot confirm the assumption that rising ontology maturity is associated with a decreasing change activity as a general rule.

5.3 The Instances Are Introduced after the Initial Design (H3)

Hypothesis 3 (H3) focuses on the development process of ontology structure and instantiation. It assumes that the structure is typically created first, followed by the introduction of individuals.

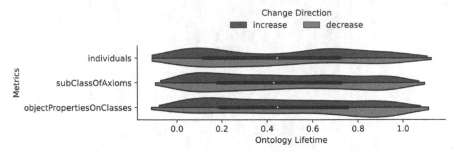

Fig. 4. Change activity of ontology metrics over time [3].

Figure 4 depicts the change activities (adding or deleting) related to sub-classes, object properties on classes and individuals. Contrary to the assumptions of H3, the data shows no distinct phase for adding structure and instances. Instead, there is a high level of change activity and instability at the beginning, with many additions and deletions for all elements, including individuals. However, after the initial phase of instability, the overall activity regarding instances decreases, while the number of commits and deletions of individuals decreases with increasing ontology maturity. The boxplot inside the violin graph indicates that the median of commits related to individuals comes shortly after the median of the other structural metrics, but the difference is relatively small.

In conclusion, we cannot confirm H3 for ontology development. Even though the end of the ontology lifecycle comes with an increase of instances, the development of structure and instances does not happen separately but jointly.

5.4 Ontology Complexity Increases with Rising Maturity (H4)

Hypothesis four (H4) posits that ontologies become more interconnected and complex as they mature. This study uses the complexity metrics *average paths per concept*, which measures the number of multi-inheritance relationships in the ontology, and the relationship diversity, measured through the ratio of inheritance and non-inheritance relationships. Both variables are plotted in their development over time in Fig. 5, where every line represents one ontology.

This left illustration for H4 (Fig. 5) incorporates several findings: At first, there seems to be significant variation among ontologies in their structural complexity, with some showing wide fluctuations over time while others remain relatively stable. The right graph shows that many ontologies exhibit significant variations in their ratio of inheritance to non-inheritance relationships. Although there is a slight trend of increasing complexity, as evidenced by a rise in average paths and relationship diversity, this trend cannot be generalized. Rather than showing consistent changes in complexity metrics, the measures appear to fluctuate widely, with many ontologies experiencing significant swings in both directions.

The second diagram (Fig. 6) shows the Pearson correlation between the complexity measures and time. It analyses whether the ontologies rise steadily in their complexity.

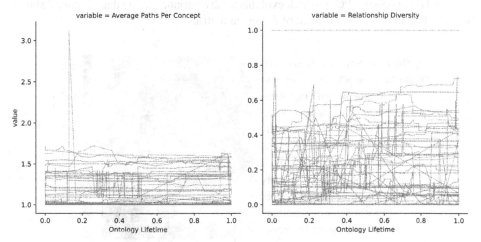

Fig. 5. Ontology complexity development over time [3].

The distribution of the Pearson correlation analysis for the complexity measures and time resembles that of H1. While most ontology files exhibit a positive correlation, indicating increasing complexity over time, no general rule can be established due to the heterogeneity in the data. Some ontologies show no correlation, and others even demonstrate a stringend decrease in complexity.

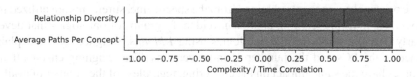

Fig. 6. Distribution of the ontology complexity in correlation with their lifetime [3].

Similar to the previous hypotheses, the results of H4 indicate that while there are indications of most ontologies becoming more complex as they mature, there is still too much contradictory evidence to accept the hypothesis fully.

5.5 A Stereotypical Development Lifecycle Can Be Identified (H5)

The last hypothesis aims to determine whether there is a generalized development process for ontologies. The assessment considers eleven compositional measures proposed in the OQual[3] [15] and OntoQA[4] [14] frameworks. These measures set metrics in relation to each other, enabling better comparisons of ontologies of varying sizes compared to count-related measurements like the number of axioms or classes. However, eleven metrics are still too numerous for efficient visual comprehension. A principal component analysis (PCA) based on the normalized metric values (0:1) reduces the measures to four principal components (PCs), which explains 86.2% variance in the data. Figure 7 shows how the PCs explain the variance of the given metrics.

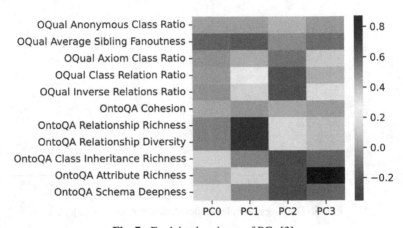

Fig. 7. Explained variance of PCs [3].

The measurements chosen for this analysis are more specific than those used in the previous analysis. Therefore, it is not anticipated that a widely accepted development process can be observed for all types of ontologies. However, it is hypothesized that if there is a typical development process, we should observe groups of ontologies that exhibit similar development patterns.

The principal components obtained from the specific measurements are utilized in an unsupervised machine learning approach to identify groups of ontologies that develop similarly. We aim to cluster the ontologies using *KMeans*, weighed by the explained variance of the PCs and the number of input versions. The weighing ensures that all ontologies have the same impact on the clustering, regardless of the number of available versions. While it is unlikely to discover a universal development process, clustering may help uncover underlying relationships between the ontologies and expose typical development patterns.

---

[3] Anonymous classes ratio, average Sibling fan outness, axiom class ratio, class relation ratio, inverse relations ratio

[4] Cohesion, relationship richness, relationship diversity, class inheritance richness, attribute richness, schema deepness

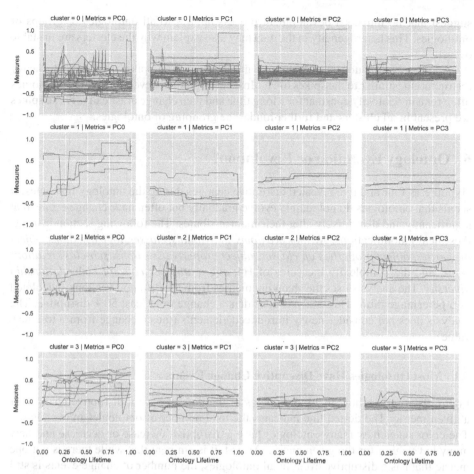

Fig. 8. Clustering based on principal component analysis (PCA) for the ontologies [3].

In order to determine the optimal number of clusters for the KMeans algorithm, multiple iterations were run and evaluated using the silhouette coefficient, which rates the quality of the clusters from −1 to 1. A coefficient around 0 indicates overlapping clusters. In this case, the analysis of the ontology dataset suggested four as the ideal number of clusters, with a silhouette coefficient of 0.381. However, it should be noted that the clustering is somewhat unstable and varies in each run. The ontologies were then assigned to the cluster that appeared most frequently throughout their versions. These four clusters represent groups of ontologies that we assume to have similar development processes.

Figure 8 reveals little evidence that groups of ontologies share a typical development process over their lifetime. In fact, ontologies that exhibit similar modeling behavior, such as those in cluster 0, generally have low overall activity. Furthermore, the graphs rarely show gradual changes that would be expected from ontologies that are improving and evolving. This observation supports the findings of the previous subsections, which suggest that no universal development process applies to all ontologies or groups of ontologies. This heterogeneity in the data may also explain why the clusters are unstable overall.

Another conspicuousness visible in the graphs is the spikes that indicate heavy restructuring, similar to the spikes of H4. Instead of gradual development, the ontologies often remain relatively constant for a long time and then change drastically. These spikes are present in all clusters and further hinder the grouping of ontologies.

6 Ontology Evolution or Revolution?

Hypotheses four and five revealed disruptive changes during the ontology lifecycles. It seems that ontologies do not mainly evolve gradually but often have change events that significantly and disruptively alter their main attributes. The following section inspects these heavy modifications. We look at *axioms, individuals, classes, logical axioms, object properties, object properties on classes, object property assertions, sub-class relationships,* and the complexity measures of H4, *avg. Paths per concept* and *relationship diversity*. The analysis uses the changing metrics from the different versions, calculated as a percentage ratio. This analysis considers a change of at least 50% disruptive. The analysis does not consider newly introduced elements (thus a change from 0 to a new value).

6.1 Most Ontologies Have Disruptive Change Events

Figure 9 visualizes how many ontologies of the dataset have a disruptive change for a given metric. The dotted line indicates the total number of ontologies in the dataset. The color states how many ontologies have a disruptive increase or decrease and how many have either for the given metric. At first, it is eminent that while there is not one metric that has a disruptive event in all ontologies, the number of change events is still relatively high. Five of the ten measures have disruptive changes in at least 35 ontologies. Moreover, as the total number is just slightly larger than the increasing or decreasing changes, many ontologies must have disruptive change events in both directions. Of the 69 ontologies, 60 have at least one disruptive change.

Most ontologies have a disruptive change event for the measures axioms and logical axioms. It is especially noteworthy as these metrics are comprised of the other measures: All summed statements in the ontology are the axioms, and all statements that incorporate logical meaning are the logical axioms (*logical axioms = axioms − annotations*). A higher number of changes in axioms and logical axioms than in the underlying measures, thus, reveals that the ontologies have significant structural change events not primarily driven by a single change measure but a combination of many. Within these combinations, the underlying atomic measures may not always reach the (arbitrary) 50% change threshold for a disruptive change, but combined, they sum up to a heavy restructuring.

However, the ontologies also have significant change events for other ontology metrics. The main components of the T-Box, the classes, sub-class relationships (sub-class axioms), defined relations (object properties), and usage of relations on classes (object properties on classes), also all often have regular, disruptive changes. The complexity measures reflect the insights of H4: The avg. Paths per concept show just little changes, the relationship diversity has a little more activity. Compared to the other measures, the complexity does not change as often.

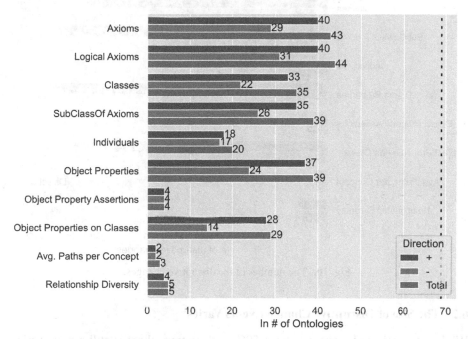

Fig. 9. The number of ontologies having at least one disruptive change for a metric.

At first, it seems that the A-Box (measured through the number of individuals and the number of object property assertions) stays more or less constant. However, only 48 ontologies define individuals. Thus, 41.7% of these ontologies have a disruptive change event in their instance count. This behavior is similar to using object properties on individuals (object property assertions). Only 13 ontologies use these axioms, and 30.8% of them have a disruptive change event in this metric.

While Fig. 9 shows how many ontologies have disruptive change events, Fig. 10 illustrates how many change events exist. Regarding the change directions, the metrics that measure the count of axioms have more disruptive increases than decreases. However, no clear trend is evident, and most ontologies with a disruptive increase also show a decrease. This tendency is similar to the findings of H1, where we experience that a majority of ontologies tend to grow, but the data generally shows much heterogeneity.

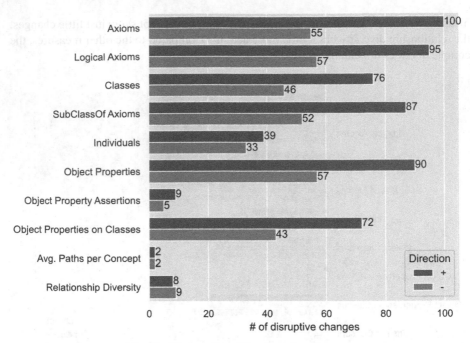

Fig. 10. The number of the disruptive changes.

6.2 The Size of Disruptive Change Events Varies

While we considered a change above 50% as disruptive, there is still a great variety regarding their size. The boxplots in Fig. 11 show the size distribution of the changes with a shift > 0.5 on the logarithmic scale. The blue boxplots indicate the size of the changes that increase the value, and the orange ones show a decrease. The decreasing values are inversed to align the scale between percentage increase and decrease $(1/x)$. This inverse operation projects a change from 3 to 6 and from 6 to 3 to a change value of 2.

The mean value of the changes that increase the size is 5.5, with a standard deviation of 18.62. The decreasing changes have a mean value of 9.83 and a standard deviation of 65.45. Thus, the standard deviation indicates a greater variety of disruptive changes that decrease a given attribute. We conclude that, in combination with the findings from the previous subsection, even though there are more ontologies with disruptive increases in attributes, the heavy changes that reduce the use of an attribute are mostly more extensive than the changes that increase it.

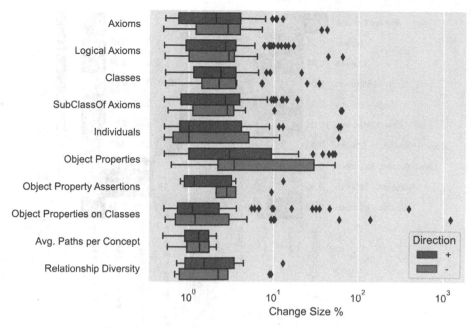

Fig. 11. The size of the disruptive changes in log scale.

6.3 Disruptive Changes Come in Various Combinations

From the number of disruptive change elements visible in Fig. 10, it is already eminent that there are more disruptive change events than ontologies. That further raises the question of whether they occur isolated from one another or simultaneously.

A first analysis identified that, for every disruptive change event, on average, these new versions have 2.8 measures involved (standard deviation: 1.94). Figure 12 below elaborates on the combinations of metrics that occur together in these change events. For example, for the measure *classes*, the heatmap shows that 92% of the disruptive change events of classes also have a significant axiom change and occur together with heavy sub-class alterations for 93% of the altered classes.

Some of the combinations are understandable by the imagination of a typical development process: When adding classes, it seems natural to directly sort them into the proper categories, thus adding sub-class relationships. Moreover, if the ontologies are more focused on building a taxonomy rather than rich description logic and do not have many annotations, the threshold for the logical axioms or axioms can easily be crossed. Similar reasoning can be established for the often-seen combinations of object property assertions and individuals. Adding the required relationships in the same process might often make sense as one creates an individual.

However, many more combinations are not as obvious apart from these highly interrelated measures. 59% of the disruptive changes in object properties also significantly affect the axioms, even though the number of object properties is often a relatively small part of their overall number. 54% of the object property changes have a disruptive change in classes, and 56% for sub-class relationships.

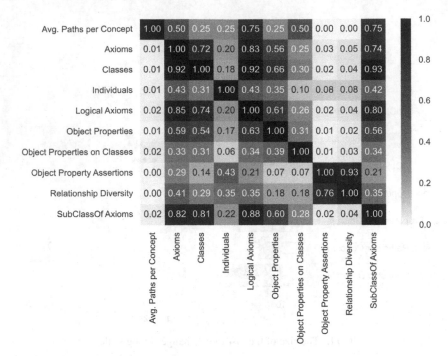

Fig. 12. Percentagewise combinations of disruptive ontology change events for a given metric.

The diversity in the previous hypothesis analysis is visible in the combination of disruptive changes. There are often rather unclear patterns, and disruptive changes often alter elements of various resorts.

6.4 Sensitivity Analysis

The threshold for identifying a change as disruptive at 50% is selected arbitrarily. It opens the question of whether the given value is a practical fit and whether a threshold change significantly impacts the overall analysis. Thus, this section repeats previous analyses for different change threshold values.

The first sensitivity analysis regards the ontologies that have disruptive changes. The diagram below presents the number of ontologies with at least one disruptive change with a variable disruptive threshold value. In this regard, Fig. 9 is an extract of the presented line diagram for the threshold value of 0.5. The graph shows that changing the value does not heavily influence the number of ontologies that have a disruptive change for a given measure. Thus, most of the ontologies have at least one sizeable disruptive event.

The next sensitivity check in Fig. 14 shows the number of changes if the level for disruptive changes is set at 25% (left) or 75% (right). While the number of total changes rises with a decrease in the threshold value, the relations between the distribution stay relatively stable, and the graph does not look fundamentally different. It seems that neither of the measures is especially affected by a greater or smaller disruptive threshold, and the number of disruptive changes decreases for all measures similarly. One

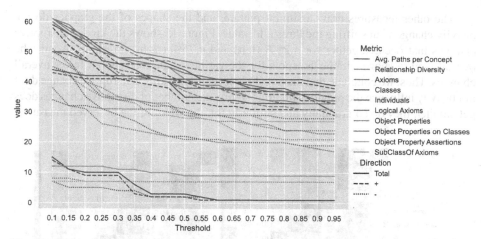

Fig. 13. The number of ontologies that have a disruptive change for the given metrics in relation to the threshold value for disruptive changes.

exemption to this finding is the measure avg. Paths per concept, which has a significant decrease in changes.

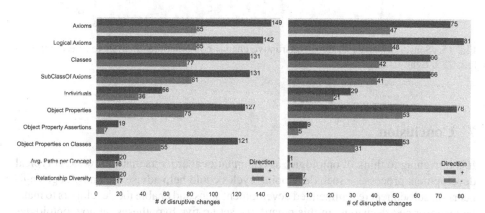

Fig. 14. The sensitivity analysis for the number of changes. (disruptive threshold: 25% left, 75% right. Cf. Figure 10).

The other measures draw a similar picture, and the shapes of the graphes do not heavily change with shifting the threshold value. Figure 15 shows the kind of disruptive changes that occur together for a 25% (left) and a 75% (right) threshold. Again, the overall picture shows similar hotspots for the various change levels but fewer overall changes. Thus, we conclude that the threshold level for marking a disruptive change does not heavily influence the previous findings. While the number of disruptive changes does get smaller, they do so gradually and similarly for almost all of the observed measures.

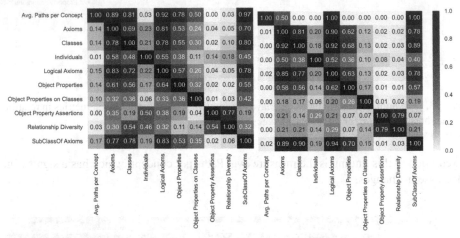

Fig. 15. Sensitivity analysis for the disruptive change combinations (disruptive threshold: 25% left, 75% right. Cf. Figure 12).

7   Conclusion

It is intriguing to think of ontologies as computational artifacts that follow stereotypical development processes. Such developing cycles could help advise the knowledge engineers on subsequent recommended development steps and enable the developers to make better-informed decisions. In this regard, we set up five hypotheses on how ontologies evolve during their lifecycle, grounded in knowledge and software engineering research, and tested them against a large body of ontology metric data.

The data does not support the existence of standard ontology development processes. While there are indications for some hypotheses, like the increase in size (H1), complexity (H4), or the decrease in development activity (H2), too many ontologies contradict the given assumptions. We further found no conclusive evidence for hypothesis two (H2), that the ontology population follows schema development, or the last hypothesis and analysis (H5), which looked at the bigger picture and examined whether standard development processes between groups of ontologies exist.

While we found no support for the given hypotheses in the data, H4 and H5 revealed an exciting finding: Often, the ontologies have few heavy change events during their lifetime and otherwise stay relatively stable. Further analysis of this phenomenon uncovered that these disruptive events are frequent for most ontology metrics and that most developed ontology files experience such change events at least once in their lifetime.

Further, a disruptive change event often does not affect a single attribute but a combination of many. For example, heavy additions or deletions of classes almost always come with heavy changes in the sub-class structure, and 66% of these class alterations also affect the object properties. The various combinations of disruptive change events are considerable and further underline the great diversity visible in the hypothesis analysis.

Rule-based artificial intelligence is developed and used in various communities with different backgrounds, needs, and application scenarios. As we have shown, the resulting ontologies reflect this heterogeneity. While they all use the same underlying technology, their way of developing these artifacts differs widely. As a result, commonly existing rules for ontology development, like they are prevalent in software engineering, do not fit the knowledge engineering context. The existence of disruptive change events indicates that the development of ontologies is less stable and often driven not only by gradual, evolutional changes but heavy restructuring.

References

1. Noy, N., Klein, M.: Ontology evolution: not the same as schema evolution. Know. Inf. Sys. (2004). https://doi.org/10.1007/s10115-003-0137-2
2. Malone, J., Stevens, R.: Measuring the level of activity in community built bio-ontologies. J. Biomed. Inform. (2013). https://doi.org/10.1016/j.jbi.2012.04.002
3. Reiz, A., Sandkuhl, K.: Debunking the stereotypical ontology development process. In: Proceedings of the 14th International Joint Conference on Knowledge Discovery, Knowledge Engineering and Knowledge Management. 14th International Conference on Knowledge Engineering and Ontology Development, Valletta, Malta, 10/24/2022–10/26/2022, pp. 82–91. SCITEPRESS - Science and Technology Publications (2022). https://doi.org/10.5220/001 1573600003335
4. Stojanovic, L.: Methods and Tools for Onology Evolution. Universitaet Fridericiana, Ph.D. (2004)
5. Zablith, F., et al.: Ontology evolution: a process-centric survey. Knowl. Eng. Rev. **30**(1), 45–75 (2015). https://doi.org/10.1017/S0269888913000349
6. Mihindukulasooriya, N., Poveda-Villalón, M., García-Castro, R., Gómez-Pérez, A.: Collaborative ontology evolution and data quality - an empirical analysis. In: Dragoni, M., Poveda-Villalón, M., Jimenez-Ruiz, E. (eds.) OWL: experiences and directions - reasoner evaluation. 13th International Workshop, OWLED 2016 and 5th International Workshop, ORE 2016, Bologna, Italy, November 20, 2016 : revised selected papers, pp. 95–114. Springer, Cham (2017). https://doi.org/10.1007/978-3-319-54627-8_8
7. Ashraf, J., Chang, E., Hussain, O.K., Hussain, F.K.: Ontology usage analysis in the ontology lifecycle: a state-of-the-art review. Knowl.-Based Syst. **80**, 34–47 (2015). https://doi.org/10.1016/j.knosys.2015.02.026
8. Rajlich, V.T., Bennett, K.H.: A staged model for the software life cycle. Computer (2000). https://doi.org/10.1109/2.869374
9. Cook, S., Harrison, R., Lehman, M.M., Wernick, P.: Evolution in software systems: foundations of the SPE classification scheme. J. Softw. Maint. Evol. Res. Pract. (2006). https://doi.org/10.1002/smr.314

10. Herraiz, I., Rodriguez, D., Robles, G., Gonzalez-Barahona, J.M.: The evolution of the laws of software evolution. ACM Comput. Surv. (2013). https://doi.org/10.1145/2543581.2543595
11. Yang, Z., Zhang, D., Ye, C.: Ontology analysis on complexity and evolution based on conceptual model. In: Leser, U. (ed.) Data integration in the life sciences. Third international workshop, DILS 2006, Hinxton, UK, July 20–22, 2006 ; Proceedings, vol. 4075. Lecture notes in Computer Science Lecture Notes in Bioinformatics, vol. 4075, pp. 216–223. Springer, Berlin (2006). https://doi.org/10.1007/11799511_19
12. Tartir, S., Arpinar, I.B.: Ontology evaluation and ranking using OntoQA. In: International Conference on Semantic Computing, 2007. ICSC 2007 ; 17–19 Sept. 2007, Irvine, California ; Proceedings ; [held in conjunction with] the First International Workshop on Semantic Computing and Multimedia Systems (IEEE-SCMS 2007). International Conference on Semantic Computing (ICSC 2007), Irvine, CA, USA, 9/17/2007–9/19/2007, pp. 185–192. IEEE Computer Society, Los Alamitos, Calif. (2007). https://doi.org/10.1109/ICSC.2007.19
13. Reiz, A., Sandkuhl, K.: NEOntometrics – a public endpoint for calculating ontology metrics. In: Şimşek, U., Chaves-Fraga, D., Pellegrini, T., Vahdat, S. (eds.) Proceedings of Poster and Demo Track and Workshop Track of the 18th International Conference on Semantic Systems co-located with 18th International Conference on Semantic Systems (SEMANTiCS 2022), 13/09/22–15/09/22. CEUR-WS, Vienna (2022)
14. Tartir, S., Arpinar, I.B., Moore, M., Sheth, A.P., Aleman-Meza, B.: OntoQA: metric-based ontology quality analysis. In: Caragea, D., Honavar, V., Muslea, I., Ramakrishnan, R. (eds.) IEEE Workshop on Knowledge Acquisition from Distributed, Autonomous, Semantically Heterogeneous Data and Knowledge Sources, Houston, 11/27 (2005)
15. Gangemi, A., Catena, C., Ciaramita, M., Lehmann, J.: A theoretical framework for ontology evaluation and validation. In: Bouquet, P., Tummarello, G. (eds.) Semantic Web Applications and Perspectives, Trento, Italy, 12/14/2005–12/16/2005. CEUR (2005)
16. Rousseeuw, P.J.: Silhouettes: a graphical aid to the interpretation and validation of cluster analysis. J. Comput. Appl. Math. **20**, 53–65 (1987). https://doi.org/10.1016/0377-042 7(87)90125-7

System to Correct Toxic Expression with BERT and to Determine the Effect of the Attention Value

Motonobu Yoshida[1]($\boxtimes$), Kazuyuki Matsumoto[2], Minoru Yoshida[2], and Kenji Kita[2]

[1] Graduate School of Sciences and Technology for Innovation, Tokushima University, 2-1, Minami-jousangima-cho, Tokushima-shi, Tokushima, Japan
c612235020@tokushima-u.ac.jp
[2] Graduate School of Technology, Industrial and Social Sciences, Tokushima University, 2-1, Minami-jousangima-cho, Tokushima-shi, Tokushima, Japan
{matumoto,mino,kita}@is.tokushima-u.ac.jp

Abstract. This paper describes an extended experiment on a system that converts sentences with toxic expressions into safe sentences, along with the evaluation and influence of the system. In recent years, toxicity on social media has created many problems. We evaluated the effectiveness of the proposed system for identifying toxic sentences using a prediction model based on Bidirectional Encoder Representations from Transformers (BERT) and then converting them into safe sentences using attention values and a score that indicates whether the sentences are appropriate after the predictive conversion. Six patterns of methods were tested, with Pattern 6 being the most effective for mitigating toxicity. This pattern is a technique that changes the way to take the top sentences of a beam search for each number of treatments, in addition to converting words with an attention value above a threshold and their adjacent words and phrases and words registered in the toxic dictionary. We used multiple indicators to judge the effectiveness of this method and evaluated its ability to make the text safe while preserving its meaning.

Keywords: Toxic expression · BERT · Classification · Text correction · Attention value

1 Introduction

In recent years, more than 80% of people in Japan have been using internet through smartphone and other devices. Therefore, the number of social media users is also increasing every year and subsequently the number of posts by people with low internet literacy and inadvertent posting of content is also increasing. An inadvertent content such as a joke that is meant to be a funny among acquaintances is spread and exposed among many people resulting in online flame wars and slander. Inflammatory speech is also increasing in politics, on both sides of issues. One example is former President Trump's aggressive and forceful comments on Twitter. In addition, spam submissions using auto-generated text by Chat-GPT, which may become popular in the future, could also be a problem.

In this study, we focus on the text posted on social media. First, a classifier based on the natural language processing model BERT is used to determine whether a post contains toxic expressions or not. Texts judged as toxic are converted to less toxic sentences by replacing the expression judged to be toxic with a safe expression. If this system can be implemented, it will be possible to prevent internet flame wars caused by unintentional posting of toxic messages and slandering of others on social media. The difference between this and our previous paper [1] is the experimental part of the conversion of toxic expressions and the multiple methods of evaluation.

This paper is organized as follows. In Sect. 2, related studies are discussed. The proposed method is described in Sect. 3. In Sect. 4, we describe the experimental results. Finally, the conclusions and future issues are explained in Sect. 5.

2   Related Works

There has been research on flame wars including the use of sentiment analysis [2,3] and real-time tweet status counts and other information to make inferences [4,5]. Other studies were condusted to create datasets for detecting abusive comments [6,7] and to classify and detect hate speech and hateful expressions [8,9]. IN addition, attempts were made to convert legal texts into simple terms using the BERT model [10].

Onishi et al. [11] judged initially whether the input text is likely to be flamed or not. Then, inflammatory words were detected with support vector machine (SVM). For the correction of detected words, they used a model trained on the distributed representation of words by word2vec, which was trained on 50 million Japanese tweets collected from Twitter. These collected tweets were preprocessed by removing URLs and hashtags. Furthermore, the predicted replies to the corrected input text were generated using a neural network-based language model. Table 1 shows an example of the actual process. The study showed good results with an F-measure of 0.74 for flame detection. However, that the corrected text may output sentences that do not make sense in Japanese is a possibility. Furthermore, another problem cited is that when the usage of a corpus is similar, words with opposite meanings may also be judged as highly similar.

In terms of sentence correction, Reid et al. [12] attempted to convert sentences independent of their types using an editing and synthesis framework called Lewis. The system determines which process is appropriate: insertion, conversion, or deletion of the text to be converted. Then, by replacing the relevant part with a SLOT, they maintained a universal style that can be processed as unsupervised data. The part of the SLOT that is kept in this style is designed for predictions using a pre-trained model to make appropriate sentence transformations.

With reference to these studies, this study uses a classifier model based on BERT to detect and transform toxic expressions in a flow similar to that of

Table 1. Example of a system for detecting and correcting flaming words system [11].

	input text	flaming words	corrected text	predicted reply
S1	情弱とキモオタは死ね！ (Die, the low information people and the creepy nerds.	情弱,キモオタ,死ね (Low information people, creepy nerds, die)	状強とオタクは苦しめ！ (Suffer, information powerhouses and geeks!)	笑わす中もらうわ寝るわ (Sleep in the midst of laugher.
S2	飲酒運転なう (Drunk driving now.)	飲酒運転 (Drunk driving)	飲酒なう (I'm drunk alcohol.)	何かのことねww (That is something lol.)

Onishi et al. [11]. The difference between flaming texts and toxic texts lies in the range of genres specified. In addition to toxic expressions, flaming texts include criminal suggestions and morally offensive content.By contrast, toxic texts are focused on slander and libel.

3   Proposed Method

The flow of the system procedure of the proposed method is shown in Fig. 1. Each of the proposed systems is explained in this section.

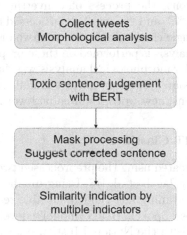

Fig. 1. Procedure of the proposed model.

3.1   Collecting Tweets

In this study, we collected tweets with Twitter API[1] The first step was to collect approximately 300,000 tweets without specifying initial conditions. Then,

---

[1] Twitter API, https://developer.twitter.com/en/products/twitter-api.

the tweets were matched with a list of words that had toxic impressions with regular expressions and the corresponding tweets were selected. The 2000 tweets collected in this way were tagged as "safe", "toxic" and "spam" by four workers.

3.2 Preprocessing of Tweets

In the pre-processing of tweets, "TweetL[2] was partially modified for pre-processing. TweetL allowed us to

– Compress multiple spaces into a single space
– Remove Hashtags
– Remove URLs
– Remove Pictograms (emoji)
– Remove mentions
– Remove link strings such as images
– Convert all to lowercase
– Convert kana to full-width characters and numbers and ASCII characters to half-width characters.
– Convert numbers to zeros
– Remove retweets
– Normalize process with neologdn

Of the above functions, the process of converting numbers to zeros was excluded in addition, "!", "?", and "w" were preprocessed by adding a process that combines them into a single character if there are two or more consecutive characters. Morphological analysis is performed on these preprocessed sentences with MeCab. The dictionary for morphological analysis was "mecab-ipadic-NEologd". As this dictionary is updated twice a week, it is suitable for analyzing tweets, where peculiar expressions, new words, and coined words are frequently used.

3.3 Creating a BERT Classifier

A BERT classifier was created using the preprocessed tweet data. BERT is a language model proposed by Jacob et al. [13] Using unlabeled data for pre-training and labeled data for fine-tuning has yielded suitable results for many tasks. In this study, the "Japanese Spoken BERT model" developed by Katsumata et al. [14] in collaboration with the National Institute for Japanese Language and Linguistics was used as a prelearning training model. This model was trained by adding a spoken Japanese corpus to WikipediaBERT[3] which was developed by the Inui Lab at Tohoku University. In this model, 80% of the 2,000 tweets that were collected and tagged were used as training data for fine tuning Fig. 2. The model was then used as a BERT classifier.

---

[2] TweetL, https://github.com/deepblue-ts/Tweetl".
[3] WikipediaBERT, https://github.com/cl-tohoku/bert-japanese.

3.4   MASK Processing Conversion with BERT

Here, the method used for MASK processing conversion by BERT is explained. This process is performed on text that is deemed toxic.

First, we performed the MASK processing transformation with attention values. The attention values are obtained from the final layer of the transformer [15] in the BERT model and then normalized using min-max normalization so that the maximum value is 1. Then, conversion is performed to MASK for words with attention values above a certain threshold (up to 0.82). The Fig. 3 outlines the process of listing words that are scheduled to be converted. Of the two lists on the right, the top one is a list of words above a certain threshold. On the other hand, the bottom list on the right is a list of the words adjacent the target word. However, if the adjacent word is a particle or auxiliary verb, it shall not be included in the list of scheduled conversions below. After this process, correction of listed words is performed by MASK predictive transform with beam search.

After this process, the words in the list of toxic impressions are converted to MASK in the same way. Then, the correction is performed by MASK predictive transformation with beam search.

In practice, conversion prediction is performed using beam search as shown in Fig. 4. The beam width is set to 3, the top three appropriate scores of sentence are saved, and the highest final score is adopted as the modified sentence. We do not perform MASK conversions on several parts of the sentence at once but perform predictive conversions one at a time, as shown in Table 2 on an example of an actual sentence. We use this approach multiple times to reduce the number

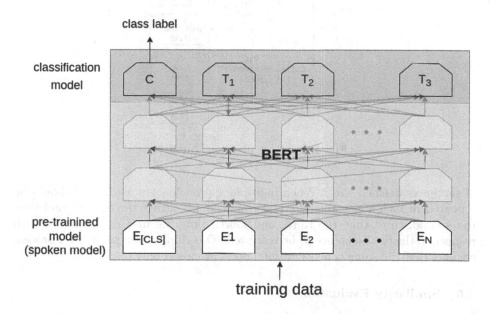

Fig. 2. Fine-tuning of BERT [1].

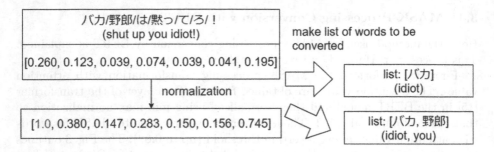

Fig. 3. Conversion word extraction with attention values.

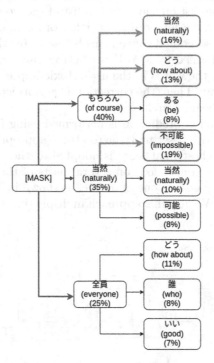

Fig. 4. Inference by beam search. [1].

of sentences deemed toxic. When multiple approaches are used, they should be repeated in such a way that the first time should extract the first, second time the second, third time the third, and fourth time the first highest score with respect to the final sentence to be retrieved. This duplication prevention process ensures that the same conversion method is proposed only once.

3.5   Similarity Evaluation

In this section, we evaluate with three evaluation indicators whether the sentences were converted into similar sentences.

Table 2. MASK conversion example. [1].

マーチ関関同立は f ラン , 低学歴でしょうに
(The mid-sized private college group would be the least educated that anyone could get into.)
↓
マーチ関関同立は [MASK], 低学歴でしょうに
(Convert "anyone could get into" to [MASK])
↓
マーチ関関同立は当然, 低学歴 でしょうに
(The mid-sized private college group, of course, would be less educated.)
↓
マーチ関関同立は当然, [MASK] でしょうに
(Convert "less educated" to [MASK])
↓
マーチ関関同立は当然, 不可能でしょうに
(The mid-sized private college group, of course, would be impossible.)

BERTScore. BERTScore is a method proposed by Zhang et al. [16] that measures the similarity between sentences with a vector representation for two sentences and the cosine similarity between each token. If one of the texts to be compared is $x = <x_1, \cdots, x_k>$ (Reference) and its vector is $<\boldsymbol{x_1}, \cdots, \boldsymbol{x_k}>$, and the other text is $\hat{x} = <\hat{x}_1, \cdots, \hat{x}_k>$ (Candidate) and its vector is $<\boldsymbol{\hat{x}_1}, \cdots, \boldsymbol{\hat{x}_k}>$, the reproduction and fit rates are obtained as in Eq. 1

$$R_{BERT} = \frac{1}{|x|} \sum_{x_i \in x} \max_{\hat{x}_j \in \hat{x}} \mathbf{x_i^T \hat{x}_j}$$
$$P_{BERT} = \frac{1}{|\hat{x}|} \sum_{\hat{x}_j \in \hat{x}} \max_{x_i \in x} \mathbf{x_i^T \hat{x}_j} \tag{1}$$

From Eq. 1, the F-measure is calculated, and the formula is presented in Eq. 2.

$$F_{BERT} = 2 \frac{P_{BERT} \cdot R_{BERT}}{P_{BERT} + R_{BERT}} \tag{2}$$

Cosine Similarity with Sentence-BERT. Sentence-BERT is a method proposed by Reimers et al. [17] that performs better on similar sentence tasks than BERT.

Two sentences are extracted by pooling the vectors u and v with BERT, respectively. Then, the similarity between the extracted vectors is calculated using cosine similarity. Figure 5 illustrates this process.

This study uses the Japanese Sentence-BERT model (sonoisa)[4]. This model uses the Tohoku University model as the pre-trained model.

BleuScore. BleuScore [18] is a method proposed to quantitatively evaluate automated translation. This indicator penalizes the inclusion of too many words

---

[4] https://huggingface.co/sonoisa/sentence-bert-base-ja-mean-tokens-v2

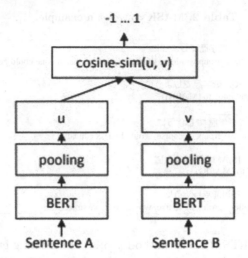

Fig. 5. Sentence-BERT architecture at inference, for example, to compute similarity scores. This architecture is also used with the regression objective function. [17].

or short sentences in the reference translation, and evaluates candidate translations based on their conformance rate. BleuScore can be calculated by the following equation.

$$BLEU = BP \cdot exp(\sum_{n=1}^{N} w_n log p_n) \tag{3}$$

Let c be the length of the candidate translation and r be the effective reference corpus length. Then, BP can be calculated as follows

$$BP = \begin{cases} 1 & if \quad c > r \\ e^{1-r/c} & if \quad c \leq r \end{cases} \tag{4}$$

As for p_n (Eq. 5), when C is the set of n-grams of candidate sentences, Count is the number of times that a sentence appears in a candidate sentence when the reference is n-grams, and $Count_{clip}$ is the number of times that the sentence appears when the maximum number of times it appears is Count, it can be expressed as follows.

$$p_n = \frac{\sum_{ngram \in C} Count_{clip}(ngram)}{\sum_{ngram \in C} Count(ngram)} \tag{5}$$

In the original paper [18], they use $N = 4$ and uniform weights $w_n = 1/N$, thus, this study used the same values.

4   Experimental Results

In this section, we describe the datasets used and performance of the classifier. The breakdown of the data used in the experiments is given in Table 3.

Table 3. Tweet breakdown [1].

Tag	Safe	Toxic	Spam
All	1,064	765	171
training data	638	459	103
validation data	213	153	34
test data	213	153	34

4.1   Classification Accuracy

First, the two pre-trained models, "WikipediaBERT" and "Japanese Spoken BERT Model" were fine-tuned with the same training data. By comparing these two models, we examined the importance of the impact of the pre-trained model. At this time, to maintain fairness and compare accuracies, both were trained for 100 epochs. The results are shown in Tables 4 and 5. The additionally trained "Japanese Spoken BERT Model" improved the overall identification accuracy.

Table 4. Accuracy of WikipediaBERT [1].

Label	Recall(%)	Precision(%)	F-measure(%)
safe	79	81	80
toxic	79	75	77
spam	68	77	72

Table 5. Accuracy of Japanese Spoken BERT Model. [1].

Label	Recall(%)	Precision(%)	F-measure(%)
safe	87	81	84
toxic	77	81	79
spam	71	89	79

We also compared the accuracy of the existing models, SVM and logistic regression. Table 6 shows the results of that comparison. Undersampling (US) adjusts to the lowest number of data instances (spam:103), while oversampling (OS) adjusts the number of data instances of each label to 1000. The oversampling method used Wordnet to convert nouns and adjectives to create sentences. It can be confirmed that BERT is superior to other models.

Table 6. Comparison with other models.

Model	Recall(%)	Precision(%)	F-measure(%)
SVM(US)	41	48	43
SVM(OS)	40	51	43
Logistic(US)	56	66	56
Logistic(OS)	51	60	52
LSTM	65	64	64
LSTM(OS)	63	63	63
BERT	82	82	82
BERT(OS)	80	82	80

4.2 Comparison of Various Patterns

In this study, we experimented with and compared the six conversion methods listed in Table 7. "Change to get beam search's top" is changing the method of taking the top ranks for each number of treatments (first time is first, second time is second, third time is third, forth time is first, more ever loop)

Table 7. Experimental patterns.

pattern	method
1	Attention words conversion only
2	Attention words with adjacent conversion only
3	Pattern1 + dangerous words conversion
4	Pattern2 + dangerous words conversion
5	Pattern3 + change to get beam search's top
6	Pattern4 + change to get beam search's top

Henceforth, the experimental methods are referred to using the numbers in Table 7.

4.3 Results of MASK Conversion by BERT

This section describes the results of the conversion process after the first processing of patterns 3 and 6 (Table 7). An example of the converted text is shown in Table 8. Compared to the pre-conversion text, the target of attack has become more ambiguous and less aggressive, however, the problem of changing the meaning has had limited improvement. In addition, the object of attention is referred to using a word or phrase that does not seem to be toxic. Including the words and phrases adjacent to the attention target word has greatly reduced the toxic, but the meaning has changed dramatically. If you want to see result of conversion, let see in my github[5].

Table 8. Text correction method.

Method	Before	Attention/Toxic words	After
pattern 3	左翼は頭いかれたやつしかおらんのか？ (Are the leftists all crazy?)	頭 / 左翼 (your thinking / leftists)	これはもういかれたやつしかおらんのか? (Is this all the crazy ones?)
pattern 6		(頭 / 左翼) + いかれ (pattern 4 + crazy)	解説は質問平穏たやつしかおらんのか? (Are all commentary opinions avoiding conflicts and troubles?

4.4 Results of the Three Evaluations

This section provides a comparison of all the methods from Table 7. First, Table 9, 10, 11 shows the mean of the distribution of each score for each pattern.

Table 9. Score average of BERTScore.

pattern	first-time	second-time	third-time
1	0.967	0.947	0.938
2	0.946	0.924	0.914
3	0.936	0.925	0.917
4	0.915	0.898	0.880
5	0.936	0.928	0.920
6	0.914	0.889	0.872

BleuScore has dropped significantly. In addition, Sentence-BERT and BERTScore are similar; however, Sentence-BERT has slightly higher values. Table 12 presents the number of changes for content deemed toxic.

The number of toxic sentences was reduced the most when the anti-duplicate treatment process (pattern 5 and 6) was applied, and this method was considered effective in correcting toxic sentences. However, since the number has not changed dramatically, other effective methods need to be considered.

[5] https://github.com/hatonobu/my_research.

Table 10. Score average of Sentence-BERT.

pattern	first-time	second-time	third-time
1	0.976	0.965	0.960
2	0.966	0.954	0.946
3	0.941	0.940	0.935
4	0.929	0.922	0.909
5	0.940	0.940	0.932
6	0.928	0.915	0.901

Table 11. Score average of BleuScore.

pattern	first-time	second-time	third-time
1	0.850	0.786	0.760
2	0.795	0.734	0.704
3	0.729	0.700	0.674
4	0.682	0.637	0.586
5	0.730	0.701	0.670
6	0.684	0.639	0.591

Table 12. Changes in the number of toxic sentences.

pattern	first-time	second-time	third-time
1	168	165	164
2	165	161	159
3	156	154	154
4	153	147	147
5	154	153	153
6	152	147	142

5   Conclusions

In this study, we constructed a system for correcting toxic sentences with BERT. Although it was a three-value classification, the accuracy of discriminating toxic sentences was 79%, with overall accuracy of 82%. In addition, we were able to construct a transformation system to mitigate the aggressiveness of texts judged to be toxic.

As most of the training data used in this study were tagged as safe, the classification accuracy for safety was considered to have been improved. Therefore, it is important to prepare more data on toxic and spam contents for comparison.

In addition, it was considered that the processing of attention tended to reduce the number of offensive sentences by including not only the focus word alone but also the adjacent words. However, it was not possible to solve the problem of the meaning changing from the original sentence. Therefore, it is considered necessary to apply some processing to the surrounding expressions of the target word. In addition, with respect to the evaluation metrics, the scores were similar for Sentence-BERT and BERTScore. It is thought that it would be effective to use BleuScore to determine the degree to which a sentence has been modified, and then use BERTScore and Sentence-BERT to determine the degree to which the meaning is the same. In addition, changing the method of taking the top ranks for each number of treatments was considered to be effective because it reduced the number of cases judged to be toxic. Finally, we conclude that the best method was Pattern 6 (Table 7), and that this method, plus new innovations, could be used to modify toxic text into safer text.

Acknowledgements. This work was supported by the 2022 SCAT Research Grant and JSPS KAKENHI Grant Number JP20K12027, JP21K12141.

Appendix

This appendix describes the distribution scores of each indicator for the third times (Figs. 6, 7, 8, 9, 10, 11, 12, 13, 14, 15, 16, 17, 18, 19, 20, 21, 22 and 23).

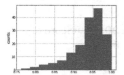 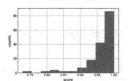 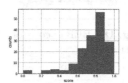

Fig. 6. BERTScore of pattern 1.   **Fig. 7.** Sentence-BERT of pattern 1.   **Fig. 8.** BleuScore of pattern 1.

Sentence-BERT distribution tends to score higher than the BERTScore. In addition, BERTScore scores are more widely dispersed. Therefore, BERTScore is considered more effective when considering the meaning of a sentence.

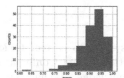 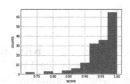 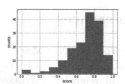

Fig. 9. BERTScore of pattern 2.   **Fig. 10.** Sentence-BERT of pattern 2.   **Fig. 11.** BleuScore of pattern 2.

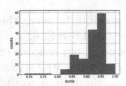

Fig. 12. BERTScore of pattern 3.

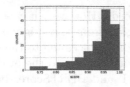

Fig. 13. Sentence-BERT of pattern 3.

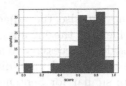

Fig. 14. BleuScore of pattern 3.

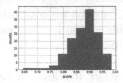

Fig. 15. BERTScore of pattern 4.

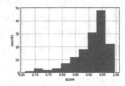

Fig. 16. Sentence-BERT of pattern 4.

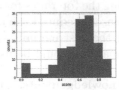

Fig. 17. BleuScore of pattern 4.

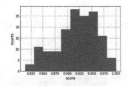

Fig. 18. BERTScore of pattern 5.

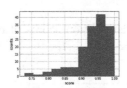

Fig. 19. Sentence-BERT of pattern 5.

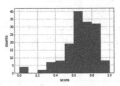

Fig. 20. BleuScore of pattern 5.

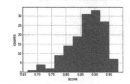

Fig. 21. BERTScore of pattern 6.

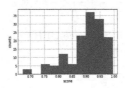

Fig. 22. Sentence-BERT of pattern 6.

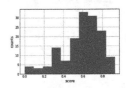

Fig. 23. BleuScore of pattern 6.

References

1. Yoshida, M., Matsumoto, K., Yoshida, M., Kita, K.: A system to correct toxic expression with BERT. In: Proceedings of the 14th International Joint Conference on Knowledge Discovery, Knowledge Engineering and Knowledge Management, pp. 92–97 (2022). https://doi.org/10.5220/0011586100003335
2. Takahashi, N., Higashi, Y.: Flaming detection and analysis using emotion analysis on Twitter. In: The Institute of Electronics, Information and Communication Engineers Technical Report, pp. 135–140 (2017)

3. Ozawa, S., Yoshida, S., Kitazono, J., Sugawara, T., Haga, T.: A sentiment polarity prediction model using transfer learning and its application to SNS flaming event detection. In: Proceedings of IEEE Symposium Series on Computational Intelligence (2016). https://doi.org/10.1109/SSCI.2016.7849868

4. Steinberger, J., Brychcin, T., Hercig, T., Krejzl, P.: Cross-lingual flames detection in news discussions. In: Proceedings of International Conference Recent Advances in Natural Language Processing (2017)

5. Iwasaki, Y., Orihara, R., Sei, Y., Nakagawa, H., Tahara, Y., Ohsuga, A.: Analysis of flaming and its applications in CGM. J. Jpn. Soc. Artif. Intell. **30**(1), 152–160 (2013)

6. Karayiğit, H., Aci, C., Akdagli, A.: Detecting abusive Instagram comments in Turkish using convolutional neural network and machine learning methods. Expert Syst. Appl. **17415**, 114802 (2021). https://doi.org/10.1016/j.eswa.2021.114802

7. Omar, A., Mahmoud, T.M., Abd-El-Hafeez, T.: Comparative performance of machine learning and deep learning algorithms for Arabic hate speech detection in OSNs. In: Hassanien, A.-E., Azar, A.T., Gaber, T., Oliva, D., Tolba, F.M. (eds.) AICV 2020. AISC, vol. 1153, pp. 247–257. Springer, Cham (2020). https://doi.org/10.1007/978-3-030-44289-7_24

8. Kapli, P., Ekbal, A.: A deep neural network based multi-task learning approach to hate speech detection. Knowl.-Based Syst. **210**, 106458 (2020). https://doi.org/10.1016/j.knosys.2020.106458

9. Watanabe, H., Bouazizi, M., Ohtsuki, T.: Hate speech on Twitter: a pragmatic approach to collect hateful and offensive expressions and perform hate speech detection. IEEE Access **6**, 13825–13835 (2018). https://doi.org/10.1109/ACCESS.2018.2806394

10. Yamakoshi, T., Komamizu, T., Ogawa, Y., Toyama, K.: Japanese legal term correction using BERT pretrained model. In: The 34th Annual Conference of the Japanese Society for Artificial Intelligence 4P3-OS-8-05 (2020)

11. Onishi, M., Sawai, Y., Komai, M., Sakai, K., Shindo, H.: Building a comprehensive system for preventing flaming on Twitter. In: The 29th Annual Conference of the Japanese Society for Artificial Intelligence 3O1-3in (2015)

12. Reid, M., Zhong, V.: LEWIS: levenshtein editing for unsupervised text style transfer. In: Findings of the Association for Computational Linguistics (ACL-IJCNLP), pp. 3932–3934 (2021). https://doi.org/10.18653/v1/2021.findings-acl.344

13. Jacob, D., Ming-Wei, C., Kenton, L., Kristina, T.: BERT: Pre-training of Deep Bidirectional Transformers for Language Understanding. arXiv preprint arXiv:1810.04805 (2018)

14. Katsumata, S., Sakata, H.: Creation of spoken Japanese BERT with corpus of spontaneous Japanese. In: The 27th Annual Conference of the association for Natural Language Processing (2021)

15. Ashish, V., et al.: Attention Is All You Need. arXiv:1706.03762 (2017)

16. Zhang, T., Kishore, V., Wu, F., Wein-Berger, K.Q., Artzi, Y.: BERTScore: evaluating text generation with BERT. In: ICLR (2020)

17. Reimers, N., Gurevych, I.: Sentence-BERT: sentence embeddings using Siamese BERT-networks. Published at EMNLP (2019). https://doi.org/10.48550/arXiv.1908.10084

18. Papineni, K., Roukos, S., Ward, T., Zhu, W.: Bleu: a method for automatic evaluation of machine translation. In: Proceedings of the 40th Annual Meeting of the Association for Computational Linguistics, pp. 311–318 (2002). https://doi.org/10.3115/1073083.1073135

Knowledge Management
and Information Systems

Machine Learning Decision Support for Production Planning and Control Based on Simulation-Generated Data

Konstantin Muehlbauer🄳, Lukas Rissmann🄳, and Sebastian Meissner(✉) 🄳

University of Applied Sciences Landshut, Am Lurzenhof 1, 84036 Landshut, Germany
Sebastian.meissner@haw-landshut.de

Abstract. Production planning and control covers various tasks to achieve an overall performance optimum of all process elements. Within these tasks, a wide variety of decisions have to be made. Progressive digitalization enables new procedures and technologies to support or automate decision-making processes. In particular, the application of machine learning can lead to considerable benefits and help to deal with increasing complexity as well as dynamics within production systems. For the development of machine learning models, a sufficient qualitative and quantitative data foundation is essential. In practice, this is often the limiting factor. Due to this problem, this article describes how a validated discrete-event simulation can generate data to train a machine learning model. The key activities and workflows for developing a machine learning decision support system based on artificially generated data are specified by a generalized framework. Based on this framework, machine learning models can be deployed in real-world operations to support decision-making regarding planning and control tasks. Their application can increase the performance of a production system, as shown in a practical example. A real-world scenario is used to validate the functionality of the activities to be executed.

Keywords: Machine learning · Decision-making · Production planning and control

1 Introduction

Planning and controlling resources and processes is an essential part of a production system. It is characterized by a high degree of complexity due to a wide variety of tasks with a high diversity of decision-making options. Furthermore, the impact on the performance of the companies' value chain is enormous. Especially in view of the increasing volatility caused by global crises and the associated cost pressure, it is essential to support planning and control tasks with regard to the achievement of relevant target variables. In this context, processes and resources must be continuously monitored and optimally utilized.

Machine learning (ML) provides promising opportunities for highly complex applications [1]. On the one hand, it can process a large amount of data for identifying insights

© The Author(s), under exclusive license to Springer Nature Switzerland AG 2023
F. Coenen et al. (Eds.): IC3K 2022, CCIS 1842, pp. 257–279, 2023.
https://doi.org/10.1007/978-3-031-43471-6_12

based on linear and nonlinear relationships. On the other hand, ML makes it possible to predict future events to take timely and enhanced measures. Nevertheless, despite the increasing amount of data that a production system generates on a daily basis, practical ML applications are still rare [2]. Similar findings about the limited real-world applications of ML are shown by other literature reviews that deal with the application of ML within production planning and control (PPC) [3, 4]. The reasons are, among others, the complex preprocessing of the data as well as the interpretation of the ML results [1]. Furthermore, in many cases, an insufficient data foundation is a major issue why ML applications are often validated utilizing a simulation rather than being validated with real-world data [5]. Artificially generated data provided by discrete-event simulations (DES) are therefore widely used for developing and verifying ML models [5–7].

DES has been applied for many years to support decision-making in long- and medium-term planning tasks within production systems [8]. These provide the opportunity to map processes as realistically as possible and thus evaluate future states. Furthermore, in view of the ongoing implementation of digital twins, simulations are increasingly used for short-term control tasks in real-time use cases [9].

This article presents an extended framework with its key activities and the process workflow for applying simulation models as data generation services. Preliminary findings about the conception of this framework and a first validation have already been published in Muehlbauer et al. [6]. In this previous work, it was answered how a generalizable framework for an ML application based on a DES has to be designed in order to be used as a decision support system in a real-world production system. Based on these findings, an enhanced sequence diagram has been developed and described using Business Process Model and Notation 2.0 (BPMN 2.0). The diagram is presented in this article. Furthermore, the validation of the approach has been extended in terms of the prediction and evaluation of various key performance indicators (KPIs) at the same time. In the case study presented, the system dynamics have also been increased by adding randomly distributed breakdowns and implementing rejects or rework. As a result, larger datasets have been required, and more sophisticated ML techniques have been applied. Concerning the preliminary findings, this article aims to answer the following research questions (RQ):

RQ: *How can a generalized framework for building a machine-learning-based decision support system with a simultaneous prediction of multiple KPIs be defined and to which extent can machine learning models optimize results?*

The article is organized as follows. Section 2, state of the art, provides an overview of the key and cross-functional tasks involved in PPC. Subsequently, the general issues and challenges encountered in PPC are examined within the context of ML applications. The principal objective of this article is to introduce a comprehensive framework. Section 3 demonstrates the proposed framework, encompassing its activities, essential steps, and overall workflow interaction. Section 4 presents a case study to validate the approach in a practical setting. Section 5 follows, highlighting the identified limitations. Finally, Sect. 6 serves as the conclusion of the article, encompassing a summary of the findings and a perspective on future research activities.

2 State of the Art

The following section will briefly introduce the relevant state of the art regarding Production Planning and Control Systems as well as their challenges and possible solutions. After the fundamentals of ML are laid out, the relevant work which applies Machine Learning inside PPC is presented.

2.1 Production Planning and Control Systems

The main task of PPC is to generate the production plan and to determine its requirements for the next period (e.g., day, week, month, etc.) [10]. The objective is to schedule the products and their quantities despite unpredictable influencing factors. There are several different models for describing and designing PPC systems. The Aachen PPC model will be discussed in more detail in this article, as it is an easy-to-understand, holistic, and established model [11]. Thereby, PPC tasks are divided into key and cross-functional tasks (see Fig. 1) [10]. One task can contain several subtasks. These are outlined in the following paragraph.

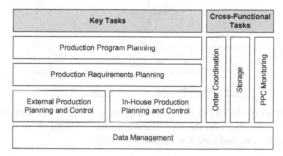

Fig. 1. Overview of the key tasks and cross-functional tasks from the Aachen PPC model [10].

Production program planning is the key task which creates the production program based on the company's sales plan. This contains the quantity to be produced for each product and each planning period. *Production requirements planning* derives the necessary material and resource requirements from the production program. Production orders are created, scheduled, and capacity requirements are calculated. *In-house production planning and control* considers lot sizing, detailed scheduling and sequence planning, as well as availability checks. The tasks of *external production planning and control* include, among others, procurement-relevant aspects, the determination of order quantities, and the selection of suppliers. The cross-functional production planning and control tasks are *order coordination, storage,* and *PPC monitoring*. These tasks serve the overall integration and optimization of the systems [10].

The focus of this work covers *in-house production planning and control* tasks since this is where numerous short-term and time-critical decisions are made, especially in day-to-day business. Furthermore, these tasks and decisions to be made in this context have an enormous influence on achieving the logistical goals of a production system.

The logistical goals are high (capacity) utilization, high adherence to schedule (schedule reliability), low work in progress, and low throughput time.

Core tasks of production control are *order release, capacity control,* and *sequencing* (see Fig. 2) [10]. Figure 2 illustrates the interdependencies between the individual tasks, as well as the control variables (work in progress, backlog, sequence deviation) and objectives (logistical goals). *Order release* determines an order's start date and time from the production point of view and thus directly triggers material provision. *Capacity control* decides the working times of resources in the production and logistics system and thus determines the short-term capacities. Determining which order is to be processed next is the task of *sequencing.*

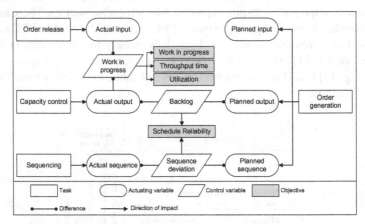

Fig. 2. Manufacturing control model with the three core tasks order release, capacity control, and sequencing, as well as the effect on the four manufacturing relevant objectives work in progress, throughput time, utilization, and schedule reliability [10].

2.2 PPC Challenges and Possible Solutions

Due to increasing challenges for production processes with regard to volatile demand fluctuations, shorter delivery times, and a higher number of variants, new approaches in PPC are required [12]. A few tasks performed within PPC have a vast solution space. Considering the high complexity, there is often an attempt to aggregate data in order to make faster and more cost-effective decisions [13]. If several production parameters and uncertainties have to be considered, an optimal solution can rarely be found [1]. Additionally, there is often a time constraint for making optimal decisions [14].

These challenges of short-term decision-making also apply to capacity management [15]. Due to the growing variability of customer demand, capacities have to be changed or the utilization of capacities has to be adjusted rapidly. This adjustment concerns working time and the number of available resources (e.g., employees or conveyors). The general goal of all areas of PPC is to increase and stabilize production and logistics performance while simultaneously reducing costs. In this context, in some cases, a decision cannot be optimized on all logistical goals (throughput, work in progress, adherence to schedule, and capacity utilization) [10]. A reason for this is, for example, that a high degree of adherence to schedule, a high degree of work in progress, and a high utilization of resources are sometimes conflicting factors [16]. To solve these problems, different approaches such as analytical methods or DES have been used for years to automate or support decision-making [5]. However, applying these classical approaches makes it apparent that the high complexity of the tasks to be performed is difficult to depict. Especially when using a DES, the decision-making process can often take longer than the available time allows. To deal with this problem, heuristic as well as other rule-based approaches are pursued, which try to find an acceptable solution faster. However, the increasing amount of daily generated process data, and the fast development of ML methods, offer new possibilities to solve tasks in the area of PPC [4]. In this way, decisions can be made faster with similar or better quality. Preliminary studies already show the positive impact of ML techniques in terms of PPC tasks performance compared to conventional methods [17].

2.3 Fundamentals: Machine Learning

ML enables computers to learn automatically by deriving information from patterns inside data [18]. ML can be separated into three categories: supervised, unsupervised, and reinforcement learning. These categories of different learning types distinguish themselves in terms of the input information and how they are trained based on the data. *Supervised learning* involves learning with different dataset features annotated with a label. Minimizing the discrepancy between real and predicted values in a given dataset is the goal [18]. In *unsupervised learning*, an algorithm learns important or valuable properties of structures within a dataset which is not labeled. A very frequently used algorithm is k-Means. In this process, respective centers are calculated by determining the number of groups in advance [19]. Thereby, groups of data points are defined which are very similar. *Reinforcement learning* derives information from an agent's interaction (by rewards and penalties) to learn actions in a particular situation [20].

A special technique of ML is deep learning (DL). DL describes different techniques for information processing of a large amount of data using artificial neural networks (ANN) with more than one hidden layer [20]. ANN consists of interconnected input, output, and hidden layers in between. Information is recorded, weighted, and evaluated within hidden layers according to its impact during training. These steps are repeated until the objective functions are minimized [20].

There are various ML algorithms, and new ones are being added constantly. Algorithms can be separated into different classes. In the context of this research, two classes of supervised learning can be distinguished, which are classification and regression. A regression model attempts to predict continuous data within a set of values [21]. On the other hand, a classification aims to predict a correct class from several classes of data [18]. An often-used neural network algorithm is a multilayer perceptron (MLP), which can be applied to classification and regression tasks. MLP feeds information only forward through an ANN and has fully interconnected layers that can process data. Convolutional neuronal networks (CNN) are an advanced technique of DL. They use different layers (e.g., convolutional and pooling layers) to analyze input data with different filters [22].

The results are stored in a matrix. The same procedure is repeated again and again on the deeper layers of the neural network. A pooling layer aggregates information on the identified features. The strongest feature of a matrix is filtered out and weaker ones are discarded [22]. In this way, it reduces the information in a matrix and transfers it to a more abstract representation. Subsequently, the output is flattened and fed into a dense layer to receive a final output [22].

2.4   Related Work: Application of Machine Learning Within PPC

Applications of ML in the field of production planning and control have increased significantly in recent years. This is also shown by the growing number of scientific publications related to ML and PPC [4]. ML approaches are particularly suitable for tasks with high uncertainty or complexity, e.g., demand planning and scheduling, which are often required in production planning and control [17]. Usuga Cadavid et al. [5] analyzed more than 90 publications to present the state-of-the-art of ML in PPC and identify further research opportunities. Publications were categorized into industry 4.0 use cases, according to Tao et al. [23]. The results of the literature study show that two-thirds of the possible research areas still need to be covered by the current literature. Among other things, it becomes clear that data from real systems are missing [5]. Further relevant topics for the development and implementation of ML in PPC were analyzed too, which are pointed out in the following. It is highlighted that supervised learning models are mainly applied as ML learning types. Widely used algorithms are decision trees and neural networks. Similar findings regarding ML classes and algorithms are provided by the literature reviews of Kramer et al. [15] and Fahle et al. [22], which are based on articles describing a real implementation of ML models within PPC tasks. When it comes to the data sources for training and testing algorithms, it becomes apparent that applications are often based on self-generated "artificial data" or data from management systems such as Enterprise Resource Planning (ERP) systems [5]. According to Usuga Cadavid et al. [5], one of the reasons for using artificial data is the difficulty of obtaining a sufficiently high-quality (quantitative and qualitative) database of companies and their processes. In this context, management systems are the only data sources in companies that can meet the requirements for a sufficient database.

The self-generated data can be computed in production and logistics systems by means of a DES. For example, the tasks and processes of a manufacturing execution system (MES) can be substituted with the help of a simulation. This enables to adapt different system settings rather easily and check the prediction accuracy of the developed ML model for different tasks within PPC [8]. Moreover, there are advantages to this application. Due to the use of a simulation model, it is possible to generate data covering several years in which only serval system variables have changed. Configurations as well as restrictions of the production and logistics systems, are therefore the same. This makes it possible to create training and test sets that contain as many different factors as possible in a reasonably balanced manner. In this way, events that occur very rarely can be reflected in the data and provide a comprehensive dataset for training an ML model [6].

Also, many authors have already dealt with identifying the necessary steps to implement an ML-based application within PPC [5]. Frequently mentioned are the core tasks of implementing an ML model (e.g., training, testing, hyperparameter tuning, etc.) [5]. Solving fundamental tasks such as data acquisition system design and data exploration (e.g., visualization and descriptive statistics) by applying ML is less frequently described in the latest research articles.

Apart from the general steps for knowledge discovery in databases, which are necessary for developing an ML model, further concrete applications of ML models within PPC are analyzed. According to Cioffi et al. [4], the application of ML helps to solve high-dimensional problems in order to optimize processes, improve the use of resources, and increase the quality of processes. Potentials for the use of ML are therefore seen primarily in the area of process and resource optimization as well as quality improvement of processes [4]. Usuga Cadavid et al. [5] state that those specific planning and control tasks, where ML in manufacturing systems is used the most, are time estimation followed by smart planning and scheduling. Thus, the main objective is to identify uncertainties early and take measures to minimize delays. In this context, the prediction of throughput times and makespans, as well as the tardiness of orders are mentioned by other authors as frequently performed tasks, too [3, 24]. For example, Bender and Ovtcharova [25] describe an approach to support lead-time prediction using AutoML. In this application, data from an ERP system and real-time data from an intelligent internet of things platform are used to predict lead times. The approach was tested using a simulation model [25]. According to Kramer et al. [17], production control and monitoring are also promising application areas. It refers to the continuous analysis of shopfloor data, which can be used to adjust parameters of physical resources automatically. Similar results are provided by the literature review of Büttner et al. [26], which describes a specific analysis of ML in terms of the Aachen PPC model. The results show that especially in the *in-house production planning and control* as well as the *production requirements planning*, ML applications are described often. In this context, the areas of detailed planning of resources and detailed scheduling of orders are specified. On the other hand, publications dealing with sequencing tasks are rarely described [26]. However, Rissmann et al. [7] analyzed different DL models to predict the amount of throughput based on different production order sequences.

With regard to the measurement of ML applications performance, mainly prediction accuracy is used. Model runtime/computational power is also considered as a measure of the ML performance. Rarely mentioned, qualitative metrics such as explainability and energy use are utilized to evaluate the ML models [17, 26].

In summary, it can be seen that ML applications are already widely used in the area of production planning and control. Nevertheless, it becomes clear that there is still a major gap in research with respect to the actual application of ML in PPC. An essential point concerns the training and testing of ML models with real data. In this context, simulation models are often used for validation. Tasks performed by ML models are mainly planning problems such as predicting throughput times or predicting the tardiness of an order. The objective is to identify uncertainties in the process on the basis of these predictions in order to subsequently take measures in a timely manner. Concrete decision support systems for specific tasks within a PPC are rarely outlined [24]. ML and DES are often applied in combination. However, simulations are increasingly used due to a lack of data. Moreover, the necessary workflow starting from the real production and logistics data via problem identification to training and testing of the ML model is described only to a limited extent. Previous findings by the authors will be addressed and expanded in the following [6]. First, the develop framework is presented.

3   Framework for Development of an ML Decision Support System Based on Simulation Data

The framework consists of different activities, which are shown in Fig. 3. BPMN 2.0 is used to describe the workflow. Different pools represent where the processes take place. Key activities of the framework are described in separate lanes: problem statement, data generation by simulation model, ML preparation and training, and ML validation.

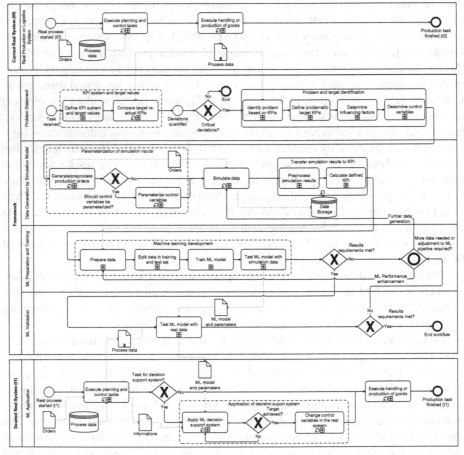

Fig. 3. Framework with specified activities for the development of an ML decision support system with simulation-generated data based on BPMN 2.0.

Problem Statement. The first pool demonstrates the current situation (t0) of the real system. Required planning and control tasks of PPCs from Sect. 2.1 are performed in this area. These serve as input information for the physical production and logistics processes. Data collected from handling or production processes are transferred to a KPI system for monitoring and controlling. Thus, deviations can be detected by comparing actual values with predefined target values for each KPI. This may reveal a potential for optimization and serve as a starting point for the framework's application. Next, it has to be analyzed whether the deviation of one or more KPIs is critical (e.g., occurs regularly or has a strong impact on process performance) or it occurs randomly and has no significant impact. If it is critical, the real problem has to be analyzed based on the changes of KPIs, process constants (e.g., number of resources, working times, etc.), and process variables (e.g., source and sink of transport tasks, activity types, etc.) [27]. This enables the definition of a target that should be improved through the use of a decision support system. Within the real system, the target has to be manifested in one or more KPIs (e.g., throughput time, throughput, failures, etc.). The factors that influence the target (e.g., process variables and process constants) or other causes have to be determined based on the domain knowledge from the real production and logistics systems [28]. Due to the fact that not all influencing factors can be directly controlled from the company's perspective, control variables have to be defined. These can be adjusted and help to modify, improve, or stabilize the target KPIs. In this step, various methods of process analysis, as well as expert knowledge, can be applied. This can be done manually (e.g., by Value Stream Mapping or Ishikawa-Diagrams) or with data-oriented approaches (e.g., by rule-based or ML approaches) [28]. The identified control variables as well as the target KPIs will be used in the following step.

Data Generation by Simulation Model. Depending on the identified target and influencing factors, there are different activities to be performed for data generation by means of a simulation model. First, it is necessary to generate diverse simulation input data (e.g., production orders, etc.). For example, data with differences in the sequence of products or in batch sizes. If the influencing factors rather refer to process variables and constants of the simulation (e.g., number of articles, conveyor capacity, etc.), these have to be parameterized in the simulation model in a further step. The simulation input data structure (e.g., production orders, resources, etc.) required for implementing a simulation model can be taken from different systems such as ERP or Warehouse Management System (WMS) [29]. This information input is used for a validated simulation model of the required production or logistics process. The model should reflect the real process in as much detail as is reasonable based on the defined target KPIs and influencing factors. Therefore, it is necessary to validate the results of a simulation model in advance. Among other things, in order to achieve an appropriate validation, it is important to use the same data structure (e.g., real production order structure) between the input data of the simulation and the real system. Methods and procedures of validation of a simulation model are not in the focus of this work and are therefore not explained in detail. Moreover, it has to be noted that by using simulations or simulations in combination with ML, several factors for inaccuracies can exist. Further research is required on this issue. These effects are not investigated in this article.

Based on the defined input data and simulation model, the required output data (e.g., KPIs or metrics for the calculation of KPIs) can be generated by simulation. By using a simulation model, it is possible to create multiple sets of data where only specific values of the system have changed. Thus, the configuration as well as the restrictions of the production and logistics systems are the same. Hence, events that occur very rarely can be reflected in the data. For determining the number of entries in the dataset required, it has to be considered that the duration of a single simulation run can be a regulating variable. Thus, it is not possible to specify the number of required entries in a dataset. This is due to different factors which can influence the number of entries: the complexity of the simulation as well as the number of process constants (e.g., number of working stations, batch sizes, working times, etc.), the complexity of the problem to be solved, or the ML task. The results of the simulation may have to be partially preprocessed according to the selected target KPIs. After data preprocessing, KPIs that cannot be calculated directly can be determined (e.g., adherence to schedule, etc.). KPIs such as throughput per day can be taken directly from the simulation results. In the end, it is important to store the inputs and associated outputs of the simulation runs in a database system (e.g., SQLite, etc.) for the next step.

ML Preparation and Training.   The generated data has to be processed using various data preparation methods. It has to be mentioned that only failed simulation runs or incorrect models can lead to erroneous data when using a validated simulation model. Nevertheless, the results should be checked. Failed simulation runs may produce incomplete or erroneous data. In addition, data argumentation as well as dimensionality reduction techniques could be performed. Also, ML clustering (e.g., k-Means, etc.) can be used to find patterns in data [6]. Furthermore, in case of a classification task, this allows to create classes which replace the initial label. To improve model performance, techniques such as principal component analysis (PCA) and up- and downsampling can be deployed. This may help to cope with imbalanced data and improve the ML result. Subsequently, it must be decided which learning type, algorithm class, and finally ML model are roughly suitable for the identified task. Supervised learning is selected as a learning type as features and labels are available. Through the description of the application scenario, an algorithm class can be specified e.g., classification or regression (Sect. 2.3). Thus, possible models can be delimited. By designating value ranges a regression problem can be adapted to a classification problem.

As displayed in Fig. 3 (ML preparation and training), it is critical to determine the output requirements of the ML model in order to evaluate the results objectively [30]. However, due to the different application scenarios within production and logistics systems, no specific requirement can be described. Nevertheless, the prediction accuracy needs to be good enough that an application of the ML model within a decision support system improves the defined target KPIs without degrading other KPIs. Hence, the quality, performance, or reliability of the production system should be increased by lower throughput times, better adherence to schedules, lower work in progress, or better utilization. The requirements can be specified in percentages or absolute numbers (e.g., > 5% more utilization of the machine, ten goods more throughput per shift, etc.). This is especially important, as low accuracy of an ML model may already cause a significant improvement of the target variable and a further improvement may yield diminishing returns.

Subsequently, the dataset can be split into training and test set. This can be done by a random training and test splitting function. The training set should contain 70% to 80% of the train and the test set 30% to 20% [19]. Afterward, the training of the selected ML models can be performed with the necessary input (features) and output (labels) data. Following this, the trained ML model must be applied to the existing test set with unknown data.

To evaluate the prediction quality, different metrics can be used depending on the selected algorithm class. For regression tasks, 'mean absolute error' (MAE) and 'mean squared error' (MSE) can be used [19]. MAE quantifies the deviation of the prediction to the observation. The MSE compares predicted with actual values and penalizes large outliers more than small ones. The 'root mean squared error' (RMSE) is similar, but positive and negative deviations do not cancel each other out. For classification, 'accuracy', 'recall', 'precision', and 'F1-score' can be used [19]. The precision value shows the true and false positive rate of all positive values. Through recall, the true positive and total positive ratio is described. F1-score is defined as the harmonic mean of the precision and recall. Accuracy shows the ratio of correct predictions compared to the total number of predictions.

A common failure during model training is overfitting. During overfitting, a model adapts too much to the given data and learns by memorizing. The ML model produced fails to generalize information and is therefore unusable for predicting unseen data. This is especially relevant if simulation data is used. By using the metrics appropriate to the use case, it should be determined whether the results obtained with the ML model are sufficient to meet the defined requirements. As shown in Fig. 3, this step leads to further iteration loops depending on the ML results. During *further data generation*, the number of simulations runs and thus, the amount of data is gradually increased. In *performance enhancement*, the settings of the ML model can be adjusted through additional data preparation steps. Also, this step can lead to testing other algorithm classes or ML models. If the ML results correspond to the previously defined requirements, the model can then be validated in the next step with real data.

ML Validation. During training, the ML model is validated with unseen simulation data. Before the ML model can be applied as a decision support system in the real-world application, the model should be validated with completely new real data (e.g., from a production and logistics process). In the proposed framework, the decision support system is used in parallel, i.e., alongside the real process. This means that the system already makes decisions on the basis of real data, but the implementation or testing is carried out by the process expert. The goal is to validate the decision support system. Depending on the result, this step leads to the execution of the corresponding feedback loops (Fig. 3). If these results match the test data results in terms of the used metrics, the ML model can be applied in the real system (t1) as a decision support system.

ML Application. In this case, the ML-based decision support system is used as a classifier. It helps to decide whether a desired KPI can be achieved with the targeted production or logistics input information or not. Through the usage of the developed ML decision support system a vast amount of possible inputs (e.g., different production plans, etc.) can be processed in seconds. A decision can trigger a new planning or release the necessary following processes. In the next section, the key activities of the framework are demonstrated by means of a case study.

4   Case Study

The following section will describe the carried-out case study in detail. Starting with its description, which not only describes the physical and simulation part of the case study but goes into detail about the conducted ML as well as retrieved baseline results. The final subsection contains the results of the case study.

4.1   Case Study Description

To validate the extended approach, a U-shaped assembly line layout of a medium-sized company was selected. This is set up as an exemplary model in the Technology Center for Production and Logistics Systems (TZ PULS) [31]. Based on the real system, a DES was created in Plant Simulation and validated against several KPIs (e.g., throughput in units, cycle time, etc.). The U-shaped assembly line layout exists for educational purposes, so the data from the educational production runs were used for the aforementioned validation. As illustrated in Fig. 4, the entire value stream is simulated with all relevant processes and tasks from goods receipt to goods issue. In the considered system, floor rollers in six different variants (three different wheel colors and two different frame types) are assembled in seven steps.

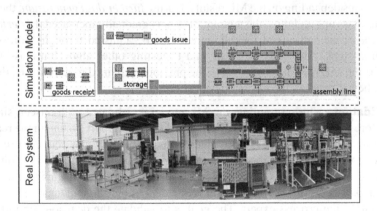

Fig. 4. Representation of the real system and DES model in the TZ PULS [7].

The variants distinguish by three different wheel colors as well as two different frame types. Demand for the high runner products is 60%, for the middle runner products 30%, and for the low runner products 10% (Table 1). The batch size in which the various products are assembled is five. At the first station, the frame types are placed on the assembly line. Followed by attaching a wheel to each wheel mount (stations 2 to 5).

Finally, the products are quality checked at station 6 and packed for shipment at station 7. Production planning and control is realized with a *heijunka board*. The provision of the necessary components is carried out with a supermarket directly at the assembly line. Replenishment orders are controlled with Kanban. Input data are production orders of the assembly line. Goods reception, storage, and goods issue are only influenced indirectly through requests within the U-shaped assembly line layout.

In order to analyze the existing process as described in Sect. 3 "Problem Statement", a KPI system was set up, consisting of five targets throughput, throughput time, work in progress, utilization, and adherence to schedule. Target values are defined on historical data. Actual KPIs were taken from educational production runs that were conducted. Based on the comparison of actual with the target KPIs, critical deviations of throughput, throughput time, and adherence to schedule could be determined.

Due to the fact that these KPIs relies on many influencing factors, it was necessary to define the scope in terms of the problem to be solved. Thus, the following restrictions were made: the solution should not require any physical changes in the material flow and be implementable in a short time without additional costs [6]. Therefore, the modification of the production order sequence within a production plan was identified as a control variable that could be changed and monitored. Hence, the aim was the evaluation of generated production plans with regard to the achievement of the defined target KPIs.

To generate data by the DES, 10,000 production plans with 751 units to be produced each were created. The maximum output quantity for one working day is 751 units per production plan. For this purpose the *numpys.random.choice* algorithm is used. The restrictions given by the educational production system are summarized in Table 1.

Table 1. Restrictions of the used production system as well as the product mix within a production plan (frame types F1 and F2 are split 50–50 for each category).

Restrictions	Product mix		
• Batch size five • 751 items of one production plan • Two shifts a day • 8 hours of working time per shift	60% high-runner	Wheel red	Frame type F1 and F2
	30% middle-runner	Wheel green	Frame type F1 and F2
	10% low-runner	Wheel white	Frame type F1 and F2

Based on the randomly generated production plans, two datasets were simulated by the DES. The two datasets differ by a best possible *scenario A* with few breakdowns and defect rate and a *scenario B* with many and longer breakdowns and with the same defect rate (Fig. 5). In Scenario B, the overall availability is significantly lower at 65% compared to Scenario A, which achieves 96%.

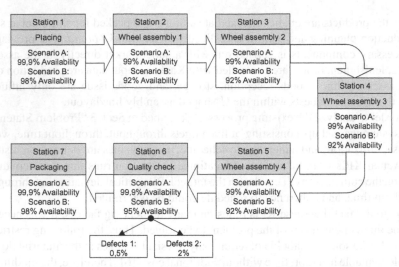

Fig. 5. Overview of the U-shaped assembly line layout incl. availability per station in percent and defects rate for scenario A and B.

After the simulation runs are done, the KPIs, which cannot be extracted directly from the results have to be derived. In this case study, only the throughput in units can be used directly. The throughput time was calculated with the help of the start and end time of each individual product. In addition, the 75th percentile of the throughput time is taken to calculate the planned end times, which in turn is used to determine the adherence to schedule. The target throughput time is based on a previous analysis with experts from the production planning domain. It was selected as the 75th percentile of all throughput times. These KPIs were determined separately for both datasets of scenarios A and B.

During data preparation, 29 simulation runs were identified with a severely decreased output. These runs had an output of approximately 10% compared to the mean output. This phenomenon was seen for scenarios A and B indicating a problem inside the simulation model. After identifying the triggering production plans (simulation input), a bug was detected within the simulation model. These production plans forced the simulation to be stuck in a loop. These runs would falsify the results. A thorough investigation of this error revealed that it occurred only in the 29 identified simulation runs. As a result, all affected simulation runs were excluded from the dataset.

Preliminary findings showed that clustering can improve ML predictions especially in a simulation environment where the data is not as diverse as in real-world applications [6]. Furthermore, these findings showed that a regression approach is not suitable. Nevertheless, a regression approach was tested. As shown in Fig. 6, during training, only the training loss decreases.

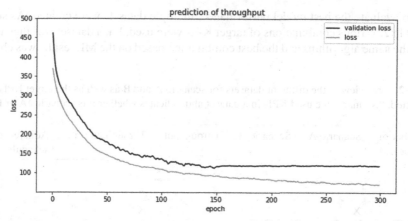

Fig. 6. Example illustration of the prediction of throughput time with a regression model: It becomes apparent that regression models performed badly and tend to overfit. The graph shows that the training loss continues to fall slightly while the validation loss remains the same.

Previously working approaches applied k-Means to cluster available data. In this case clustering with k-Means yielded no usable clusters. Hence, a manual approach was selected. For each target KPI, a threshold was used to create two classes. These resulting clusters represent good and bad results for each KPI. To find the exact threshold, multiple model trainings were analyzed. As displayed in Fig. 7, 10% was found optimal. The result of that clustering is utilized in the following classification task.

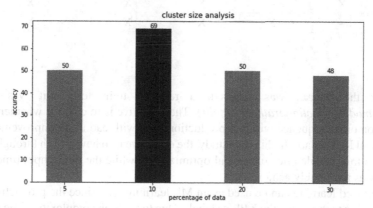

Fig. 7. Comparing model performance using various thresholds to determine the optimal cluster size.

To evaluate the best model performance, multiple datasets were created. As shown in Table 2, various combinations of target KPIs were used. Each dataset was then tested with the same algorithms and the best combination based on the ML results was chosen.

Table 2. Overview of the different datasets for scenario A and B as well as the target KPIs to be predicted. "X" marks the used KPIs in a dataset and indicates whether it is scenarios A or B.

Number of Datasets	Scenario A	Scenario B	Throughput	Throughput time	Adherence to schedule
1	X	–	X	–	–
2	–	X	X	–	–
3	X	–	–	X	–
4	–	X	–	X	–
5	X	–	–	–	X
6	–	X	–	–	X
7	X	–	X	X	–
8	–	X	X	X	–
9	X	–	X	–	X
10	–	X	X	–	X
11	X	–	–	X	X
12	–	X	–	X	X
13	X	–	X	X	X
14	–	X	X	X	X

After the dataset was selected, a random train test split was applied (*sklearn.model_selection.train_test_split*). The objective is to classify whether a given production order sequence within a production plan will lead to an improvement with regard to all KPIs or not. In this case study, the objective is to have a high throughput and adherence to schedule after successful optimization, while the throughput time should be as low as reasonably achievable.

Supervised learning can be used as an ML learning type since the production plans can be used as features and the KPIs as labels. Due to the high complexity of the problem to be solved, the application of ANNs is necessary. For the application within this case study, an MLP and a CNN model were tested for classification. To set a baseline, Fig. 8 demonstrates each unique KPI with its aforementioned clusters.

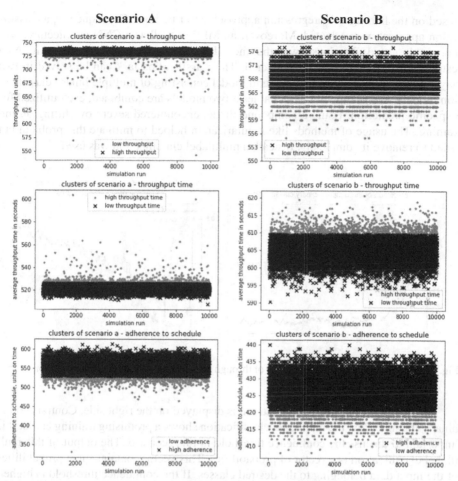

Fig. 8. Representation of the classes determined by clustering for the KPIs throughput, throughput time, and adherence to schedule. The Y-axes of scenarios A and B differ due to the different maximum and minimum values as well as the dispersion of the data.

To validate the ML model as mentioned in Sect. 3 (ML preparation and training), the following requirements of each working day and scenarios A and B were defined: the average throughput in units as well as the adherence to schedule should be increased and the average throughput time should be decreased. The results of the classification for each ML model and dataset (few and many breakdowns) are presented below.

4.2   Results of the Case Study

Verification of the approach is done by comparing the prediction with the corresponding simulation results. As displayed in Table 2, datasets with one, two, or three labels were available. Furthermore, as previously mentioned, a regression approach was tested. The regression approach showed bad results in combination with severe overfitting (Fig. 6).

Based on the findings, the regression approach was ruled out. Consequently, a classification approach was selected. Moreover, an MLP as well as a CNN architecture, was thoroughly tested. Results showed that the MLP suffered from severe overfitting. As a result, a CNN architecture was selected. The classification task can be solved in two ways. The first of which is a compound model consisting of multiple binary classification models. In a compound model at least two models are combined, each utilized for a specific prediction. Using a compound model encountered severe overfitting during training. The usage of methods like regularization helped to mitigate this problem but failed to remove it completely. Instead, a multilabel classification was used.

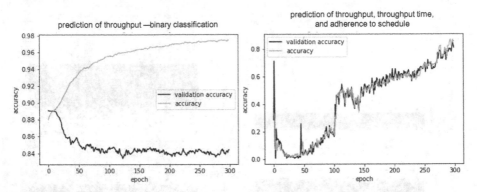

Fig. 9. Results of a binary classification of throughput (left) vs. a multilabel classification (right).

In Fig. 9, the multilabel classification is displayed on the right side. Contrary to the binary classification, the multilabel classification shows a promising training curve. It is important to discuss the confidence threshold in this scenario. The output of this multilabel classification is a vector of probabilities. This vector contains three probabilities of the input data belonging to the desired classes. If the confidence threshold is higher, the precision value increases, whereas the recall will decrease. The threshold was determined by approximating several test runs. In this scenario, the threshold is set to 0.99 for an optimal balance.

After training, the evaluation of the model is necessary. As explained in Sect. 3, there are multiple evaluation metrics for a classification task. For the case study, the evaluating metrics are displayed in the following table.

Table 3. Final model classification report of the three target KPIs throughput (0), throughput time (1), and adherence to schedule (2).

KPIs	Precision	Recall	F1-score	support
Throughput (0)	0.90	0.28	0.42	1776
Throughput time (1)	0.91	0.26	0.40	1792
Adherence to schedule (2)	0.93	0.20	0.33	1794

As displayed in Table 3, the precision for the class throughput is between 90% – 93%. Support annotates the total amount of positive values for each category. As this is only an abstract representation of the results, the application of the model to the test set is visualized in the following Fig. 10.

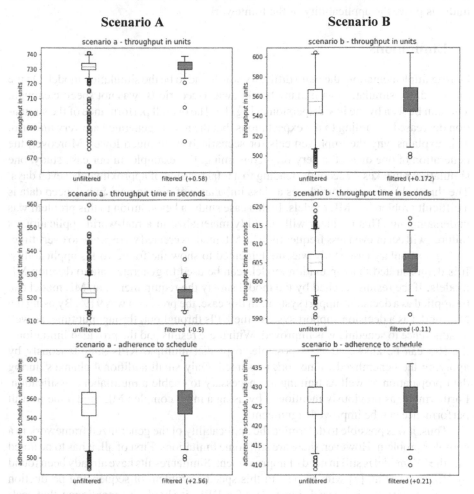

Fig. 10. Presentation of the achieved results for the three KPIs throughput, throughput time, and adherence to schedule of scenarios A and B.

Figure 10 shows that the output is improved by using the proposed framework. As shown through the application of the ML model, the dispersion was reduced. The absolute improvement of each individual KPI is relatively small but the focus of the article was to improve all KPIs at once. It has to be mentioned that the mean values for the positive cluster are relatively close to the overall mean. The throughput in units was increased by 0.6 units with the mean of the positive cluster at 1.2 units. The throughput time was reduced by 0.5 seconds with the mean being at 0.8 seconds. The adherence to schedule increased by 2.6 units with a mean of 0.4 units. From 1,995 production plans in the validation dataset 356, were selected by the ML model. It is expected by focusing on a single KPI a higher absolute improvement could be achieved. As illustrated by the improvement numbers in Fig. 10, scenario A yielded better results compared to scenario B. This is probably due to the low dispersion of data in scenario B. Nevertheless, the findings prove the applicability of the framework.

5 Limitations

During implementation, the main difficulty was found to be the simulation model. On the one hand, the simulation with many breakdowns (scenario B) was not specific enough. This can be seen by the low dispersion in Fig. 10. The overall performance of the simulation decreased according to the expectations, but the results generated are very uniform. This explains why the improvements for scenario B were much lower. Moreover, the generation of one dataset is very time-consuming. For example, in our case study, one simulation run takes 30 seconds, leading to a total runtime of approximately seven days. The threshold selection introduces a class imbalance of nine to one. Imbalanced data is a difficult problem for ML models. In this case study, a key solution to this problem was undersampling. This problem will certainly materialize in a real-world application as failures will occur even less frequently. The ML models created were prone to overfitting.

An exemplary case study was implemented to show the framework's applicability. It is demonstrated that simulation models can be used to generate data to develop ML models. If the results reached by the model satisfy the requirements, an ML model can be applied as a decision support system. In this case, the precision was 91%. By using the ML model as a decision support system, the KPIs throughput, throughput time, as well as adherence to schedule was improved. With these results and the provided limitations, the RQ can be answered: it is possible to predict multiple KPIs simultaneously by applying the generalized framework presented. Only small additional changes during data preparation as well as training are necessary to enable a multilabel classification. Furthermore, as previously mentioned by using a more complex ML model the overall performance can be improved significantly.

Thus, it was possible to determine the applicability of the generalized framework to a complex problem. However, there are still some limitations. First of all, it has to be noted that the ML model is still in need of improvement. Similar results have already been found by Rissmann et al. [7] with respect to this specific problem of sequencing production orders. Despite the increased dynamics of a DES, it should be mentioned that real-world systems still contain further fluctuations. Therefore, further investigations should show how the application works on more extensive random problems (e.g., failures, downtimes, etc.) in real-world production and logistics systems.

6 Conclusion and Outlook

Based on the previously published findings, this article presents an extended generalized framework [6]. This framework is designed to develop machine learning-based decision support systems for planning and control tasks within production systems according to critical KPIs. The core is the generation of artificial data by means of a DES, which is used to train and test ML models. The aim is to create sufficient realistic data in a short time and to significantly accelerate the actual use of machine learning within PPC. In this way, ML models can also be developed in processes with limited data or insufficient data quality or even for processes in planning stages. Building on the initial findings, the application of the approach was validated by means of a realistic exemplary case study. In the case study, a decision support system was developed. Based on a production plan the system selects those that simultaneously optimize three relevant KPIs: throughput, throughput time, and adherence to schedule. The results show that ML can support tasks within PPC and helps to reduce optimizing effort.

In future research, the approach should be further tested and improved using an industrial application example. Further research steps are developing methods to counteract data imbalance. Also, a further exploration of a data-driven problem identification and optimization approaches based on KPIs, process variables (parameter), and process constants is needed.

References

1. Wuest, T., Weimer, D., Irgens, C., Thoben, K.-D.: Machine learning in manufacturing: advantages, challenges, and applications. Product. Manufact. Res. **4**, 23–45 (2016). https://doi.org/10.1080/21693277.2016.1192517
2. Woschank, M., Rauch, E., Zsifkovits, H.: A review of further directions for artificial intelligence, machine learning, and deep learning in smart logistics. Sustainability. **12**, 3760 (2020). https://doi.org/10.3390/su12093760
3. Alemão, D., Rocha, A.D., Barata, J.: Smart manufacturing scheduling approaches—systematic review and future directions. Appl. Sci. **11**, 2186 (2021). https://doi.org/10.3390/app110 52186
4. Cioffi, R., Travaglioni, M., Piscitelli, G., Petrillo, A., De Felice, F.: Artificial intelligence and machine learning applications in smart production: progress, trends, and directions. Sustainability. **12**, 492 (2020). https://doi.org/10.3390/su12020492
5. Usuga Cadavid, J.P., Lamouri, S., Grabot, B., Pellerin, R., Fortin, A.: Machine learning applied in production planning and control: a state-of-the-art in the era of industry 4.0. J. Intell Manuf. **31**, 1531–1558 (2020). https://doi.org/10.1007/s10845-019-01531-7
6. Muehlbauer, K., Rissmann, L., Meissner, S.: Decision support for production control based on machine learning by simulation-generated data: In: Proceedings of the 14th International Joint Conference on Knowledge Discovery, Knowledge Engineering and Knowledge Management, pp. 54–62. SCITEPRESS - Science and Technology Publications, Valletta, Malta (2022). https://doi.org/10.5220/0011538000003335
7. Rissmann, L., Muehlbauer, K., Meissner, S.: Application of deep learning based on a simulation model to classify production orders. In: Proceedings of the 34th European Modeling and Simulation Symposium (EMSS 2022). Rom (2022)
8. Pfeiffer, A., Gyulai, D., Kádár, B., Monostori, L.: Manufacturing lead time estimation with the combination of simulation and statistical learning methods. Procedia CIRP. **41**, 75–80 (2016). https://doi.org/10.1016/j.procir.2015.12.018
9. Kritzinger, W., Karner, M., Traar, G., Henjes, J., Sihn, W.: Digital twin in manufacturing: a categorical literature review and classification. IFAC-PapersOnLine. **51**, 1016–1022 (2018). https://doi.org/10.1016/j.ifacol.2018.08.474

10. Lödding, H.: Handbook of Manufacturing Control: Fundamentals, Description, Configuration. Springer, Berlin (2013). https://doi.org/10.1007/978-3-642-24458-2
11. Schuh, G., Stich, V., eds: Produktionsplanung und -steuerung 1. Springer Berlin Heidelberg, Berlin, Heidelberg (2012). https://doi.org/10.1007/978-3-642-25423-9
12. Fottner, J., et al.: Autonomous Systems in Intralogistics – State of the Art and Future Research Challenges. Bundesvereinigung Logistik (BVL) e.V., DE (2021). https://doi.org/10.23773/2021_2
13. Schuh, G., Stich, V., eds: Produktionsplanung und -steuerung 1: Evolution der PPS. Springer Berlin Heidelberg, Berlin, Heidelberg (2012). https://doi.org/10.1007/978-3-642-25423-9
14. Kunath, M., Winkler, H.: Integrating the digital twin of the manufacturing system into a decision support system for improving the order management process. Procedia CIRP. **72**, 225–231 (2018). https://doi.org/10.1016/j.procir.2018.03.192
15. Reuter, C., Brambring, F.: Improving data consistency in production control. Procedia CIRP. **41**, 51–56 (2016). https://doi.org/10.1016/j.procir.2015.12.116
16. Nyhuis, P. (ed.): Beiträge zu einer Theorie der Logistik. Springer, Berlin Heidelberg (2008). https://doi.org/10.1007/978-3-540-75642-2
17. Kramer, K.J., Rokoss, A., Schmidt, M.: Do we really know the benefit of machine learning in production planning and control? a systematic review of industry case studies. (2021). https://doi.org/10.15488/11296
18. Domingos, P.: A few useful things to know about machine learning. Commun. ACM. **55**, 78–87 (2012). https://doi.org/10.1145/2347736.2347755
19. Joshi, A.V.: Machine Learning and Artificial Intelligence. Springer, Cham (2020). https://doi.org/10.1007/978-3-030-26622-6
20. Goodfellow, I., Bengio, Y., Courville, A.: Deep Learning. The MIT Press, Cambridge, Massachusetts (2016). http://www.deeplearningbook.org
21. Han, J., Kamber, M.: Data Mining: Concepts and Techniques. Elsevier, Burlington, MA (2012). https://doi.org/10.1016/C2009-0-61819-5
22. LeCun, Y., Bengio, Y., Hinton, G.: Deep learning. Nature **521**, 436–444 (2015). https://doi.org/10.1038/nature14539
23. Tao, F., Qi, Q., Liu, A., Kusiak, A.: Data-driven smart manufacturing. J. Manuf. Syst. **48**, 157–169 (2018). https://doi.org/10.1016/j.jmsy.2018.01.006
24. Fahle, S., Prinz, C., Kuhlenkötter, B.: Systematic review on machine learning (ML) methods for manufacturing processes – Identifying artificial intelligence (AI) methods for field application. Procedia CIRP. **93**, 413–418 (2020). https://doi.org/10.1016/j.procir.2020.04.109
25. Bender, J., Ovtcharova, J.: Prototyping machine-learning-supported lead time prediction using autoML. Procedia Comput. Sci. **180**, 649–655 (2021). https://doi.org/10.1016/j.procs.2021.01.287
26. Büttner, K., Antons, O., Arlinghaus, J.C.: Applied machine learning for production planning and control: overview and potentials. IFAC-PapersOnLine. **55**, 2629–2634 (2022). https://doi.org/10.1016/j.ifacol.2022.10.106
27. Muehlbauer, K., Wuennenberg, M., Meissner, S., Fottner, J.: Data driven logistics-oriented value stream mapping 4.0: a guideline for practitioners. IFAC-PapersOnLine. **55**, 364–369 (2022). https://doi.org/10.1016/j.ifacol.2022.09.051
28. Wuennenberg, M., Muehlbauer, K., Fottner, J., Meissner, S.: Towards predictive analytics in internal logistics – an approach for the data-driven determination of key performance indicators. CIRP J. Manuf. Sci. Technol. **44**, 116–125 (2023). https://doi.org/10.1016/j.cirpj.2023.05.005
29. Knoll, D., Prüglmeier, M., Reinhart, G.: Materialflussanalyse mit ERP-Transportaufträgen*/Material flow analysis using transport orders. wt. **107**, 129–133 (2017). https://doi.org/10.37544/1436-4980-2017-03-25

30. Vernickel, K., et al.: Machine-learning-based approach for parameterizing material flow simulation models. Procedia CIRP. **93**, 407–412 (2020). https://doi.org/10.1016/j.procir.2020.04.018

31. Blöchl, S.J., Schneider, M.: Simulation game for intelligent production logistics – the pull® learning factory. Procedia CIRP. **54**, 130–135 (2016). https://doi.org/10.1016/j.procir.2016.04.100

FAIRification of CRIS: A Review

Otmane Azeroual[1](✉) (iD), Joachim Schöpfel[2] (iD), Janne Pölönen[3] (iD),
and Anastasija Nikiforova[4,5] (iD)

[1] German Centre for Higher Education Research and Science Studies (DZHW), 10117 Berlin,
Germany
azeroual@dzhw.eu
[2] GERiiCO Laboratory, University of Lille, 59653 Villeneuve-d'Ascq, France
[3] Federation of Finnish Learned Societies, 00170 Helsinki, Finland
[4] Institute of Computer Science, University of Tartu, 51009 Tartu, Estonia
[5] European Open Science Cloud Task Force "FAIR Metrics and Data Quality", 1050 Brussels,
Belgium

Abstract. While the topics of CRIS and FAIR are not new, after decades of
research on CRIS, CRIS and their FAIRness remain a relatively overlooked dimension
of CRIS. To address this problem, we conduct a systematic literature review
(SLR) that connects the fragmented knowledge accumulated through the observation
of CRIS development/maturing dynamics and attempts to make them or
their elements FAIR. Based on the SLR we assemble the overarching framework
that expands the theoretical foundations of CRIS and their FAIRness based on the
existing practices.

Keywords: FAIR · Research Information Management System · Research
Information System · RIS · CRIS · Systematic Review

1 Introduction

The FAIR principles were originally developed as guidelines for the effective and efficient
management of research data and stewardship as part of the open science policy
framework, with a "specific emphasis on enhancing the ability of machines to automatically
find and use the data" in data repositories [1]. In a short time, FAIR has established
itself in research, supported by scientific institutions, funding bodies, academic networks[1]
etc., in particular in the European Union whose research and innovation funding
programme emphasises the management of data and other outputs in accordance with
the FAIR principles[2].

This paper extends our IC3K 2022 paper, which can be found at this link: https://doi.org/10.5220/
0011548700003335

[1] Cf. The GO FAIR initiative https://www.go-fair.org/

[2] Cf. OpenAIRE https://www.openaire.eu/how-to-comply-with-horizon-europe-mandate-
for-rdm

F. Coenen et al. (Eds.): IC3K 2022, CCIS 1842, pp. 280–298, 2023.
https://doi.org/10.1007/978-3-031-43471-6_13

The FAIR principles describe concise and domain-independent recommendations for a wide range of scientific results. They consist of fifteen interconnected but independent and separable elements which are basically a consolidation and a comprehensive rephrasing of earlier approaches to move toward a machine-friendly research infrastructure [2]. Some principles apply only to data or metadata, others to both; they are designed for human and machine readability. Their short and general definitions should enable a low-threshold entry ([1]; see Appendix 1). In short, the FAIR principles can be described as follows[3]:

- F for Findability means that metadata and data should be easy to find for both humans and computers.
- A for Accessibility means that the users need to know how metadata and data can be accessed, possibly including authentication and authorisation.
- I for Interoperability means the ability of data or tools from non-cooperating resources to integrate or work together with minimal effort; the data need to interoperate with applications or workflows for analysis, storage, and processing.
- R for Reusability means that metadata and data should be well-described so that they can be replicated and/or combined in different settings (reuse).

The FAIR principles have become central to the discussion and implementation of open science policies, and they are increasingly being applied to other "digital objects" [3] such as institutional repositories and large infrastructures like the European Open Science Cloud (EOSC) and the German national research data infrastructure (NFDI), but also to metadata, identifiers, catalogues and software, to the processing of electronic theses and dissertations [4], as well as for the assessment of technological behaviours [5]. Recently, a white paper [6] made the point that in fact, FAIR principles cover all types of digital objects, metadata, and infrastructures but as FAIR defines principles not standards, "they do not propose a mechanism to achieve the behaviours they describe"; also, the white paper calls for an "open discussion around FAIRness governance" and accurate FAIRness assessment metrics and tools.

Current research information systems (CRIS) are a particular category of research infrastructures and as such, are impacted by FAIR principles. CRIS, also called RIS (research information systems) or RIMS (research information management systems), are used to organize and process research information, i.e., information on research, as for instance people (researchers / scientists), organisations, and outputs. CRIS encompasses the process of managing this research information throughout its life cycle, from planning, generation, selection, evaluation and storage to preparation for subsequent use. Research can hardly take place without this strategic information, and as the amount of data to be evaluated is increasing, it is necessary to develop strategies for dealing with the research information [7]. For this purpose, CRIS are introduced to collect, store, process, develop, network and manage (incl., use and, more importantly, reuse) data on research.

CRIS are not research data repositories but contain data on research that have strategic value and may be sensitive and potentially even harmful when it is about persons. For

---

[3] Cf. GO FAIR description https://www.go-fair.org/fair-principles/

all these reasons, and because these systems communicate with other research infrastructures like institutional repositories, human resource or financial systems, interoperability, transparency, and quality - both data quality and system quality are essential features. This is where the FAIR principles become a promising asset.

CRIS (or RIS, or RIMS) can be seen as a one-stop-shop for researchers when it comes to the registration, management and online exposure, e.g. through CV or profile pages, of information about their research. This information may include but is not necessarily limited to information on the projects they are involved in, their funding, the organisations and researchers participating in them, the equipment used, the time spent for the research or the results the research yields, with the information on the data being created and used in the research. Registration of datasets in the CRIS brings the added value that they can be linked to the publications based upon them, the project they belong to, the researchers creating and working with the data, and to software or other tools used in analysing the data, or the organisations involved in the research [8] and [9]. Linking the datasets automatically and directly to the extensive and rich metadata of other research objects and attributes present in the CRIS, is crucial for the FAIRness of the data, and thus for the Open Science as whole. Jetten et al. (2019) suggest that this is also applicable to the Data Management Plan (DMP) intended to hold key information on the management and preservation of the research data throughout the research life cycle, and as a result CRIS should consider DMP as one of its components and treat them in the same way as the datasets, including linking it to the rest of the information on the research it is part of.

An analysis of studies produced by the euroCRIS community reveals a growing awareness of FAIR principles by CRIS stakeholders [10]. EuroCRIS[4] is an international not-for-profit association founded in 2002 in order to bring together experts on research information in general and CRIS in particular. The mission of euroCRIS is to foster cooperation and knowledge-sharing across the research information community and to promote interoperability of research information through the Common European Research Information Format (CERIF). It provides the framework for information exchange across a broad variety of stakeholders, for example researchers, research managers and administrators, research councils, research funders, entrepreneurs and technology transfer organisations. Papers from the euroCRIS international CRIS conferences (held every other year) and its membership meetings (held twice a year) show that FAIR principles are already applied to some systems; yet, FAIRness is a bidirectional process, insofar as CRIS can contribute to improve the FAIRness of data and infrastructures, and FAIR principles push further improvements to the underlying CRIS. FAIR research information management is required.

The 2022 analysis was based on a review of 14 papers from different euroCRIS conferences and meetings between 2016 and 2022. In order to provide more insight on the relation between CRIS and FAIR, we conducted a systematic review with the two major scientometric databases, Scopus from Elsevier and the Web of Science from Clarivate. The results are discussed against the 2022 findings and the development of the FAIR landscape. The purpose is twofold: To connect the fragmented knowledge accumulated through the observation of CRIS development and attempts to make them

---

[4] euroCRIS https://eurocris.org/

or their elements FAIR; and to assemble an overarching framework that expands the theoretical foundations of CRIS and their FAIRness.

2 Methodology

In order to identify relevant literature, the review was carried out by searching digital libraries covered by Scopus and Web of Science (WoS) Core Collection, which index the majority of well-known publishers. This was done employing Preferred Reporting Items for Systematic Review and Meta-analyses Method (PRISMA).

The search query was defined as a combination of terms "current research information system"/"CRIS" and "FAIR", where CRIS term has been provided with various alternative namings found in the literature and based on our own experience, including "Research Information System", "Research Information Management System". Similarly, FAIR abbreviation was supplied with the lists of the respective principles, "findability", "accessibility"," "interoperability" and "reusability", as well as "findable", "accessible", "interoperable", "reusable".

For all of the keywords we identified, synonyms were found and included in the query. Only articles in English were considered, but statistics on the most popular non-English studies were also collected. In terms of coverage, reviews, books, editorials, notes and conference reviews were excluded, and further analysis of articles, conference papers, book chapters, short surveys and letters was carried out.

For the period covered by these searches, we set 1994 as the start date without limiting the end date. It also allows us also to get an insight of the trends in the popularity of these topics over the years and to obtain the most complete set of studies on these topics for further analysis, as well as find out how (or whether) the concept evolved over time.

The initial search was conducted in February, 2023 on all elements of the articles (abstract, title, keywords and body) without limiting the areas to which they belong. However, this returned articles with a prevailing predominance of medical and healthcare research that was not related to the subject of interest. Given the original set of results we obtained, we decided to limit the scope of the search to the article title, keywords, and abstract in order to limit the number of articles to those where these objects were the primary object of study, rather than mentioned in the body, e.g., as a future work. We enriched the resulting sets with additional studies using the snowball method.

("Research Information System" OR "Research Information Management System" OR "CRIS" OR "Current Research Information System") AND ("FAIR" OR ("findable" AND "accessible" AND "interoperable" AND "reusable") OR ("findability" AND "accessibility" AND "interoperability" AND "reusability")).

Figure 1 shows the results of the query.

After conducting the search and filtering out the papers in accordance with the process described above (see Fig. 1), we come up with twelve papers. This is the corpus of our review study. The articles were then reviewed according to the developed protocol (see Appendix 2) which is based on [11].

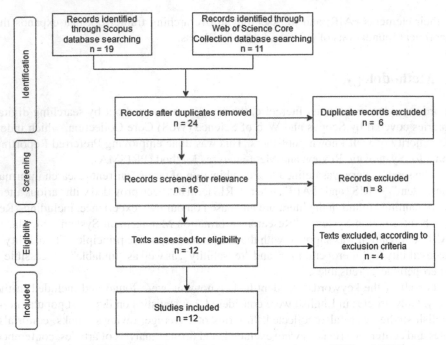

Fig. 1. PRISMA flow diagram of the systematic review on CRIS and FAIR.

3 Results

First, it should be mentioned that there is a relatively small number of relevant studies. Twelve articles are a quite small corpus. Two papers are also part of our review conducted in 2022 [10]. This means that our review identified only nine papers that had not been retrieved in 2022, when the review was limited to the euroCRIS community and repository. Merging both reviews, we get a corpus of 26 original and relevant papers, published between 2004 and 2022.

The coverage is European - papers have been published by authors from Finland, Germany and the Netherlands (two articles per country) but also from Belgium, Estonia, France and Sweden. This is not surprising, as both topics - research information systems and FAIR principles - are mainly discussed in Europe and constitute the pillars of Open Science promoted in the European Union as a driver of science and development as a whole.

Surprisingly, there is no evolution over the years, no steady increase in the long term but a sudden rise in awareness: ten of the twelve papers have been published since 2019. All papers present results from applied research, without a theoretical or conceptual approach. This means for instance that they either simply do not define CRIS, or they are rather limited to a short and general description, such as "used to collect information about research organisations' scientific publications" [12], "developed to provide researchers, research managers, innovators, and others with an overview of research activity in a specific domain" [13] or "(developed) to maintain a wide array of research information consistent, well-structured and up-to-date" [14].

While some papers are based on case studies with local or commercial systems (PURE, Converis), others make assumptions regarding CRIS as a particular category of software.

Most studies cover all FAIR principles, while studies such as [8] and [15] show how CRIS can improve potential reuse, while [16] focus on interoperability.

3.1 FAIRification of CRIS

Implementing FAIR workflows can improve the FAIRness of CRIS. Here, the "Implementing FAIR Workflows" project [17] can be mentioned as one of the most expressive examples. It aims at the integration of services and platforms to existing and well-accepted global research infrastructure, in particular the different open identifier systems through which metadata of scholarly artefacts are aggregated and shared. According to the authors, *"The combination of active sharing on the researcher's side and the effective metadata curation on the services and platform side, will provide the foundation for connectivity among researchers, institutes, funders, and research outputs (and) encourage researchers (...) to adopt workflows that ensure the FAIRness of all research outputs by design, instead of as an afterthought"*. The idea is that by applying the FAIR principles *from the inception of the research project, "all the different entities of research information get related to each other"* [17]. The challenge, however, is how stakeholders can contribute to workflows (bridges), while the main issue reported by the authors is metadata curation and, above all, adoption of persistent identifiers.

Meadows et al. (2019) [18] describe persistent identifiers (PIDs) - for people (researchers), places (their organisations) and things (their research outputs and other contributions) – as "foundational elements in the overall research information infrastructure" and essential for their interoperability and the findability of their content (data). PIDs are good for CRIS: "Instead of spending time on frustrating administrative tasks like online form-filling during grant application or manuscript submission, researchers could simply grant access to their ORCID record and enable data-sharing with the various research information systems with which they interact". Yet, the relation between PIDs and CRIS is bidirectional, as the PIDs' metadata should be FAIR, i.e., open, interoperable and well-defined, with provenance information; and this information can partly be provided by CRIS. Or with [10], "the improvement of FAIRness is a bidirectional process, where CRIS promotes FAIRness of data and infrastructures, and FAIR principles push further improvements to the underlying CRIS".

Assuming that an agreed understanding of the concepts of research information is crucial for research evaluation and policy, [13] presents "an approach to systematically develop and document (...) definitions of research information (and) discussed alternatives and related arguments". The purpose is "to support existing (research information) standardisation initiatives", thus improving the implementation of FAIR principles in CRIS.

Following a series of online workshops with experts on research information and FAIR principles, a qualitative analysis of the expert discussion confirms the relevance and challenge of FAIR for CRIS [14]. The main purpose of the discussion is the FAIRification of CRIS and, as a result, of the whole ecosystem of research information. The main means and methods to get there are standardised metadata, PIDs, open formats and protocols (e.g., CERIF), data quality and curation, and multilingual vocabulary.

3.2   FAIRification of Workflows and Other Infrastructures

Implementing FAIR principles can improve the quality, usefulness and acceptance of CRIS. On the other side, CRIS can contribute to the FAIRification of workflows and other infrastructures. Similar to [16, 19] put forward the potential and ability of CRIS to improve data quality and more generally, FAIRness of other systems, especially in the emerging landscape of EOSC: *"these systems have a very relevant role to play in the ongoing process for putting together any RIM e-infrastructure such as the European Open Science Cloud"*. They describe the CRIS contribution on two levels, the richness of contextual information, and interoperability (the I in FAIR) through standardisation: *"This is not only for the wealth of valuable contextual research information they are able to provide, but also because they would bring along the concept of the three pillars of interoperability: standard definitions of concepts, standard persistent identifiers and a standard exchange format such as CERIF"*.

A Dutch case study from the Radboud University argues that a one-stop-shop CRIS solution will help implement a FAIR data policy, *"making Open Science as feasible as possible"*, especially by adding a data management plan (DMP) module to the institutional CRIS [8]. Their main argument is that "the fact that CRIS's hold interlinked information of datasets, with a multitude of other information objects and attributes, makes them real 'treasure chests' for an international FAIR data network, such as e.g. envisaged by the European Open Science Cloud (EOSC), as each of these objects and attributes represent (interconnected) parameters for finding, interpreting and judging (the value and/or use of) the dataset, its accessibility and its reusability". Also, the highly standardised CRIS format and data can contribute to improve the interoperability of the whole ecosystem. Hauschke et al. (2021) [14] provide additional evidence how a local CRIS can provide data for global knowledge graphs.

Another case study from The Netherlands confirms the role of the data quality and standardisation provided by CRIS for the interoperability of research data management, by the adoption of common standards for data exchange such as CERIF and Dublin Core for publications, or OpenAIRE for datasets [20].

Even without a complete research information system, the standardised CRIS data format can improve FAIRness of research infrastructures. A case study from the Swedish University of Agricultural Sciences illustrates how a CERIF based archive structure will manifest itself in the different information package stages of the OAIS model and advocates "that if CERIF is employed in relevant archive processes, a FAIR compliant archive can be easier to achieve" - in this case, a digital archive of student theses [21].

A German case study from the University of Erlangen-Nuremberg illustrates how CRIS can improve the FAIRness of research data management [15]. Based on a combination of a software tool run on the researchers' local computer and the institutional CRIS, the workflow is broken into four steps: selection of curated data, generation of technical file metadata on the local machine, upload of metadata into the institutional CRIS and enrichment towards DataCite Metadata Schema (4.4), upload to the institutional data repository. Some of the DataCite recommended properties were made mandatory, especially the description of the data which is essential to future re-use (the R in FAIR).

3.3 CRIS as an Input for RDM FAIRness Assessment

A Finnish case study on research data management in a computer science department reveals another functional role of CRIS [12]. As these systems are used to collect information about research organisations' scientific publications, and insofar the publications listed in CRIS provide detailed descriptions how the affiliated researchers acquire and share research data, they can provide information about FAIR research data management. Rousi (2022) [12] describes how research data acquisition and exchange/share occurring within a particular research organisation can be investigated by using CRIS publication data and concludes that the CRIS-based research design seems to hold a good promise to improve the understanding of how research data is shared within research organisations. In other words, CRIS can contribute to the understanding and the assessment of FAIR practice. Furthermore, the findings suggest that research organisations, such as university departments, may include subfields that have their own cultures of data sharing.

4 Discussion

The topic of CRIS and the FAIR guiding principles is not well covered in the literature. Also, the majority of contributions comes from the euroCRIS community and, less, from the EOSC, which is not really surprising, considering the fact that the FAIR principles have been introduced by people from the EOSC system, while euroCRIS seems to be the only organisation and forum worldwide for research and discussion on research information management systems, with experts who bring their knowledge and expertise from their own national, local, regional, and international CRIS.

This review based on Scopus and the WoS confirms the findings of a former review of papers published by the euroCRIS repository [10], especially the sudden rise of awareness since less than five years on the relation between CRIS and FAIR, and the bidirectional nature of this relation: implementing FAIR principles will improve the quality, usefulness and acceptance of CRIS, as well as their interoperability with other infrastructures, especially with repositories; and the high degree of standardisation of CRIS can improve the FAIRness of the whole ecosystem of research information (workflows, other infrastructures...), through the provision of reliable, standardised data and metadata. Additionally, this review reveals a third level of the CRIS and FAIR relationship, i.e., the potential production of relevant data for the monitoring and assessment of the FAIRness of other infrastructures.

In the following, we will discuss three topics: the assessment of FAIRness of the CRIS themselves, the ecosystem of CRIS, and the potential factors for the FAIRification of CRIS. The conclusion will make some recommendations for further research and development of research information management systems.

4.1 Assessing the FAIRness of CRIS

The reviewed papers agree that CRIS can and should be compliant with the FAIR principles in order to improve their quality, usefulness, acceptance and interoperability with other infrastructures. However, no paper describes or designs so far a specific protocol or checklist, not to say about the (semi-)automated tools, for the assessment of FAIRness of these systems whether the FAIR goals are being achieved and where there is a need for improvement.

Our main suggestion would be to explore if the community-driven approach developed by the FAIR Metrics Group[5] is appropriate and can be helpful to develop a specific tool for the assessment of FAIR maturity of CRIS [22]. Their *"scalable, automatable framework for the objective and quantitative evaluation of the level of FAIRness of digital objects"* defines 15 "maturity indicators" which cover most of the FAIR Principles and sub-principles and can be assessed individually. In addition to these maturity indicators that refer to the community-authored specifications that delimit a specific automatically-measurable FAIR behaviour, this framework consists of compliance tests in the form of small Web apps that test digital resources against individual maturity indicators, and the Evaluator, which is *"a Web application that registers, assembles, and applies community-relevant sets of Compliance Tests against a digital resource, and provides a detailed report about what a machine "sees" when it visits that resource"*. This framework is work in progress, with some failures and missing criteria, and apparently it has not been tested so far with research information management or similar systems. But it seems promising as a standard methodology for a given community - European Open Science Cloud, especially because of its flexibility; our suggestion would be to experiment the framework with some particular CRIS and then adjust it to the specificities of these systems and their community (euroCRIS with CERIF standard).

Beyond this community-driven framework, other tools and procedures have been developed for assessing FAIRness (see [23]). For instance, the FAIR Data Maturity Model proposed by a working group within the Research Data Alliance (RDA)[6] is not subject-specific and allows the separate evaluation of 41 essential, important or useful indicators covering all 15 FAIR principles. The method seems interesting for data suppliers (e.g., CRIS operators) but unsuitable for data or system users.

Other methods seem less relevant, because they are too specific to data repositories (see [24, 25]); nevertheless they may be inspiring for the development of a CRIS specific approach. But in any case, we should be aware of the large variety of infrastructures' FAIRness and keep in mind that "partly FAIR may be fair enough" [26].

4.2 Ecosystem

The reviewed papers confirm that research information management is not an isolated activity but functionally and technologically embedded in and dependent on other activities, such as human resource and account management, academic publishing, data management and sharing, and so on. A CRIS is not a stand-alone system, not a data silo, but

---

[5] FAIR Metrics Group repository https://github.com/FAIRMetrics/Metrics

[6] FAIR Data Maturity Model https://www.rd-alliance.org/groups/fair-data-maturity-model-wg

always interconnected to numerous and heterogeneous other systems, to institutional and research data repositories, library catalogues, bibliographic databases, financial and human resource management systems, and so on; also, it has been addressed as a middleware, as a software that acts as a bridge between operating systems, databases and/or applications [27]. It is part of an ecosystem. FAIR principles pave the way for a more systematic data exchange [28]. Unlike other "digital objects", the FAIRification of CRIS has to be considered from a systemic angle, as they need FAIR data, produce FAIR data and contribute to the assessment of FAIRness.

This means that the FAIRification of CRIS cannot be achieved without considering the entire ecosystem, as well as all of its internal and external components, referring to both the data (data type, volume, structure) and the systems, features and workflows, and stakeholders: all stakeholders in the research ecosystem should and can contribute with "collaborative actions to build bridges and remove the huge amounts of administrative work that currently is needed for making research FAIR, specifically the data collection, structuring, and quality assurance" [17].

The challenge is to identify all stakeholders and to determine how they can be involved in the process of improving FAIRness; this will include "information scientists, librarians, PID providers, researchers, research funders, research information experts, and scientometricians, data providers, CRIS managers, CRIS data (re)users" [14], with especially "data providers" and "data (re)users" being large categories that have to be defined for each particular system.

The stakeholder analysis should take place periodically to identify new players in the game (if any) and their role, needs and requirements. The input received should complement the list of requirements expected to be reviewed for FAIRification of CRIS, making it aligned with the user needs and expectations, starting with basic features, and those more advanced and supportive facilitating FAIR research.

Related aspects, which should also be treated as part of the CRIS ecosystem, refers to data literacy and other digital skills that stakeholders are expected to have, making sure actions are taken to provide them with information and training on both research information management and FAIR principles, and on the role they can play in this process [8].

Such a collaborative action under a systemic perspective is not limited to local (institutional) environments but should take into account the global PID landscape (persons, outputs, organisations...) and, especially for European institutions, the EOSC with its marketplace and initiatives for further standardisation, interoperability and richness of contextual information of research infrastructures [8, 16]. Furthermore, as Chen & Jagerhorn (2022) [17] state, this FAIRification of CRIS would facilitate the generation of knowledge graphs which would offer, for instance, "Institutional Repositories and CRIS-systems great opportunities to take advantage afforded by the PID infrastructure by contributing to and drawing from the wealth of publicly available metadata of scholarly records and their relationships, which not only increase the FAIRness of the research outputs but also provide users with the means to tap into the valuable insights regarding the usage and impact of their work".

Who should take the lead in this necessary collaborative action? The reviewed papers do not suggest any governance solution but from a CRIS point of view, it seems realistic that CRIS provider and manager should work closely work together in order to improve FAIRness of their systems, that this work should rely on relevant working groups and projects in the field (e.g., EOSC, RDA, COAR[7]), and that the overall progress should (or could) be coordinated by the euroCRIS community.

4.3 Factors for further FAIRification of CRIS

As stated in the introduction, the FAIR principles have become central to open science policies especially in European countries. Applied as a standard to all kinds of digital objects, they do not, however, propose a "mechanism to achieve the behaviours they describe" [6]. Depending on the particularities of a given digital object (infrastructure or other), depending also on its specific environment (ecosystem), the implementation of the FAIR principles and the achievement of FAIR maturity will be more or less slow and challenging. What does this mean for research information management? Which are the favourable factors, the strengths and opportunities for the FAIRification of CRIS, which are its barriers? Based on the reviewed papers and other research, here are some general variables, bearing in mind that this is a draft, in need of more discussion and insight, and that such a general approach cannot replace a detailed analysis of a specific system in its particular and unique context.

Favourable Factors. Related to research information management and its systems (CRIS), four variables appear helpful and favourable for the fsurther implementation of FAIR principles:

- The existence of a dynamic international CRIS community, committed to open science, data quality and standardisation; especially euroCRIS is a forum of discussion, case studies, and coordination.
- The reality of accepted standards for data format and terminology, on the international level (e.g., CERIF, CASRAI) as well as on national levels (e.g., KDSF in Germany), will contribute to the interoperability of CRIS.
- The central position of CRIS in the environment of research infrastructures and other academic systems, where CRIS play an essential role as data providers and are therefore particularly concerned with interconnectedness and interoperability.
- The development and supply of open systems in the CRIS market, compliant with (some) FAIR principles (e.g., DSpace).

In the wider environment of research information management, at least three other variables create opportunities and will (can) contribute to the FAIRification of CRIS:

- The role of EOSC and its strong commitment to FAIR which will foster further standardisation and interoperability of European CRIS.
- The FAIRification of interconnected infrastructures, such as institutional and research data repositories. Providing data for CRIS or (re)using CRIS data, their achievement of FAIR maturity will necessarily affect the further development of CRIS.

---

[7] Confederation of Open Access Repositories https://www.coar-repositories.org/

- Finally, the existence of some major, largely accepted persistent identifiers (e.g. DOI for data and publications, ORCID for persons) contributes to the FAIRification of research information management, in particular to findability and interoperability of their data.

Unfavourable Factors. Other variables appear rather unfavourable for the FAIRification of CRIS. Some of them are rather "universal" insofar they are barriers to all change and must be addressed as such, like for instance lack of investment or funding, missing human resources (or skills), or lack of motivation (fear of change). Among the more specific unfavourable variables, we have identified six issues:

- The heterogeneity of research information management systems: there is no globally accepted definition or concept of CRIS, and institutions make use of a large variety of tools for their research information management, such as Excel spreadsheets, repositories, commercial solutions but also Google Scholar. This will be a major barrier to the FAIRification of CRIS as a special category of research infrastructures.
- A Eurocentric community: the CRIS community is not a global, international community but mainly rooted and based in Europe. This, along with the Eurocentric roots of the FAIR principles, will be a second barrier to the FAIRification of CRIS around the world.
- The heterogeneity of many data and metadata standards will not be helpful for the FAIRification of CRIS. Many standards depend on research communities with their needs and terminology, on domains, on countries with their specific laws and rules. Even if EOSC for instance tries to come up with some sort of domain-agnostic uniformity, this is rather a set of minimum requirements in order to remain sufficiently flexible and compliant with the special challenges of each community.
- The market share of important and high-quality proprietary systems (e.g., PURE, Converis) may be a barrier to FAIR maturity of CRIS.
- Privacy and confidential data: one part of the CRIS data is impacted by the General Data Protection Regulation and other privacy laws or have a confidential (strategical) character, and therefore cannot be made accessible or reusable.
- Finally, institutions but also regional or national authorities may prioritise local, specific solutions, with a low degree of standardisation, that are only partly interoperable with other systems.

Other factors in the wider environment of research information management may slow down the FAIRification of at least one part of CRIS:

- As mentioned above, the achievement of FAIR maturity by research infrastructure is above all a European initiative, which means that in other parts of the world, research infrastructure may be much less interested and concerned.
- One part of the connected systems is not directly or not at all impacted by the debate on FAIR principles, such as in particular human resources and account management systems. As research information management partly depends on these systems, this will slow down the FAIRification of CRIS.

- For some central elements of CRIS, persistent identifiers are missing or not generally accepted, e.g., for research projects and activities (RAiD), organisations and funding. Community-specific identifiers are not really helpful for interoperability and findability. Also, even accepted identifiers like ORCID experience a slow uptake, which limits their usefulness for CRIS.
- Finally, as for other initiatives in favour of FAIR maturity, the research information management systems come up against the two obstacles described by [6]: lack of governance, and lack of assessment tools. You can't improve what you don't measure; so how to achieve FAIR maturity of CRIS without a reliable way to assess a CRIS' FAIRness?

5 Conclusion

The topics of CRIS and FAIR are not new, however, after decades of research on CRIS, CRIS and their FAIRness remain among the most unauthorised and relatively overlooked dimensions of research information management. To address this problem, we conducted a systematic literature review that connects the fragmented knowledge accumulated through the observation of CRIS development and attempts to make them or their elements FAIR. The review produced three results:

- Implementing FAIR principles can improve the quality, usefulness and acceptance of CRIS, as well as their interoperability with other infrastructures, especially with repositories.
- FAIRness of CRIS can contribute to the FAIRification of the whole research infrastructure ecosystem, through high-quality, reliable and standardised data on research. Here, data quality and persistent identifiers play a central role.
- CRIS can contribute to the assessment of FAIR maturity of other research infrastructures.

The paper deals with the implementation of the FAIR principles within CRIS. The compliance with them can be ensured through (1) a CRIS that is tailored to the subject-specific and general needs of research groups, (2) development and maintaining sustainability of next-generation repositories for research information, code and other research artefacts, including research outcomes, and (3) the development of training and support services for a CRIS based on a feedback of involved stakeholders and keeping CRIS up-to-date and in line with the current trends in the area of CRIS and digital technologies as a whole.

FAIR thus forms complementary building blocks for the CRIS projects in the field of research information. Supporting the entire life cycle of research information - from generation to archiving and re-use - with expertise and the associated tools, is essential for an efficient CRIS that complies with the FAIR principles. In summary, the FAIR principles aim to ensure a sustainable CRIS by keeping research information safe for reuse and enabling access to it. The FAIR principles were developed for this.

Nevertheless, the achievement of CRIS FAIRness is not a simple "act of will", and our paper provides a draft inventory of favourable and unfavourable factors that may foster but also slow down the process of FAIRification. The very next future will show if and how the CRIS community will be able to meet the challenge of FAIR and turn it into an opportunity for future development of the research information management.

Appendix 1: FAIR Principles

Source: Wilkinson et al. (2016).
  To be Findable:

- F1. (meta)data are assigned a globally unique and eternally persistent identifier.
- F2. Data are described with rich metadata.
- F3. (meta)data are registered or indexed in a searchable resource.
- F4. Metadata specify the data identifier.

  To be Accessible:

- A1. (meta)data are retrievable by their identifier using a standardized communications protocol.

  - A1.1 the protocol is open, free, and universally implementable.
  - A1.2 the protocol allows for an authentication and authorization procedure, where necessary.

- A.2 metadata are accessible, even when the data are no longer available.

  To be Interoperable:

- I1. (meta)data use a formal, accessible, shared, and broadly applicable language for knowledge representation.
- I2. (meta)data use vocabularies that follow FAIR principles.
- I3. (meta)data include qualified references to other (meta)data.

  To be Re-usable:

- R1. Meta(data) have a plurality of accurate and relevant attributes.

  - R1.1 (meta)data are released with a clear and accessible data usage license.
  - R1.2 (meta)data are associated with their provenance.
  - R1.3 (meta)data meet domain-relevant community standards.

Appendix 2 - Review Criteria

(See Table 1).

Table 1. Developed protocol

Category	Metadata	Description
Descriptive information	Article number	A study number, corresponding to the study number assigned in an Excel worksheet
	Complete reference	The complete source information refers to the study (in APA style), including the author(s) of the article, the year in which it was published, the article's title and other source information
	Year of publication	The year in which the study was published
	Journal article/conference paper/book chapter	The type of the paper, i.e. journal article, conference paper, or book chapter
	DOI/Website	A link to the website where the study can be found
	Number of citations (Google Scholar), WoS and/or Scopus later	The number of citations of the article in Google Scholar, Web of Science and Scopus digital libraries
	Availability in Open Access	Availability of an article in the Open Access or Free/Full Access
	Keywords	Keywords of the paper as indicated by the authors (in the paper)
	Relevance for our study (high/medium/low)	What is the relevance level of the article for this study?
Approach- and research design-related information	Objective/Aim/Goal/Purpose & Research Questions	The research objective/aim, and established research questions

(continued)

Table 1. (*continued*)

Category	Metadata	Description
	Research method (including unit of analysis*)	The methods used to collect data in the study, including the unit of analysis that refers to the country, organisation, or other specific unit that has been analysed such as the number of use-cases or policy documents, number and scope of the SLR etc
	Study's contributions	The contributions of the study, as stated by the author(s)
	Qualitative/quantitative/mixed method	Whether the study uses a qualitative, quantitative or mixed methods approach?
	Availability of the underlying research data	Whether the paper has a reference to the public availability of the underlying research data e.g. transcriptions of interviews, collected data etc., or explains why these data are not openly shared?
	Period under investigation	Period (or moment) in which the study was conducted (e.g., January 2021-March 2022)
	Use of theory/theoretical concepts/approaches? If yes, specify them	Does the study mention any theory/theoretical concepts/approaches? If yes, what theory/concepts/approaches? If any theory is mentioned, how is theory used in the study? (e.g. mentioned to explain a certain phenomenon, used as a framework for analysis, tested theory, theory mentioned in the future research section)
Quality-related information	Quality concerns?	Whether there are any quality concerns (e.g. limited information about the research methods used)?

(*continued*)

Table 1. (*continued*)

Category	Metadata	Description
RIS vs FAIR-related information	The primary object of the study	Is this study rather about CRIS in the context of FAIR? Or FAIR in the context of CRIS? I.e. what is the focus of the study
	CRIS definition	How is CRIS defined? What elements/components constitute it? What are the actors and/or stakeholders involved? Data sources variety?
	The scope of FAIR principles	Whether all FAIR principles are addressed or rather some of them? If some – which ones?
	CRIS	What type of CRIS system is addressed? Which country or region does it belong to?
	The role of FAIR principles in CRIS	How is the contribution of FAIR principles addressed? What are the benefits of FAIR principles in CRIS?
	The role of CRIS in the FAIR context	Whether the role of CRIS in the FAIR context is addressed? What benefits does the CRIS topic bring to the general FAIR area?
	Governance of FAIR in CRIS	How is the FAIRness of CRIS governed? Who is involved? How? What elements are involved?
	Level (if relevant)	What is the level of the study? Theoretical? Applied?
	Additional comments	
New papers	Other potentially relevant papers	Did you find any potentially relevant papers in the references section?

References

1. Wilkinson, M.D., et al.: The FAIR Guiding Principles for scientific data management and stewardship. Sci. Data **3**(1), 160018 (2016). https://doi.org/10.1038/sdata.2016.18
2. Mons, B., Schultes, E., Liu, F., Jacobsen, A.: The FAIR principles: first generation implementation choices and challenges. Data Intell. **2**(1–2), 1–9 (2020). https://doi.org/10.1162/dint_e_00023
3. Wittenburg, P.: Large Research Infrastructure Building using FAIR Digital Objects. Autumn 2019 EuroCRIS Strategic Membership Meeting (WWU Münster, Germany, Nov 18–20 (2019). http://hdl.handle.net/11366/1223
4. Ivanović, D., Ivanović, L., Layfield, C.: FAIRness at University of Novi Sad - Discoverability of PhD research results for Non-Serbian scientific community. Procedia Comput. Sci. **146**, 3 (2019). https://doi.org/10.1016/j.procs.2019.01.071
5. Mornati, S.: Enhancing interoperability: the implementation of OpenAIRE Guidelines and COAR NGR Recommendations in CRIS/RIMS. OR19 Workshop on Repository/CRIS Interoperability (2019). http://hdl.handle.net/11366/1008
6. Wilkinson, M.D., et al.: Community-driven governance of FAIRness assessment: an open issue, an open discussion. Open Res. Europe **2**(146), 146 (2022). https://open-research-eur ope.ec.europa.eu/articles/2-146/v1?src=rss
7. Zawacki-Richter, O.: The current state and impact of Covid-19 on digital higher education in Germany. Hum. Behav. Emerg. Technol. **3**(1), 218–226 (2021). https://doi.org/10.1002/hbe 2.238
8. Jetten, M., Simons, E., Rijnders, J.: The role of CRIS's in the research life cycle. A case study on implementing a FAIR RDM policy at Radboud University, the Netherlands. Procedia Comput. Sci. **146**, 156–165 (2019). https://doi.org/10.1016/j.procs.2019.01.090
9. Schöpfel, J., Prost, H., Rebouillat, V.: Research data in current research information systems. Procedia Comput. Sci. **106**, 305–320 (2017). https://doi.org/10.1016/j.procs.2017.03.030
10. Azeroual, O., Schöpfel, J., Pölönen, J., Nikiforova, A.: Putting FAIR principles in the context of research information: FAIRness for CRIS and CRIS for FAIRness. In: Proceedings of the 14th International Joint Conference on Knowledge Discovery, Knowledge Engineering and Knowledge Management (IC3K 2022) - KMIS; ISBN 978-989-758-614-9; ISSN 2184-3228, SciTePress, pp. 63-71 (2022). https://doi.org/10.5220/0011548700003335
11. Zuiderwijk, A., Chen, Y.-C., Salem, F.: Implications of the use of artificial intelligence in public governance: a systematic literature review and a research agenda. Gov. Inf. Q. **38**(3), 101577 (2021). https://doi.org/10.1016/j.giq.2021.101577
12. Rousi, A.M.: Using current research information systems to investigate data acquisition and data sharing practices of computer scientists. J. Librarian. Inform. Sci. 096100062210930 (2022). https://doi.org/10.1177/09610006221093049
13. Riechert, M.T.: RIDAL – a language for research information definition argumentation. Data Sci. J. **16** (2017). https://doi.org/10.5334/dsj-2017-005
14. Hauschke, C., Nazarovets, S., Altemeier, F., Kaliuzhna, N.: Roadmap to FAIR research information in open infrastructures. J. Libr. Metadata **21**(1–2), 45–61 (2021). https://doi.org/10. 1080/19386389.2021.1999156
15. Walther, M., Wagner, M.: FAIR research data integration in CRIS at FAU Erlangen-Nürnberg. Procedia Comput. Sci. **211**(C), 246–250 (2022). https://doi.org/10.1016/j.procs.2022.10.198
16. Sicilia, M.-A., Simons, E., Clements, A., Castro, P.D., Bergström, J.: FAIRness of research information. Procedia Comput. Sci. **146**, 1–2 (2019). https://doi.org/10.1016/j.procs.2019. 01.070
17. Chen, X., Jagerhorn, M.: Implementing FAIR Workflows along the research lifecycle. Procedia Comput. Sci. **211**(C), 83–92 (2022). https://doi.org/10.1016/j.procs.2022.10.179

18. Meadows, A., Haak, L.L., Brown, J.: Persistent identifiers: the building blocks of the research information infrastructure. Insights UKSG J. **32** (2019). https://doi.org/10.1629/uksg.457
19. Baird, N.: How CERIF-based CRIS can help to identify the factors that contribute to the creation of value by R&D. In: Nase, A., Van Grootel, G. (eds.) Putting the Sparkle in the Knowledge Society: 7th International Conference on Current Research Information Systems. Leuven, Belgium: Leuven University Press (2004)
20. Farinelli, C., Zigoni, A.: Extending the value of a CRIS with research data management. Procedia Comput. Sci. **211**, 187–195 (2022). https://doi.org/10.1016/j.procs.2022.10.190
21. Engelman, A., Enkvist, C., Pettersson, K.: A FAIR archive based on the CERIF model. Procedia Comput. Sci. **146**, 190–200 (2019). https://doi.org/10.1016/j.procs.2019.01.076
22. Wilkinson, M.D., et al.: Evaluating FAIR maturity through a scalable, automated, community-governed framework. Sci. Data **6**(1), 174 (2019). https://doi.org/10.1038/s41597-019-0184-5
23. Thompson, M., Burger, K., Kaliyaperumal, R., Roos, M., da Silva Santos, L.O.B.: Making FAIR Easy with FAIR tools: from creolization to convergence. Data Intell. **2**(1–2), 87–95 (2020). https://doi.org/10.1162/dint_a_00031
24. Dunning, A., De Smaele, M., Böhmer, J.: Are the FAIR data principles fair? Int. J. Digit. Curation **12**(2), 177–195 (1970). https://doi.org/10.2218/ijdc.v12i2.567
25. Bonaretti, S., Willighagen, E.: Two real use cases of FAIR maturity indicators in the life sciences. BioRxiv (2019). https://doi.org/10.1101/739334
26. Mons, B., Neylon, C., Velterop, J., Dumontier, M., da Silva Santos, L.O.B., Wilkinson, M.D.: Cloudy, increasingly FAIR; revisiting the FAIR Data guiding principles for the European Open Science Cloud. Inf. Serv. Use **37**(1), 49–56 (2017). https://doi.org/10.3233/ISU-170824
27. Jeffery, K.G., Asserson, A.: CRIS: Research organisation view of the e-infrastructure. In: CRIS2008: 9th International Conference on Current Research Information Systems (Maribor, June 5–7) (2008)
28. Boeckhout, M., Zielhuis, G.A., Bredenoord, A.L.: The FAIR guiding principles for data stewardship: fair enough? Eur. J. Hum. Genet. **26**(7), 931–936 (2018). https://doi.org/10.1038/s41431-018-0160-0

Measuring Augmented Reality and Virtual Reality Trajectory in the Training Environment

Amy Rosellini[1,2]( ) (iD)

[1] University of North Texas, Denton, TX 76201, USA
amy.rosellini@gmail.com
[2] New Western, Irving, TX 75039, USA

Abstract. Corporate learning professionals understand that technology has changed the way we learn, work and interact with one another. The last vestige of the corporate training environment left mostly unchanged was in-person training. Until the last decade, in-person training with real world simulation was understood to achieve the highest knowledge transfer through experiential learning. With COVID-19 and the prevalence of hybrid work, companies started relying on technology in more ways, including how virtual simulation can replace in-person training. As augmented and virtual reality enter more workplaces across the United States, there is an opportunity to learn from the industries and workplaces who have utilized augmented and virtual reality in corporate training for over a decade. The healthcare, aviation, construction and military have utilized augmented and virtual reality in the training environment for a number of years. These industries are increasingly replacing live simulation and in-person learning with augmented and virtual reality. This study investigates aviation, one of the industries at the forefront of augmented and virtual reality programs in corporate training. Flight attendants are the population tasked with safety and security of passengers on commercial airlines. In this study, in-flight virtual reality training is compared to in-flight real life simulation training to understand what impact, positive or negative, virtual reality has on knowledge transfer.

Keywords: Virtual reality · Knowledge transfer · Behavior change · VR · Aviation · Training

1 Introduction

Augmented Reality (AR) technology and Virtual Reality (VR) technology research remains relatively new in many industries with articles dating back only 25 years [7]. As virtual and hybrid work are more pervasive since the COVID-19 pandemic, many companies began investing more resources into technology tools that will enhance the learning environment. With the advent of increased technology replacing in-person training, more research is needed to investigate how AR technology is proven successful in real world behavior change [11, 13]. Current AR and VR technology research investigates healthcare, mining, and construction industries but fails to compare the VR and AR technology to traditional learning environments that include real-life simulation and in-person training.

F. Coenen et al. (Eds.): IC3K 2022, CCIS 1842, pp. 299–308, 2023.
https://doi.org/10.1007/978-3-031-43471-6_14

The current research is an extension of a VR study presented at the Proceedings of the 14th International Joint Conference on Knowledge Discovery, Knowledge Engineering and Knowledge Management and Information System [22]. The current research builds upon the study of the VR training simulation and establishes a methodology of how to investigate both augmented reality (AR) and VR technology, while defining both AR and VR, to better understand how and when they should be tested for effectiveness in companies.

Knowledge is a competitive advantage for organizations, and AR/VR technology is increasingly a source of knowledge transfer in firms [2, 14, 16]. While AR/VR technology emerges, research is needed to understand when to incorporate new technologies into the learning environment. AR/VR technology emerged in the last few decades with different methods of implementing the technology into the training environment. The literature identifies the need to perform a thorough and consistent method for measuring how AR/VR technology is integrated, when it is integrated and how it interacts with real-life simulation training to determine effectiveness [1, 17].

Recent studies have taken steps to create a methodology introducing an experimental design that allows companies to determine the effectiveness of AR/VR technology [19, 22]. While studies are being conducted utilizing this experimental design, an opportunity exists to determine recommendations of when the methodology should be implemented to determine the effectiveness of AR/VR technology use in the training environment.

Further steps must be taken to help companies know how and when to measure the effectiveness of the AR/VR technology in the training environment. Companies are implementing AR/VR technology without a clear direction to determine when and if AR/VR integration should be integrated into the training and how it should interplay with the real-life simulation that industries have already adopted. As more research is conducted, companies will learn if training is most effective when real-life simulation is utilized, AR/VR technology is utilized or when the two simulations are conducted in tandem.

The research included provides an overview of AR/VR technology. It sets to answer the questions: What methodology helps companies measure the effectiveness of AR/VR technology in training? What is the effectiveness of AR/VR technology compared to real life simulation in the training environment? How does AR/VR technology training result in real world behavior change?

This paper begins with an understanding of the terms AR and VR technology, then proceeds to examine the history of AR and VR starting as artificial reality. The earlier study presented at 14th International Joint Conference on Knowledge Discovery, Knowledge Engineering and Knowledge Management and Information Systems 3 summarizes the peer reviewed research of VR technology in manufacturing, healthcare, and aviation. This paper examines both AR and VR technology uses in aviation providing a more comprehensive history of how AR and VR technology has evolved specific to the aviation industry as it pertains to this flight attendant study.

2 Understanding the Terms

Defining the terms Augmented Reality (AR) and Virtual Reality (VR) technology is necessary as new companies are adopting these technologies. The circumstances around hybrid work and how employees learn provide an opportunity for companies to embrace an understanding of these terms and how to incorporate new technology into the corporate training environment.

2.1 Defining Augmented Reality and Virtual Reality

Augmented Reality (AR) and Virtual Reality (VR) technology research remains relatively new in many industries. As virtual and hybrid work became more popular with COVID-19, many companies began investing more resources into technology tools that will enhance the learning environment. With the advent of increased technology replacing previously utilized in-person resources, companies should understand the history of augmented reality and its growing uses in the learning environment at companies. Learning and education appear to be one of the greatest fields of research for AR, but VR is better researched in a variety of applications [7].

The difference in the definitions of AR and VR is the location of the participant relative to the real-world. While AR is defined as "a mediated reality where the visual perception of the physical real-world environment is enhanced by means of computing devices", VR places the participant in a simulation where they are made to feel or perceive they are in a real-world environment [4] p. 284. VR is defined as being immersed in an environment with the "perception to be present in [the] environment" and with an ability to interact with the environment [7] p. 2086. Table 1 provides a list of the many terms associated with live and simulated realities reliant on computer-generated realities and provides examples in the real estate industry of how the different realities are utilized.

Table 1. Terms of reality, virtual reality and augmented reality [9].

Reality	Augmented Reality	Virtual Reality	Mixed Reality	Augmented Virtuality	Virtuality
The actual world that we experience with all of our senses.	Information and data overlaid on top of the actual world.	A complete digital representation of the actual world.	The introduction of possible elements into an actual world.	The introduction of actual elements into a possible world.	An imaginary world that mostly follows the rules of the actual world.
An actual house.	A realty app provides details of an actual house.	A 3D image of actual furniture. A virtual tour of an actual house.	Simulation of different furniture, virtual or new, in an actual house.	Staging of actual furniture in a new house.	A 3D model for a new house or of new furniture.
Key concept: Physical co-presence of people and objects.	Key concept: Add utility to physical co-presence.	Key concept: Enable perceived presence and full immersion.	Key concept: Adaptation of actual scenarios.	Key concept: Participation in possible scenarios.	Key concept: Vision of a completely different world.
Real			Possible		
Actual Reality Continuum			Virtual Reality Continuum		

2.2 History of Augmented Reality and Virtual Reality

In 1962, Sensorama provided a simulated experience of riding a motorcycle through Brooklyn; the simulation was created by Morton Heilig. In 1965, the first AR technology was designed at Harvard University by Ivan Sutherland where he and his students presented three-dimensional graphics to users through the display in a helmet. The U.S. Air Force designed the first flight simulation in 1982 and the 1980s continued with the increased commercialization of computer devices leading to glove sensor and ocular devices [7]. In 1985, AR was utilized when the participant's body was displayed on a screen through camera capture [15]. In the 1990s, the term "augmented reality" was first utilized by Caudell and Mizell in the aviation industry. As Boeing scientists, Caudell and Mizell utilized AR technology in a training environment where workers used AR to connect wiring harnesses [6].

Industries like healthcare, aviation, military and construction have incorporated technology into in-person training since the early 1990s [3, 17]. Recent growth of AR training in the workplace has increased to retail, sports and telecommunications. In the last five years, Wal-Mart purchased over 1 million Oculus headsets for employee training; Verizon utilized virtual reality (VR) to train on workplace safety, and Stanford utilized technology to teach football players about movement on the virtual football field [12, 18]. As the usage of VR technology spans new fields and training environments, more testing is needed to understand how VR technology is utilized in early adopting fields like healthcare and aviation to begin working towards best practices.

2.3 Peer-Reviewed Research of Augmented and Virtual Reality

Augmented reality articles number over 9,900 in the Web Science Core collection as of 2018. Its presence in research is more recent in history to that of VR technology, with virtual reality spanning almost three decades of research and including over 21,000 articles [7]. The presence of new technologies like AR and VR in the current world allows for the entrance of VR and AR technology into training and education, which has some limitations. The lack of research within the educational field is one of the primary obstacles for companies looking for conclusive proof that the investment in VR and AR technology will provide a return on investment to employers [23].

The integration of AR and VR technology blended with real-life training allows companies to maximize the learning styles of individuals while improving overall behavior change of workers [22]. Given the concentration of AR and VR technology research in the last five years, more data must be collected and analyzed to understand how VR technology impacts behavior change to a greater or similar degree to classroom simulations [20].

A recent study investigating the utilization of VR and AR technology in professional maintenance found the technology to decrease training time, decrease training cost and improve effectiveness. The study also set out to determine whether real-life training, VR training, or AR training was more effective. The outcome of the study cited that AR and VR outperformed real-life training in complex tasks, with AR slightly outperforming. For one-step tasks, real-life simulation training outperformed both AR and VR [25].

2.4 Virtual Reality in the Aviation Industry

The aviation industry utilizes real-life simulation in training that includes testing and verification of the training environment to maximize knowledge transfer. The United States Air Force was one of the first integrators of alternate reality technology, and aviation continues to find new ways to integrate technology into training based on positive response from the participants. In a recent study in the United States, 310 aviation students students identify VR technology as useful, enjoyable, and positively impacting learning [10].

Some work has been done to determine effectiveness of VR training in the aviationa industry. In 2017, the efficacy of different VR technology display screens was researched to understand the effectiveness of VR technology in the training environment [5]. The researchers find that knowledge and self-efficacy improve utilizing all types of VR technology. The study included examination of the group prior to training, immediately after training, and two weeks post-training.

In 2018, a German aviation study made a step forward for the research comparing the real-life simulation environment to the VR technology flight simulation. The flight study compares the speed and accuracy of pilots in both real-life and VR environments. The result of the study showed pilots spent more time in VR technology to engage cockpit instrumentation than they did in the hardware flight simulation [19]. While the study is inconclusive on the effectiveness of comparing real-life to AR/VR technology, this study is impactful in that it begins the comparison between real-life and technology training.

The 2020s have led to greater discovery in how impactful VR technology is in the training environment compared to real-life simulation. In 2021, Dymora et al. find that VR technology leading to higher test scores in pilot training [8]. In the same year, a pilot training showed increase effectiveness with VR technology in measuring cognitive ability, situational awareness, and prospective memory [23]. As testing continues with VR and AR technology in training, it is imperative that the AR/VR technology training be compared to real-life simulation environments that appeal to all learning styles [22].

3 Methodology in Measuring Effectiveness of VR Technology

Current aviation training environments that include VR technology are showing results that show more effective knowledge transfer in the VR environment than in real-life simulation. AR and VR technologies continue to spread through the training environments in new industries, is it important to understand how knowledge transfer is occurring and how the new technologies compare in effectiveness with their real-life simulation counterpart [1].

The 2018 Oberhauser et al. held a flight study of 38 pilots in Austria with an experimental design. The study compared the pilot training outcomes in real-life hardware simulation versus VR simulation. The study tested half the group on real-life simulation first and the other half on VR-simulation first. None of the pilots tested had utilized VR technology previously. The outcome of the study resulted in VR technology showing some slower response times. Another outcome was that overall demand upon the pilots – both physical and mental – was much higher with VR technology than with the real-life hardware simulation. Demand upon the pilots was determined through a survey administered post-training [19].

The experimental design comparing real-life simulation to VR technology simulation was used in a second study measuring over 12,000 flight attendant behaviors post-training. There were a few adjustments to the methodology from the pilot study. In the Rosellini study, the first group of flight attendants completed training with both VR technology and in a real-life hardware simulation [22]. Like the pilot study, half of the first group completed VR technology simulation first while the other half of the group completed real-life hardware simulation first. The flight attendant study took a different approach with the second group. In the flight attendant study, the second group did not complete VR technology simulation.

In the flight attendant study, researchers utilized the knowledge transfer management measurement model which suggests behavior observation as a more reliable measure for knowledge transfer than survey [21]. The flight attendant study included behavior drills where both groups of flight attendants were observed performing the job tasks post-training. The behavior drills assigned scores to each flight attendant and measured against each other using an Independent Samples Test with IBM SPSS to measure the differences in scores between the two groups.

4   Results of VR Technology versus Real-Life Simulation

The study of over 12,000 flight attendants measured the knowledge transfer of flight attendants when utilizing both VR technology and real-life hardware simulation. Both groups performed training drills immediately following the training. The group that received both real-life simulation and VR technology simulation scored 5.73% higher than the group who received only the real-life simulation training. This is one of the first studies of its kind to test flight attendants' skills post-VR training while comparing them to a control group that has not received VR simulation training [22].

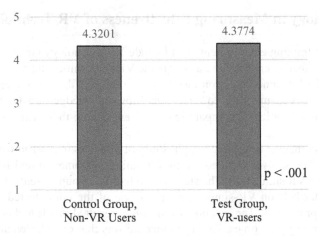

Fig. 1. Non-VR Technology users and VR-technology users in the training environment [21].

The combined scores of the group of flight attendants that did not utilize VR technology simulation prior to their behavior drills was 4.3201. The combined scores of the group of flight attendants that utilized both VR-technology and real-life hardware simulation prior to their behavior drills was 4.3774. The p value showed a statistically significant relationship between the two data sets (Fig. 1).

4.1 The Timing of VR Technology Simulation in the Training Environment

The flight attendant study failed to test user behavior drills based on the timing of VR technology. The first group of flight attendants experience both VR technology and real-life hardware simulations, but half the group received VR first and half the group received real-life simulation first. It is necessary for companies to begin investigating the order of AR/VR technology to learn how the order of training impacts knowledge transfer. This will be discussed more in the next section.

4.2 VR Technology Simulation Resulting in Behavior Change

Unlike the pilot study conducted in 2018, flight attendant speed is not measured in the behavior drills. The behavior drills measure accuracy of job skills that include securing doors and handling emergency equipment. While the pilot study effectively measured change in response time, it measured change in response time while the pilot is in the training environment [19]. In the flight attendant study, the behaviors post-training were measured rather than the behaviors measured in the training environment [22].

The benefit of the flight attendant study methodology and results is that the flight attendant study focuses less on how VR technology works in the training environment and focuses on how VR technology impacts behavior post-training. The results of the flight attendant study paired with the experimentation of the pilot study begin to show companies a framework for measuring how VR technology simulation results in real world behavior change.

4.3 Findings in Non-VR Participants

In this study, the median scores of flight attendants were measured for a control group that did not participate in VR training. A surprising finding was a significant drop in median score in a group of non-VR trained participants over time. Figure 2 illustrates how the median score dropped in non-VR training participants over a two-year period [22].

This finding was both a surprise in the study and also serves as a warning to companies when deploying both VR/AR technology integration to provide balanced resources to both VR/AR integrated training environments as well as non-VR/AR integrated training environments to appropriate behavior change post-training.

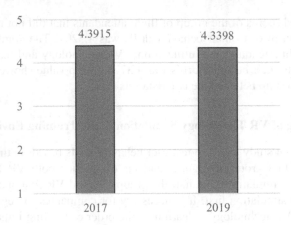

Fig. 2. Non-VR Technology users in 2017 versus 2019 [22].

5   Next Steps

The outcome of the pilot and flight attendant studies provide a methodology for companies to follow to investigate their AR/VR technology integrations in the training environment. More studies are needed to determine when and how the technology integration is successful in addition to testing populations based on the order in which they perform AR/VR technology simulation and real-life simulation.

The U.S.-based airline from the Rosellini study is continuing the methodology described above to test flight attendant skills based on the order in which they complete VR technology simulation [22]. With further testing, the airline contributes to research in this field providing a framework for future aviation companies and other industries to follow.

In light of the pervasive AR/VR technology use in the training environment, government bodies like the Federal Aviation Administration (FAA) and the European Aviation Safety Agency will benefit from understanding the effectiveness of AR/VR training and when it is most effective in the training process. As future studies and research is conducted, the methodology by which AR/VR technology simulation is conducted will gain consistent design. The consistency of testing across industries is important to building a framework for how companies integrate and measure the impact of AR/VR technology in the training environment.

6   Conclusion

AR/VR technology continues to be utilized across industries to train employees. With workplace environments changing to allow for remote and hybrid work, AR/VR technology provides companies the opportunity to train employee skills in a hybrid or remote work environment. The benefit of the simulated technology environment allows companies to create an at-work training environment in a home environment.

As the original Rosellini VR study found, simulated reality benefits all learning styles. This paper defines the methodology for companies to track and measure the success of their AR/VR technology programs post-training and analyze how behaviors change because of the AR/VR training. As companies utilize the methodology to test the success of their simulated technology training, they will likely measure the success of the simulated program compared to the cost of in-person, on-site training. The initial high cost of AR/VR equipment may be lower than the ongoing cost of in-person trainers, travel for employees to attend in-person training, and additional in-person training costs.

References

1. Abivj, J., Parker, J., Murphy, J., Eudy, M.: A review of the evidence for training effectiveness with virtual reality technology. Virtual Reality **25**, 919–933 (2021)
2. Ahn, J., Chang, S.: Assessing the contribution of knowledge to business performance: the KP3 methodology. Decis. Support Syst. **36**(4), 403–416 (2004)
3. Azuma, R.: A survey of augmented reality. Presence: Teleoper. Virtual Environ. **6**(4), 355–385 (1997)
4. Bottani, E., Vignali, G.: Augmented reality technology in the manufacturing industry: a review of the last decade. IISE Trans. **51**(3), 284–310 (2019)
5. Buttussi, F., Chittaro, L.: Effects of different types of virtual reality display on presence and learning in a safety training scenario. IEEE Trans. Visual Comput. Graphics **24**(2), 1063–1076 (2018)
6. Caudell, T.P., Mizell, D.W.: Augmented reality: an application of heads-up display technology to manual manufacturing processes. In: Proceedings of the 25th Hawaii International Conference on System Sciences, vol. 2, pp. 659–669. IEEE, USA (1992)
7. Cipresso, P., Giglioli, I.A.C., Raya, M.A., Riva, G.: The past, present, and future of Virtual and Augmented Reality research: a network and cluster analysis of the literature. Front. Psychol. **6**(9), 2086 (2018)
8. Dymora, P., Kowal, B., Mazurek, M., Romana, S.: The effects of virtual reality technology application in the aircraft pilot training process. Mater. Sci. Eng. **1024**(1), 1–9 (2021)
9. Farshid, M., Paschen, J., Eriksson, T., Kietzmann, J.: Go boldly!: Explore augmented reality (AR), virtual reality (VR), and mixed reality (MR) for business. Bus. Horiz. **61**(5), 657–663 (2018)
10. Fussell, S., Truong, D.: Accepting virtual reality for dynamic learning: an extension of the technology acceptance model. Interact. Learn. Environ. 1–18 (2021)
11. Gabajová, G., Furmannová, B., Medvecká, I., Krajčovič, M., Furmann, R.: Virtual training application by use of augmented and virtual reality under university technology enhanced learning in Slovakia. Sustainability **11**(23), 66-77 (2019).
12. Incao, J.: How VR is transforming the way we train associates. Retrieved from: walmart.com on June 12, 2019. (2018)
13. Jia-Ye, C., Ruo-Fan, W., Cui-Yu, W., Xin-Dong, Y.: Xiao-Zhi, L,: The influence of learners' cognitive style and testing environment supported by virtual reality on English-speaking learning achievement. Sustainability **13**(21), 11751–11765 (2021)
14. Jordão, R., Novas, J.: Information and knowledge management, intellectual capital, and sustainable growth in networked small and medium enterprises. J. Knowl. Econ. 1–33 (2022)
15. Krueger, M.: Videoplace: a report from the artificial reality laboratory. Leonardo **18**(3), 145–151 (1985)
16. Kuah, C.T., Wong, K.Y.: Knowledge management performance measurement: a review. Afr. J. Bus. Manage. **5**(15), 6021–6027 (2011)
17. Nee, A.Y.C., Ong, S.K., Chryssolouris, G., Mourtzis, D.: Augmented reality applications in design and manufacturing. CIRP Ann. Manuf. Technol. **61**(2), 657–679 (2012)

18. Noguchi, Y.: Virtual reality goes to work, helping train employees. National Public Radio homepage. https://www.npr.org/2019/10/08/767116408/virtual-reality-goes-to-work-helping-train-employees. Accessed 3 Feb 2023
19. Oberhauser, M., Dreyer, D., Braunstingl, R., Koglbauer, I.: What's real about the virtual reality flight simulation? Comparing the fidelity of a virtual reality with a conventional flight simulation environment. Aviat. Psychol. Appl. Hum. Factors **8**(1), 27–34 (2018)
20. Popov, O., et al.: Immersive technology for training professional development of nuclear power plants personnel. In: Proceedings of the 4th International Workshop on Augmented Reality in Education, vol. 4, pp. 1–25. CEUR, Ukraine (2021)
21. Rosellini, A.: Knowledge transfer model to measure the impact of formal training on sales performance. In: Proceedings of the International Conference on Knowledge Management: Knowledge Discovery and Data Design Innovation, vol. 14, pp. 127–144. World Scientific, USA (2017)
22. Rosellini, A.: Virtual reality (VR) technology integration in the training environment leads to behavior change. In: Proceedings of the 14th International Joint Conference on Knowledge Discovery, Knowledge Engineering and Knowledge Management and Information Systems, vol. 3, pp. 200–207. Scitepress, Malta (2022)
23. Van Benthem, K., Herdman, C.M.: A virtual reality cognitive health screening tool for aviation: managing accident risk for older pilots. Int. J. Ind. Ergon. **85**, 103169 (2021)
24. Velev, D., Zlateva, P.: Virtual reality challenges in education and training. Int. J. Learn. Teach. **3**(1), 33–37 (2017)
25. Xiao-Wei, L., et al.: Research on training effectiveness of professional maintenance personnel based on virtual reality and augmented reality technology. Sustainability **13**(21), 14351–14373 (2022)

DroNit Project: Improving Drone Usage for Civil Defense Applications

Diego Passos[2,3]([envelope]) [ORCID], Carlos Alberto Malcher Bastos[1], Roberto Saeger[2],
Bruno Hilário[2], Raphael Guerra[2], Walace Medeiros Barbosa[4],
Yuri Sisino dos Santos Felipe[4], Thais Belloti Loureiro[4], Gilvane dos Santos Dias[4],
Hullysses Sabino[5] [ORCID], and Fernanda G. O. Passos[1,6] [ORCID]

[1] Engineering School, Universidade Federal Fluminense, Niterói, Brazil
camalcherbastos@id.uff.br, fernanda@midiacom.uff.br
[2] Institute of Computing, Universidade Federal Fluminense, Niterói, Brazil
{dpassos,rguerra}@ic.uff.br, {rsaeger,brunohilario}@id.uff.br
[3] DEETC, Instituto Superior de Engenharia de Lisboa – ISEL, Lisbon, Portugal
[4] Civil Defense Department, City Hall of Niterói, Niterói, Brazil
[5] Geosciences Institute, Universidade Federal Fluminense, Rio de Janeiro, Brazil
[6] Atlântica Instituto Universitário, Oeiras, Portugal

Abstract. *Drones* find several usages in the modern world, including smart agriculture, providing Internet connectivity, delivering goods, and entertainment. They also find applicability in smart cities, enabling or improving activities such as surveillance, city planning, disaster management, and traffic monitoring. The usefulness of drones stems from their ability to access difficult regions, but also from the possibility of customization by means of different sensors and actuators: depending on what kind of accessories they carry, drones can perform a number of different tasks, broadening their applicability. However, this potential can be hindered by a number of hurdles, including technical, regulatory or even social issues. This paper describes the work of the *DroNit* project, which aims to improve the applicability and efficacy of drones in the context of the activities of the Civil Defense Office of the city of Niterói, Brazil. We describe how the office currently uses drones and discuss the main issues they faced throughout the years. We also discuss other possible applications of drones that could help the work done by the Office and study what are the currently standing obstacles. Finally, we discuss technical solutions that are currently under development by the DroNit project and report on preliminary results.

Keywords: Drones · Unmanned aerial vehicle · Smart cities · Civil defense · Information management · Knowledge management systems

---

This work is supported by the PDPA program of the City Hall of Niterói.

F. Coenen et al. (Eds.): IC3K 2022, CCIS 1842, pp. 309–333, 2023.
https://doi.org/10.1007/978-3-031-43471-6_15

1 Introduction

Drones, also known as Unmanned Aerial Vehicles (UAVs), are aircraft that operate without a human crew. They can be either autonomous or controlled remotely by a human pilot. Their ability to fly without humans on board enables missions that would be otherwise impossible—either due to excessive risks or simply the impossibility of reaching certain regions. One example is the usage of drones for monitoring volcanic environments [19]. They can also speedup processes such as the delivery of services and goods, as in the notorious case of the Amazon prime air service [22].

Drones can also carry different loads, including a vast array of sensors and actuators which can be connected to the same communication channel used for controlling the drone, rendering them accessible from the ground station during the flight. While the canonical example are cameras in recreational drones, sensors can span a wide range of purposes, such as smoke detectors, temperature sensors, speakers, or headlights. Thus, drones can perform a number of tasks, as long as the proper set of sensors and actuators are employed. Examples of fields with successful usage of drones include agriculture, entertainment, industry, military, surveillance, maritime rescue and security inspection of construction sites [2,9]. Recently, drones have also been proposed for several uses in smart cities [1,14].

Niterói is a medium-sized city—with about 500 thousand inhabitants—in the state of Rio de Janeiro, Brazil. The City Hall of Niterói is currently implementing a number of smart-city initiatives through a research and development program called *Applied Projects Development Program* (PDPA) [20]. This program is a partnership between the City Hall and Universidade Federal Fluminense (UFF). It aims at studying and developing solutions for the real-world problems faced by the city.

One of the projects supported by the PDPA is the DroNit, which has the goal of studying how drones can be used for enhancing or enabling important services performed by the City Hall. Even before the PDPA, the City Hall of Niterói already used drones for a number of purposes. More specifically, in recent years, its Civil Defense Office has been using drones in some of the services it provides to the local population. Thus, the DroNit project has been particularly focused on optimizing the drone usage for the main tasks of the Civil Defense Office.

Among the usages of drones by the Civil Defense Office of Niterói, one can cite their expertise in disaster-response missions. In those missions, drones uses include aiding in searches and identifying vulnerable constructions. Drones are also used by the Office for periodically assessing risk areas and checking for unauthorized constructions. In both cases, drones enable a quicker data acquisition process, in comparison to the traditional approach of sending crews to the places of interest.

Despite their already successful employment by the Civil Defense Office, the usage of drones still faces a range of challenges. Those include technical issues—*e.g.*, limitations in the communication range and flight autonomy—, but also issues related to the current legislation and how it affects the processes of the Civil Defense Office. There are even cultural and social issues related to the acceptance of drones by the population [21]. All those factors still limit the potential benefit that drones can have in practice.

This paper reports some of the efforts and preliminary results of the DroNit project. We describe several drone-aided activities currently performed by the Civil Defense Office and discuss how drones have enabled made them more effective. We also identify limitations or inefficiencies on how those applications are currently conducted, as well as related technical and legal challenges. We further describe other activities performed by the office that currently do not employ drones, but that could be aided or improved by this technology. Finally, we discuss solutions proposed by the DroNit project using information and knowledge management, as well as other techniques, for coping with the aforementioned challenges and enabling a more widespread usage of drones by the Civil Defense Office.

This paper is an extended version of our initial report [3]. In that previous work, we focused on an overview of the experience of Niterói's Civil Defense Office in using drones in different situations, based on interviews conducted with their staff. The previous paper also generically discussed ideas to broaden and improve the usage of drones by the office. In this extended version, we complement that study by reporting concrete solutions developed within the DroNit project for the following challenges: (i) how to use drones to complement or replace satellite images for evaluating vegetation coverage? (ii) how to plan missions taking into account realistic communication range restrictions and constructions to enable a safer operation of the drones? (iii) how to properly coach drone pilots to safely fly the aircraft under critical conditions, including poor communication? and (iv) how to improve the range of flight of the drones, allowing for larger areas to be covered?

Aside from those particular solutions, this paper also contributes to the state of the art by raising awareness for innovative uses of drones that can be applied in the context of smart cities. Moreover, it shows the existing gaps in current drone technologies, pointing to open issues in the area.

The remainder of the text is organized as follows. Section 2 provides a primer on drones. Section 3 presents a case study of Niterói's Civil Defense Office, describing its typical tasks that are—or could be—aided by drones. In Sect. 4 we highlight the main challenges identified with the usage of drones for the activities of the Office and also discuss ideas for how the drones' usefulness for the Civil Defense may be improved. In Sect. 5 we describe how the DroNit project is tackling the issues highlighted in Sects. 3 and 4 and report some preliminary results. Section 6 briefly overviews the related literature. Finally, Sect. 7 concludes the paper.

2 Drone Types and Characteristics

Typology, i.e., type of aircraft, is the most basic drone characteristic. Fixed-wing, single-rotor, multirotor, and fixed-wing hybrid are the most usual typologies [11]. Fixed-wing drones resemble airplanes, in the sense that they have rigid wings that provide lift as long as they move forward. Rotor-based drones use vertical propellers, similarly to a helicopter. The difference between single- and multirotor drones lies on the number of such propellers.

Rotor-based drones have very precise maneuverability. They can also remain relatively stable in a certain position, thus being suitable for applications that involve photography. Multirotor drones are more stable than their single-rotor counterparts, and the number of propellers usually correlates with their load capacity [9]. Conversely, fixed-wing drones can achieve significantly higher speeds and carry much more load. They also excel in terms of range. They are, however, harder to pilot and unsuitable for missions that involve fine maneuvers or stops in particular positions.

Consumer-grade drones are usually small. They can weight as little as a few hundred grams and measure less than 30 cm in their largest dimension. Drones for more specialized applications, such as agriculture, tend to be larger and heavier, as they often need to carry more weight, requiring more and/or larger propellers. Drones for military applications can be as large as some manned aircraft, weighting several hundred kilograms [9].

Even within the same typology, drones may vary significantly in terms of autonomy. Consumer drones tend to use electrical propellers powered by batteries, thus offering relatively short flight times (typically below one hour, for entertainment drones). Internal combustion engines can be found in some larger, more specialized drones and usually allow much longer autonomy.

Another important aspect is the type of communication channel used between the drone and the ground station. Even drones that do not send any sensored data back to the ground station usually need to at least receive commands from the pilot[1]. Thus, the reliability of the communication channel is an important factor and it also influences the flight range of the aircraft. Frequently, open standards, such as the IEEE 802.11 [10], are used, but some vendors opt for proprietary technologies—e.g., DJI uses its own technology called OcuSync [24]. Even when a proprietary technology is used, consumer drones usually operate on unlicensed radio bands alongside multiple competing devices. That may severely degrade the quality of the communication, further limiting the drone's range.

In terms of payload, consumer-grade drones usually have severely restricted capacity, limiting their ability to carry sensors and actuators. Those drones are usually equipped with a simple camera for visible light, which can be used for both aiding the pilot in controlling the flight and for recording video and taking photos. For more specialized tasks, other types of payload may be attached. For example, some manufacturers offer models with multispectral cameras—e.g., an infrared or thermal camera. For mapping the topography of a region and/or buildings, a LIDAR might be useful. Other examples include temperature sensors and smoke detectors, which can be used for detecting fires.

While less common in consumer-grade drones, actuators can also be part of the payload. Drones for agriculture often contain tanks that allow it to carry liquids for irrigation or application of pesticides. In other scenarios, headlights or speakers could be interesting to generate alert signals or to disseminate information or warning messages.

Sensors and actuators can be controlled either manually by the pilot or in automated fashion. In the first case, they must be connected somehow to the ground station— perhaps using the same communication channel employed for the telemetry/control of

[1] While some drones may have a few autonomous flight capabilities (e.g., avoiding collisions, returning home under certain conditions), the most usual mode of operation is remotely piloted drones.

the drone. In the second case, an alternative is to use some kind of standalone device for controlling the sensor/actuator also included in the drone's payload.

3   Understanding the Needs of the Civil Defense of Niterói

This section provides an overview of the Civil Defense Office of Niterói. Here, we review both the general responsibilities of the office, as well as the particular tasks for which it already employs drones. The information contained in this section is mainly based on interviews we conducted with the staff of the Office. The goals of those interviews were multifold. For one, we wanted to understand the needs of the office and how drones could help. We also wanted to assess the overall experience of the staff with drones, with a particular focus on what were their main complaints and difficulties.

3.1   Daily Activities and Roles of the Office

A municipal law[2] regulates the Civil Defense Office of Niterói city and its protection services provided to the citizens. Generally speaking, the role of a Civil Defense Office is protect the population against civil disturbances, including natural disasters. This may comprise both reactive and proactive actions. Reactive actions take place in response to a particular occurrence—*e.g.*, a natural disaster. Proactive actions are usually a continuous effort to avoid or mitigate the effects of such events. A more detailed list of actions/roles of a Civil Defense Office—particularly based on the responsibilities defined in the municipal law of Niterói—can be seen in Table 1.

Table 1. Main roles of the Civil Defense office of Niterói [3].

Id.	Role	Reactive	Proactive
1	Identify and map risk areas, monitor slope/hill stabilization works		✓
2	Inspect risk areas avoiding occupations		✓
3	Inspect buildings, evacuating areas of risk or vulnerable buildings	✓	✓
4	Inform the population about risk areas, extreme events, protocols	✓	✓
5	Perform simulated exercises		✓
6	Collect, distribute and control supplies in disaster situations	✓	
7	Assess damages and losses of disaster affected areas	✓	
8	Develop citizen awareness of disaster prevention		✓
9	Encourage economic and production restructuring of affected areas	✓	
10	Train human resources for civil defense and protection actions		✓
11	Provide data and information to the national system	✓	

In practice, the Office will have a set of different concrete actions it must perform in order to achieve its general goals. However, those may differ substantially between

---

[2] Law n° 3561 published on December 18, 2020, available (in Portuguese) in http://leismu nicipa.is/dvfyk.

offices of different cities due to a number of local peculiarities. For instance, the climate and topography of a city directly influence the concerns and actions of its Civil Defense Office, because they are strongly related with the type of natural event that may take place in that particular region. Even cultural trends of the population may play an important role on defining the responsibilities and specific daily actions of a particular Civil Defense Office.

Niterói is located in a coastal region with tropical climate. Temperatures are typically high almost all year, especially during the summer, when storms are frequent. The city also has an uneven topography, with several hills and plains. Coupled with the relatively high population density, a significant portion of city's constructions are located on or near those hills. As such, Niterói is very susceptible to mudslides, particularly during the summer. When those mudslides occur, they usually disrupts population displacement, destroy houses and, unfortunately, lead to deaths. Illegal constructions are especially susceptible to that, as they are often built on unstable terrains and without the proper permits demanded by the City Hall.

Therefore, avoiding illegal constructions is one of the main concerns for the Civil Defense Office of the city. To that end, the Office continuously monitors the city perimeter for early signs of unauthorized constructions. Another related action is the monitoring of the vegetation coverage of hills and other areas vulnerable to mudslides, as lack of proper vegetation increases the probability of such events. The Office also has processes in place to monitor the city for signs of terrain instability.

Currently, all those monitoring tasks are performed by means of satellite images received periodically and reviewed by technicians. They analyze the images looking to identify and measure deforestation areas. Aside from the aforementioned impacts on possible mudslides, that analysis is also important because, according to the Office, more than 50% of the total area of the city comprises environmental protection areas. Those satellite images are also used to look for illegal constructions.

While those preventive measures contribute to avoiding mudslides, they still occasionally occur. In those cases, the Civil Defense Office is also tasked with handling the emergencies or helping other public forces. Emergency response actions include assessing the damage, helping evacuate the affected area, looking for survivors, and providing logistics so that supplies can be delivered to the location.

Another seasonal issue in Niterói are natural wildfires due to the typically high temperatures. Those fires pose a significant threat to the population and, as such, they are a concern to the Civil Defense Office. To cope with that, the office continuously maps and monitors areas that are deemed susceptible to fires. Part of this process comprises identifying vegetation that is particularly dry.

Fire balloons are another significant concern. The construction and release of this kind of balloon is a common form of cultural expression in Brazil, including the city of Niterói. Nevertheless, fire balloons represent a serious risks, because their paths and flight time are unknown and contingent on the direction and speed of the wind in that particular moment. Thus, their landing spot is not easy to predict, and when they land, they can cause fires. Because of their risks, releasing fire balloons is a punishable offense according to the Brazillian law. For all those reasons, the Civil Defense Office of Niterói dedicates significant effort to detecting, capturing and handling the consequences of illegal fire balloons.

Even though the main duties of the Civil Defense Office of Niterói are related to the well-being of the population of the city, it also frequently collaborates with its counterparts from other municipalities. It is a common practice for offices from one city to contribute with the response actions in other locations, especially in cases of large-scale disasters.

3.2   Current Use of Drones

The Civil Defense Office already employs drones for several purposes. That has led to the creation of a *drone operation crew* within the staff of the Office composed by personnel trained to pilot these aircraft for both preventive and emergency missions.

One of the tasks of the drone operation crew is complementing the analysis done by means of satellite images. When technician finds evidence of irregular constructions, for example, the drone missions are performed in the location in question taking more detailed pictures. Those pictures are then further analyzed to either confirm or dismiss the existence of an illegal construction.

The drone operation crew is also deployed during natural disasters or wildfires. In those cases, their main goal is to provide support for other teams. For example, the drones can be used to assess the extent of the area affected by the disaster. They can also help determine other potentially useful information, such as available access routes for ground crews.

Notable Uses of Drones by the Office.   Despite the importance and effectiveness of the preventive work done by the Civil Defense Office, for the general population, the work of the office becomes more apparent when emergency situations arise. Those are also the situations in which drone usage by the office has been more pronounced thus far. Even though the drone operation crew has been created for only a few years now, it has already accumulated a significant track record of successful operations with drones.

As an example, in 2019, a fire started in a forest area in the neighborhood of Charitas, in Niterói[3]. Fighting the fire is, of course, a responsibility of the fire department. However, the Civil Defense Office provided support to the operation in many ways. Among those, it conducted survey flights in order to precisely estimate the extension of the area affected by the fire. Those surveys also enabled the response units to identify the most critical fire spots, as well as the most likely directions the fire could spread. That allowed the fire department to concentrate efforts and resources, effectively reducing the damages caused by the fire. Moreover, by means of those aerial images, it was also possible to identify access routes for the ground crews to reach the most critical spots.

At the end of 2021, severe rain storms hit the state of Bahia[4]. By the beginning of 2022, the damage caused by the rain required a series of emergency response actions and the Civil Defense Office of Niterói sent a team to provide support. Among other

---

[3] More details (in Portuguese): http://www.sma.niteroi.rj.gov.br/index.php?option=com_content&view=article&id=5966:2019-08-05-19-01-40.

[4] More details: https://edition.cnn.com/2021/12/26/americas/brazil-bahia-flooding-w/index.html.

tasks, they used drones to help assess hills and other areas under the risk of mudslides. The drones were used to gather high resolution images that were later analyzed by geologists and engineers to pinpoint risk areas.

Shortly thereafter, a heavy storm hit the nearby city of Petrópolis. The city infrastructure was severely damaged and over 150 people died[5]. Similarly to the episode in Bahia, Niterói's Civil Defense Office provided support to the local authorities by sending a team. In particular, this team helped identify areas in risk of mudslides, as well as buildings in risk of collapse. Another consequence of the storm was that several vehicles were dragged towards a river and sunk. Among those vehicles, there were two buses with passengers. Eventually, the drone operation crew of the Civil Defense Office of Niterói was called upon to help in the searches of missing people. The usage of drones in the operation allowed the search to move quickly and, thus, to cover more area.

A similar collaboration with local authorities happened in June 2022, when heavy rains caused destruction in the state of Pernambuco, in the Northeast of Brazil. As in the previous episodes, Niterói's Civil Defense Office lent its expertise with drones to help inspect mudslide risk areas and assess the safety of buildings.

Products. Several products are generated by Niterói's Civil Defense Office by means of their actions in the city and the services provided to other cities. These products can be generated in response to demands of other municipal departments—*e.g.* Fire Department—regarding the services provided by the Office. But, ultimately, those products are responses to demands of the population.

In loco data are often recorded by drones of the Civil Defense Office in order to obtain, store and register data (products) regarding incidents. The products are filtered and dispatched to the responsible government departments to facilitate preventive or corrective actions. Information related to types and uses of impacted properties, infrastructure and buildings, geographical aspects, such as landslide propensity data and pedology, among others, comprise these products.

3.3   Demands of Drone Usage

While the Civil Defense Office of Niterói already has vast experience with the usage of drone for several purposes, there are other possible use cases, as well as the possibility of improving the usefulness of these aircrafts in their day-to-day tasks.

One example is the inspection of constructions. Currently, those inspections are performed only *in situ*, requiring technicians to physically attend each building. This activity could be more agile and cost-effective by means of periodical drone surveys, provided they could take sufficiently detailed images to allow at least a preliminary remote evaluation—more detailed *in situ* inspections could be made in case images were inconclusive or if signs of issues were detected. This would effectively increase the frequency of inspection of each building, reducing risks of accidents.

Another yet unexplored usage of drones is during events with large concentration of people, such as protests or concerts. In this case, drones could be equipped with loud

---

[5] More details: https://www.bbc.com/news/world-latin-america-60401611.

speakers so that audio messages could be disseminated with alerts or other types of safety instructions. Sound alarms are already used in Niterói in the form of static sirens located in regions with propensity to mudslides to alert the population about emergency situations. Drones can make that system more dynamic, allowing such alerts to be generated even in locations where the static siren system has not yet been deployed.

Drones could also be used by the Office for transporting essential supplies—such as medication or drinkable water—during emergence operations. Due to their ability of reaching difficult areas quickly, they could be employed as a first response before ground crews arrive.

There are also some activities for which the Office already employs drones in minor roles that could be expanded. For instance, when identifying risk areas and irregular constructions, drones are only used for confirming or detailing the analysis based on satellite images. However, those images are not available in real-time, are unusable in cloudy days and the spatial resolution could not be enough to distinguish specific features. Thus, drones could be used beyond a simple confirmation tool, instead being also the primary source of images used for this task, mitigating the aforementioned issues.

The role of drones could also be expanded in their usage for handling fire balloons. Today, they are mostly used to track the route of the balloon, trying to anticipate where it is going to fall and, therefore, allowing the preparation of a proper response. However, during our interviews, the Office staff has shown interest in the idea of using drones in a more active fashion. One of the ideas was to use the drone to drag or direct the balloons to safer areas. Alternatively, the drones could be used to attempt a controlled take down of the balloon whenever it was deemed to be over a safe location.

We also note that drone missions can be simulated ahead of time. This could be explored by the Civil Defense Office for the purposes of training or even planning real missions. Flight simulations could be conducted for a same overall mission, but considering different deployment strategies, so that the optimal drone usage could be selected, increasing the effectiveness of the devices.

4 Challenges and Insights

Despite the current popularity of drone applications, the tasks performed by the Civil Defense Office of Niterói have a number of particularities, making them significantly different from traditional drone uses. Because of that, we were able to identify several challenges that need to be addressed for a more effective use of drones by the Office. We also identified many lessons learned from the existing experience of the Office with drones. This results in a wide range of topics that deserve further investigation, particularly for proposals of information and knowledge management and development of appropriate information systems.

4.1 Issues and Challenges

The autonomy of the drones used by the Civil Defense Office ranges from 15 to 20 min of flight, according to reports from the staff. They also identified that environmental factors—such as wind velocity and temperature—have significant impact on that autonomy. Such a short autonomy impairs missions that involve either long flight times or large areas to be covered—*e.g.*, searching for survivors of natural disasters. This is mitigated to a certain degree by the usage of backup batteries, but that still requires frequent returns to ground station for battery replacement, delaying the missions. Moreover, replacing the battery requires powering-off the drone, which further increases delay, although that could be mitigated by using hot-swap batteries. Recharging depleted batteries on the field can also be a challenge, as power outlets are not always available.

Aside from influencing the autonomy of the drone, the weather can impede missions all together, as most common drone models cannot fly under rain. In those cases, the mission—or, at least, the usage of the drones—must be postponed until better weather conditions occur. Nevertheless, as explained in Sect. 3, several emergency missions performed by the Civil Defense Office of Niterói are related to the occurrence of heavy rain.

Another limiting factor is the communication range for the wireless channel used between the drone and the ground station. Several factors influence this range, including the communication technology, the existence of obstacles, the frequency of operation, and interference levels. Currently, the drones used by the Civil Defense Office are off-the-shelf models that use radios operating on unlicensed bands—usually, the 900 MHz, 2.4 MHz, and 5 GHz ISM bands. Those bands are generally crowded in most urban areas, especially due to the popularity of technologies such as Wi-Fi and Bluetooth. As a consequence, devices operating under those frequency bands often face significant levels of interference, degrading the quality of communication, particularly in densely populated areas. Unsurprisingly, pilots of the Civil Defense Office reported multiple times during our interviews that they had experienced instabilities while controlling the drones, which may be caused by poor communication between the aircraft and the ground station.

Birds were also reported as a significant concern by the staff of the Office. Several missions had to be aborted because the drones were attacked by certain species of birds—perhaps because they felt threatened by the device. Pilots reported that this is particularly problematic for missions in which the drone flies far away from the ground station, because the lack of visual contact with the aircraft makes it harder to anticipate the birds approaching. This can put the drone, animals and people nearby in risk.

During the interviews, we also identified that the needs of the Civil Defense Office often conflict with restrictions imposed by the Brazillian drone legislation. For example, certain regions of Niterói are located relatively close to the Santos Dumont airport. Whenever the Office needs to conduct flights in one of those regions, the legislation requires it to register the mission beforehand with the competent department and wait for the proper permission. For certain missions, that kind of delay might not be tolerable. Moreover, off-the-shelf drones automatically recognize the vicinity of airports and are programmed to avoid entering those areas.

Despite the agility of drones to reach difficult areas, the staff of the Civil Defense Office reported that some of the products generated by drone missions can actually take significant time (*e.g.*, weeks) to be produced. The issue is not the drone flight itself, but full set of procedures and protocols associated with generating those products. The mission needs to be planned—and, sometimes, authorized—and executed for collecting data. This data is then accessed by technicians and processed in the office to generate reports and conclusions. Accelerating the production of those reports would allow the office to take action faster to address the incidents, thus improving the quality of the services provided to the population. In some cases, that might mean even saving lives.

Pilot training is another aspect to be considered, particularly because several drone missions occur under difficult conditions—e.g., significant wind. Missions may also involve pushing drones to the limit regarding their autonomy and range. In order to avoid issues, pilots need to be aware of the limitations of the particular model they operate, as well as how to handle instabilities and other issues during non-ideal flight situations.

We also note that a fundamental challenge is choosing the right drone model. A large number of different models is available in the market, and those can differ significantly in several aspects, including size, flight autonomy, load capacity, and accessories. Given the very heterogeneous objectives of the desirable drone uses by the Civil Defense Office, it is unlikely that a single model is adequate for all purposes. For example, when searching for missing persons in dense vegetation, long autonomy and thermal cameras are more valuable than the capacity of dragging large objects. This capacity, however, is valuable for the application of directing fire balloons to safer areas. Generally speaking, the very particular set of requirements of the Civil Defense applications point away from the most common off-the-shelf models. Indeed, more modular drones that can be easily modified according to specific needs of a certain mission would be desirable.

4.2   Recommendations for More Effective Drone Usage

The DroNit project is currently proposing a series of potential solutions for the demands and challenges highlighted in Subsect. 4.1. Our main recommendations are summarized in Table 2, and associated to the respective challenges and demands. They are further detailed in the remainder of this section.

For the issue of battery autonomy, one possible solution is the employment of a multi-UAV system, also called a *drone swarm* [5]. This strategy can mitigate the problem of covering larger areas by replacing the single drone approach with a group of drones autonomously coordinated to explore a certain region. One may also consider the deployment of strategic battery charging points throughout the city or mission site. Those charging points do not need to be permanent structures. Instead, they can simply comprise vehicles parked in strategic positions, which can be done only when effectively required (*e.g.*, during response to natural disasters). Planning a effective placement of those charging points, subject to realistic placement restrictions, is an interesting and important problem that can be further investigated. Battery hot-swap—changing the drone's battery without restarting their electronic components and, consequently, the previously defined mission—can also reduce the down-time.

The problem of flying under bad weather conditions requires efforts from different perspectives. One point is, of course, choosing a drone that is waterproof or splash-proof, but that is not trivial, as most off-the-shelf drones are not designed with that requirement in mind. An alternative for the Civil Defense Office would be to develop a custom drone with this capability, but that involves an engineering expertise that is not the attribution of the Office. Another aspect of this problem is the proper training of the

Table 2. Summary of the main recommendations for each challenge or demands identified [3].

Challenges/Demands	Recommendation Summary
Battery autonomy	Multi-UAV (*i.e.*, using multiple drones to cover an area), define points in ground for battery swap, hot-swap
Weather conditions	Investing in waterproof or splash-proof drones
Network communication	Study and use of LPWAN, 5G, FANET
Choosing drones	Survey of readily available drones on the market and sensors
Regulation and Legislation	Reduce bureaucratic processes, flexibilize rules for emergency
Training agents	Use simulators of drone flight
Mapping risk areas	Use of infrared/multispectral camera, humidity sensors, embedded in the drone
Handling fire balloon	Study techniques and procedures to extinguish or redirect balloons
Building surveillance	Define protocols for the drone structural inspection, knowledge management
Warning sound messages	Define message and protocol in missions according to historical situations
Supply delivery	Specify drone capable to transport supply. Define protocols
More agile processes	Automate procedures to provide (*quasi*) real-time responses while *in situ*

pilots for controlling the drones under such conditions, which will be discussed later in this paper.

In terms of enhancing the communication between the drone and the ground station, several different paths can be investigated. One possibility is considering alternative communication technologies that may be better suited for the needs of the Civil Defense Office. The so-called *Low Power Wide Area Networks* (LPWAN) [4]—such as LoraWAN—are designed to operate over long distances and with low battery consumption. Nevertheless, they offer relatively low bit-rates, being targeted at applications that generate low volumes of traffic. That might be suitable for the transmission of commands or telemetry between the drone and the ground station, but may not support video feedback, unless bandwidth demands are significantly reduced. Other technologies, such as 5G, can offer both high performance and long range, but the antenna placement of such networks is often optimized for covering the ground—where most of the users of the mobile operators are. That can be a challenge for their application for enabling drone communications [18]. Moreover, 5G creates a dependence on the infrastructure provided by carriers, which may be affected by natural disasters, for example. Another possibility is the usage of a *Flying Ad Hoc Network* (FANET), *i.e.*, the usage of a multi-UAV system to extend the communication range by means of multi-hop aerial communication between drones [5].

With respect to choosing a drone for a specific purpose, it is fundamental to conduct a thorough survey of the current market. While most off-the-shelf drones nowadays are target at the entertainment segment—photography and videography—, there are companies that specialize on drones for more particular niches, such as agriculture. Those specialized drones have widely different characteristics in comparison to the more usual models, often excelling at weight capacity. Another possible route is that of customized drones. It is possible to find kits of parts to assemble drones, allowing one to customize certain aspects to fit particular purposes. Moreover, such custom drones are usually highly modular, which bodes well for the heterogeneous usages of the Civil Defense Office.

The reports provided by the staff of the Civil Defense Office also highlight the need for more streamlined bureaucratic processes between the office and the competent govern departments. That is particularly important in case of emergency missions. Because the Civil Defense is a government service, rules for emergence flights in civilian prohibited areas could, perhaps, be flexibilized, provided, of course, that they do not endanger the population. Thus, any flexibilization would require an additional effort from the part of the Civil Defense Office, such as stricter licenses for their pilots. Special processes and systems could also be put in place so that the authorization requests made by the Civil Defense Office could be handled faster.

From the discussion above, it is clear that properly training the staff of the Civil Defense Office to operate the drones is of paramount importance. Because there are so many possible use cases for these aircraft, drone related drills should be included as part their training. In this particular aspect, we argue that the usage of simulators as part of the training could be particularly helpful. A simulator with good models on the many aspects involved in a drone flight could be used to expose pilots to several duress situation that might arise during real missions. A systematic training program can include simulated missions under strong winds, with low battery capacity, under communicating failures, among other challenging situations. Exposing the pilot to these situations before they actually occur can be decisive for the success of the actual missions. Nevertheless, this requires the simulator to be rather precise in its depiction of this kind of condition.

As discussed in Subsect. 3.3, mapping and surveillance of risk areas are two of the most common tasks performed by the Civil Defense Office—both routinely and during disaster response. While the Office already has processes in place for those purposes, we argue that drones can also be used to assess the condition of the soil and vegetation by means of multispectral images. This can complement the current satellite-based approach used by the Office. In a first moment, satellite images can be used for an overall evaluation that would yield a list of large potential risk areas. Based on that, drones equipped with multispectral cameras would be sent to survey those areas, providing more detailed images that can be used for more precisely mapping issues. Other types of sensors can also be carried by the drones—such as an air humidity sensor—providing more information that satellite images could.

Using drones for handling fire balloons is currently a technically challenging task. Those balloons are generally large causing significant drag if one tries to push or pull them, rendering the task impossible for typical off-the-shelf drones. An alternative could be trying to take the balloon down when it naturally traverses an area deemed to be safe—such as the sea or a lake. An idea is to try to cool down the heat source of the balloon, which could be attempted with either water or chemicals. But those would have to be carried during flight, which, in turn, requires a drone with a significant load capacity. Moreover, a system for delivering the water or chemicals to the heat source of the balloon would have to be developed. Because of all those reasons, we believe such a solution would require a multidisciplinary effort for designing and eventually equipping a proper drone with suitable actuators for this task.

We also argue that some of the processes involving drones in the Civil Defense Office could be automated to provide (*quasi*) real-time responses. We identified many information that can be processed *in situ*—rather than being processed later in the office—taking advantage of the computing and communication capacities of the drone itself. Specially for custom drones, it is possible to envision scenarios in which data from the drone's sensors would be processed either locally or directly sent to a cloud server, automatically yielding *information* instead of the *raw data* collected nowadays. This would accelerate the generation of the products of the Civil Defense Office, such as reports and alerts, allowing faster action to handle incidents. Taking the example of the inspection of risk areas, agents can compute information on risk points, based on images, still in the field.

It is also important to define action protocols for each specific task, such as building surveillance, warning sound messages and supply delivery, as to allow drones to be effectively used in practice. Those protocols should define important stages of knowledge management and decision-making, such as the processes of acquiring data, generating, storing and disseminating the information and knowledge, and making decisions based on acquired knowledge. Effective information and knowledge management techniques, especially designed for the problems discussed, are therefore crucial for optimizing processes in the office.

Table 3 summarizes the current use of drones in the Civil Defense Office by roles (see Table 1) and also the recommendations for future drone usage. The difference between the current and future use of drones by the office is highlighted in the fourth column, labeled as "Future Drone's Use".

5 Preliminary Results of the DroNit Project

Aside from the general recommendations aforementioned in Subsect. 4.2, the DroNit project has also been working on more specific solutions for optimizing drone usage by the Civil Defense Office of Niterói. In this section, we summarize the main points of study and report on the preliminary results achieved thus far.

5.1 Using Drones to Complement Satellite Images

Satellite images analysis is a routine task performed by the Office for several purposes. One particularly important is assessing the vegetation coverage state of the city area. In the current process adopted by the Office, when new images are received, they are geoprocessed by Geographic Information Systems (GIS) to generate a NDVI (Normalized Difference Vegetation Index) [25]. The NDVI is a graphical representation of the extension and density of the vegetation coverage of a region. It can be calculated by the ratio between the difference and sum of the spectral response of vegetation in the Red and Near Infrared (NIR) range, as follows:

Table 3. Summary of drone usage by the Civil Defense Office and recommendations for the future [3]. Role Id. refers to the numeration on Table 1. Current and Future Drone Usage indicate if drones are or could be used in the future by the Office, respectively.

Role Id.	Current Drones' Use	Summary of the Current Drone Usage	Future Drones' Use	Recommendation
1	yes	Inspect risk areas using conventional cameras	yes	Map and identify risk areas using infrared cameras
2	yes	Inspect risk areas using conventional cameras	yes	Inspect risk areas using infrared cameras
3	no	–	yes	Define protocols to include drones in building inspection
4	no	–	yes	Send sound alert messages to the civilians
5	no	–	yes	Apply drones in exercise drills; use simulators of drone flights
6	no	–	yes	Transport supplies for a risk area, if needed
7	yes	Capture conventional images of areas hit by disasters	yes	Automate the current process and improve evaluation
8 9	Not applicable			
10	no	–	yes	Drones as a tool to assist in the training of human resources
11	no	–	yes	Data and procedures using drones can feed the national system

$$NDVI = \frac{NIR - Red}{NIR + Red} \qquad (1)$$

From an image with both Red and NIR bands, this formula can be applied to each pixel, resulting in a value that ranges from -1 (absence of vegetation) to $+1$ (dense vegetation). Those values can then be mapped to colors or brightness intensities, resulting in a new version of the original image that highlights areas with vegetation. A difference between two NDVI images taken at different moments can also be used to analyze the vegetation heath and detect loss of vegetation coverage, often associated with illegal deforestation.

Thus, NDVI analysis is very useful, but it comes with a few caveats. As explained in Subsect. 3.3, those satellite images can be obstructed by clouds and they take some time to be acquired. Thus, detecting signs of vegetation coverage loss might be delayed. Moreover, the accuracy of this detection depends on the limited resolution of the original images.

In order to deal with those caveats, the DroNit project has been developing a drone-based solution for generating NDVI vegetation coverage analysis. The idea is that drone missions can be used to acquire multispectral images of one or more regions of interest which are then used to generate the correspondent NDVI images.

We are currently prototyping this solution by equipping a drone with a Raspberry Pi and a Pi Camera NoIR v2 module. This camera module does not have an IR filter, commonly found on CMOS image sensors, and thus can capture NIR information. The Raspberry Pi itself can process the raw image frames acquired by the camera to generate the NDVI images, which are later uploaded to servers in order to maintain a historical database of the vegetation evolution in the city perimeter.

While this solution does not replace the need for satellite images, it provides a useful complement, as it allows particularly important areas to be surveyed independently of the availability or quality of the satellite images. Moreover, it also allows a finer analysis of target areas, since the drone images can be acquired from a relatively short distance.

5.2   Improving the Safety and Effectiveness of Drone Missions

As discussed in Subsect. 4.2, several issues were identified associated with this general objective of making drone missions safer and more effective. Among those, two that stand out are planning of the missions and training of the pilots.

One of the early conclusions of the DroNit project was that those issues can be solved, or at least aided, by the usage of simulations. However, this conclusion assumes that the simulator can accurately represent several aspects of the drone flights. Those aspects include (i) the energy usage and battery capacity of the drone; (ii) the range and quality of the communication between the drone and the ground station; (iii) the physical interactions between the drone and the world around it (*e.g.*, how it reacts to wind); and (iv) the existence and characteristics of other relevant objects for the mission, such as buildings and other obstacles.

We conducted a preliminary study of available simulators which reveled that there are, indeed, many possible choices. Those include commercially simulators, such as DJI's *Flight Simulator*[6] and *Real Flight*[7], as well as open source alternatives, such as the SITL (Software In The Loop) ArduPilot[8]. SITL ArduPilot is a build of the autopilot ArduPilot used in several drone models that allows testing the behavior of code in a simulated environment. Thus, it only simulates the drone itself, and not the world around it. For that reason, it is often coupled with a physical world simulator, such as Gazebo[9] or AirSim[10]. Both those simulators create a virtual environment for the simulated drone to fly in. Those environments correspond to a 3D representation that can include details such as terrain elevation and objects—*e.g.*, mountains and buildings. Gazebo and Airsim are also responsible for simulating physical interactions of the drone, such as how it responds to wind or collisions with other objects.

Despite the many available options, we were not able to find a simulator that accurately modeled all the required aspects for planning critical Civil Defense missions and

---

[6] Available at: https://www.dji.com/br/simulator.

[7] Available at: https://www.realflight.com/.

[8] Available at: https://ardupilot.org/.

[9] Available at: https://gazebosim.org/home.

[10] Available at: https://microsoft.github.io/AirSim/.

training its pilots. In particular, simulators such as *Flight Simulator* and *Real Flight* focus mainly on the developing the piloting skills, but do not include models for the drones energy consumption or possible failures in communication. The SITL ArduPilot does include an energy consumption model, but it proved to be quite simplified in our preliminary tests (*e.g.*, certain drone models would consume the same amount of energy regardless of whether their propellers were on or off). The SITL ArduPilot also does not simulate the communication channel between the drone and the ground station. Instead, it simply assumes control messages arrive by a socket, regardless of the position of the drone with respect to the ground station. Finally, while Gazebo and Airsim provide accurate simulations of the physical interactions of the drone, they require a virtual world map of the simulated flight area, including the description of objects, such as buildings. For a proper usage by the Civil Defense Office of Niterói, there would have to be such a map available for the whole city, something that currently does not exist. Furthermore, creating such a map is not trivial, especially regarding modeling the relief, buildings and other constructions.

To cope with those limitations, several solutions were developed by the DroNit project in order to make a simulation environment composed of the SITL ArduPilot and Gazebo suitable for the needs of the Civil Defense Office. Those are described in more detail below.

Communication Models. Figure 1a illustrates the typical architecture used in a SITL ArduPilot simulation. Aside from SITL ArduPilot itself, it also requires a physical simulator for modeling the interactions between the drone and the outside world, such as Gazebo. It also requires a software component to act as the ground station during simulations. As an example, Fig. 1a assumes the usage of MavProxy[11], which offers an interface for the user to interact with the simulated drone. Commands or actions performed in MavProxy are sent to the simulated drone in the form of messages following the MAVLink protocol [15].

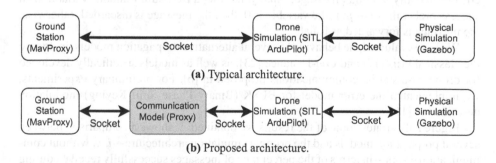

(a) Typical architecture.

(b) Proposed architecture.

Fig. 1. Architectures of a simulation environment based on ArduPilot and Gazebo. (a) shows the typically employed architecture, while (b) shows the architecture proposed for incorporating more accurate communication models.

---

[11] Available at: https://ardupilot.org/mavproxy/.

In the simulated environment, all three pieces of software communicate by means of sockets, either TCP or UDP. Since the most common scenario involves all three pieces of software running in the same computer, message losses are unlikely regardless of protocol. Moreover, even if some UDP datagrams were to be lost during simulation, those losses would not be caused by current simulation state (*e.g.*, factors such as the current distance between the drone and the base station), but simply by unrelated events within the hardware used to run the simulations. Further notice that the SITL ArduPilot does not apply any communication error models to the incoming messages.

To add potential packet losses to the communication between the ground station and the simulated drone, we changed the typical architecture to the one shown in Fig. 1b. A software component hereinafter called *Proxy* is placed between the simulated ground station (MavProxy) and the simulated drone (SITL ArduPilot). That can be achieved by simply configuring MavProxy and SITL ArduPilot to establish a socket communication with the Proxy, instead of with each other. Hence, every message sent from the ground station to the simulated drone (or vice-versa) will pass through the Proxy, allowing it to perform selective discards to simulate channel losses. We opted for this architecture—instead of modifying either MavProxy or the SITL ArduPilot—in order to increase modularity, as well as to avoid introducing any unwanted side-effects by means of modifications to either existing software.

When the proxy is started, it receives a number of information regarding the simulated scenario. One of those is the geographical coordinates of the ground station. The proxy implements a parser for the MAVLink protocol and parses each message that it receives. If it is a message from the drone to the base station, it checks if the message contains an update of the coordinates of the drone. If so, it extract the coordinates, computes the current distance from the drone to the ground station and saves it for later processing. Based on the currently known distance between the drone and the ground station, it apply a propagation model and estimates the strength of the signal that would reach the receiver for that message, as well as the SNR (Signal-to-Noise Ratio). From the SNR and the size of the message, it applies an error model to estimate the packet error probability p for that message. Finally, it draws a Bernoulli Random Variable with success probability $1 - p$: if the variable is 0, then the message is discarded; otherwise, the message is forwarded as usual.

We have evaluated the behavior of several alternative propagation models, including the classical Friis [17] and Log-Distance [23], as well as models specifically developed for drone-base station communications proposed in [6]. For preliminary experiments, we implemented the error model for BPSK (Binary Phase Shift Keying) modulation described in [16].

Figure 2 illustrates some of the results we obtained. It shows a comparison between several propagation models and the original simulation architecture—*i.e.*, without communication errors—in terms of the percentage of messages successfully received during simulations. For these results, we simulated a typical mission of about 10 min in which the drone flew over a predetermined route in a neighborhood of Niterói. As shown in Fig. 2, certain propagation models are more pessimistic than others. Notably, the Friis propagation model is rather optimistic and resulted in no message losses throughout our experiments. The Log-Distance and the Line-of-Sight (LoS) and Obstructed Line-Of-Sight (OLoS) models proposed in [6] are much more pessimistic, causing severe

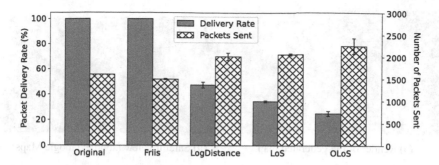

Fig. 2. Comparison of the message delivery rates measured with each propagation model evaluated, as well as with the original simulation architecture.

message losses, especially in the middle portion of the mission—during which the drone effectively lost communication with the ground station. Preliminary experiments we have been conducting with real drones suggest the LoS and OLoS models are more representative of the true behavior.

Process for Generating Realistic Maps. Maps describe the natural relief and other objects present in the simulations. While drone simulators generally supply maps, those are either from arbitrary locations or even completely artificial. Thus, a well-defined process to generate realistic maps of a region of interest is important to allow the proper planning of real missions.

To that end, the DroNit project developed a semi-automatic process to generate maps with both relief and building information for usage in drone simulations. This process required geoprocessing procedures that were performed in the free Geographic Information System QGIS[12]. Process starts by converting the line-type shapefile (contour lines) with the relief elevation data of the interest region converted to a point-type shapefile and then converting it to a raster file in TIFF (Tagged Image File Format). Then, a polygon-type shapefile of the Niterói's building lots were downloaded from the Geoinformation Management System[13]. This is a online portal of the Niterói City Hall that can be used to obtain information regarding environmental, administrative and infrastructure aspects. Based on the list of lots and the information on the height of the buildings on each lot, one can create a raster with approximate elevation data of each building in the area of interest. Based on the list of lots and the information about the height of the buildings on each lot, the shapefile was edited with approximate elevation data for each building in the area of interest. Then, this shapefile were also converted to raster format. Those two raster files were combined with QGIS *Merge* tool. The result is a Digital Surface Model containing both natural geographical elevation data and approximate building data that can be loaded in Gazebo. Final resulting file contained high spatial resolution and still ran smoothly in Gazebo. Elevation data is used to simulate events such as collisions and the 3D map is also rendered to the user during simulation, providing a visual feedback of the obstacles to the pilot.

---

[12] Available at: https://www.qgis.org/.

[13] Available in Portuguese: https://www.sigeo.niteroi.rj.gov.br/.

(a) Render of the generated map.   (b) Satellite view (source: Google Maps)

Fig. 3. Render generated by Gazebo of the custom map with both relief and building elevation data created with the proposed methodology, along with a satellite view of the same area.

As an example of this process, we generated a map for the area surrounding one of the *campi* of Universidade Federal Fluminense, in Niterói. A render of this map generated by Gazebo during a simulation can be seen in Fig. 3a. The elevated structures in a more square shape at the center and at the left of the figure correspond to constructions. Conversely, in the far right of the figure it is possible to see a less uniform elevation, which corresponds to a hill. Figure 3b shows a satellite view of the same region for comparison.

This process is not perfect, as it does not take into account the precise architecture of the buildings—instead assuming they are cube-like shapes. But it provides a relatively quick methodology based on free software and data that is usually available from the City Hall and yields scenarios that account for the main obstacles in a possible drone route or in the field of view of the drone's camera when photographing a certain subject.

5.3 Improving the Communication Range of Drones

The Brazilian legislation does not allow drones to fly autonomously. Therefore, the pilot must have either visual contact of the drone or a video feedback generated by a camera. This effectively introduces a limitation on the maximum range of a drone mission, as the communication channel between the drone and the ground station must have enough QoS (Quality of Service) to allow the video feedback to provide enough *situational awareness* to the pilot. As the quality of wireless communication degrades with the distance, at some point this requirement is not met anymore.

Thus, one of the ways of increasing the drone range is by working to reduce the amount of bandwidth required for the video feedback. With lower bandwidth requirements, the wireless link between the drone and the ground station will remain feasible even at larger distances. Moreover, with bandwidth requirements are sufficiently low, some LPWAN technologies might become feasible, resulting in added range.

The bandwidth required by a compressed video stream can be reduced in a number of ways. Notably, resolution and frame rate, along with parameters of the compression itself—*e.g.*, the proportions of P, B and I frames types—, can be manipulated to achieve lower bitrates. However, reducing the bitrate by such means has the side effect of reducing the quality of the reproduced video.

Motivated by that, one of the lines of investigation of the DroNit project is evaluating how far the bitrate of the video feedback can be pushed down, while still allowing a proper situational awareness for the pilot. For that purpose, we have conducted preliminary experiments in a simulated environment with pilots of different backgrounds where we manipulate quality parameters of the video feedback and register how that has affected the ability of controlling the aircraft. Each round of the experiment consisted in asking the pilot to perform the *UAV Reaper Mk 9* mission available in the well-known *Great Planes Flight Simulator 7.5*. However, the video feedback was manipulated in real-time by a software written in C++ using the OpenCV library that selectively dropped frames in order to achieve a configurable target frame rate. For each pilot, we repeated the experiment several times with decreasing frame rates.

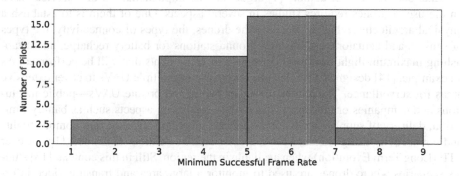

Fig. 4. Overall distribution of the minimum frame rate for which each pilot in the experiment was capable of piloting the aircraft.

In total, 32 pilots of different backgrounds took part in the experiments. Figure 4 summarizes the overall results. It shows the distribution of the minimum frame rate that allowed each pilot in the experiment to successfully complete the mission. Even at 8 FPS, all pilots, regardless of their background, were able to complete the mission. For lower frame rates, the pilots started to show more difficulty in controlling the aircraft. Still, 93.75% of the volunteers still were able to pilot the aircraft with as little as 6 FPS. Below that, success rate fell sharply, and only 2 of the 32 pilots were able to complete the mission with a video feedback of only 2 FPS.

When the results are broken-down by the background of the pilots, we noticed that the two most successful groups were professional drone pilots and gamers—on average, pilots from those groups achieved success with frame rates as low as 3 FPS. Recreational drone pilots, on the other hand, needed an average of at least 4.73 FPS to succeed in the mission.

While preliminary, those results suggest that (i) the typical frame rates used in video streaming—*e.g.*, 24 or 30 FPS—can be significantly reduced for this application, while still allowing proper situational awareness; and (ii) as expected, proper training of pilots allows for further reduction in the quality of the video feedback required for successfully controlling the aircraft. In general, that points towards a feasible—and significant—reduction of the bandwidth requirement for the communication channel between the drone and the ground station, facilitating the increase of the usable communication range.

6 Related Work

There is a vast literature available on the usage of drones for applications in smart cities. Jensen [12], for example, explores the connectivity issues related to the use of drones in smart cities and discusses how drones can improve applications such as surveillance, object detection, general purpose distributed processing applications, data collection, route planning, tracking delivery, navigation and collision prediction.

Like our work, other authors [1] argue that the implementation of a service based on the use of drones requires studies in several aspects. One of them is to establish a physical architecture, that is, choosing the drones, the types of connectivity, the types of sensors and actuators, establishing ground stations for battery recharge, and establishing maximum flight time considering the measurements that will be performed. As an example, [14] designed a framework for the use of multiple UAVs to cover extensive areas for surveillance. The authors consider public and private UAVs—public institutions and companies or citizens, respectively—analyzing aspects such as battery limitation, delivery of supplies, collision avoidance, global positioning, autonomous flights and connectivity using standard for vehicular communication (IEEE 802.11p) or over LTE (Long Term Evolution) when available in the region. Still in this context, [13] studies scenarios where drones are used to monitor a large area and transmit video information to a remote control unit using multiple hops. To maintain a strong connectivity between drones and the control unit, the authors used wireless mesh networks (IEEE 802.11 s) at fixed positions on the ground to increase the node redundancy for routing.

Giordan et al. [7] present a review of drones applied to natural hazards around the world such as landslides, floods, earthquakes, volcanic activity and wildfires. They are used to collect data from inaccessible regions, typically from images from conventional cameras, but also, in some cases, from thermal sensors and multi-spectral cameras. These RPA-gathered data are then georeferenced and processed in order to provide, for instance, environmental and geological studies, mapping different active processes at the Earth's surface and analysis of river channel vegetation.

More recently, Gohari et al. [8] systematically reviewed the literature of using drones for monitoring and surveillance in smart cities, classifying the papers into seven categories: transportation, environment, infrastructure, object or people detection, disaster management, data collection and other. Air pollution (environment) and traffic monitoring (transportation) are the aspects more studied in the recent literature. In the disaster management category, the main areas are human body detection, evacuation map building, fire detection, firefighting management and search and rescue. They also associate the categories according to the number of UAVs (multiple or single), type of UAV (mostly, with rotary wings) and the aerial sensors on board (mostly, conventional camera).

Despite being addressed by several authors and papers, the issue of how to effectively use drones for improving services in smart cities remains open on several fronts.

In particular, we note that before this and our previous work [3], little attention had been given to the particular issues of the Civil Defense usage of drones in their missions. More specifically, in this paper we tackle a number of very particular usages drones can have in this context, as well as several technical issues that must be overcome in practice.

7 Conclusion

Drones offer an impressive combination of mobility, sensing, actuation, communication and processing capabilities. Given their relative low cost and easy access, they can be valuable tools in a number of different domains. Particularly, they lend themselves well for several tasks in the context of smart cities. However, those usages might involve complex procedures, interoperability between different systems, as well as cooperation between multiple parties. In that context, drones and their applications to smart cities may benefit from information and knowledge management systems.

One concrete success case of using drones in smart cities can be found on Niterói's Civil Defense Office. For the past few years, the office has been pioneering the usage of drones for a plethora of rescue and risk prevention activities in Brazil. This paper reported on the experience of the Office in using those devices. It presented an overview of their current use cases, showing how drones have been or could be helping the Office succeed at its missions. We also documented issues reported by the Office's pilots and technicians during their years using drones, as well as other usages envisioned for those devices. We further analyzed current technical challenges that lie ahead of those future uses and discussed possible paths for realizing the drones' full potential for the Civil Defense Office.

That analysis revealed the existence of challenges in both technical and legislative aspects of drone usage. From the technical perspective, for instance, autonomy and flight range are often obstacles. While autonomy range can be tackled by more efficient battery technology and communication range issues can be mitigated by the proliferation of 5G, regulatory obstacles also need to be overcome. That depends on the modernization of the relevant legislation, but also of the cooperation between the regulatory bodies and the Civil Defense Office to find safe, yet streamlined processes, for the authorization of time-critical missions and the usage of specialized drones.

This paper also reported on preliminary results of several technical solutions being developed in the context of the DroNit project. In particular, we discussed the issue of generating NDVI images from pictures acquired from drones in an automated fashion for the analysis of vegetation coverage. We also reported on methodologies and tools developed for creating more realistic simulation environments that can be used for both planning missions and training pilots. Finally, we presented preliminary results of a study targeted at improving the range of drone missions by means of manipulating the quality of the video feedback stream provided to the pilot.

While the early results on all those fronts are encouraging, we acknowledge the need for future investigation in several aspects. Regarding the usage of drones for NDVI analysis, we are in the process of evaluating our prototype. This will help answer questions such: as how does the quality of the raw frames acquired by the inexpensive Pi Camera affects the generated NDVI? Does the solution require a second RGB camera to be carried by the drone? How does the resolution of the vegetation detection by this process compares to what is achieved today with satellite images? In terms of the proposed simulation environment, we would like to improve our communication models by also adding realistic delays to the messages transmitted between the drone and the ground station. We believe this realistic delay can be important, especially for the training of pilots. We also intend to investigate more complex propagation models that take into account obstacles, such as the natural relief and buildings, as that information is readily available during simulations. Finally, we would like to use our early results on the possibility of decreasing the quality of the video feedback to build a proof-of-concept drone with a larger communication range based on a technology such as IEEE 802.11ah.

References

1. Alsamhi, S.H., Ma, O., Ansari, M.S., Almalki, F.A.: Survey on collaborative smart drones and internet of things for improving smartness of smart cities. IEEE Access **7**, 128125–128152 (2019)
2. Ayamga, M., Akaba, S., Nyaaba, A.A.: Multifaceted applicability of drones: a review. Technol. Forecast. Soc. Chang. **167**, 120677 (2021)
3. Bastos, C.A.M., et al.: Drones for civil defense: a case study in the city of niterói. In: Proceedings of the 14th International Joint Conference on Knowledge Discovery, Knowledge Engineering and Knowledge Management - KMIS, pp. 72–82 (2022)
4. Chaudhari, B.S., Zennaro, M., Borkar, S.: LPWAN technologies: emerging application characteristics, requirements, and design considerations. Future Internet **12**(3), 46 (2020)
5. Chen, W., Liu, J., Guo, H., Kato, N.: Toward robust and intelligent drone swarm: challenges and future directions. IEEE Netw. **34**(4), 278–283 (2020)
6. Feng, Q., McGeehan, J., Tameh, E., Nix, A.: Path loss models for air-to-ground radio channels in urban environments. In: 2006 IEEE 63rd Vehicular Technology Conference, vol. 6, pp. 2901–2905 (2006)
7. Giordan, D., Hayakawa, Y., Nex, F., Remondino, F., Tarolli, P.: Review article: the use of remotely piloted aircraft systems (RPASs) for natural hazards monitoring and management. Nat. Hazard. **18**(4), 1079–1096 (2018)
8. Gohari, A., Ahmad, A.B., Rahim, R.B.A., Supa'at, A.S.M., Abd Razak, S., Gismalla, M.S.M.: Involvement of surveillance drones in smart cities: a systematic review. IEEE Access **10**, 56611–56628 (2022)
9. Hassanalian, M., Abdelkefi, A.: Classifications, applications, and design challenges of drones: a review. Prog. Aerosp. Sci. **91**, 99–131 (2017)
10. IEEE Standards Committee: IEEE Std 802.11-2016 (Revision of IEEE Std 802.11-2012): IEEE Standard for Information technology-Telecommunications and information exchange between systems Local and metropolitan area networks-Specific requirements - Part 11: Wireless LAN Medium Access Control (MAC) and Physical Layer (PHY) Specifications, December 2016
11. Jayaweera, H.M., Hanoun, S.: A dynamic artificial potential field (D-APF) UAV path planning technique for following ground moving targets. IEEE Access **8**, 192760–192776 (2020)
12. Jensen, O.B.: Drone city - power, design and aerial mobility in the age of "smart cities." Geographica Helvetica **71**(2), 67–75 (2016)
13. Katila, C.J., Di Gianni, A., Buratti, C., Verdone, R.: Routing protocols for video surveillance drones in IEEE 802.11s wireless mesh networks. In: 2017 European Conference on Networks and Communications (EuCNC), pp. 1–5 (2017)

14. Kim, H., Mokdad, L., Ben-Othman, J.: Designing UAV surveillance frameworks for smart city and extensive ocean with differential perspectives. IEEE Commun. Mag. **56**(4), 98–104 (2018)
15. Koubâa, A., Allouch, A., Alajlan, M., Javed, Y., Belghith, A., Khalgui, M.: Micro air vehicle link (MAVlink) in a nutshell: a survey. IEEE Access **7**, 87658–87680 (2019)
16. Lacage, M., Henderson, T.R.: Yet another network simulator. In: Proceedings of the 2006 Workshop on NS-3 (2006)
17. Lassabe, F., Canalda, P., Chatonnay, P., Spies, F., Baala, O.: A Friis-based calibrated model for wifi terminals positioning. In: Sixth IEEE International Symposium on a World of Wireless Mobile and Multimedia Networks, pp. 382–387 (2005)
18. Lin, X., et al.: Mobile network-connected drones: field trials, simulations, and design insights. IEEE Veh. Technol. Mag. **14**(3), 115–125 (2019)
19. de Moor, J.M., et al.: Insights on hydrothermal-magmatic interactions and eruptive processes at Poás volcano (Costa Rica) from high-frequency gas monitoring and drone measurements. Geophys. Res. Lett. **46**(3), 1293–1302 (2019)
20. Reis, L.C.D., Bernardini, F.C., Ferreira, S.B.L., Cappelli, C.: An ICT governance analysis for the digital and smart transformation of Brazilian municipalities. In: DG.O2021: The 22nd Annual International Conference on Digital Government Research, pp. 327–338 (2021)
21. Sabino, H., et al.: A systematic literature review on the main factors for public acceptance of drones. Technol. Soc. **71**, 102097 (2022)
22. Shavarani, S.M., Nejad, M.G., Rismanchian, F., Izbirak, G.: Application of hierarchical facility location problem for optimization of a drone delivery system: a case study of amazon prime air in the city of san francisco. Int. J. Adv. Manuf. Technol. **95**(9), 3141–3153 (2018)
23. Siddiqui, S.A., Fatima, N., Ahmad, A.: Comparative analysis of propagation path loss models in LTE networks. In: 2019 International Conference on Power Electronics, Control and Automation (ICPECA), pp. 1–3 (2019)
24. Swinney, C.J., Woods, J.C.: The effect of real-world interference on CNN feature extraction and machine learning classification of unmanned aerial systems. Aerospace **8**(7), 179 (2021)
25. Tucker, C.J., Townshend, J.R., Goff, T.E.: African land-cover classification using satellite data. Science **227**(4685), 369–375 (1985)

Innovation Processes and Information Technologies: A Study of Boutique Hotels in Valletta, Malta

Kristina Buhagiar[✉] [ID], Lisa A. Pace [ID], and Sandra M. Dingli [ID]

The Edward de Bono Institute for Creative Thinking and Innovation, University of Malta, Msida, Malta

{kristina.buhagiar,lisa.a.pace,sandra.m.dingli}@um.edu.mt

Abstract. Service innovation has come to represent an essential underpinning necessitated for enhanced value creation, competitiveness, idiosyncrasy, and long-term survival in contemporary contexts. Given the importance of this construct, a substantial corpus of the literature has developed and been devoted towards exploring this phenomenon. Despite increasing interest in this field, however, theoretical approaches solely dedicated towards service innovation have yet to materialize, while scholars remain divided on fundamental aspects of service innovation, e.g., the developmental paths through which innovation emerges. Compounding these issues, explorations aimed at investigating service innovation in the context of tourism enterprises remain nascent, while limited attention has been placed on investigating the role of ITs and ICTs in the innovation processes of tourism enterprises. To counteract these shortcomings and based on Buhagiar et al.'s [51] conceptual model of service innovation, this paper investigates the micro-foundation processes deployed in boutique hotels in Valletta, Malta, to reconfigure knowledge resources and establish innovation outcomes. Concurrently, this research explores the inflection points at which ITs and ICTs are deployed in the innovation processes of boutique hotels in Valletta, Malta, and examines how such technologies influence the innovation activities of these hotels.

Keywords: Service innovation · Innovation process · Web 2.0 · ITs · Boutique hotels

1 Introduction

In 2022, Malta's accommodation sector was worth approximately €486.6 million, it was responsible for employing around 7,294 individuals, and it comprised circa 215 enterprises [1]. Despite the value of this sector, however, studies aimed at exploring innovation in the context of boutique hotels, which reflects a niche yet growing global phenomenon, remain scarce [see, for example, 2, 3], both in Malta and in other geographic locations. Furthermore, while boutique hotels make for a novel and relevant context to explore the developmental paths through which service innovation occurs, especially since the sector, at a global level, is anticipated to be valued at $115.80 billion

© The Author(s), under exclusive license to Springer Nature Switzerland AG 2023
F. Coenen et al. (Eds.): IC3K 2022, CCIS 1842, pp. 334–356, 2023.
https://doi.org/10.1007/978-3-031-43471-6_16

by 2032 [4], the necessity of this research is further substantiated by recent critiques of the literature on service innovation. First, as expressed by Freni [5], "despite the amount of research on the subject [service innovation], the debate has evolved along lines not always shared by all the scholars who, frequently, propose different conceptualizations, definitions and theories regarding service innovation; there is no common core concept at the moment" [p. 154]. As a result, service innovation has come to mirror an ill-defined and poorly understood construct [6]. Moreover, empirical analysis on service innovation has largely occurred in silos and void of cumulative knowledge development, leading to a fragmented field of exploration [6]. As a result, service innovation has come to represent "everything and nothing at the same time" [7, p. 95], while the paths through which service innovation develops remain underexplored [8, 9]. Compounding this, only a paucity of studies have investigated the role of technologies in the innovation processes of accommodation provisions [see, for example, 10–15], with Kroh et al. [16] having concluded that "to date, research does not fully understand the underlying mechanisms through which IT improves the firm's innovation performance" [p. 720]. To overcome these shortfalls, this study aspires to:

1. Explore how innovation develops in boutique hotels in Valletta, Malta through knowledge resources.
2. Investigate the role of ITs and ICTs in the innovation processes of boutique hotels in Valletta, Malta.

This paper is an extended version of Buhagiar's [7] published paper and results, however, in this specific paper, emphasis is placed on the role of ITs and ICTs in the innovation processes of boutique hotels. Thus, this paper both compliments and broadens Buhagiar's [7] multi-level analysis of the innovation process.

The novelty of this paper is two-fold. First, this paper presents an in-depth overview of the innovation process, this counters the reductionist models often set forth in the innovation literature, where innovation tends to be portrayed as a simplified construct, and the innovation process is generally reduced to five or six straightforward processes [see, for example, 8, 9, 25, 63]. Thus, the innovation process illustrated in this paper portrays the innovation process for what it is, i.e., complex and exhaustive, leading to a realistic representation of the state, nature and structure of innovation activities in boutique hotels. Second, this study directly addresses Kroh et al.'s [16] call for additional investigations on the use of ITs in the innovation process.

The results and implications presented in this study are of significance to both scholars and practitioners alike. For scholars, the innovation process model presented in this study may be used as a basis to test innovation processes in other accommodation provisions, allowing for the development of a process model with sector-wide applicability. For practitioners, this model may be used to guide innovation efforts. Likewise, practitioners may choose to use the large array of idea generation stimuli detailed in the model as a basis to kickstart innovation efforts. Second, this paper demonstrates how Web 2.0 technologies are deployed in boutique hotels to facilitate innovation processes. These findings may support micro- or small-sized enterprises with limited financial resources better manage both creativity and innovation processes. Last, this paper extends the literature in the field by detailing the mechanisms through which different ITs and ICTs contribute towards innovation processes in boutique hotels.

This paper is structured into six sections. Starting with Sect. 2, a critical discussion on the literature pertaining to knowledge resources and innovation, and knowledge management and information and communication technologies is presented. Following this, Sect. 3 addresses the philosophical assumptions and the methodological underpinnings applied in this investigation to collect and analyze empirical data. Section 4 presents a detailed discussion on the results of data analysis, with importance placed on discussing both the micro-foundation processes deployed in boutique hotels to attain innovation outcomes, and the role of ITs and ICTs in the innovation process. Section 5 presents the discussion and conclusion of this research, and Sect. 6 addresses the limitations of this study and areas for future research.

2 Theoretical Background

Section 2 presents a critical review of the literature grounding this study. In this Section, two core streams of the literature are discussed. First, Sub-Sect. 2.1 discusses the literature on knowledge resources and innovation. This is followed by Sub-Sect. 2.2, where a review of the literature on knowledge management and information and communication technologies is presented.

2.1 Knowledge Resources and Innovation

As economic landscapes become increasingly more complex to navigate, unpredictable, fragile, and turbulent, with a good example of this reflected in the Covid-19 pandemic, which exerted unforeseeable negative impacts on SMEs [see, for example, 17, 18], and as societal problems expand, e.g., climate change, decolonization, poverty, and food and water scarcity [19], the importance and relevance of innovation has become increasingly pervasive.

In the tourism industry and specifically, the accommodation sector, which is the focus of this research, innovation, particularly technology-based innovation has played a key role in advancing the global consumer environment, it has changed the methods through which consumers travel, it has influenced the purchasing and consumption behaviors of customers, and exerted an impact on post-purchase evaluations [20]. Furthermore, innovation in tourism and hospitality has been found to increase performance efficiency and customer experiences [20], it has been associated with higher degrees of added value, and it has been denoted to enhance competitive differentiation at the destination-level through strategies characterized by novelty [21]. Given that hotels comprise the largest sub-sector in the tourism industry, with revenues in this [hotel] sector reaching circa $362.90 billion in 2022 [22], innovation has come to represent "a major topic of interest in the field [hospitality and tourism]" [20, p. 2]. However, despite increasing traction in this domain of investigation [see, for example, 20, 21, 23, 24], "academic studies in the field of tourism innovation are still new compared to other sectors" [23, p. 16]. As a result, the theoretical foundations of innovation in accommodation provisions are still subject to debate.

Despite this shortcoming, increasing importance in the literature on innovation is being attributed to the role of knowledge resources in the innovation process. For example, in one of his seminal works, Nonaka [25] stressed that "innovation can be better understood as a process in which the organization creates and defines problems and then actively develops new knowledge to solve them" [p. 14]. Likewise, Quintane et al. [26] stated that "knowledge is a pre-requisite for the innovation process to occur" [p. 936], and Grant [27] expressed that "knowledge is the preeminent factor of production—it is [the] main source of productivity in the advanced economy and the primary basis for generating economic rent" [p. 542]. Thus, in contemporary knowledge economies intellectual capital has become the core resource necessitated for value creation [28, 29].

Similar to traditional definitions of innovation [6], this study positions innovation to reflect novel combinations of new or existing knowledge resources, with innovations including both the outcome of innovation efforts, and the knowledge-based processes deployed and exploited by individuals to attain such outcomes [26]. The relevance and importance of knowledge resources in the innovation processes of tourism organizations has been substantiated by several studies.

For example, a number of empirical analyses have reported and provided substantiating evidence for the presence of positive relationships between knowledge acquired through customers and innovation activities. In this respect, Sørensen and Jensen's [30] research on interactive and unstructured service encounters between hotel employees and customers located in a boutique hotel in Copenhagen, Denmark, found that customer-employee interactions enhanced knowledge creation processes, with knowledge generated via these interactions having led to the development of in-house information utilities. Similarly, in hotels in Spain, knowledge and feedback derived through customers was found to enhance service innovations and improve the overall competitiveness of hotels [31]. Likewise, Tefera and Dlamini's [32] analysis of small- to medium-sized hotels in Eswatini, Africa, found that personnel in the explored hotels, including hotel owners, directors, middle managers, supervisors, and hotel staff, predominantly generated ideas through customer feedback and by visiting other entertainment establishments. Likewise, several other studies have provided evidence to substantiate the link between employee-customer interactions in hotels and innovative behaviors [see, for example, 33, 34].

While customers and access to their knowledge resources have been found to play a core role in the innovation processes of hotels, a number of studies have also illustrated how innovations in accommodation provisions tend to be catalyzed by knowledge acquired through networks. For example, Saxena's [35] empirical analysis of tourism stakeholders in the Peak District National Park located in the United Kingdom, revealed that networks and relational ties between stakeholders acted as an avenue for entrepreneurial activities and the development of new resources. Likewise, Halme's [36] empirical analysis of tourism networks in Alcúdia, Spain, revealed that networks acted as a basis to counteract common problems in the tourism sector, e.g., environmental degradation, with these networks having provided tourism stakeholders with the means to develop common strategies to counteract prevalent problems in the sector. The pivotal role played by networks in the innovation processes of tourism enterprises have been further substantiated by several studies [see, for example, 37, 38], with networks emerging to reflect "a repository of competence and knowledge, and parts of this knowledge are unique and inimitable, and crucial for the development of products and services" [39, p. 6].

In addition, from an intra-organizational perspective, several studies in the tourism literature have denoted how individual-level and group-level intra-organizational knowledge resources and collaborative routines tend to play a fundamental role in the innovation processes of accommodation provisions. For example, at the individual-level, Engen and Magnusson's [40] analysis of front-line employees revealed that employees generally generated novel ideas through daily work routines and by reporting problems. Moreover, Liu and Cheng's [41] empirical analysis of B&B owners in Taiwan revealed that at the individual-level, B&B owners often relied on several [knowledge-based] stimuli to generate ideas including, for example, the owners' lifestyle, customers, market information, external knowledge, business expansion needs, policy, and familiar partners. Furthermore, Nieves et al.'s [42] research concluded that within hotels, observation and imitation often represented viable paths to identify innovation opportunities. In addition to the preceding, a number of scholarly articles have also illustrated how intra-organizational knowledge sharing routines are generally necessitated to exploit individual-level knowledge. For example, Engen and Magnusson [40] illustrated that intra-organizational group discussions were generally necessitated to share knowledge, generate ideas, and validate ideas. Similarly, Hu et al.'s [43] empirical analysis of international hotels located in Taiwan concluded that intra-organizational knowledge sharing activities exerted a positive impact on service innovation performance, and Nordli's [44] analysis of Norwegian tourism organizations revealed that cross-functional teams generally aided in organizational innovation.

Given the fundamental role of knowledge resources in accommodation provisions, scholarly works have also illustrated the importance of knowledge management capabilities in hotels. In this regard, Salem's [45] analysis of chain-managed hotels located in Egypt revealed that knowledge management capabilities positively impacted both organizational performance and innovation within the investigated hotels. Likewise, Baytok et al.'s [46] exploration of thermal hotels located in Turkey revealed that knowledge management processes generally aided in the acquisition of competitive advantages, while such processes also enhanced service quality and consistency. With knowledge and the management of this resource reflecting an increasingly vital basis for innovation in tourism enterprises, information and communication technologies are progressively featuring as promising tools for enhanced knowledge management practices. This is further discussed in the following section.

2.2 Knowledge Management and Information and Communication Technologies

Technologies, including but not limited to, information technology (IT) and information and communication technologies (ICTs), have exerted an impact on the operations and strategic management of hospitality and tourism enterprises [47]. For example, the inception of the internet not only catalyzed boundary-less economic ecosystems, however, it has also transformed the competitive dynamics prevalent within markets [48]. Due to intensified rivalry and exponential ubiquity, which reflect byproducts of interconnectivity, tourism organizations are increasingly compelled to cultivate idiosyncratic strategies for enhanced differentiation [48], with technologies often positioned to represent essential components and drivers of heterogeneity. By way of implementing and exploiting technologies, tourism organizations generally reap several benefits, including augmented processes, and flexibility in establishing customizable services and experiences [12]. Furthermore, technologies have also been found to provide tourism organizations with access to unprecedented data, information, and knowledge concerning customers and market conditions [48]. A subsequent frontier where technology has proven to be instrumental in tourism organizations is in the realm of knowledge management.

According to Okumus [14], "knowledge can be seen as one of the key assets for hospitality organizations. Therefore, KM [knowledge management] can help hospitality organizations create and sustain a competitive advantage. Use of IT applications can assist in creating, storing, transferring and using tacit and explicit knowledge" [p. 64]. Through IT tools and applications for knowledge management, tourism organizations purposefully prioritize interconnectivity between employees and customers, and among employees in different departments, with these technologies often aiding in information and knowledge sharing, while concurrently contributing towards the development of an organizational memory [11, 13, 49, 50]. Through enhanced knowledge management processes and systems, hospitality organizations increasingly benefit from access to relevant, up-to-date, and easily accessible information, which is positioned to facilitate these organizations solve problems and concurrently attain their goals [49].

Given the rapid development of technology, tourism organizations may implement a variety of IT and ICT-based knowledge management tools, these include, for example, employee competence databases, video conferencing tools, data mining tools, decision support tools, enterprise portal sites, groupware for communal discussions, and customer relationship management programs [14]. Each of these tools may be deployed in tourism organizations for a variety of knowledge management purposes. For example, hospitality organizations generally implement intranets and expert systems to capture and store both tacit and explicit knowledge, they have also been found to implement databases and intranets to facilitate discovery processes [14]. Likewise, these organizations implement video conferencing tools, and electronic meeting systems to facilitate knowledge sharing activities among employees [14]. Through these tools, tourism organizations are able to locate and create new knowledge, while they are also able accumulate tacit knowledge [14]. Furthermore, these tools aid in providing hospitality organizations with richer insights concerning customers and their respective needs [14]. For example, Neuhofer et al.'s [12] analysis of Hotel Lugano Dante's guest relationship management system, which provided the hotel with an overview of the entire customer journey, equipped the hotel with the ability to manage all service encounters, it also enhanced personalization, and empowered employees to anticipate and respond to the changing needs of guests. According to the authors, by way of this software, "experiences are no longer static and pre-designed in advance by the hotel provider, but are dynamically co-created and personalized between guests and employees at the service encounter in real time" [12, p. 249]. Similarly, Bharwani and Mathew's [10] analysis of luxury hotels in India revealed that smart IOT in-room technologies, e.g., virtual concierges, robotics, and self-service technologies, promoted guest engagement while simultaneously improving satisfaction levels. In addition, the author's [10] results also revealed that "at a more macro-level, technology can be used for understanding emerging trends in the hospitality industry as a whole and tailoring service innovations to match customer demand to create superlative guest experience" [p. 173].

The benefits of IT tools in hotels have also been explicated by Nieves and Oso-rio's [13] empirical analysis, which found that in hotels located in Spain, organizational knowledge influenced the integration capabilities of the investigated hotels, while the deployment of IT tools in hotels was found to exert an indirect impact on the integration capabilities of such hotels. Furthermore, IT tools were noted to exert a direct impact on management innovations within the explored accommodation provisions [13]. The author's results also illustrated that "IT development in service firms and management innovation performance is more strongly pronounced when the company has a greater knowledge integration capability of its organizational knowledge" [13, p. 30]. There-fore, these results accentuate the close interrelationship between IT use and integration capabilities in hotels, with innovation emerging as somewhat contingent on a hotel's fluidity and proficiency in both IT tools/systems and knowledge integration capaci-ties. Likewise, Jalilvand et al.'s [11] analysis of hotels situated in Iran revealed that the deployment of IT tools led to effective coordination, collaboration, enhanced effi-ciency, and the development of co-creational value in hotel supply chains. According to the author's results, IT competence in hotels also allowed for augmented supplier relationships, expedited decision-making capacities, and enhanced operational as well as financial performance [11]. Moreover, Sigala and Chalkiti's [15] analysis of Greek tourism professionals revealed that social media usage, e.g., microblogs, personal blogs, and social networks, positively impacted creativity, with social media platforms used as a basis to acquire, co-create, and share new knowledge.

Despite the important role of knowledge resources in the innovation processes of hotels, and in spite of the far-reaching benefits of ITs and ICTs in hotels, to date, a holistic picture or process model grounded in empirical data, which illustrates the paths through which knowledge resources are transformed into innovation outcomes at the micro-foundation level, and in the context of accommodation provisions, has yet to materialize. In part, this gap in the literature may be due to the nature of innovation, with innovation in service organizations often recognized to represent "a complex construct, the emergence of which is perceived as heterogeneous, situated and path-dependent on hard-to-replicate intra- and inter-organizational knowledge resources and processes" [51, p. 119]. While the complexity interlinked to service innovation may represent one potential obstacle which may have impeded the development of process models in this context, this shortcoming has been exacerbated by on-going debates concerning the definitional framing of service innovation [see, for example, 5, 6, 52], conceptual confusion regarding the underlying foundations of service innovation [see, for example, 6, 53], and a prevalent manufacturing-bias in innovation studies [see, for example, 6, 52, 54, 55]. As a result, this has led to a scenario where "knowledge has been built in silos and not through cumulative knowledge development" [6, p. 114]. Second, compounding the limitations of the literature on service innovation, the literature on tourism is comparatively nascent, with this field of investigation having emerged in the last 40 years [56], and the literature on innovation in this context having emerged even more recently, in 1992 [21]. Furthermore, according to Singh et al. [57] most explorations on innovation have focused on investigating this phenomenon in the healthcare and IT sectors, "while few studies have investigated hospitality" [p. 510]. In addition to these obstacles, and notwithstanding the fact that the literature on ITs and ICTs has increased [see, for example, 24, 58–61], there is an overarching divide between this literature and the literature on service innovation process modelling [see, for example, 25, 62, 63]. As a result, not only is the structure and nature of the innovation process of hospitality organizations underexplored, however, limited attention has been placed on investigating the role of ITs and ICTs in this process. To counteract these shortcomings, this study aimed to investigate the following research questions:

1. How does innovation develop in boutique hotels in Valletta, Malta through knowledge resources?
2. What is the role of ITs and ICTs in the innovation processes of boutique hotels in Valletta, Malta?

3 Methodology

Section 3, which comprises two sub-sections, presents the philosophical foundations and the methodological underpinnings applied in this research to collect and analyze data. Starting with Sub-Sect. 3.1, an overview of the conceptual model applied in this research and the corresponding philosophical assumptions employed are addressed. Following this, Sub-Sect. 3.2 presents a discussion on the research design and the data collection techniques applied in this study to collect data from research participants, this is followed by a discussion on the data analysis protocol employed to evaluate and interpret data.

3.1 Conceptual Model and Philosophical Underpinnings

In order to explore the innovation processes of boutique hotels in Valletta, Malta, and to understand the role of ITs and ICTs in this process, this study applied Buhagiar et al.'s [51] conceptual knowledge-based model of service innovation [see Fig. 1 below]. This model was selected, applied, and tested in this research for two core reasons. First, the model's theoretical assumptions position knowledge to mirror the most important of the firm's resources [27]. This assumption directly aligns to Research Question 1, where the core unit of analysis is knowledge. Second, the model was designed to provide a comprehensive conceptual representation of the micro-foundation processes deployed in tourism organizations to transform knowledge resources into innovation outputs, there-fore, the model was perceived to act as an exhaustive and sound basis upon which to test innovation processes.

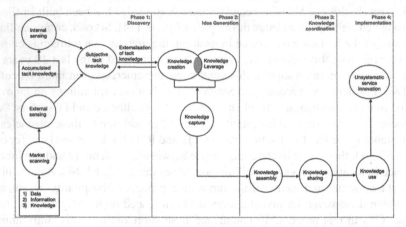

Fig. 1. Knowledge-based model of service innovation [Source: 51, p. 121].

To investigate Buhagiar et al.'s [51] model and to explore the research questions established in this study, the philosophical underpinnings applied in this research com-prised a constructivist interpretive paradigm. This philosophical orientation was selected as it is able to account for the socially constructed nature of knowledge resources and innovation processes, while it places significant emphasis on exploring the role and impact of context and situatedness on innovation activities [64, 65].

3.2 Research Design, Data Collection Technique and Data Analysis

In line with the philosophical underpinnings of the constructivist interpretive paradigm, the research design implemented in this study was that of the qualitative methodology. This methodological approach was selected as it provided the basis necessitated for research participants to detail knowledge-based micro-foundation processes from a per-sonal, in-depth, and context-dependent perspective [66]. Thus, this approach enabled the researchers to capture and account for the subjective, heterogeneous, and social nature of knowledge-based processes and innovation. To collect data, the researchers estab-lished a semi-structured interview template based on Buhagiar et al.'s [51] model and an extensive narrative literature review of scholarly articles on innovation in tourism organizations. The interview template used to collect data in this study comprised six core sections, and 36 questions. The scope of each section comprising the interview template is outlined in Fig. 2 below.

The sample populations comprising this study included both boutique hotel owners and managers. In this regard, the researchers chose to interview boutique hotel owners as several studies have explicated the impact of owners, their decision-making rights, and centralized power on innovation processes [see, for example, 67, 68]. Similarly, boutique hotel managers were selected for inclusion in this study as these individuals have been acknowledged to play a core role in strategy development activities [see, for example, 69], and they have also been found to impact the culture and climate for innovation in organizations [see, for example, 63, 70]. In order to identify relevant boutique hotels, and boutique hotel owners and managers, the researchers applied both purposive and convenience sampling techniques.

Interview section and title	Aim of section
Section 1: Demographic data	This section aimed to investigate the demographic composition of interviewees, including their age, level of education, (prior) industry experience, and the number of years in the respective role in the boutique hotel being explored.
Section 2: Assessing the external environment prior to and during Covid-19	This section was established to explore the industry dynamics present in the boutique hotel sector in Valletta, Malta, prior to and during Covid-19. Questions in this section aimed to investigate the nature of the boutique hotel sector in Valletta, Malta, the trajectory of the sector's development, and whether and how industry dynamics, and changes in these dynamics due to Covid-19, may have impacted micro-level and firm-level processes for knowledge transformation and innovation.
Section 3: Role and importance of innovation and knowledge resources in boutique hotels	This section aimed to investigate the meaning interviewees attributed towards the terminology 'innovation' in boutique hotels in Valletta, Malta. In addition, this section sought to gain an understanding of the different role/s personnel in boutique hotels in Valletta, Malta, played in the innovation process.
Section 4: Innovation process prior to Covid-19	This section directly explored the micro-foundation and firm-level processes implemented by interviewees in boutique hotels in Valletta, Malta, to transform knowledge resources into innovations prior to Covid-19.
Section 5: Innovation process during Covid-19	Similar to section 4, this section sought to investigate the micro-foundation and firm-level processes implemented by interviewees in boutique hotels in Valletta, Malta, to transform knowledge resources into innovations, however, during Covid-19.
Section 6: Innovation process when developing the boutique hotel	This section, which was specifically designed for boutique hotel owners, aimed to investigate how knowledge resources were transformed into innovation/s prior to the opening of each respective boutique hotel.

Fig. 2. Scope of the sections in the interview template.

Following submission of the interview template and letters of consent to the Research Ethics Board at the University of Malta, data collection took place between the 4th August 2021 and 2nd May 2022 in Valletta, Malta. In total, 25 interviews were conducted with boutique hotel owners and managers from 14 boutique hotels located in Valletta, Malta. Out of these 25 interviews, 7 interviews were held virtually due to Covid-19 restrictions, and 18 interviews were held in-person. Interviews were audio recorded and conducted in the English language. Each interview lasted approximately 74 minutes, and the total number of recorded minutes equated 1,923.98 minutes. In order to analyze data, each interview recording was transcribed in-verbatim. Following transcription, the researchers applied six rounds of coding to analyze data, including open coding, axial coding, structural coding, provisional coding, causation coding, and the constant comparative method. Based the results obtained through semi-structured interviews, the following section sets forth a discussion concerning the core findings which emerged through data collection and analysis efforts.

4 Results

Section 4 presents a discussion on the results of the empirical findings collected and analyzed in this research. This Section comprises three sub-sections. Starting with Sub-Sect. 4.1, a discussion on the attributes comprising the research participants involved in this study is presented. This is followed by Sub-Sect. 4.2, where a discussion on the individual-level processes deployed by boutique hotel employees and owners to transform knowledge resources into innovation outcomes is presented. Last, Sub-Sect. 4.3 explicates how research participants used ITs and ICTs in the innovation process.

4.1 Sample Attributes

In total, 14 boutique hotels (BHs) located in Valletta, Malta, comprised this study, with hotels having opened between 2014 and 2021. From the 14 hotels, 25 interviews were conducted. In this regard, 16 interviews were held with boutique hotel managers (BHE) and 9 interviews were held with boutique hotel owners (BHO). From the 14 hotels, the authors managed to conduct interviews with both BHOs and BHMs in 9 hotels, while interviews with 2 BHMs were held in 2 hotels, and interviews with only 1 BHM were held in 3 boutique hotels. The average of age interviewees was 41 years of age, while the sample comprised more male participants (n = 16 interviewees) than female participants (n = 9 interviewees). Furthermore, 9 respondents in the sample were foreign nationals, while the majority of respondents were Maltese nationals (n = 16 interviewees). In addition, out of the 25 interviewees in this study, 18 interviewees comprised prior experience in the tourism sector while, for 7 interviewees, their current role in the respective boutique hotel mirrored the start of their experience in the sector. Out of the 14 BHs investigated hotels in this research, three differing ownership structures were identified, these are independently owned boutique hotels, which comprised 9 hotels (BH1, BH2, BH3, BH4, BH5, BH6, BH7, BH8, BH9), chain-owned boutique hotels, which consisted of 2 hotels (BH10, BH11), and multi-sector group-owned boutique hotels, which encompassed 3 hotels (BH12, BH13, BH14). Due to the ethical protocol endorsed in this study, pseudonyms have been allocated to hotels and interviewees, these are outlined in Table 1 below.

Table. 1. Pseudonyms allocated to hotels and interviewees

Acronym	Meaning
BH	Boutique Hotel
BHO	Boutique Hotel Owner
BHE	Boutique Hotel Manager

Based on the ownership structures of BHs, to distinguish hotels, these have been attributed numbers ranging from 1 to 14, e.g., boutique hotel 1 equates BH1. Likewise, to interlink BH owners and managers to their respective hotels, the same numerical logic was applied, i.e., the manager of BH1 is denoted by the acronym BHE1.1, similarly, the owner from this respective hotel is referred to as BHO1.1.

4.2 Knowledge-Reconfiguration Micro-Foundation Processes

This section sets forth a critical discussion concerning the individual-level processes deployed by BHEs and BHOs to transform knowledge resources into innovation outcomes. Due to the small sample size of respondents in this study, the results discussed in the following sections lack generalizability, thus, these findings are only applicable to the investigated BHs.

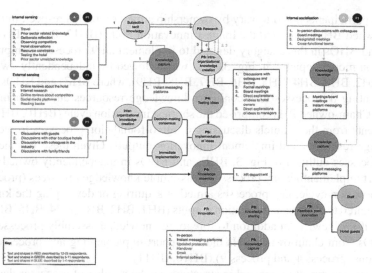

Fig. 3. Micro-Foundation Knowledge Processes Implemented in Boutique Hotels in Valletta, Malta. [Updated and adapted from: 7, p. 100].

Path A: Internal Sensing		Path B: External Sensing	
Travel	• Acted as a basis for copying and adapting ideas to fit the local context (imitated innovation) • Acted as a source of inspiration for the development of new ideas • Acted as a source of learning, with accumulated knowledge used at a later date to improve the hotel	Online reviews about the hotel	• Acted as a basis for identifying problems in the hotel and developing solutions for improvement • Acted as a basis to understand customer expectations and to adapt by refining the service on offer • Customer suggestions acted as a source of new ideas
Prior sector related knowledge	• Lessons learned and ideas developed by respondents in previous contexts directly imported into new hotel contexts (imitated innovation) • Prior knowledge acted as a guide for the development of viable ideas	Internet searches	• Acted as a basis to identify the latest trends in the industry • Acted as a source of inspiration to stimulate the development of ideas • Acted as a basis to identify areas for improvement
Deliberate reflection	• Acted as a basis to challenge long-held assumptions and conventional ways of doing things	Online reviews about competitors	• Acted as a basis to understand the weaknesses of competitors and develop ideas for better service offerings • Acted as a basis to unravel customer expectations and develop ideas to satisfy customer expectations
Observing competitors	• Acted as a basis for copying ideas (imitated innovation) • Acted as a source of inspiration for the development of new ideas • Acted as a benchmark to improve service offerings	Social media platforms	• Acted as a source of inspiration for the development of new ideas
Hotel observations	• On-site observations led to the identification of areas for improvement	Reading books	• Acted as a source of inspiration for the development of new ideas
Resource constraints	• Spatial constraints acted as a catalyst for the development of novel ideas		
Testing the hotel	• Feedback gained through testing the hotel acted as an avenue for identify areas for improvement		
Prior sector unrelated knowledge	• Unrelated knowledge gained through different experiences acted as a basis to identify areas for improvement in the hotel		
Path C: External Socialisation		Path D: Internal Socialisation	
Discussions with guests	• Customers provided hotel personnel with in-person feedback on areas for improvement • Customers provided hotel personnel with an overview of daily experiences, leading to the development of new service provisions or collaborations with market actors	In-person discussions with colleagues	• Acted as a method to co-create new knowledge and develop ideas
Discussions with other boutique hotels	• Acted as a basis to share common problems and to co-create solutions	Board meetings	
Discussions with colleagues in the industry	• Ex-colleagues acted as a soundboard to discuss ideas, market trends, and industry changes	Designated meetings	
Discussions with family/friends	• Acted as an avenue to acquire different perspectives • Acted as a source of inspiration for the development of new ideas	Cross-functional teams	

Key:
- Text in RED: described by 12-25 respondents.
- Text in GREEN: described by 5-11 respondents.
- Text in BLUE: described by 1-4 respondents

Fig. 4. Idea Generation Processes in Boutique Hotels in Valletta, Malta. [Source: 7, p. 100].

In line with Fig. 3 above, in this study, at the individual-level, BHEs and BHOs (n = 25 respondents) reported implementing, in total, 9 processes to transform knowledge resources into innovation outcomes, with the total number of processes implemented by research participants noted to vary by ownership structure. In this respect, multi-sector group-owned BHs comprised the longest innovation cycle (BH12, BH13, BH14), with BHEs and BHOs in this category denoted to implement all 9 processes comprising the innovation model depicted in Fig. 3. This was followed by independently owned BHs (BH1, BH2, BH3, BH4, BH5, BH6, BH7, BH8, BH9), where BHEs and BHOs reported implementing 8 processes to reconfigure knowledge resources and attain innovation outputs. Chain-owned BHs comprised the shortest innovation cycle (BH10, BH11), with respondents from these hotels discussing 6 micro-foundation processes to reconfigure knowledge resources and implement innovation outputs. Given these variances, from the 9 processes outlined in Fig. 3, BHEs and BHOs in independently owned BHs did not report implementing any processes to assemble knowledge resources (process 6) in their innovation cycle, i.e., processes aimed at acquiring or developing the knowledge bases required to effectuate innovation outputs (BH1, BH2, BH3, BH4, BH5, BH6, BH7, BH8, BH9). Likewise, in addition to foregoing knowledge assembly processes, BHEs and BHOs from chain-owned BHs did not report implementing any processes to test innovations (process 4 and process 9) (BH10, BH11).

Despite the impact of ownership structures on the number of processes deployed in BHs to transform knowledge resources into innovation outputs, 5 processes emerged as central to the innovation cycles of all BHs (BH1, BH2, BH3, BH4, BH5. BH6, BH7, BH9, BH10, BH11, BH12, BH13, BH14), these included idea generation processes (process 1), research processes (process 2), intra-organizational knowledge creation processes (process 3), decision making processes (process 5), and implementation processes (process 7). Subsequent to the preceding processes, BHs infrequently implemented knowledge assembly processes (process 6) and knowledge sharing and capture processes (process 8) (BH12, BH13, BH14), while these hotels seldom implemented processes to test ideas (process 4) (BH2, BH12, BH13) and acquire feedback post-innovation (process 9) (BH2, BH5, BH7, BH8, BH12).

What these results illustrate is that notwithstanding the fact that innovation in BHs may be grounded in 5 fundamental processes, ownership structures in BHs seemed to exert an influence on the nature and structure of the innovation process. In this respect, multi-sector group-owned and independently owned BHs comprised the longest innovation cycles, with several steps implemented to gauge innovations prior to their rollout and following their implementation. Alternatively, in chain-owned BHs, innovation cycles were comparatively shorter, this is due to the fact that such hotels seem to have adopted a 'first-to-market' stance, with testing, both pre- and post-innovation, seemingly not realized in these accommodation provisions. Furthermore, these results also illustrate that while common patterns of actions may be interlinked to the innovation processes of BHs, effectively, several paths may be used to transform knowledge resources into innovation outputs. Thus, innovation processes in BHs align to the principles of equifinality, where numerous paths may be used and applied by BHEs and BHOs to transform knowledge resources into productive resources, i.e., innovation outputs. A perfect example of this is elucidated in the idea generation process (process 1), where BHEs and BHOs (n = 25 respondents) discussed using 21 stimuli to generate ideas. Therefore, although knowledge resources were found to underpin the innovation processes of BHs, and despite the fact that innovation processes in BHs may be disaggregated into 5 core processes, in itself, innovation in BHs represented a highly complex, heterogeneous, and situated construct.

Further compounding the complexity of the innovation process in BHs is the fact that 'igniting' innovation via creative ideas emerged as inherently contingent on the subjective tacit knowledge of employees and their motivations to share ideas with intra-organizational personnel (process 3), see Figs. 3 and 4. Thus, unless BHEs and BHOs are willing to externalize their ideas, these ideas will inherently remain in the minds of such individuals. The human-centric and personal nature of idea generation processes (process 1) and externalization processes (process 3) in BHs implies that BHs are somewhat contingent on intellectual capital to kickstart innovation activities. The personal, subjective, and complex nature of idea generation processes was explicated by several respondents in this research, with BHEs and BHOs suggesting that what resides within one's mind may prove to be invaluable for cultivating innovations, however, ultimately, unless [verbally] externalized, these ideas cannot be capitalized. For example, BHE12.1 asserted that "I have adopted ideas that I got from a hotel in Austria, [and] a hotel in Rome, but that is something I would do out of my own will, because I am very passionate about it". Similarly, BHE8.1 stated that "it is the experience that brings the change and the innovation". Likewise, BHE1.1 stated that "I always like to challenge myself, and I always, twice a week, I spend around 30 min speaking to myself during the evening trying to understand what can I do to improve, and what is the next step". Aside from reflecting the extent to which idea generation processes are 'individualized' and bound to one's cognition, these findings also illustrate that idea generation processes are most likely to occur in a sporadic and unprecedented manner. Therefore, in BHs, innovations emerged as contingent on both the "cognitive capacities of boutique hotel owners and managers/supervisors, as well as their willingness to externalize and share their subjective tacit knowledge with other personnel" [7, p. 99].

Based on these findings, certain inferences concerning the micro-foundation processes used to transform knowledge resources into innovation outcomes in BHs in Valletta, Malta, may be drawn. First, in the investigated BHs, intellectual capital and the capacity of such capital to generate and externalize ideas, proved to mirror invaluable resources necessitated to kickstart innovation activities. Second, in BHs, knowledge resources reflected the core productive resource grounding the innovation process, with idiosyncratic combinations and recombinations of both explicit and tacit knowledge resources used by BHEs and BHOs to identify innovation opportunities and seize such opportunities. Third, processes 1 to 3, as outlined in Fig. 3, mirror highly personal, subjective, and heterogeneous processes, as a result, in the majority of BHs, these processes were found to ensue in an unmethodical manner, with BHEs and BHOs noted to use a combination of paths to develop and externalize (share) novel ideas. Counter to this, processes 4 to 9 reflected comparatively linear and impersonal processes. Fourth, while innovations in BHs may be rooted in 5 core processes, in this study, ownership structures and variances in such structures, were denoted to impact the number and types of processes implemented in BHs to transform knowledge resources into innovation outcomes.

4.3 Role of IT and ICTs in the Innovation Processes of Boutique Hotels

In this research, ITs and ICTs, especially Web 2.0 technologies, were predominantly used by BHEs and BHOs in three processes comprising Fig. 3, these are idea generation processes (process 1), research processes (process 2), and during knowledge sharing and capture processes (process 8).

During the idea generation phase (process 1), BHEs (n = 13 respondents) and BHOs (n = 7 respondents) predominantly relied on the internet and several social media platforms, i.e., Web 2.0 technologies, to stimulate idea generation processes, and to identify trends in the market and opportunities for innovation. For example, BHE1.1 stated that "nowadays you have access to so much information on the internet that it is amazing. You can understand trends, you can understand the opinion of people". Likewise, BHE14.1 asserted that "I like to read a lot, I read a lot of blogs, and I try to keep up to date with the latest trends, the latest innovations, and to be honest, I am constantly looking at new ways of doing things". The internet, and the different functionalities of this portal, which provided respondents with the ability to read blogs, customer reviews, and access different interest groups, was found to act as an invaluable starting point for innovation activities, with this type of ICT ultimately empowering respondents to either "copy-and-paste" successful innovations implemented in other contexts, or to act as a trigger for creative thinking. In addition to the internet, several respondents discussed how social networking sites and digital communication platforms acted as a basis to inspire ideas. For example, BHE2.2 asserted that "well, sometimes, you go through the social media, I mean, I am on TikTok, and Instagram, and sometimes you see something and you're like 'oh, okay, this is a good idea to try for breakfast'". Similarly, BHO11.1 asserted that "I do a lot of research on Instagram and Pinterest, you know? Jien naf [I don't know], luxury bathrooms, for example, and you try look things up". In this research, different ITs and ICTs, including but not limited to, different content on the internet, blogs, LinkedIn, Facebook, Instagram, Pinterest, and TikTok, proved particularly essential to generate ideas via external sensing activities (path B Fig. 3), with access to online reviews [about the respective hotels] featuring as the most essential method to mine for ideas, identify consumer needs and areas for improvement in the respective hotels (see Fig. 4). Moreover, due to the ubiquitous and domestic nature of these ICTs and ITs, i.e., Web 2.0 technologies, with these platforms presenting themselves as practical and widely used components of every-day-life, respondents asserted that whether out of deliberate action or not, at some point they would likely stumble across targeted posts. For example, BHO7.1 stressed that "nowadays, if you go on Instagram or Facebook, you can't help but be bombarded into seeing what everybody else is doing, whether it's something in the culinary field, or hotel trends, or designs in hotels, or facilities. The media is constantly giving you information about what is happening out there". Thus, even sublime and not necessarily intentional exposure to different online platforms provided respondents with some sense of understanding of current trends in the sector.

Another method through which ITs and ICTs supported idea generation processes in BHs is by facilitating intra- and inter-organizational socialization activities. Particularly in independently owned BHs, instant messaging platforms, such as WhatsApp, were used as a basis to share ideas, discuss communal problems, and as a basis to co-create solutions with inter-organizational actors from other BHs (n = 7 respondents). For example, BHO5.1 asserted "today it is very easy, we [BHs in Valletta] have groups on WhatsApp where we chat all the time, we exchange data and information with each other". Likewise, other respondents used group chats as a means to communicate with personnel in wider networks (n = 2 respondents). For example, BHE13.1 stated that "I mean, I am on a group chat with some other people, some are still here in Valletta, some have moved because they changed their positions and jobs, still in the industry but moved out of Valletta. We used to share some thoughts, some concerns". Several BHEs (n = 8 respondents) and BHOs (n = 3 respondents) also reported discussing ideas with intra-organizational personnel through social media platforms (internal socialization and leveraging processes). For example, BHE2.2 stated that "so if me and BHE2.1 decided to get the new cushions and the runner, for example, maybe we did not tell everybody that it will be changed, and we decided to do it, we got the sample, we tried it out, we took pictures and said 'okay, what do you all think about it?' in the group chat". Group chats on commonly used social media platforms, e.g., Facebook messenger and WhatsApp, proved particularly invaluable in independently owned and chain-owned boutique hotels. However, in multi-sector group owned BHs (BH12, BH14), dedicated intranets to facilitate internal communications were preferred to the preceding platforms.

In addition to facilitating idea generation processes, ITs and ICTs were also deployed in BHs to aid BHEs (n = 7 respondents) and BHOs (n = 6 respondents) explore and understand the viability of an idea (process 2). For example, BHE4.1 stated that "the other day, we got an idea, for example, we thought about changing toiletries, so then you start researching and you start finding what people are using, you know". Likewise, BHE8.1 asserted that "in online searches usually, when I know that I need to implement something, for example, I start to look and maybe because I start to look for that thing, something else comes up from the research". Therefore, in BHs, ITs and ICTs further facilitated innovation activities by acting as a basis to validate or challenge an idea, while these technologies also helped BHEs and BHOs become aware of any alternative products/services on the market.

Last, ITs and ICTs also assisted BHEs (n = 8 respondents) and BHOs (n = 2 respondents) share knowledge regarding implemented innovations (process 8). Therefore, these technologies, particularly, instant messaging platforms, emails, and intranets, proved to reflect an invaluable medium to facilitate the dissemination of knowledge. In this regard, BHO6.1 stated that "but a lot of things are done via WhatsApp, so while before you would have needed more documents like a book where you write things down, here we just write things down on our group on WhatsApp". Likewise, BHO8.1 stated that "I would say most communication is WhatsApp related, and WhatsApp is just so easy and you know, communicative, so that really works". Therefore, in the innovation processes of BHs, ITs and ICTs proved to represent a facilitative tool for knowledge sharing and capture processes (process 8), while simultaneously allowing for shared knowledge to be codified and stored on one platform.

Based on the preceding results, several inferences about the role played by ITs and ICTs in the innovation processes of BHs in Valletta, Malta, may be drawn. First, ITs and ICTs specifically, Web 2.0 technologies, acted as a medium to facilitate idea generation processes, with a number of different ITs and ICTs deployed by BHEs and BHOs to identify market trends and innovation opportunities. Likewise, these tools proved to facilitate intra- and inter-organizational knowledge sharing processes among and between ecosystem actors and hotel personnel. Thus, these tools acted as mechanisms for the integration of knowledge resources and co-value creation. Second, ITs and ICTs facilitated BHEs and BHOs in research processes, with the internet allowing respondents to examine the validity of an idea and the potential for alternative ideas. Last, ICTs and ITs aided BHEs and BHOs disseminate knowledge regarding an implemented innovation, with these tools used to codify and store explicit knowledge.

5 Discussion and Conclusion

Based on the results obtained in this study, in the investigated BHs, at a micro-foundation level, innovation was found to reflect a complex process involving combinations and recombinations of knowledge resources. These findings align to prior research on service innovation [see, for example, 71–73]. Thus, in the context of BHs, innovation reflected "highly complex knowledge processes" [72, p. 347] where, through new knowledge, BHs were able to effectively react to market changes and determine their future via innovation outcomes [51]. Moreover, this study also confirms the importance of knowledge resources in contemporary economic ecosystems, substantiating the necessity and value of theoretical lenses which prioritize the investigation of knowledge resources, e.g., the knowledge-based view [see, for example, 27]. While this study aligns to the literature regarding the importance of knowledge resources in innovation processes, in comparison to the innovation process models set forth in the literature [see, for example, 25, 62, 63], and in contrast to Buhagiar et al.'s [51] conceptual model, the findings obtained in this research [see Fig. 3] elucidate that generic innovation process models, most especially conceptual models, are often limited in their ability to capture the complex, personal, and subjective nature of innovation activities. Furthermore, the linear disposition of the innovation processes commonly depicted in these models tends to lead to overly simplistic and reductionist illustrations of innovation. Contrarily, the findings established in this research indicate that innovations in BHs are capable of occurring though a multitude of different paths, with equifinality in this process indicating that a variety of novel trajectories may be followed to combine and recombine knowledge resources into innovation outcomes. Furthermore, unlike the innovation process models set forth in the literature, which often neglect to provide any insight into the stimuli used to generate ideas, this research has outlined that a wide range of stimuli (21 stimuli) may be used to incite ideation processes. Moreover, as asserted by Grant [74], "if the primary productive resource of the firm is knowledge, and if knowledge resides in individual employees, then it is employees who own the bulk of the firm's resources" [p. 119]. As a result, in BHs, the rate of innovations evolved as partly contingent on and determined by "the motivations of hotel employees and owners to: 1) engage in innovation opportunity identification activities and 2) externalize/share their subjective tacit knowledge with colleagues" [7, p. 102]. Last, and a factor which often goes unaccounted for in the literature on innovation process modelling, is the great degree of influence ownership structures are capable of exerting on the complexity and length of innovation cycles. In this regard, the findings of this research extend Crossan and Berdrow's [67] research by explicating how variances in BH ownership altered the paths through which knowledge resources were reconfigured.

In addition to extending and enriching the literature on innovation process modelling, this research has also shed light on the role of ITs and ICTs in the innovation processes of BHs. In this regard, the findings of this study illustrated that comparative to the advanced ITs and ICTs reported to be implemented in other tourism contexts [see, for example, 10, 12, 14], during innovation processes, BHs in Valletta predominantly relied on 'domestic' ITs and ICTs, i.e., Web 2.0 technologies, which reflect free tools and applications, e.g., the internet, WhatsApp, and Facebook, which require no formal training, are available to mass target audiences, and are easy to use. Therefore, while several scholarly articles have outlined that the future of the tourism industry is rooted in, for example, big data, AI, virtual reality, and augmented reality [10], when it comes to the innovation process itself, and BHs located on a small island state like Malta, preference seems to be given to already available ITs and ICTs, which respondents are likely to already use for daily communications. These results align to Matassi et al.'s [75] empirical analysis, which revealed that middle-aged adults often used WhatsApp for work responsibilities and communication. Similarly, these findings also substantiate Terkan and Serra's [76] conclusions which revealed that WhatsApp, for example, improved employee-employee communications, work performance, and productivity. Extending these findings, however, this study has illustrated that idea generation processes, which are necessitated to stimulate the innovation process, significantly rely on creative inspiration derived through an array of different ITs and ICTs, such as TikTok, Pinterest, Instagram, etc. These findings imply that 1) ICTs and IT tools aid in opportunity identification activities and, furthermore, 2) at any given moment through, for example, targeted adverts, idea generation may occur. Thus, just like hotels are contingent on employees to develop and share ideas, the creative capacities of employees seem to be influenced by ICTs and ITs. Moreover, the findings of this research also substantiate Jalilvand et al.'s [11] results, with ITs and ICTs in BHs in Valletta, Malta, having been found to facilitate knowledge sharing processes between intra- and inter-organizational actors while, concurrently, these tools were also denoted to aid in the co-development of solutions and ideas. Likewise, these results also align to Sigala and Chalkiti's [15] findings, which revealed that social media platforms positively impacted creativity.

To conclude, the novelty and significance of this research lies in a holistic picture of the innovation processes adopted in boutique hotels in Valletta, Malta, to transform knowledge resources into innovation outcomes. Through empirical data, this research has added layers of nuance and complexity to generic innovation process models, resulting in a comprehensive innovation process model which captures a snapshot of the numerous paths through which innovation is capable of evolving [see Fig. 3]. Furthermore, this research has illustrated the intersection points at which ITs and ICTs aid in innovation processes, and how such tools inherently facilitate the development and validation of ideas, and knowledge sharing processes. Moreover, this study has outlined that in the context investigated in this research, social media or Web 2.0 technologies, seem to be favored by respondents. As a result, Web 2.0 technologies emerged to play a dual and often overlooked role, as platforms used for personal purposes and as platforms with the potential to significantly aid in stimulating and cultivating innovation activities in BHs.

6 Limitations and Areas for Future Research

One of the core limitations of this study is the small sample size used in this research to gather data, which severely restricts the generalizability and transferability of the findings presented in this paper. To overcome this limitation, future studies could seek to apply the same model to a larger sample size and in different contexts, this would assist in providing a more comprehensive overview of the innovation processes deployed in different types of accommodation provisions, e.g., star-rated hotels. A second limitation of this study is related to the types of respondents selected for inclusion in this research, with this study only accounting for hotel managers and owners. To extend the results presented in this study, future researchers could explore how front-line employees contribute towards the innovation activities of accommodation provisions, this would add an additional level of detail to the current model proposed in this research. A third limitation of this study is that despite the large number of stimuli identified during idea generation processes, this research did not place any emphasis on exploring whether and how different stimuli relate to certain types of innovation outcomes, e.g., product innovations, process innovations, etc. An exploration of this kind would be invaluable in assisting practitioners better understand how to manage and control idea generation processes for deliberate types of innovation outcomes. Future studies could also seek to explore the benefits and drawbacks of technology on employee motivation and innovation, especially since such technologies inherently imply that employees are 'connected' to their jobs 24/7. These insights could support a better understanding of the impact of being always connected on innovation performance.

References

1. Statista: Key figures on the hotel industry in Malta in 2022. https://www.statista.com/statis tics/1312360/key-figures-hotel-industry-malta/
2. Pirnar, I., Kamali, Y.C., Eris, E.D.: Soft innovation in hotel services: case of Izmir City. Int. J. Tourism Cities 6(4), 1025–1043 (2019). https://doi.org/10.1108/IJTC-05-2019-0072
3. Truong, N., Dang-Pham, D., McClelland, R., Nkhoma, M.: Exploring the impact of innovativeness of hospitality service operation on customer satisfaction. Oper. Supply Chain Manage. Int. J. 13(3), 307–319 (2020). https://doi.org/10.31387/oscm0420272
4. Future Market Insights: Boutique Hotels Types Market Outlook -2022–2032. https://www.futuremarketinsights.com/reports/boutique-hotel-sector-outlook
5. Freni, G.: Service Innovation: A Literature Review of Conceptual Perspectives. New Metropolitan Perspectives: Post COVID Dynamics: Green and Digital Transition, between Metropolitan and Return to Villages Perspectives, pp. 154–163 (2022)
6. Gustafsson, A., Snyder, H., Witell, L.: Service innovation: a new conceptualization and path forward. J. Serv. Res. 23(2), 111–115 (2020). https://doi.org/10.1177/1094670520908
7. Buhagiar, K.: Innovation in boutique hotels in Valletta, Malta: a multi-level investigation. In Proceedings of the 14th International Joint Conference on Knowledge Discovery, Knowledge Engineering and Knowledge Management (IC3K 2022), pp. 95–106. https://doi.org/10.5220/001158550000335
8. Song, L.Z., Song, M., Di Benedetto, C.A.: A staged service innovation model. Decis. Sci. 40(3), 571–599 (2009). https://doi.org/10.1111/j.1540-5915.2009.00240.x

9. Toivonen, M., Tuominen, T.: Emergence of innovations in services. Serv. Ind. J. **29**(7), 887–902 (2009). https://doi.org/10.1080/02642060902749492

10. Bharwani, S., Mathews, D.: Techno-business strategies for enhancing guest experience in luxury hotels: a managerial perspective. Worldwide Hosp. Tour. Themes **13**(2), 168–185 (2021). https://doi.org/10.1108/WHATT-09-2020-0121

11. Jalilvand, M.R., Khazaei Pool, J., Khodadadi, M., Sharifi, M.: Information technology competency and knowledge management in the hospitality industry service supply chain. Tour. Rev. **74**(4), 872–884 (2019). https://doi.org/10.1108/TR-04-2018-0054

12. Neuhofer, B., Buhalis, D., Ladkin, A.: Smart technologies for personalized experiences: a case study in the hospitality domain. Electron. Mark. **25**, 243–254 (2015). https://doi.org/10.1007/s12525-015-0182-1

13. Nieves, J., Osorio, J.: Using information technology to achieve management innovation. Academia Revista Latinoamericana de Administración **32**(1), 20–39 (2019). https://doi.org/10.1108/ARLA-02-2016-0037

14. Okumus, F.: Facilitating knowledge management through information technology in hospitality organizations. J. Hosp. Tour. Technol. **4**(1), 64–80 (2013). https://doi.org/10.1108/17579881311302356

15. Sigala, M., Chalkiti, K.: Knowledge management, social media and employee creativity. Int. J. Hosp. Manag. **45**, 44–58 (2015). https://doi.org/10.1016/j.ijhm.2014.11.003

16. Kroh, J., Luetjen, H., Globocnik, D., Schultz, C.: Use and efficacy of information technology in innovation processes: the specific role of servitization. J. Prod. Innov. Manag. **35**(5), 720–741 (2018). https://doi.org/10.1111/jpim.12445

17. Engidaw, A.E.: Small businesses and their challenges during COVID-19 pandemic in developing countries: in the case of Ethiopia. J. Innov. Entrepren. **11**(1), 1(2022). https://doi.org/10.1186/s13731-021-00191-3

18. Juergensen, J., Guimón, J., Narula, R.: European SMEs amidst the COVID-19 crisis: assessing impact and policy responses. J. Indust. Bus. Econ. **47**, 499–510 (2020). https://doi.org/10.1007/s40812-020-00169-4

19. United Nations. Global Issues. https://www.un.org/en/global-issues

20. So, K.K.F., Kim, H., He, Y., Li, X.: Mapping service innovation research in hospitality and tourism: an integrative bibliometric analysis and research agenda. Cornell Hosp. Quar. **00**, 1–18 (2022). https://doi.org/10.1177/19389655221101023

21. Gomezelj, D.O.: A systematic review of research on innovation in hospitality and tourism. Int. J. Contemp. Hosp. Manag. **28**(3), 516–558 (2016). https://doi.org/10.1108/IJCHM-10-2014-0510

22. Statista.: Hotels – Worldwide. https://www.statista.com/outlook/mmo/travel-tourism/hotels/worldwide

23. Işık, C., Aydın, E., Dogru, T., Rehman, A., Sirakaya-Turk, E., Karagöz, D.: Innovation research in tourism and hospitality field: a bibliometric and visualization analysis. Sustainability **14**(13), 7889 (2022). https://doi.org/10.3390/su14137889

24. Shin, H., Perdue, R.R.: Hospitality and tourism service innovation: a bibliometric review and future research agenda. Int. J. Hosp. Manag. **102**, 103176 (2022). https://doi.org/10.1016/j.ijhm.2022.103176

25. Nonaka, I.: A dynamic theory of organizational knowledge creation. Organ. Sci. **5**(1), 14–23 (1994). https://doi.org/10.1287/orsc.5.1.14

26. Quintane, E., Mitch Casselman, R., Sebastian Reiche, B., Nylund, P.A.: Innovation as a knowledge-based outcome. J. Knowl. Manag. **15**(6), 928–947 (2011). https://doi.org/10.1108/13673271111179299

27. Grant, R.M.: Reflections on knowledge-based approaches to the organization of production. J. Manage. Govern. **17**, 541–558 (2013). https://doi.org/10.1007/s10997-011-9195-0

28. Dean, A., Kretschmer, M.: Can ideas be capital? Factors of production in the postindustrial economy: a review and critique. Acad. Manage. Rev. **32**(2), 573–594 (2007). https://www.jstor.org/stable/20159316
29. Drucker, P.: Post-Capitalist Society. Routledge. (1993/2012)
30. Sørensen, F., Jensen, J.F.: Value creation and knowledge development in tourism experience encounters. Tour. Manage. **46**, 336–346 (2015). https://doi.org/10.1016/j.tourman.2014.07.009
31. Santos-Vijande, M.L., López-Sánchez, J.Á., Pascual-Fernandez, P.: Co-creation with clients of hotel services: the moderating role of top management support. Curr. Issue Tour. **21**(3), 301–327 (2018). https://doi.org/10.1080/13683500.2015.1078781
32. Tefera, O., Dlamini, W.: Effect of innovation, knowledge sharing and trust culture on hotels' SMEs growth in eswatini. African J. Hosp. Tour. Leisure **10**(3), 881–894 (2020). https://doi.org/10.46222/ajhtl.19770720-138
33. Li, M., Hsu, C.H.: Linking customer-employee exchange and employee innovative behavior. Int. J. Hosp. Manage. **56**, 87–97 (2016). https://doi.org/10.1016/j.ijhm.2016.04.015
34. Xu, F.Z., Wang, Y.: Enhancing employee innovation through customer engagement: the role of customer interactivity, employee affect, and motivations. J. Hosp. Tour. Res. **44**(2), 351–376 (2020). https://doi.org/10.1177/1096348019989304
35. Saxena, G.: Relationships, networks and the learning regions: case evidence from the Peak District National Park. Tour. Manage. **26**(2), 277–289 (2005). https://doi.org/10.1016/j.tourman.2003.11.013
36. Halme, M.: Learning for sustainable development in tourism networks. Bus. Strateg. Environ. **10**(2), 100–114 (2001). https://doi.org/10.1002/bse.278
37. Sigurðardóttir, I., Steinthorsson, R.S.: Development of micro-clusters in tourism: a case of equestrian tourism in northwest Iceland. Scand. J. Hosp. Tour. **18**(3), 261–277 (2018). https://doi.org/10.1080/15022250.2018.1497286
38. Toader, V., Bota, M., Negrusa, A., Gavriletea, M., Tutunea, M.: Networks, clusters and innovation in Romanian tourism. Int. J. Arts Sci. **6**(2), 81–89 (2013)
39. Hjalager, A.: A review of innovation research in tourism. Tour. Manage. **31**(1), 1–12 (2010). https://doi.org/10.1016/j.tourman.2009.08.012
40. Engen, M., Magnusson, P.: Casting for service innovation: the roles of frontline employees. Creat. Innov. Manage. **27**(3), 255–269 (2018). https://doi.org/10.1111/caim.12263
41. Liu, C.W., Cheng, J.S.: Exploring driving forces of innovation in the MSEs: the case of the sustainable B&B tourism industry. Sustainability **10**(11), 3983 (2018). https://doi.org/10.3390/su10113983
42. Nieves, J., Quintana, A., Osorio, J.: Knowledge-based resources and innovation in the hotel industry. Int. J. Hosp. Manag. **38**, 65–73 (2014). https://doi.org/10.1016/j.ijhm.2014.01.001
43. Hu, M.L.M., Horng, J.S., Sun, Y.H.C.: Hospitality teams: knowledge sharing and service innovation performance. Tour. Manage. **30**(1), 41–50 (2009). https://doi.org/10.1016/j.tourman.2008.04.009
44. Nordli, A.J.: Information use and working methods as drivers of innovation in tourism companies. Scand. J. Hosp. Tour. **18**(2), 199–213 (2018). https://doi.org/10.1080/15022250.2017.1343682
45. Salem, I.E.B.: Toward better understanding of knowledge management: correlation to hotel performance and innovation in five-star chain hotels in Egypt. Tour. Hosp. Res. **14**(4), 176–196 (2014). https://doi.org/10.1177/1467358414542265
46. Baytok, A., Soybali, H.H., Zorlu, O.: Knowledge management processes in thermal hotels: an application in Afyonkarahisar Province, Turkey. J. Econ. Soc. Stud. **4**(1), 159–182 (2014)
47. Law, R., Leung, D., Chan, I.C.C.: Progression and development of information and communication technology research in hospitality and tourism: a state-of-the-art review. Int. J.

Contemp. Hosp. Manag. **32**(2), 511–534 (2020). https://doi.org/10.1108/IJCHM-07-2018-0586

48. Buhalis, D., Leung, R.: Smart hospitality—interconnectivity and interoperability towards an ecosystem. Int. J. Hosp. Manag. **71**, 41–50 (2018). https://doi.org/10.1016/j.ijhm.2017.11.011

49. Gronau, N.: The knowledge café–a knowledge management system and its application to hospitality and tourism. J. Qual. Assur. Hosp. Tour. **3**(3–4), 75–88 (2002). https://doi.org/10.1300/J162v03n03_05

50. Hallin, C.A., Marnburg, E.: Knowledge management in the hospitality industry: a review of empirical research. Tour. Manage. **29**(2), 366–381 (2008). https://doi.org/10.1016/j.tourman.2007.02.019

51. Buhagiar, K., Pace, L.A., Dingli, S.M.: Service innovation: a knowledge-based approach. In: Proceedings of the 13th International Joint Conference on Knowledge Discovery, Knowledge Engineering and Knowledge Management (IC3K 2021), pp. 119–125. https://doi.org/10.5220/0010652900003064

52. Peixoto, M.R., Paula, F.D.O., da Silva, J.F.: Factors that influence service innovation: a systematic approach and a categorization proposal. Eur. J. Innov. Manage. ahead-of-print No. ahead-of-print (2022)

53. Snyder, H., Witell, L., Gustafsson, A., Fombelle, P., Kristensson, P.: Identifying categories of service innovation: a review and synthesis of the literature. J. Bus. Res. **69**(7), 2401–2408 (2016). https://doi.org/10.1016/j.jbusres.2016.01.009

54. Carlborg, P., Kindström, D., Kowalkowski, C.: The evolution of service innovation research: a critical review and synthesis. Serv. Ind. J. **34**(5), 373–398 (2014). https://doi.org/10.1080/02642069.2013.780044

55. Gallouj, F., Savona, M.: Innovation in services: a review of the debate and a research agenda. J. Evol. Econ. **19**, 149–172 (2009). https://doi.org/10.1007/s00191-008-0126-4

56. Kim, C.S., Bai, B.H., Kim, P.B., Chon, K.: Review of reviews: a systematic analysis of review papers in the hospitality and tourism literature. Int. J. Hosp. Manag. **70**, 49–58 (2018). https://doi.org/10.1016/j.ijhm.2017.10.023

57. Singh, S., Akbani, I., Dhir, S.: Service innovation implementation: a systematic review and research agenda. Serv. Ind. J. **40**(7–8), 491–517 (2020). https://doi.org/10.1080/02642069.2020.1731477

58. Agegnehu, M., Lemi, K., Mulatu, F.: Factors influencing the adoption of information communication technology (ICT): In selected, rated, hotels in Addis Ababa, Ethiopia. J. Process Manage. New Technol. **7**(4), 13–23 (2019)

59. Ko, C.H., Pei, L., Tsai, Y.H.: A study of employees' perception of information technology adoption in hotels. Int. J. Organ. Innov. **8**(3), 231–238 (2016)

60. Sarmah, B., Kamboj, S., Rahman, Z.: Co-creation in hotel service innovation using smart phone apps: an empirical study. Int. J. Contemp. Hosp. Manag. **29**(10), 2647–2667 (2017). https://doi.org/10.1108/IJCHM-12-2015-0681

61. Urbinati, A., Chiaroni, D., Chiesa, V., Frattini, F.: The role of digital technologies in open innovation processes: an exploratory multiple case study analysis. R&D Manage. **50**(1), 136–160 (2020). https://doi.org/10.1111/radm.12313

62. Hollebeek, L.D., Andreassen, T.W.: The SD logic-informed "hamburger" model of service innovation and its implications for engagement and value. J. Serv. Mark. **32**(1), 1–7 (2018). https://doi.org/10.1108/JSM-11-2017-0389

63. Tidd, J., Bessant, J.: Strategic Innovation Management. Wiley, United Kingdom (2014)

64. Jarzabkowski, P.: Strategy as Practice: An Activity Based Approach. SAGE Publications Ltd (2005). http://dx.doi.org/https://doi.org/10.4135/9781446215777

65. Weick, K.: The Psychology of Organizing, 2nd edn. Addison-Wesley Publishing Company, US (1969/1979)

66. Denzin, N. K., Lincoln, Y. S.: The SAGE Handbook of Qualitative Research, 5th edn. SAGE Publications Inc, USA (2018)
67. Crossan, M.M., Berdrow, I.: Organizational learning and strategic renewal. Strateg. Manag. J. **24**(11), 1087–1105 (2003). https://doi.org/10.1002/smj.342
68. Gutierrez, E., Sandstrom, G.O., Janhager, J., Ritzen, S.: Innovation and decision making: understanding selection and prioritization of development projects. Paper presented at the 2008 4th IEEE International Conference on Management of Innovation and Technology, Bangkok, Thailand (2008). https://doi.org/10.1109/ICMIT.2008.4654386
69. Garrido-Moreno, A., Lockett, N., García-Morales, V.: Paving the way for CRM success: the mediating role of knowledge management and organizational commitment. Inform. Manage. **51**(8), 1031–1042 (2014). https://doi.org/10.1016/j.im.2014.06.006
70. Goodman, M., Dingli, S.M.: Creativity and Strategic Innovation Management: Directions for Future Value in Changing Times, 1st edn. Routledge (2013)
71. Galanakis, K.: Innovation process. Make sense using systems thinking. Technovation **26**(11), 1222-1232 (2006). https://doi.org/10.1016/j.technovation.2005.07.002
72. Peschl, M.F., Fundneider, T.: Designing and enabling spaces for collaborative knowledge creation and innovation: from managing to enabling innovation as socio-epistemological technology. Comput. Hum. Behav. **37**, 346–359 (2014). https://doi.org/10.1016/j.chb.2012.05.027
73. Nonaka, I., Takeuchi, H.: The Wise Company: How Companies Create Continuous Innovation. Oxford University Press, New York (2019)
74. Grant, R.M.: Toward a knowledge-based theory of the firm. Strateg. Manag. J. **17**(S2), 109–122 (1996). https://doi.org/10.1002/smj.4250171110
75. Matassi, M., Boczkowski, P.J., Mitchelstein, E.: Domesticating WhatsApp: family, friends, work, and study in everyday communication. New Media Soc. **21**(10), 2183–2200 (2019). https://doi.org/10.1177/1461444819841890
76. Terkan, R., Serra, I.C.: How whatsapp changes the way business work? Int. Rev. Manag. Mark. **10**(5), 179 (2020)

Author Index

F. Coenen et al. (Eds.): IC3K 2022, CCIS 1842, pp. 357–358, 2023.
https://doi.org/10.1007/978-3-031-43471-6

Printed in the United States
by Baker & Taylor Publisher Services

Printed in the United States
by Baker & Taylor Publisher Services